Dr Ida Glaser and Hannah Kay, scholars of both the
expressed their thoughts in their new book *Think*
Genesis, Transfiguration, Transformation compre
Readers of both faiths will find it amazingly relevant. It is a superb and deeply
theological analysis of the Bible and the Qur'an. This book looks at some of
the main themes of the Bible and the Qur'an in a deeper sense. So it will be
useful both in the academic arena and also for general readers. The book
reminds us how essential it is to explore and know the other faith and I hope
it will help build bridges between people of different faiths. The writers' aim
is clearly not to create confrontation but to promote dialogue about admitted
truth between the followers of the two faiths. Thus I believe that this book will
also surely help Muslim Background Believers in Bangladesh and beyond.

Anwar Al-Azad
Vice-Principal, Institute for Classical Languages, Dhaka, Bangladesh

This is an extraordinary book. It is not an introduction to Islam, still less
a "how to" manual on Christian-Muslim dialogue, or instruction on how
Christians might share their faith with Muslims – though the authors could
teach us quite a bit about all three of these topics. Rather, this book looks
squarely at how Muslims, in all their remarkable diversity, look at a wide
variety of things – events or stances or people that are treated both in the
Qur'an and in the Bible (e.g. creation, fall, Moses, Elijah, Jesus, the cross), law
(shariah), people of God (*ummah*), the nature of holy books (Qur'an, Bible),
and more – and ask how Christians should think about all these matters if
they carefully study them out of the framework of the Christian Bible. What
is characteristic of this study is its zeal to get things right, to be truthful and
accurate. Highly recommended.

D. A. Carson
Research Professor of New Testament, Trinity Evangelical Divinity School, IL, USA

Here is a very fresh and original way of helping Christians to engage with
Muslims and Islam. Approaching the Bible with all the disturbing questions
raised by the study of the Qur'an and of Islam, Ida Glaser and Hannah Kay
come up with refreshingly new ways of understanding familiar biblical themes
and texts. Because they have taken the trouble to understand how Muslims
interpret the Qur'an, and because they also appreciate rabbinic interpretation

of the Old Testament, they are able to recognise where there is genuine common ground between Christian and Islamic beliefs and where there are really significant and crucial differences. They have a remarkable lightness of touch which enables them to explain quite difficult ideas very simply – but without over-simplification. While readers therefore will appreciate the thorough academic study which undergirds this book, they won't be able to escape the personal challenges which are presented on every page about how Christians should think about Muslims and Islam.

Colin Chapman
Formerly lecturer in Islamic Studies at the Near East School of Theology, Beirut, and visiting lecturer at the Arab Baptist Theological Seminary, Beirut, Lebanon

Thinking Biblically about Islam is an outstanding book. Ida Glaser is a uniquely qualified author – academically, spiritually and personally. Drawing on decades of first-hand experience with several Muslim cultures as well as on thorough academic knowledge of both the Bible and the Qur'an, she invites the reader to think seriously about Islam in light of Christian Scriptures. What makes her book special is not only her academic and professional competence but her exceptional humility, honesty and grace in dealing with extremely difficult and sensitive issues. Her book offers no simplistic solutions to complex problems, nor easy answers to tough questions. She takes the reader through an adventure of learning step by step to think anew in a Christ-like way about Islam and Muslims, offering rich resources of prayerful reflection and personal experience. It is the rare combination of academic excellence and spiritual sensitivity that gives her book such a unique quality. In a time of reductionist slogans about Islam, be they motivated by panic and fear, or naiveté and ignorance, a book like *Thinking Biblically about Islam* is a more than welcome invitation to godly wisdom, loving concern and informed balance, so urgently needed in the contemporary troubled world.

Pavel Hosek
Head of Religious Studies Department
Protestant Theological Faculty, Charles University, Prague

I am thrilled to see this solidly evangelical book which encourages us to think about Islam through the eyes of God and to 'listen to Him' (Luke 9:35). This book has deepened my own Christian belief through this process too.

Thinking Biblically about Islam is an excellent resource for any Christian to think and understand Islam from different points of view. I specially recommend it for ministers and lay people who work with Muslims or have Muslim background Christians in their congregations.

Mohammad Reza Eghtedarian
Curate for Liverpool Cathedral and Sepas

Thinking Biblically about Islam, is opportune, rigorous and challenging.

It is a very timely contribution to today's world. As worldwide events prompt a cacophony of competing voices and assertions about Islam and Muslims, more urgently than ever we need to be able to respond biblically – and this book shows us a way to do so. Rather than raucously competing opinions, it is a delight to encounter so many voices brought in conversation in one book. We hear the authors' voices clearly, as well as Muslim voices: and the reader's own voice and experience is constantly invited into the discussion through the questions in each part.

With characteristic rigor, the authors read the Bible and Qur'an with detailed attention to the background and structure of the texts. The book exemplifies the reminder that authentic interpretation has to take account of the worlds "behind the text," "of the text" and "in front of the text." The event and characters of the transfiguration are a central theme to examine what the Bible and the Qur'an say about God and people.

To read this book is to be challenged to listen better to ourselves, to others, and particularly to the Bible and what it calls us to in living obediently as God's people. It is accessible to people with little background in Islam. At the same time it will stimulate those with more experience to think anew about biblical texts and their implications for how we live and relate to Muslims in the world today.

I highly recommend it to church leaders, Bible teachers and all Christians engaged with Muslim (and other religious) communities.

Moyra Dale
Adjunct Research Fellow, Melbourne School of Theology

Thinking Biblically about Islam is one of the most exhaustive and thorough works I have seen on the subject of the gospel in church and culture. It reminds all who proclaim Jesus as Lord of the central theme of his teaching. The authors have suggested that thinking biblically strengthens acting biblically. Christians around the world must allow what they love and cherish to guide their actions, and not their hates and/or fears. This book gives a historical and theological understanding of Islam from its modest beginning in the Arabian Peninsula. The spread of Islam to other parts of the world with its eventual encounter with the rich heritage of the Judeo-Christian faith is captured in the book. These understandings break the barrier that has hitherto excluded peaceful co-existence and even more importantly sharing the gospel message in our societies. It calls on true believers in Christ to 'think biblically about Islam' and about all of life. An extraordinary work – highly recommended!

Sylvester Dachomo
Registrar and Senior Lecturer in Islam and Global Christianity,
Gindiri Theological Seminary, Jos, Nigeria

Thinking Biblically about Islam is a wonderful book about the amazing grace of God in Muslim-Christian interaction. It is about the heart of God which grieves for all human beings to be saved. In the time of 4 C's (crisis, chaos, confusion and challenges) like today, Ida Glaser and Hannah Kay have inspirationally demonstrated with academic integrity and theological clarity that God's heart for human beings was revealed on the mount at the transfiguration as well as at the cross on the mount of Calvary.

This is a triply interwoven story incorporating the God in the Bible and the Qur'an (similarities and differences through the lens of the Bible), stories of Muslims and Christians in history, and stories of both authors on a journey with the presence of God.

This is a must-read book. Glaser gently and yet powerfully invites everyone to know the heart of God and love him, and to love their neighbours – Muslim, Christian, or anyone – by transformation (or transfiguration) of oneself through the cross of Jesus. This is an awakening and unavoidable call of God for his church today.

Matthew Jeong (Keung-Chul)
Ambassador for Interserve
Director of 'Islam Partnership', South Korea
Professor of World Religions at Hap-Dong Theological Seminary, South Korea

Christians and Muslims have over the centuries tried to make sense of each other's beliefs mainly through the lenses of their respective scriptures. In this encounter, the Christian reflections on Islam have been complicated by the virtual absence of direct references to Islamic beliefs in the Bible. In *Thinking Biblically about Islam*, Ida Glaser and Hannah Kay employ a thematic approach to address some of the most pertinent and vexing theological questions at the heart of Christian-Muslim understanding and offer very clear and persuasive responses and ways to respond. The depth of central biblical themes, the breadth and scope of understanding of Islam, and the compelling nature of the arguments are self-evident. *Thinking Biblically about Islam* is long overdue and a timely contribution in the current climate of intense intra-Christian debate on what to make of the Qur'an, Muhammad and whether Muslims and Christians worship the same God, among others. The non-polemical tone and dispassionately evangelical engagement of the issues make this book a must read for every theological student, academic and practitioner interested in Christian-Muslim understanding. All readers, whatever their theological convictions, will find much to stimulate their thinking in this book.

John Azumah
The Lausanne Movement's Senior Associate for Islam,
Professor of World Christianity and Islam
Director of International Programs, Columbia Theological Seminary, USA

Thinking Biblically about Islam

Langham
GLOBAL LIBRARY

Thinking Biblically about Islam

Genesis, Transfiguration, Transformation

Ida Glaser

with Hannah Kay

GLOBAL LIBRARY

Published 2016 by Langham Global Library
an imprint of Langham Creative Projects

Langham Partnership
PO Box 296, Carlisle, Cumbria CA3 9WZ, UK
www.langham.org

ISBNs:
978-1-78368-912-5 Print
978-1-78368-910-1 Mobi
978-1-78368-911-8 ePub
978-1-78368-129-7 PDF

British Library Cataloguing in Publication Data
A catalogue record for this book is available from the British Library

ISBN: 978-1-78368-912-5

Cover & Book Design: projectluz.com

The image featured on the cover has been adapted from the *Icon of the Transfiguration* by Theophanes the Greek, early 15th century, tempera on wood, located in the Tretyakov Gallery in Moscow. Image is available under Public Domain License. Credit: Theophanes the Greek. Original Image: https://commons.wikimedia.org/wiki/File:Transfiguration_by_Feofan_Grek_from_Spaso-Preobrazhensky_Cathedral_in_Pereslavl-Zalessky_(15th_c,_Tretyakov_gallery).jpeg

CONTENTS

Acknowledgements

Writing this book has been a long, hard journey, but I've learnt a great deal on the way, and I look back on the road with thankfulness.

Hannah Kay accompanied me for most of the way, helped me to put together many years of thinking, and enriched the book with her own experience and observations.

Colleagues at The Centre for Muslim–Christian Studies, Oxford, and especially the 'Reading the Bible in the Context of Islam' research team, encouraged me and gave me some rigorous discussion of ideas.

Towards the end, Tom E. Taylor helped with the editing, and Iram Sarwar, Guy Gray and Richard Croft commented on the manuscript.

The biggest 'thank you' has to go to all the people who appear in the stories in this book (not least my husband, David). All the stories are about real people and about things that really happened, although sometimes details have been changed. I am thankful to God for the amazing variety of people in his world, and for the way he has brought such riches into my life and into Hannah's life through them.

Ida Glaser
Oxford, 2015

Introduction

Thinking Biblically about Islam

I appeal to you therefore, brothers, by the mercies of God, to present your bodies as a living sacrifice, holy and acceptable to God, which is your spiritual worship. Do not be conformed to this world, but be transformed by the renewal of your mind, that by testing you may discern what is the will of God, what is good and acceptable and perfect. (Rom 12:1–2)

Why This Book?

This book is primarily written for Christians who want to think biblically about Islam. We hope that others will also read it, because we believe that it is important that all sorts of people should study what it might mean to 'think biblically'.

This is not a book about how to do Christian–Muslim dialogue, although both the writers believe that dialogue is important, and that 'thinking biblically' is an important basis for dialogue. It is not a book about how Christians can share the gospel with Muslims, although both the writers believe that Muslims are as much in need of the gospel as are all other human beings, and that 'thinking biblically' is an important basis for witness.

Nor is this book an introduction to Islam and to Muslims: we will be assuming that readers have already gained some knowledge of Islam.[1] However, we believe that 'thinking biblically' is an important basis for

---

1. There are many good introductions to Islam, by Muslims and by non-Muslims. There are also many that introduce only one kind of Islam, and many that are very biased and unbalanced in their approach. We would recommend Daniel W. Brown, *A New Introduction to Islam*, 2nd ed. (Oxford: Wiley-Blackwell, 2009) and Mahmoud Ayoub, *Islam: Faith and History* (Oxford: Oneworld, 2004).

learning, so we do aim to equip Christians to study Islam and to understand Muslim people.

Nor does this book attempt to give a full biblical analysis of Islam, or an analysis that will apply to all Muslims everywhere. Rather, it offers a framework for thinking and for taking to the Bible the questions raised by Christian interaction with Islam and with Muslims.

This book follows Ida's earlier *The Bible and Other Faiths*, which is subtitled *What Does the Lord Require of Us?*[2] In that book it was argued that we cannot necessarily expect to know what God thinks of other people, but we can always expect that he will show us what he wants of us. In this book, we are going to try to 'think biblically' about Islam; but our prayer is that this will result in Christian people finding out how God wants them to relate to Muslims, and being transformed by the Holy Spirit into the likeness of Jesus Christ.

Why Think Biblically?

Both of us want to think biblically because we want to please our heavenly Father. We want to honour the Lord Jesus Christ and to have our minds transformed by the Holy Spirit. We believe that the Bible is God's written Word, and is our main tool for learning what is 'good and acceptable and perfect' in God's eyes. The Word of God enables us to understand who Jesus is as we allow the Spirit to shape and test our thinking.

The purpose of the biblical mind is not that we 'may discern how God thinks about other people', but that we 'may discern what is the will of God' for our own living as his children, as we see in Romans 12:1–2 (quoted at the beginning of this Introduction). A biblically transformed mind starts and flows from our offering an acceptable sacrifice to God. We respond to God's mercy, to the one acceptable sacrifice of Christ (that Paul has been explaining earlier in Romans) by offering our very selves.

Romans 12 continues, 'For by the grace given to me I say to every one among you not to think of himself more highly than he ought to think.' Paul wants us to think correctly about ourselves, about our particular place within the body of Christ, and about the importance of right relationships within that body. Only after this is established does he go on to questions about

---

2. Ida Glaser, *The Bible and Other Faiths: What Does the Lord Require of Us?* (Leicester: Inter-Varsity Press, 2005).

how to treat other people. He considers how we treat opponents, governing authorities and neighbours. His summing up is in terms of 'the law'. In the first part of Romans, Paul has explained very clearly that the law could not save people, and so we might think that he had a negative view of the law. But here, as in Romans 6, he reminds his readers that faith in Christ demands a higher, not a lower, standard of law-keeping. Twice in Romans 13:8–10 he will insist that love is the fulfilment of the law.

Paul's teaching is an outworking of Jesus' teaching and life. Jesus himself calls us to love – to love one another, to love our neighbours and to love our enemies. That is his 'new commandment' (John 13:34; 15:12–13), it is his summary of the law (Matt 22:36–40), and it is his standard for all the children of God (Matt 5:43–48). We see this love demonstrated by Jesus himself as we consider how he lived and died.

How will we know whether we are 'thinking biblically'? By the fruit of love, bringing joy, peace, patience, kindness, goodness, faithfulness, gentleness and self-control.

Who Is Writing, and Who Is Reading?

There are many different Christian opinions on how to understand Islam. One of the main reasons for this variety is that there are so many Christians who have had different experiences of different interpretations of Islam and of different Muslims in different places. Just as Christianity has many denominations and many groups within those denominations, so Islam has many different sects and different movements within those sects. Just as people who call themselves 'Christian' come from many cultures and nations and have different personalities and passions, so people who call themselves 'Muslim' come from many cultures and nations and have different personalities and passions. Therefore, there will be a wide range of experiences and knowledge of Islam and of Muslims among Christians.

An important part of this book is that we relate stories from our experiences, and we invite you to think about them and to think about your own experiences. We start here by reflecting on some of the contexts in which we, the authors, have encountered Muslims and have seen how Muslims and Christians relate to each other. As you read our stories below, think about how they compare with your own experiences and with the situation in your own country. How do your experiences and the experiences of the people you know affect the way that you think about Islam and about Muslims?

Ida's Story: Teaching in Northern Nigeria

I have lived among Muslims in many contexts, from teaching physics in peaceful Malaysia and the beautiful Maldives to working for a church in deprived inner-city Newcastle upon Tyne, England – an area where Muslim friends received regular racial abuse, where I was physically attacked by a white youth who broke into my home, and where the husband of one of my Muslim friends was murdered in a racist attack.

While writing this book, I have been working in the academic world of Oxford, meeting and teaching Muslims and Christians from all over the world. I also spent some time teaching at The Theological College of Northern Nigeria, and that made me think hard about 'thinking biblically about Islam'. I wrote the following reflection while I was there:

Students and staff from a town that has just been overrun by people from the Boko Haram group are waiting for news of their families. A neighbour telephoned her uncle, and one of the Boko Haram people answered the phone and said, 'We have just killed him.' Her brother and her mother have fled to a nearby mountain. That family is Christian, but Muslim families are also fleeing. So are some of the Nigerian army and some of the traditional Muslim leaders. 'Boko Haram started by attacking Christians,' say some of my students. 'Now, they have killed most of the Muslim leaders who have spoken against them in the mosques, and they are also attacking any other Muslims who disagree with them.'

A student tells me of an attack on his village in a different area. 'Houses were burned and I heard that fifty people died. My uncle died, and his family have fled. The village is deserted now,' he says. 'Who attacked them?' I ask, 'and why?' 'It was some Fulani men,' he answers. 'They were helped by some local people who had converted to Islam and are very fanatical.' We discuss whether the motivation might have been to spread Islam or, more likely, to empty the village so that they could take the land.

It is not always easy to distinguish fact from rumour. Here, in the Jos area, it is peaceful, but many people think that the peace depends on keeping Muslims and Christians apart. Following a period of violence, I am told, both Christians and Muslims 'ethnically cleansed' their areas, pushing the 'others' out. Now, Christians live on one side of the main road and Muslims live on the other side. Each group is afraid to go into the other's area. 'They have a plan,' says one of the Christian students. 'We used to be friends, but now we can't trust them. It's best to keep apart.' He quotes Matthew 5:39: 'We turned the other cheek,' he says, 'but they slapped that one too. We don't have any more cheeks to turn.'

'That sort of fear is unnecessary,' says one of the foreign staff. She takes me to a project near the central mosque, where Muslims and Christians are happily and deliberately working together on educational projects. Every participant has to begin with a course that tells their life story and addresses the trauma that so many have lived through. An elderly Muslim leader there introduces me to a visiting Christian pastor. 'We are brothers,' he says.

I am told about projects to help Christians to relate in love towards their Muslim neighbours. One uses Jesus' call to us to love God and our neighbours (Matt 22:37–40), his teaching about true righteousness (Matt 6:1–4) and the believer's role as light in the world (Matt 5:14–16), and the example of Daniel living and learning in a foreign land (Dan 1).[3] Another starts from Jesus' challenge to the religious leaders in John 8:31–47 and challenges Christians not to follow the devil's ways of violence and lies but, rather, to follow Jesus in love and in truth, using the example of his relationships with Samaritans.[4]

And Boko Haram? Some students think that they are an example of what Islam 'really' is and of what Muslims 'really' intend to do in the country. Others say, 'They seem to have nothing to do with Islam. I hear that they are drunk half the time, or on drugs.' One student prays, 'Lord, if we were really honest, we would say, "Do to them what they have done to our churches." But we pray instead, "Lord, have mercy on them and grant them repentance!"'

And I pray, 'Lord, help me to be faithful in my attempts to think biblically about Islam! Help me to write a book that will enable all these people to hear your voice through your Word!'

Hannah's Story: England, India and Pakistan

One Sunday afternoon, some representatives from the local mosque were visiting men in our neighbourhood in a suburb of England. My husband opened the door to them and they started to talk. Just then, our flatmate, Greg, returned. As soon as he saw the men outside our house, he dropped his bags, rolled up his sleeves and looked set to

---

3. 'InReach': see www.inreachministry.wix.com/inreach.
4. 'Love Language': material not yet published.

fight. 'What's going on?' he demanded, in a voice angrier than I had ever heard him use before.

In conversations with us, Greg often used to tell us, 'I'm not religious, but I respect everyone.' On that day, though, his underlying feelings towards Muslim men came out and reminded me that everyone has a different attitude to Muslims and Islam.

My grandmother has rarely met Muslims. 'We're all the same, really,' she says in her sweet, kind voice. 'We all worship the same God; I don't see why we need to discuss religion with them.' Where I live now, Muslims are a minority. A lady in the library where I work thumped a copy of the Hindu Bhagavadgita. 'These people are good people. We should respect Muslims more.' People at church meet Muslims at work, as neighbours and at the school gates. They often comment on how nice they are: 'I think my neighbour might be Muslim – he's called Muhammad,' Sue told me. 'He's such a gentleman.'

In parts of inner city Bradford, Muslims are the majority. The older people at the church where I used to go have seen their home city change as more and more Pakistanis have arrived. Although that church is surrounded by Pakistani households and businesses, church members tend to avoid the subject, and seem sad when the subject of Islam comes up. Some told me they grew up in this neighbourhood and, with obvious resentment, relate how they had to move. 'It used to be a lovely area,' Betty told me.

Meanwhile, my younger, secular colleagues were fascinated by the Muslim assemblies held every Friday at the school we taught at. 'I heard that "Islam" means "peace"', Sharon told me. 'I feel so peaceful when you all pray – I love you guys' assemblies,' she continues, including my Bible-story assemblies in the same category. However, it irritates her when, in the staffroom, Muslim colleagues take the moral high ground on marriage, dating and homosexuality.

There is confusion in the school as to what makes a person a Muslim or a Christian. When I wore shalwar kameez, my pupils' parents asked, 'Are you Muslim?' I explained that neither knowledge of Urdu nor Punjabi clothing made one Muslim. The dinner ladies further confused the issue by asking staff, 'Are you having the Muslim meal or the English one?' to differentiate between spiced food and mashed potato.

I grew up in India. There, broad-minded Hindu teachers and friends described 'the Muslim period of history' (the Mughal Empire) in romantic terms. Islam brought beautiful art, architecture and poetry to the subcontinent. Films we watched together portrayed the women as especially alluring in flowing headscarves or praying, with their eyes raised heavenwards, in white marble spaces. When violence broke out against Muslims, liberal newspapers and academics denounced it. Muslims, to them, were a poor, maligned minority.

On the other side of the border, however, in Pakistan, things are different. The 2 per cent of the population that define themselves as Christian have a more troubled experience of Muslims. Many of those I know keep their distance. Saira, with whom I lived in an apartment block, never spoke to her Muslim neighbours, even when they shared the space on the roof to enjoy the winter sunshine. There is a level of distrust among them, so that they are wary of getting too close. Many mothers don't let their children play out on the streets. Some phone to call a rickshaw driver from the Christian community rather than going with the one on the street outside. Some churches admit to not really wanting Muslims to come to the services, 'for security reasons'. But all of this is only natural given the attacks on churches in the past, or how quickly an accusation of blasphemy against Christians turns into a highly charged court case.

Still, I rarely met Pakistani Christians whose impression of Muslims was all bad. School friends and happy college days with Muslim students or good workmates meant that most could testify to some Muslims being really good people. 'I love Shi'ahs – they're so brave,' my Urdu teacher told me, and a tear came to his eyes as we translated the story of Ali together. Two sisters I am friends with go into a school and a hospital every day, the only Christians there, and never have a bad word to say about their Muslim colleagues.

To Think About

What have been your personal experiences of Muslims? What do the Christians in your community think about Islam? How do they feel towards the Muslims they know? And towards other Muslims in your country?

Today, a European convert to Islam sent me (Ida) an article on love and compassion in Islam. Every surah in the Qur'an except one, it points out, begins with the words, 'In the name of God, the Lord of Mercy, the Giver of Mercy'. Today, too, a Christian living in Iraq posted on his Facebook page, 'Over 1,500 people killed by "the Islamic State" yesterday.'

How to you respond to these different presentations of Islam?

What Are We Thinking About?

About what are we thinking when we think about Islam? Where do we start in trying to understand a faith that is followed by such a variety of people in such a variety of circumstances, and that can produce such opposites of compassion and violence?

There are several dimensions of Islam that urgently demand our attention. Here we introduce five:

We could begin with *Islam as a faith*, asking how we might understand the worship, ethics and theology of different human beings. We might choose to focus on the Islamic concept of Allāh and compare the teachings of the Qur'an with the teachings of the Bible. However, we are aware that Islam is more than just a private belief system or personal set of morals.

We might start with *the links that Islam makes between faith and power*. The Islamic calendar began when Muhammad and his followers moved from Mecca to found a community under Islamic law in Medina. Since that time, there have been close links between Islam and politics, and today it is almost impossible to separate politics from religion in most places where Muslims are in power. The political dimension of Islam was an underlying factor in the creation of Pakistan and Bangladesh; it is also the basis for international relations for many Islamic states, the grounds for debating the viability of democracy in the Middle East, and the framework for the distribution and exercise of power in many current conflict situations.

We could focus on *the role of shariah law*. Sometimes, laws from the Qur'an and Hadith are the basis of a Muslim society's legal system. Sometimes, the shariah forms an alternative to the national judicial system. How would the Bible suggest we think about shariah in the political arena? Moreover, because shariah regulates every aspect of some Muslims' lives, we need to be aware that, when we think about Islam, we are considering even the tiny details of Muslims' lives – from what time they wake up to the direction they lie in to sleep; from how and what they eat to how they brush their teeth; from what they wear to how they pray. Are there biblical models for understanding regulations like these?

Islam is understood and experienced by most Muslims as a whole way of life. So we could look at *the role of Islam in forming the culture of Muslim societies*. It lays down social codes and can determine all sorts of relationships, such as whom to marry, whose home to live in, which people of the opposite sex to interact with, or employer–employee relations. It also forms the basis for aesthetics, governing what kind of art and architecture is an appropriate expression of belief in God. Where, then, is the overlap between these cultures and biblical cultures that will help us gain a biblical perspective on the cultural implications of Islam?

We could also think about *Islam as a challenge to Christianity*. Uniquely as a world religion, Islam claims to complete the Judaeo-Christian faiths. It offers alternative accounts of many characters in the Bible – even of Jesus – and sees their ministries as fulfilled in Muhammad. We might, therefore, want to understand Islam as a critique of Christianity. Indeed, even in the West, where Muslims are in a small minority, Christian leaders often describe Islam as a real challenge to Christianity. It is listed alongside other major worldviews, such as secularism, materialism and relativism, that oppose a biblical faith in Christ. The statistics and the view from the streets confirm this feeling, as more and more people who have grown up in Europe and North America are converting to Islam.[5] How might we think biblically about such challenges?

Given the wide range of knowledge and experiences of Islam and of Muslims among Christians, it is not surprising that Christians have started at different places in their thinking about Islam. They have also used different parts of the Bible as a basis for their thinking. For example, they have used:

- Elijah and the prophets of Baal as a basis for a ruthless challenge to Islam
- Joshua as a basis for dealing with struggles over land or as a picture of spiritual warfare
- Daniel and Revelation as frameworks for understanding the place of Islam in the unfolding of history
- John the Baptist's and Jesus' confrontations with the Pharisees as a basis for polemics
- Paul's two years at the hall of Tyrannus in Ephesus as a basis for apologetic debate
- Peter's sermons to Jews as a basis for starting dialogue from the Qur'an

---

5. In the UK, for example, it was estimated in 2011 that there could be as many as 100,000 converts from all ethnic backgrounds. See Catrin Nye, 'Converting to Islam: The White Britons Becoming Muslims', BBC News UK, 4 January 2011, http://www.bbc.co.uk/news/uk. This statistic is based on a number of sources, including a 'survey of more than 250 British mosques, census data from 2001 and conversion figures in Europe'.

- Cornelius and the Samaritan woman at the well as bases for personal evangelism
- The Sermon on the Mount as a model for dealing with law-based religion
- Hagar, Tamar, Leah and Rachel as a basis for understanding Muslim women
- Jesus' dealings with the Samaritans as a basis for challenging prejudice
- Passages about false prophets and the antichrist as a basis for dealing with Islam's denials concerning Jesus

You might have noticed, in what we have said so far, that we have distinguished between 'Islam' and 'Muslims'. 'Islam' refers to the faith, and 'Muslim' refers to the person who belongs to the faith. This distinction will become important as the book develops. We will not start by trying to find something in the Bible that is similar to Islam, but by considering how the Bible understands human beings. We will seek to understand Islam mainly by comparing biblical teaching with Islamic teaching.

To Think About

Before reading further, take some time to note down any questions you already have about interacting with Muslims. It may be that this book will not answer them. But after you have read this book, we hope you will be able to use the frameworks offered to find answers in the Bible.

What Is in This Book?

Thinking Biblically about Islam divides into four parts:

- In part 1, we consider how to approach reading the Bible. In particular, we focus on Genesis 1 – 11, an important starting point for thinking biblically about anything in God's world. God's world today includes millions of Muslim people.
- In part 2, we focus on the Gospel accounts of the transfiguration of Jesus. We do this to begin to think about how Jesus relates to Moses and Elijah – to the law and to the prophets, and to contending for the One True God – from a biblical point of view. Monotheism, prophethood and law are central in Islam.

- In part 3, we consider how the Qur'an relates to this understanding of Jesus, Moses and Elijah. This forms a basis for considering how our studies in parts 1 and 2 can help us to 'think biblically' about Muhammad, the Qur'an, the shariah and the political dimensions of Islam.

- In part 4, we consider Jesus' priorities, and how the disciples and we ourselves respond to the transfiguration account; and we ask again what God requires of us.

Parts 1 and 2 together provide a framework for approaching the Bible that can help us to read Scripture more faithfully and move towards a better understanding of other faiths, so enabling us to think more biblically about Islam. These two parts offer, first, a biblical basis for understanding Muslims as human beings and, second, a biblical basis for understanding Islam as a faith.

From our study of Genesis 1 – 11 we will see that the most essential truth about Muslims is that they are human beings, so we can expect to see the whole variety of human nature among Muslims that we see in the portrayal of human nature in the Bible. Muslims are normal: when the Bible speaks of human beings, Muslims are included.

We will compare what we have read in the Bible with parallel Islamic material, especially in the Qur'an. This will enable us to see both similarities and differences between Islamic thinking and biblical thinking, and so to begin to develop a biblically based view of the ideas that make up Islam.

The other passage to be explored in detail is Luke's account of the transfiguration. This choice needs some explanation.

Standing at the centre of all three Synoptic Gospels, lifted high and dressed in dazzling white, is Jesus, transfigured. Set on an unnamed mountaintop, the incident seems to rise above the geography of Jesus' life. Two men of old 'appear in glory', and something of eternity breaks into history on earth. The cloud that covers them and the voice that speaks from it give a rare and breathtaking glimpse of the transcendence of Christ. Peter tries to enclose the three men in tents, but they will not be contained. He doesn't know what to say and is afraid. Those with Jesus did not speak of this event until later. The event was shrouded in silence.

Many of Jesus' people today still speak little about the transfiguration. It is a strange and other-worldly story that seems difficult to understand. However, what is central to the structure of biblical texts is often central in significance, and what is strange demands a closer look. In each of Matthew,

Mark and Luke's accounts, the transfiguration marks a crucial turning point: as Jesus descends the mountain, he turns towards Jerusalem and the cross. We must give this story the importance it requires and investigate it.

The transfiguration is about Jesus, Moses and Elijah. The presence of Moses shows that the story finds its place in Israel's history of covenant, law, land and nationhood; Elijah positions it in relation to prophetic history and zeal. In the transfiguration, we start with Jesus, Moses and Elijah all talking together; they look the same. Then, we see Jesus become brighter than Moses and Elijah, they disappear, and Jesus is left, and goes on his way to the cross. This book is organized around the idea that Islam effectively reverses this process. It removes the death of Jesus and his divine sonship, and then puts him back on the same level as Moses and Elijah.

Given the prophetic–legal foundations of Islam, the transfiguration's presentation of how Jesus relates to the law and the prophets becomes a compelling theme for a Christian theology of Islam. For this reason, part 2, on the transfiguration, includes study of the Bible's accounts of Moses' and Elijah's ministries as recorded in Exodus and the books of Kings, and part 3, on thinking about Islam, includes study of Moses and Elijah in the Qur'an. The Qur'an's and the Bible's stories of Moses are more similar than are their accounts of any other man. His importance is underlined by the similarities between Muhammad's life and his. Elijah's story is referred to in the Qur'an only once, but, as an example of the long succession of prophets sent by God, he too is important. We will find that the qur'anic stories omit aspects of Exodus and Kings that point to the transfiguration.

The final step in Islam's reversal of the transfiguration is in Muslims regarding Muhammad as the final prophet: he is more like Moses and Elijah than he is like Jesus. In practice, they listen to him and not to Jesus. So, as an incident that relates Jesus to the models of law and prophethood, the transfiguration is of crucial importance in allowing us to see Islam through New Testament eyes.

It is for the above reasons that we pursue our framework for thinking biblically about Islam in the shadow of that great cloud on the mountain top. The voice from that cloud declares, 'This is my Son, my Chosen One; listen to him' (Luke 9:35). When we take the Bible seriously, we allow our thoughts on this subject, as with any issue, to be governed by it, to 'listen to *him*'. In part 4, we will try to do just that: we will follow Jesus and his disciples down from the mountain and ask what the gospel requires of Christians in their relationships with Muslims today.

When the Bible's teaching on a subject is hard to discern, 'listening to him' involves careful study. When its conclusions are contrary to our instinctive attitudes, it requires us to wrestle with the Word and with our thinking. This book aims to help filter out some of the noise the world generates about Islam and to allow us to tune into the Son's voice.

Two Preliminary Points:

Point 1: Truth

A very important foundation for 'thinking biblically about Islam' is to decide to think about Islam as it really is, in all its variety, rather than about only a particular version of it that a particular Christian or Muslim website wants us to see; in other words, we want to be truthful.

Thinking and speaking truthfully is certainly biblical: the Ten Commandments given through Moses tell us, 'You shall not bear false witness against your neighbour' (Exod 20:16), and Jesus summed up the Law and the Prophets like this: '. . . whatever you wish that others would do to you, do also to them, for this is the Law and the Prophets' (Matt 7:12). If we would like Muslims to think and to speak truthfully about us, Jesus implies, we should also try to think and to speak truthfully about them.

Of course, it is very difficult – even impossible – to think about the whole variety of Islam and of Muslims, but we can at least recognize that, if we want to think biblically about any particular Muslims we meet, we need first to find out who they are and what they believe, rather than assume they fit into a general pattern called 'Islam'. Furthermore, if we want to think about any particular aspect of Islamic faith, we need to recognize that different Muslims may understand it and apply it in different ways.

In the course of this book we will be referring to different sorts of Muslims who live in different places and think in different ways. We offer here a short overview for readers who are not familiar with the variety that is found within Islam.

Forming nearly a quarter of the world's population, the 1.6 billion Muslims of the world represent the whole range of humanity. They are as varied as the places they come from: from the edges of the Sahara Desert to the lush islands of South East Asia, from remote valleys and plateaux in the Himalayas to teeming mega-cities of Asia, from southern Europe to sub-Saharan Africa.

It is hardly surprising, given their hugely varied ethnic backgrounds, that Muslims express their distinctive forms of Islam in different ways. There are two main sects of Islam: Sunni (up to 90 per cent of the total Muslim population) and Shi'ah. Their different practices, institutions and structures of authority are underpinned by different understandings of the role of Muhammad's family that date back to the decade following Muhammad's death. Sunnis accepted a series of different successors to Muhammad (caliphs) as leaders of the Muslim people, while the Shi'ites believed that Muhammad's own descendants should be their leaders (imams).

Besides these two branches of Islam are many smaller sects, often based in specific regions. The Ibadis in Oman and Zanzibar follow a variety of Islam. The Ahmadiyyas (also known as Qadiyyanis) follow an interpretation of Islam based on the teachings of a nineteenth-century Indian leader. They can be found in many parts of the world, but many Muslims regard them as non-Muslims.

There are also many groups and movements within Sunni and Shi'ite Islam. The different Shi'ite groups accept different imams. Most believe that the last imam has disappeared and will return towards the end of the world; but the Ismailis see the living Aga Khan as their leader. Sunnis are often described in terms of which of four different 'law schools' they follow: in different areas, there have been different ways of interpreting the requirements of the Qur'an and the Hadith. Within both Sunni and Shi'ite Islam can be found 'Sufis' – people who seek direct experience of God through religious practices and through following a holy person who might be called 'sheikh' or 'pir'.

In addition, there is a wide range of cultural influences on belief and practice across the Muslim world. Some Muslims seek to base every area of their lives on the Qur'an and certain Hadith, and are careful not to be influenced by the culture that surrounds them. Other Muslims accept much of the local culture even if it is not, strictly speaking, Islamic. So in South Asia, for example, many Muslims enjoy the same music, films, fashions and wedding ceremonies as their Hindu counterparts.

Muslims practise their religion in a variety of different ways and have different views on which are acceptable under Islam. For example, in some regions, it is unacceptable to revere Muslim saints; in other places, it is the norm. Proportions of Muslim populations that wear amulets to protect themselves from evil or that visit religious healers also range widely.

Political views are another area of wide variation. Some Muslims are committed to democratic processes, while others would use violence to bring about change. Many more would prefer to keep their heads down and keep the peace for the sake of stability. For some, their political persuasion is more important than their religious identity. Political views are affected by the political climates in which Muslims live.[6] In forty-nine countries, Muslims are the majority, but a fifth of Muslims live as minorities. Of these, some are subject to persecution. In parts of India, for example, sporadic Hindu right-wing violence is targeted at Muslims. The 6 million Rohingya people have a particularly tragic history as an unwanted group, unable to gain status in either Bangladesh or Myanmar.[7]

So Muslims find themselves in all sorts of situations around the world, alongside everyone else in the human race. A few are fabulously rich. However, they are in the minority: nearly all the Muslim-majority countries are in the less-developed regions of the world. Many Muslims are displaced – the majority of refugees are Muslims – affected by conflict, drought or natural disasters.

Finally, as with all people, the young and the old approach their lives differently. On the one hand, some young Muslims adopt a much more radical form of Islam than their parents. On the other hand, research suggests that, across nearly all the Muslim world, the younger generation is less likely to read the Qur'an, to pray and to attend the mosque.

A Story: A Drink to Break the Fast

It had felt like a long day in the office, a long time since their pre-dawn breakfast. Food they could manage without during this month of fasting, but when their boss blamed them for errors in calculations they'd never even worked on, the junior engineers were all agreed: they missed their cigarette breaks.

Anyway, it would be a good iftar tonight; Oibek was newly married and his wife made a good pan of plov. Meanwhile, they would try to stay focused on their screens and avoid the attention of their boss altogether.

Towards sunset, they started showing up at Oibek's place. They strode in, a whole lot more confident now that they were away from the boss, and sat around the *dastarkhwan* spread on the floor.

---

6. Interesting details can be found in 'Muslim-Majority Countries', Pew Research, 27 January 2011, http://www.pewforum.org/2011/01/27/future-of-the-global-muslim-population-muslim-majority/.

7. Subir Bhaumik, 'Nobody's People in a No-Man's Land', Aljazeera, 16 August 2012, http://www.aljazeera.com.

Zainab had placed little glasses at each of their places. They fingered them absent-mindedly as they tried to outdo each other making jokes about the project managers.

Soon, their guest came – Sadiq from overseas. He was older than them, and couldn't speak their language, but it was only right to invite him, they had considered, given that he was a Muslim alone and away from his family at this special time. Besides, he was such a pleasant gentleman. They made polite conversation with him and were glad when the hands of the clock told them the fast was over. They could have a drink. Oibek unscrewed a bottle and began to fill everyone's glass with a shot of vodka.

Sadiq's back stiffened. Everyone noticed. Some took a nervous sip, but no one shouted out the toast to Oibek and Zainab they would otherwise have made.

'So . . . would you prefer a soft drink, sir?' Oibek tentatively offered.

'Thank you, that would be nice . . . but you boys carry on, I'll be fine.'

The next day, in the office, Oibek took Sadiq aside and began to apologize. 'Sir, we just didn't think . . . we forgot you might not appreciate . . . this thing.' He could not bring himself to name the drink.

'Son, it's totally fine.' He placed his hand on Oibek's arm. 'You've grown up in a different place. Your parents couldn't give you the good upbringing we give in my country. You have all done so well to stay Muslim after so long under Soviet rule. I am very impressed.'

To Think About

What surprises you about this story? What do you learn about the variety of Muslims in the world, and about how Muslims from different places might relate to each other? How do the Christians in your area treat other Christians who have different practices?

Are there Muslims from different communities around you? Do you see differences in how the different generations express their identity and faith? How do different groups relate to each other?

Point 2: God

One question that people often ask is, 'Do Muslims and Christians worship the same God?' This can be a misleading question, as it expects an answer of either 'Yes' or 'No'. However, it needs an answer of both 'Yes' and 'No'.

On the one hand, the Qur'an clearly intends to refer to the One God who created all things and who is the God worshipped by Jews and Christians. On the other hand, there are some important differences, not least the fact that an Islamic view of God does not allow for the idea that God is Father, Son and Holy Spirit. By the end of this book, we hope that readers will have gained deeper understanding of the similarities and differences between Muslim and Christian views of God, and will be able to think about this question for themselves.

Here, we need to deal with a slightly different question, as we need to decide about what words we should use in our study. We have used the word 'God' to refer to the object of Islamic beliefs as well as of Christian beliefs: the question is, 'Is it right to refer to Allāh of the Qur'an as 'God', using the same word that we use to refer to the God of Israel as revealed in the Bible?'

The word 'Allāh' is the Arabic word for 'God': this book is being written in English, so we will use 'God' to translate the Arabic 'Allāh'. If we were writing in Arabic, we would have to use 'Allāh' to translate the English word 'God', just as Arabic Bibles use 'Allāh' to translate the Hebrew word *elohim* and the Greek word *theos*.

Some Muslims use 'Allāh' as a proper name for God even when they are speaking English. They want to make a difference between God as Muslims understand him and God as Christians understand him. In Malaysia, there is a big controversy about whether and how Christians should be allowed to use the word 'Allāh' – it is a word that is only for Muslims, say some Muslims. However, 'Allāh' was in use among the Arabs long before the time of Muhammad.

The word *allah* is related to the Syriac or Aramaic word *'Ĕlāhā*. This was the word used by the Christians with whom Muhammad would have spoken. It is related to the Hebrew *elohim* and can be found in the Syriac portions of the Old Testament in Daniel and Ezra. It is the word for God that Jesus would have used in Aramaic.

An old tradition states that 'Allāh' comes from the Arabic *al-ilāh*, where *al* is the definite article and *ilāh* is an object of worship or a god. 'Allāh' would then mean 'the one object of worship' or 'God'. This is similar to the New

Testament's use of *ho theos* (literally, 'the god'); just as there were many gods worshipped in Arabia before the rise of Islam, so there were many gods worshipped by the Greeks of the first century AD. In both cases, the word used for the many gods is applied to the One God by books that teach monotheism. Christians have followed the New Testament pattern: the gospel spread, they appropriated local words such as the Teutonic word 'god', then they gradually adjusted the meaning of the word to convey the God of the Bible.

Putting these ideas together, we can see that it is appropriate for Christians to use the word 'Allāh' when talking to Muslims in Arabic or other Muslim languages, and then to explain what the One Creator and Judge of all peoples is like. Similarly, we can use 'God' in English and then discuss what he is like. As far as language is concerned, it is more important to listen to what particular people believe about the Creator than to argue about what to call him. As far as theology is concerned, there can be no doubt that Muslims are intending to speak about the being who created everyone and everything when they use the word 'Allāh', and that is the being whom, in English, Christians call 'God'.

With these preliminary points considered, we are now ready to start looking at Genesis 1 – 11.

Part 1

Genesis

Genesis 1 – 11 is about peoples: who they are, what they are and where they came from. Out of this account of people emerges a family history which fills the rest of Genesis. This family, in turn, becomes a whole nation, a people whose story goes on to fill the rest of the Torah. 'Why did God call this family and this people? Who are they? Where did they come from? What are they?' These are the questions being answered by the Genesis family story. One of the clearest indications that the relatedness of people is the author's focus is the phrase repeated throughout the book, 'These are the generations of . . .' (KJV). The book relates the 'generations' first of all 'of the heavens and the earth' (2:4), then 'of Adam' (5:1), 'of Noah' (6:9), 'of Shem, Ham, and Japheth', Noah's sons (10:1), 'of Shem' (11:10), 'of Terah' (11:27), 'of Ishmael, Abraham's son' (25:12), 'of Isaac, Abraham's son' (25:19), 'of Esau' (36:1, 6) and, finally, 'of Jacob' (37:2).

The Hebrew word translated 'generations' is *toledoth*. The root meaning of the word has to do with people being born. Readers have long discussed exactly what it means in Genesis, and translations vary. The NIV renders it 'account', because each *toledoth* formula introduces the next part of the account, but the ESV continues to use the word 'generations' to emphasize that the accounts are about generations of related people. Both are right: Genesis is a genealogy, telling us how people are connected, but it does that by relating the stories, or 'accounts', of the people who are important for its purposes.

There are clues to those purposes in what the *toledoth*s include and in what they omit. As we would expect, Abraham's ancestors and those of his descendants who will be the ancestors of the Jewish people are included. But those descendants of Abraham who are *not* the ancestors of the Jewish people are also included, even those who are the ancestors of Israel's enemies! We see, then, that Genesis is not only about the Jews, but about the whole of humanity. Omitted – and this is a surprise – is Abraham himself: there is no *toledoth* of Abraham. There is, it seems, something special about Abraham.

So Genesis is, on the one hand, about the whole world of human beings into which Abraham is called; and, on the other hand, about the family through which Abraham's call will bear fruit. By the end of the book, in chapter 49, we see that branch of the family called the children of Israel (Jacob), but we see them living among another people, having saved the lives of the Egyptians and many others (50:20). In short, the good news in Genesis is, as Paul points out quoting Genesis 12:3, that God promises that 'in [Abraham] shall all the nations be blessed' (Gal 3:8). Genesis is not only about people, but also about blessing.

We begin our study with Genesis 1 – 11 because it tells us who the people are whom God planned to bless through Abraham, and why they needed this plan of blessing. It tells us about all people, which included Jews and non-Jews, and continues to include all peoples – Muslims, Jews, Christians, Hindus, Sikhs and everyone else.

We will do three things through our study of Genesis 1 – 11:

- First, we will model *a way of reading the Bible*. There are many different ways to approach the Bible, and we need to choose one that is appropriate to our concerns.
- Second, we will discern a framework for thinking biblically about *Muslim people*. Since Muslims represent the whole range of human experience and culture, Genesis 1 – 11's understanding of *human beings* and their religious nature will give us a framework for thinking about them.
- Third, we will set out towards developing a method for thinking biblically about *Islam*. We need a way of thinking about *religious beliefs and practices*, and for comparing Islamic faith to biblical faith.

In Genesis 1 – 11 we see God's intention for people: how, in God's good order, we were made to be. We then see how his design was marred when the first people tried to take control, and this is followed by a description of the world outside Eden, which is the world in which, subsequently, all human beings have lived and still live today. The whole direction of biblical history is built on these early chapters. This, then, is the place to begin any study of human relationships with God, with each other or with the environment, work, possessions, knowledge or power. This will give us the framework for thinking about Muslims as human beings.

In chapter 2 we will compare some of the stories in Genesis 1 – 11 with parallel stories from the Qur'an in order to compare Islamic and biblical ideas. Here, though, we introduce a method for approaching the Bible, which we can then apply to Genesis 1 – 11 in chapter 1.

A Multi-Layered Approach to Reading the Bible

How do we choose between the different ways of using the Bible? Do they depend only on the situation? If so, how is it that sincere Christians can come to opposite conclusions about any particular subject? One of the answers is that people approach the Bible in different ways. There is a lot of work to be done, not only in understanding the different aspects of Islam, but also in deciding which part of the Bible is relevant to which aspect of Islam, and then in understanding what it means. Then we need to ask how that part of the Bible relates to other parts, and how each part should be interpreted.

Ida's *The Bible and Other Faiths* suggests how we can best go about reading the Bible with questions about people of other faiths in mind. Here, we use the method of reading described in that earlier work. This section gives an overview of that method.[1]

Our method of reading is to look at any biblical text from three perspectives, and then to develop understanding through seeking to obey whatever we learn.

Perspective 1: Looking at the World behind the Text

Many readers are geographically far removed from the setting of the events recorded in the Bible, and we are all living in a different age entirely. So the thoughtful reader's first task is to *look at the world in which the Bible was written*, which is known as 'the world behind the text'. This is like looking through the text as a window on the world in which it was written.

The story of Israel and the church is historical and the characters were real actors in history, not just symbols for deeper meanings or morals. We

---

1. For more details, see ch. 3, 'Reading the Bible', in Glaser, *The Bible and Other Faiths*, 63–64, 99.

read about them as real people. That is why they are named and their fathers are named on page after page of the genealogies, such as those mentioned above. They also lived in real places. Many copies of the Bible include maps, for we want to know about the landscape they lived in, to try to enter their world. And so, when we first view any biblical passage, our eyes must focus on the sociology, geography and biographies of the times. It is as if we look through the Bible as a window on the past.

Therefore, the first step in our method is to ask what the world was like in which the writer wrote any given passage. Archaeology and ancient literature can provide important background detail. We can also learn from what the passage itself tells us about the time and place in which it is set. That will help us to hear it as the author and first hearers would have understood it. What did the words, sentences and stories convey to them? What pictures did they conjure up? What were the implications for their lives? What echoes of other stories could they hear?

Since we are reading the Bible here in the context of Islam, we will particularly keep our eyes open for parallels between the Bible's historical background and Muslim societies. For instance, we will see similarities between religions of the time and some elements of Islam: their legal and political dimensions, family and social structures, and interactions between nations.

Perspective 2: Looking at the World of the Text

The next step is to *pay attention to the composition of the text itself*. This is what scholars call studying 'the world of the text'. We need to consider what a passage means in the context of the book it is in and in relation to the rest of the Bible; we need also to look carefully at the nature and structure of the text. This is like looking at the text as a picture, seeing its details and enjoying its beauty.

The Bible includes many different types of literature. It was written by singers, poets, storytellers, historians and lawyers. They used Hebrew, Aramaic and Greek words well. The Sons of Korah, psalmists, give us a glimpse of the craft and emotion involved in conveying the message of the Bible:

> My heart overflows with a pleasing theme;
>> I address my verses to the king;
>> my tongue is like the pen of a ready scribe (Ps 45:1).

To understand any particular passage, we need to look at the texts they were inspired to compose as an art historian might study a painting, asking how it is patterned, why certain techniques were used and what the significance is of the symbols and idioms. This will help us hear the message they brought to their first audiences and readers. We will notice what was important to them, feel the impact of certain details and be alert to the action below the surface of the text.

Perspective 3: Looking at the World in Front of the Text

The next stage is to *ask the significance of the message to ourselves and our world and to how we relate to it*. This is finding the meaning of the text for the 'world in front of the text'. It is like looking into the text as a mirror in which we can see ourselves and our situations.

For any particular Bible passage, we can be sure that many others have already read it in their 'world in front of the text', and it can be helpful to consider their readings.

- The various books of the Bible often refer to each other. In the Old Testament, the prophetic books often give interpretations of the historical books. In the New Testament, the writers often give interpretations of the Old Testament. Jesus himself applies much Old Testament teaching to his first-century world and to himself.
- Many events of the Bible are dealt with in the Qur'an, so we can see the Qur'an as offering readings of the Bible in its own 'world in front of the text'. To study this thoroughly, we would also have to read the Bible in the context of its pre-Islamic rabbinic and Syriac Christian interpretations, as these were in circulation during the development of Islam.
- At different times in history, Christians have used texts to help them think about their various experiences of Islam in their 'worlds in front of the text'.
- Muslims in different times and places have also read and commented on the Bible, and continue to do so.

Clearly, there is not space in this book to give much attention to all these traditions, but we will be consciously reading the Bible in the context of Islam. This is particularly important since Islam is the only world religion to have its own accounts of the events and people foundational to Christian faith. The Qur'an, in which they are found, describes these accounts as the true ones. As we will see, reflecting on the similarities and differences between the Qur'an and the Bible will be fruitful for our understanding of the Bible itself, even as we seek to understand Islam better.

With our eyes wide open to the world and writing of the Bible, we also look at today's world, as in a mirror. For this, we need to make an accurate assessment of the current situation and speak truthfully about 'our neighbours', as we have already noted (Exod 20:16). Then, we need to see ourselves in the mirror of the Bible. 'First take the log out of your own eye,' Jesus exhorts us (Matt 7:5), so that we can help those around us, without hypocrisy, to deal with specks in their eyes. There is a danger that, as readers, we write ourselves into the role of hero in every story and ignore our own failings as individuals or as churches. On the other hand, in these politically correct times in Europe, some readers may need to take care not to automatically cast themselves as 'the baddy' in relation to religious minorities. A multifaceted reading of the Bible will enable us to make a more accurate assessment.

Perhaps the most important step in the 'world in front of the text' is putting into practice what we learn. Jesus himself points out that we must desire to obey God if we want to know what is true (John 7:17), and 1 John exhorts us not only to know the truth but also to 'do' the truth (1 John 1:6). Obedience takes our faith to new levels, and, with it, our understanding.

1

A Created, Fallen, Religious World

Genesis 1 – 11 offers a powerful framework for thinking about all religious people, including Muslims and Christians. In this chapter, we will read Genesis 1 – 11 keeping in mind our specific questions about how to understand Muslims as human beings belonging to a particular religious faith. We will focus on the worlds behind the text and of the text, but we will keep inviting you to ask, 'How do these worlds relate to Muslims in today's world "in front of the text"?'

We start by looking at the context in which Genesis was written. It was a religious world. Texts and archaeological finds dating from the same era as Genesis show that people believed in many gods. The various cultures had different stories about the creation of the world, battles between the gods and their complex relationships. These gods and their stories seem to have been the basis for many practices of ancient cultures. However, it is interesting that Genesis deals with all these beings by writing them out of the script: apart from brief mentions of household gods in the Jacob story,[1] and of the priest of On in the Joseph story,[2] today's reader would hardly guess at their existence.

Genesis 1 has much in common with other creation stories from the same period.[3] It is because the stories are broadly similar that the differences

---

1. Rachel stole her father's 'household gods' and hid them under the saddle she was sitting on when he came looking for them (Gen 31:17–35).

2. He became Joseph's father-in-law when Joseph married Asenath, his daughter, in Egypt (Gen 41:45).

3. Both the Babylonian epic *Enuma Elish* and the *Epic of Atrahasis* have the gods create man to work the land and to allow themselves to rest. In the latter poem, the god Ea suggests making a substitute for the gods and, with the Mother goddess, adds clay to the corpse of a god and spits on it. Wombs give birth to seven pairs of humans. The idea of creating man from the ground in some form, as in Gen 2, is prevalent in many other Sumerian and

stand out clearly and appear significant. In the Genesis account of the origin of the world, there is but one creator God of all. There are no warring, jealous, lustful or hungry deities: the One God is good, and in control of everything. The sun and the moon are not gods: God created them. There are no sea gods or mountain gods: the One God made both the sea and the land. In other creation stories, human beings play active parts in creation, sometimes as relatives of the gods, and sometimes as those who provoke the gods. In Genesis, however, humans are neither the playthings nor the helpers of the gods: the One God needs neither. People are simply part of God's creation.

When read with an awareness of the world behind the text, the beginning of Genesis offers a powerful framework for understanding the world as a multi-religious place. From Genesis 1 – 2, we learn about the religious nature of human beings. From Genesis 3, we learn how that religious nature went wrong through the 'fall' of human beings. Genesis 4 – 11 then describes the world after the fall, which is the world we live in. It is a religious world, and each part of Genesis 4 – 11 describes a different aspect of religious humanity after the fall.

Genesis 1 – 3: Humans are Religious Beings

The story of the creation of men and women is well known: human beings are made by the One God and for relationship with the One God. In Genesis 1, he makes male and female people 'in his own image' (v. 27). He blesses them, speaks to them, provides for them and gives them tasks. This means that we would expect to find a measure of awareness of the Creator in every human being; people are naturally religious.

What God then gives to the people he has created establishes some of the deepest aspects of human nature. In Genesis 2 he gives them land; he 'planted a garden in Eden, in the east, and there he put the man whom he had formed' (v. 8). The chapter goes on to describe the geographic significance of Eden in relation to rivers that flow out of it and the precious resources around it. People are *placed*, grounded, connected to a space they call their own. This territorial aspect of people and communities is still true today, discerned in our attachment to home and our yearning for it.

Babylonian accounts. P. Bienkowski and A. Millard, eds., *Dictionary of the Ancient Near East* (London: British Museum Press, 2000), 81.

God's first charge to the male and female to be 'fruitful and multiply' (1:28) puts the desire and responsibility to be creative, productive and significant right at the heart of what it means to be human. God also gives people dominion over all the other species and charges them to 'fill the earth and subdue it' (1:28). The desire and the responsibility to walk confidently in the world, ordering it and exercising authority, is also intrinsic to human nature.

God created male and female. After he made woman, God 'brought her to the man' (2:22). The togetherness they experienced is part of who people are by God's design. With God in their midst, people move towards being in community, here described as completely uninhibited: 'the man and his wife were both naked and were not ashamed' (2:25).

Other creation stories from the time of Genesis tell of deities who gave power and land to particular peoples. Each story serves to strengthen a particular community's claims to certain places. The Genesis writer counters the prevailing idea that links people and power to a territorial god by showing how land, authority and family are gifts from the One God of all the earth.

Genesis 3, however, describes how things went wrong. Instead of enjoying the land and exercising authority under God, the human beings took things into their own hands and abused the fruit of the land, motivated by the desire to become like God. Their relationships with God, with each other and with the animals and land were spoiled. Their power had to be limited (3:22) and they lost their garden home. Genesis 3:14–19 describes the power struggles and pain that would henceforth mark relationships between humans and animals, men and women, and humans and the earth.

Ever since this time, people have reflected something of God's good design while also being tainted by the sin first seen in Adam and Eve. All religious communities are part of this world, and so we can expect them to reflect aspects of both the good creation and the fallen state. They have the need and the capacity to relate to God, but, like every other aspect of human nature, this has been marred. Neither Muslims nor Christians are exceptions.

Muslims, like Christians and everyone else in the world in front of the text, are created in God's own image. Classical Islam has problems with this idea (as we will see later), but, according to Genesis, this is how God sees people, and it has implications for how people see him. God dignified Adam with purpose, spoke to him and blessed him with companionship, and people today are made for a similar relationship with God. So Muslims, like all other humans, have an instinctive feel for their creator and a capacity to hear him.

Hannah's Story: The Child Who Prayed

Sitting on a rickshaw, I splash through the backstreets of the city through grey drizzle, past bare trees and cosy shop fronts decked out in green and gold tinsel and coloured lights. People are getting ready for the birthday of their prophet on Sunday. At dusk, the town fills with his chanted praise.

I am travelling to a school-cum-boarding house for poor girls located down a narrow alley. Helena and I are ushered into the heart of the house to visit the head of this Qur'an school. When we enter, her phone is ringing and she ignores it, because she is performing her prayers. Ten minutes later, she is still praying.

Hostel girls come in and out. They sit for a while and play with the head's daughters. The youngest one, rosy-cheeked and four years old, starts to imitate her mother, splaying her little fingers as she places her palms on the mat and bows her head. Then she jumps up with a squeal, as if uncurling from a game of hide-and-seek, ready to copy her mother's upright posture.

Baji lives with her husband and three daughters in a single room and shares the rest of the house with girls from needy homes who come and study with her. She teaches the Qur'an in return for donations towards their upkeep.

'No one taught me to pray as a child,' Baji tells us when she at last makes herself comfortable on a cushion and watches her daughter roll up her little mat. 'I was the only one in my village to pray.'

Baji grew up in the mountains to the north. She describes how, aged seven, she would rise before dusk, creep from under the family quilt and slip outside into the bite of the cold morning air. There she bowed her head to the frozen ground. 'I just knew Allāh was there,' she says, 'and I wanted to talk to him.' Getting up early meant she was the one who had to blow on the embers of last night's fire, which would sting her eyes with smoke, and start the breakfast preparation. Her family laughed at her at first. 'No one in the village used to believe in Allāh. But now they do.'

Baji's devotion to God has never abated. In a women's study group, over tea, she joins in the talk about husbands. There are all sorts of complaints about their various foibles and vices. We're all shocked to hear that Baji is married to a man who in the past didn't pray. 'He used to tell me to relax and come back to bed,' she says. 'But he didn't stop me, and I prayed to God for the strength to be an example to him.' We nod in approval, subdued as we reflect on our own prayer lives and marriages. 'He is a man of prayer now.'

> **To Think About**
>
> Baji wanted to talk to God.
>
> What first made you want to know God? How does your story about seeking God compare to hers? How does Genesis 1 – 3 help you to understand her yearning for God?
>
> Baji calls God 'Allāh'.
>
> In what ways are her prayers similar to yours? In what ways are they different? How might that demonstrate different understandings of the nature of God?

Genesis 4 – 11

As we saw above, Muslims, like Christians and everyone else in the 'world in front of the text', are included in the 'fall'. We can expect them to exhibit all the aspects of fallen human nature that others do. Like any other system, Islam is likely to encourage some of these aspects and discourage others. Genesis 4 – 11 describes the world outside Eden: while Genesis 1 – 2 describes the world before the fall, Genesis 4 – 11 describes the world after the fall. It is a world that includes Muslims.

Christians have sometimes attempted to understand Islam biblically by identifying Ishmael as the father of the Arabs and therefore as a pattern through whom all Muslims can be understood.[4] There is some value in this, as Muslims themselves see Ishmael as their forefather in faith. However, such an approach can be too narrow: Ishmael is but one of the human beings whose nature is described in Genesis 1 – 11. If we are to be true to Genesis, we need first to look at human nature as a whole: Genesis 1 – 11 tells us about all human beings, including Muslims.

The world described by Genesis 4 – 11 is a religious world. Archaeologists have learned that in the world of Mesopotamia 'behind the text', the widespread belief that people were servants for the gods led to them constantly offering food, drink, clothes and other useful or precious things. There were daily

---

4. A recent example can be found in Tony Maalouf's excellent study of Ishmael, *Arabs in the Shadow of Israel: The Unfolding of God's Prophetic Plan for Ishmael's Line* (Grand Rapids: Kregel, 2003).

offerings at mealtimes, occasional festival offerings, and thank-offerings or offerings made as part of a request. Certain places besides temples have been identified as being specifically used for sacrifices.[5] This is the background to the account of Cain and Abel's and Noah's sacrifices in Genesis 4 and 10 respectively.

Looking at the 'world of the text', these chapters can be considered as a 'chiasmus': that is, the shape of the narrative can be seen as an X, which is the Greek capital letter 'chi'. The centre of the X is the central point of the narrative, and the writer has arranged ideas that reflect each other symmetrically either side of that point. So the pattern of the narrative can be described as:

A B C B' A'

There are many chiasmus structures in the Bible, and we will study others later in this book. In the case of Genesis 4 – 11 we have:

A Cain and Abel (Gen 4)
   B Genealogy of death (Gen 5)
      C Noah (Gen 6 – 9)
   B' Genealogy of life (Gen 10)
A' Babel and the nations (Gen 11)

A and A' – Cain and Abel and the Babel story – are important for our study because they describe early religious acts, and C – the Noah story – must be important because it takes up so much space and is at the heart of the chiasmus. We will explore these passages in detail below.

In this book, we will not look at the details of Genesis 5 and 10, which are labelled B and B' in the chiasmus; but these chapters are also important for our study because they tell us about how human beings are related to each other. As we saw at the start of part 1, the whole of Genesis is built around the relatedness of people and God's promise to Abraham in chapter 12:3. The Bible sees history in terms of God's desire to bless all families and peoples: this is foundational to any biblical thinking about Muslims.

Genesis 5 and 10 remind us that all human beings have the same nature and are dependent on each other. We have called B a 'genealogy of death' because Genesis 5 says of each person (with one exception), 'and he died'. No other Old Testament genealogy tells us that; each simply assumes that people died. But Genesis 5 is the first record of deaths after Cain's murder of

---

5. Bienkowski and Millard, *Dictionary of the Ancient Near East*, 248.

Abel. It reminds us not only that we are a human family, but also that we all die because we are all descended from Adam. Genesis 10, B', is usually called 'the Table of Nations', but we have called it a 'genealogy of life' because the multiplication of the people is the fulfilment of God's blessing in Genesis 1:28: at last, the people are filling the earth. God's blessing is further underlined by the beautiful ordering of the peoples, and by his giving them all their living places. Genesis 10 reminds us that all the ethnic groups to which we belong are included in God's promise to Noah.

Cain and Abel: Humans Seek God

Although the first people were sent out of the garden of Eden, they were not cast out from God's care. Eve testified that it was 'with the help of the LORD' that she bore her first son, Cain (Gen 4:1). Adam and Eve's sons worked the land and tended the flocks under the 'curse', but they still knew that God existed and that he mattered. In fact, the first story recorded of the first human beings born outside Eden begins with a 'religious' act: 'In the course of time, Cain brought to the LORD an offering of the fruit of the ground, and Abel also brought of the firstborn of his flock and of their fat portions' (4:3–4).

This has established a pattern in history and forms a foundational element in our framework for understanding religion. People may be fallen, but the religious instinct to reach out to the divine remains. God also continues to be involved in the lives of people. We do not only relate as husband to wife, parent to child or brother to brother, but, created in the image of God, we have enough likeness to our creator to want to relate to him. From the Cain and Abel story, we learn that human beings are likely to seek relationship with God through forms of sacrifice.

The 'religious' act is followed immediately by the first 'religious' argument and violence. So far, the story outside Eden has been one of creation, new life and multiplication. Suddenly there is a dark new element: Cain kills his brother. There is no reference to a tempter: this violence springs unaided from the human heart. Cain acts out of his own jealousy and rivalry. Instead of directing his anger at God, who, after all, was the one who rejected his produce, he directs his anger towards his innocent brother. And God lets it happen: he does not save the life of the brother whom he has accepted, but allows him to be cruelly slaughtered. Then, in the Genesis 5 genealogy that follows, comes the announcement, uniquely among biblical genealogies (as noted above), 'and he died' of each of Adam's descendants,[6] as if death is an extraordinary fact. God's warning to Adam (Gen 2:17) has proved right: the cycle of death has set in.

The story of Cain and Abel suggests some of both the positive and the harmful aspects of all religious enterprise that we still see in the 'world in front of the text'. There are a number of dimensions of Islam that can be seen as parallel to Cain and Abel's attempts to reach God through sacrifice – from the actual understanding of the Eid sacrifice as substitutionary in some popular thinking, to more orthodox teaching about how the hajj can wipe out sin. The ritual prayers, fasting, almsgiving and pilgrimage are not, in Muslim understanding, sacrifices: Muslims see them as part of a life of obedience to God. However, they are all ways of seeking to please God, and a life of obedience is, at its best, an offering of oneself to God. In view of the Cain and Abel story, then, it is not surprising that there is not only debate but also violence associated with different Islamic understandings of what might be acceptable to God.

Two Goats for a Village

There was some debate as to whether it was one thousand or ten thousand sins that got cancelled out by every hair of the goat that was sacrificed. The older men seemed to think it was only a thousand, but, either way, they reckoned the two goats for the village would be enough this year. They had certainly all had plenty of meat to eat. 'We couldn't afford more this year, so we hope it will be enough.'

'But why would God forgive according to the hairs on a goat?' the visitor asked.

'Well, we do *neki*, too – one good deed for every sin – and it balances out . . . *Inshallah*.'

---

6. With one strange exception: that of Enoch in vv. 21–24: 'When Enoch had lived for 65 years, he fathered Methuselah. Enoch walked with God after he fathered Methuselah for 300 years and had other sons and daughters. Thus all the days of Enoch were 365 years. Enoch walked with God, and he was not, for God took him.' It raises the possibility of another way to enter eternity: without dying.

> **To Think About**
>
> This was a conversation in a rural area of South Asia. What attempts do Muslims you know make to reach God? How do these compare to the ways in which other people try to reach God?
>
> 'We hope it will be enough,' said the elders. At what times do you hope that you have done 'enough'?

God and Sacrifice

The next thing that we learn from Genesis 4 is good news: God accepts Abel and his sacrifice. The story is so familiar that we expect it, but, in its place in Genesis, God's acceptance is a surprise. The human beings have sinned, and God has told them the consequences. The consequences are so severe that Christians often call them 'curses'.[7] Outside Eden, we wonder whether the humans have lost the blessing of God altogether. The births of Cain and Abel 'with the help of the LORD' give some hope. But the gates of Eden have been shut, so will human beings ever again hear God's voice or experience his presence? Will he respond to the sacrifices? We do not know how Abel knew that his sacrifice was accepted, but he did know, and so did Cain. God must have communicated with him in some way. We learn that, even in this fallen world, God accepts some sacrifices and some of the people who make sacrifices.

Genesis 4 leaves open the question of what makes Abel's sacrifice acceptable and Cain's sacrifice unacceptable. Is it the nature of the sacrifice or the attitude of the person who brings the sacrifice, or is it simply God's sovereign decision? Either way, the story makes it clear that not every sacrifice is acceptable to him: not every religious act pleases God. Neither man knows what sacrifice God wants: people are only allowed to approach God on his terms. Hebrews 11:4 suggests that it was not the kind of sacrifice that mattered, but the faith of the sacrificer. There are some hints of this in Genesis, in that Abel brought the best that he could; but it is not until the New Testament that we can see clearly the faith that distinguished him from his brother. Only God sees the heart.

---

7. In fact, the human beings are not said to be cursed. The word 'curse' is used only of the serpent and of the ground (Gen 3:14, 17).

To Think About

Is it possible that some of the sacrifices offered by Muslims might be acceptable to God from a biblical perspective?

The Bible includes many stories of individuals outside Israel whose prayers are heard by God, as well as many stories of people within Israel whose sacrifices are repulsive to God. Can we expect God to respond to the agonies of some Muslims as he did to Hagar (Gen 21:15–19), or to the prayers, fasting and almsgiving of others as he did to those of Cornelius (Acts 10)? Might he speak also to those who are inclined to violence, as he did to Cain and to Saul of Tarsus?

Read the accounts of God hearing the prayers of these people outside the covenant community. On what basis did God respond? What does this do to our ideas about prayerful Muslims?

God and Cain

Following the murder, God speaks to Cain, the angry, rejected, violent one (v. 6–7, 9–15). In contrast, and perhaps surprisingly, God has not spoken at all to Abel, and the writer has included none of Abel's speech. So this story is not about the innocent victim but about God's patience with the wicked murderer. We might be surprised that God does nothing to protect Abel; but we may also be surprised that he does do something to protect Cain.

God exiles Cain rather than killing him, and even marks him to prevent anyone attacking him. Earlier, God had said that death would be the consequence for disobedience, warning Adam and Eve concerning the tree of the knowledge of good and evil that 'in the day that you eat of it you shall surely die' (2:17). However, shockingly, it is the innocent Abel who has died and Cain's life is, for now, spared, given value and documented. He remains creative, starting a family and building a city. His descendants establish further aspects of civilization – music and metal work – and nomadic farming (4:17–22). The descendants of this sinner act on God's commission to work and subdue creation. God still gives gifts to this family and allows it to prosper.

God opens up the possibility of change and hope with the question 'If you do well, will you not be accepted?' (v. 7). Often in the Bible, God prolongs the lives of people who have committed terrible sins, giving them time to repent and change. Return to God is open to the 'Cains' of the world.

Ultimately, though, if they choose not to take the opportunity offered, they are judged.

To Think About

Holding this text up as a mirror on the world of your community in front of it, where might you 'see' Muslims in this Cain and Abel account? Are attempts to reach God and/or violent behaviours unique to them, or are these common to other sections of your community?

Babel: People, Land and Power

The story of Cain and Abel comes at the beginning of the Genesis 4 – 11 chiasmus, and we have labelled it A. The matching story at the end of the chiasmus is A': the story of the tower of Babel. While A is about religious individuals, A' is about the religion of a whole group of people. The story shows us that the link between religion and power is normal in a fallen world, but that it can greatly displease God. This forms the second element to our framework for understanding religion in our world and it will in particular help us to understand the aspects of Islam that connect power with religion.

'Babel' is the Hebrew word usually used for 'Babylon'; the story of Babel in Genesis 11 is the first mention in the Bible of the sort of religion that will be called 'Babylon' through the rest of the Bible, right up to its final judgement in Revelation 18. The story introduces what Ida calls in *The Bible and Other Faiths* 'the dangerous triangle' of people, power and land. There, Ida describes how the connections between these elements are, on the one hand, part of God's good creation: he created people to relate to each other, and he put them in a land over which they had dominion. On the other hand, when people try to push God out of the triangle, or to use religion to establish power for their own group in their own land, it becomes dangerous – so dangerous that God will not tolerate it.[8]

The writer of Genesis tells the story of people on the Shinar plain. Genesis is not clear as to whether they are the only people on earth at this stage, but it does present the story as dealing with something that affects 'the whole earth' (11:1). It seems to be rewriting the Babylonians' own story of their

---

8. Glaser, *The Bible and Other Faiths*, 63–64, 99.

origins, turning it on its head and bringing it crashing down on them with a significance for all humanity.

Other historical evidence about the 'world behind' this text indicates that the ancient Babylonians did indeed build a highly impressive temple as part of their imperial regime, and that they also imposed their language on the peoples whom they conquered. In the middle of the Temple of Marduk in Babylon was a tall ziggurat tower (now no longer standing) which is often identified as the tower of Genesis 11.[9] The establishment of this temple features as the climax to the Babylonian creation epic. In that story, the Babylonians build the temple as a home for their god Marduk and the other gods under him. The gods then come to live in it, and the people feed them and serve them. The gods then lead them out to conquer other nations in battle. As there is no reference to any other gods in Genesis 1, there is no explicit mention of a temple or of gods in Genesis 11. However, Genesis does tell us that the aim of building the tower was to reach heaven: the aims of the construction project were religious. The first readers of Genesis would certainly have recognized the allusion to Babylon.

The individual religious acts of Cain and Abel led to the first religious violence. The account of the religious building of the Babel community deals with people who use religion to propagate power over other people. The people described in Genesis 11:1–3 were tribal: they wanted a place and a name for their own group. As migrants from the east who had 'found' this plain and settled there, perhaps they needed to build a power base to show their dominion of the land. Outside Eden, as we have already seen, people's relationships with one another, as well as with the Lord, were marred. With God no longer the centre of this group's communal life, they feared being 'dispersed over the face of the whole earth' (11:4). These were the motivating factors behind baking bricks to construct the tower of Babel.

In the way of Adam and Eve, Cain, and the sons of God in Genesis 6,[10] here again people overstepped the limits God had set and tried to become like him. The Babel tower was a boast in brickwork, designed to reach the

---

9. Avraham Negev, ed., *The Archaeological Encyclopedia of the Holy Land*, 3rd ed. (New York: Prentice Hall Press, 1990), 50.

10. 'When man began to multiply on the face of the land and daughters were born to them, the sons of God saw that the daughters of man were attractive. And they took as their wives any they chose. Then the LORD said, "My Spirit shall not abide in man for ever, for he is flesh: his days shall be 120 years." The Nephilim were on the earth in those days, and also afterwards, when the sons of God came in to the daughters of man and they bore children to them. These were the mighty men who were of old, the men of renown' (Gen 6:1–4).

heavens, crossing over into God's place. Religion such as this which bolsters political power and advances one group's claim to the land does not reach God. The irony was that God had to come down even to see it.

The very thing the people in Babel feared – dispersal – happened to them as part of God's judgement, and he ensured they would never again be able to say to each other, 'Come let us . . .' about any more plans, for he came and 'confused their language' (11:4, 7). In short, Genesis 1 – 11 ends with another failure of human religion: people have not been able to approach God on their own terms. All sorts of people, all descended from Noah, fill the earth but are now confused with different languages, and some are cursed by Noah with slavery. God has judged them once again, but he has tempered his judgement, just as he did with Adam, Eve and Cain, with an element of protection in the limits he places on them. One of the things that God was doing at Babel was protecting people from further imperial arrogance, for this tower building was 'only the beginning of what they will do' (11:6).

This tower was the first monument of what has become part of normal religion ever since, for all religions contain elements of tribalism or territorialism. Islam shares this normal aspect of religion. From the time of the *hijra*,[11] it has had a political dimension. As Genesis 11 tells us, the fusion of religion and power is so potentially dangerous to creation that God himself will not let it develop beyond certain limits. It is therefore not surprising that Islam's political dimension has been one of its greatest challenges to Christians throughout its history. Neither is it surprising that Christian and Western empires have eventually collapsed.

Domes and Domination

Nestled in the sun-baked hills of Andalusia in southern Spain is the golden brickwork of the Alhambra. Its fluted edging, arched alcoves and geometric tile-work now seem unusual in Europe, but for nearly eight centuries this area was part of an Islamic empire. Between the eighth and eleventh centuries, Al-Andalus covered the whole peninsula. Arabic calligraphy rimming the interiors testifies to this palace having been built to the glory of God, 'Al Ghalib', the 'One Who Overcomes'. Plastered over this, however, is the branding

---

11. The *hijra* was Muhammad's 'migration' from his home in Mecca, where his mission was opposed, to Yathrib, later called Medina, 280 miles to the north. Muhammad became the civil as well as religious leader of the town, bringing law and order to a place of tribal conflict. The Islamic calendar numbers years from this move *Anno Hagirae* (the year of the *hijra*), A.H.

of another place, another civilization and another religion entirely. There is a large crown-shaped seal proclaiming the 're-conquest' of this territory by the Catholic monarchs Isabella and Ferdinand.

Nearby, in the city of Córdoba is the curiously named 'Great Mosque-Cathedral'. A vast prayer hall contrasts with the narrow winding streets outside. The polished floor glistens and reflects the arches that extend in elegant red and white across the entire space. Everything is arranged parallel to the mihrab, decorated in gold. Moorish caliphs have added features over the centuries since AD 784, when the site was first turned into a mosque. Previously it had been the site of a Roman temple, then a church. In the middle of it all, iron bars within the central arches mark out a structure with a different aesthetic, built to different proportions. Candlesticks, saints in flowing robes, Grecian columns and baroque flourishes announce that this is not part of the mosque. High up, a statue holds aloft a cross. Here, in the middle of the mosque, Charles V of Spain built the Cathedral of Córdoba.

For four centuries there had been intermittent power struggles between the northern kingdoms, fighting in the name of Christianity, and Islamic kingdoms to the south. The surrender of Granada in 1492 marked the end of any Islamic rule in Europe. These and other buildings reflect the power struggles.

The Hagia Sophia (Church of Holy Wisdom) in Istanbul, Turkey, was for nearly a thousand years at the centre of Eastern Orthodox Christianity and the largest cathedral in the world. Under a massive dome were mosaics, silver walls covered in icons of saints and ornate reliquaries. When the Ottoman Turks under Sultan Mehmed II took Constantinople in 1453, they were impressed by it, although it was no longer in use. Plastering over the mosaics and removing statues, relics and icons, they made it into their mosque. Outside, minarets were added, and inside, a mihrab was built with the minbar by its side. Round emblems were hung at the base of the dome proclaiming the names of the four imams, together with the salutation on each, 'May God be pleased with him'. Since 1935, Hagia Sophia has been a museum, reflecting the secularism of modern Turkey.

To Think About

How do Christians and Muslims express power through buildings in your area?

In this picture of the great church of Hagia Sophia in Istanbul, you can see the Islamic plaques and the minbar from which imams preached their Friday sermons.[12]

Right up to the final coming of God's kingdom in the new heavens and new earth of Revelation 21 – 22, there will continue to be tension between, on the one hand, the creation blessings of people being given land with responsibility, and, on the other hand, the danger of fallen people-land-power-based religion. We feel it throughout the Old Testament, not only in the accounts of the powerful peoples of Babylon, Assyria and Persia, but also in the power struggles within Israel. The Babylonians and other imperial powers worship non-gods and cause terrible suffering for precious people made in the image of God. At the same time, however, God uses them, sends prophets like Daniel and Jonah to them, and, as Jesus points out (Luke 4:25, 27) – and as we shall see in detail later – sometimes blesses them more than he does their Israelite peers.

Later in the history of Abraham's family, when it has become an entire nation, God chooses Israel as his own people, establishes them in a land and

---

12. Photograph © Paul Windsor, used with permission.

gives them a ruler. However, his chosen people often fall into wrong worship, into seeking power for themselves and into tribal rivalry, and they are sent into exile: they lose their land and their power, and their very survival as a people is threatened. They will repeat the pattern of Genesis 11. By New Testament times, they still do not have the promised peace of being a people in a land under a righteous ruler and with their hearts set on God. They are longing for just this, but most expect the promise to be fulfilled through a conflict that uses power to establish their religion and their people in their land. It is into just this set of tensions, in the context of Roman rather than Babylonian rule, that Jesus comes and that the Gospels speak. We shall explore more of this in chapters 6 and 13, when we will look at what was in the minds of the first Gospel readers as they heard about the transfiguration of Jesus.

Noah and the Flood: Dealing with Evil

The flood story is at the heart of the introduction to biblical history found in Genesis 4 – 11. As is well known, there are other ancient flood stories from different parts of the world.[13] God's responses in the Genesis account stand out starkly in contrast to those of the gods in the other flood stories because only here is the flood the direct result of God's will in his impassioned reaction to human wickedness. The destruction the flood brings is judgement on humanity.

The Genesis account offers two ways of dealing with pervasive human wickedness: flood or sacrifice. Here is the first main revelation of the tension in God's heart between these two responses to sin, a tension which continues to be felt throughout the biblical narrative. It is the underlying motivation in all God's dealings with his people and is finally resolved on the cross.

God himself struggles with the problem of evil: what people do on earth touches God's heart. Later we will see that there is debate about how this can be so and what it means, but here it is clear that God is affected by people's

---

13. The Sumerian King List records the gods' decision to send a flood and that one man, Ziusudra, survives and becomes immortal. Some of this is in common with the Babylonian *Epic of Atrahasis*, in which people's noise becomes so loud that the gods decide to send an annihilating flood. Atrahasis, a man, receives from the god who created people a dream warning him to build a boat. This saves him and his family and the animals aboard while the flood wipes out everything else. When he emerges, he makes to the gods sacrifices which they come down to eat. This story was remodelled to create several versions, including the *Epic of Gilgamesh*, which also has details of the boat coming to rest on a mountain in north-eastern Mesopotamia and the release of birds. From Bienkowski and Millard, *Dictionary of the Ancient Near East*, 119.

actions. So when God saw 'that the wickedness of man was great in the earth, and that every intention of the thoughts of his heart was only evil continually' (6:5), he responded with troubled emotions: he was 'sorry that he had made man on earth, and it grieved him to his heart' (v. 6). The word 'grieve' here carries a sense of pain, echoing the same words for Eve's childbearing agony (3:16) and men's back-breaking toil (5:29).

What is so amazing in the Genesis account is that we as readers are offered a glimpse of God's heart. Moreover, it is displayed in a way we can recognize and to which we can relate. Only in the most intimate relationships does one share the deepest feelings of one's heart – and that is what God is doing with readers here. When we come to explore the qur'anic story of Noah, we will see that this revelation is a key to understanding the difference between biblical and qur'anic scripture.

The chiasmus structure within this text shows us that the form of this judgement was the deliberate reversal of the very act of creation. However, the creator God would not entirely abandon his creation. In chapter 8 there is a description of creation re-emerging after the flood. The pattern is emphasized by repetitions:

> 1:6–7: The waters are separated.
> 7:11: The waters break their bounds.
> 8:2: The bounds are set again.

> 1:9–10: The waters are cleared from the dry land.
> 7:19–20: The dry land disappears.
> 8:5–14: The dry land reappears.

> 1:11–12: The plants are made.
> 8:11: The plants reappear.

> 1:20–26: The animals and human beings are made.
> 7:21–23: The animals, including human beings, are killed.
> 8:15–19: The animals, including human beings, reappear.

Recalling that 'wind' and 'spirit' are both *ruach* in Hebrew, when we read that 'God made a wind blow over the earth, and the waters subsided' (8:1), we hear a restarting of creation, when 'the Spirit of God was hovering over the face of the waters' (1:2). This is the centre of the chiasmus, with everything hinged on the point that 'God remembered Noah' (8:1). Re-creation begins; there is a fresh start. Noah and his family come out of the ark together with the animals onto the dry land, and God gives them the same blessing and charge that he gave to Adam and Eve: 'Be fruitful and multiply and fill the earth' (9:1).

The first action recorded of the first humans to be born was sacrifice: the first action recorded of Noah after his emergence from the flood is also sacrifice. However, the flood had not wiped away bloodshed and wickedness, and the sacrifice did not mean that the human heart had changed. On the contrary, the same terms used before the flood to describe the wickedness of human hearts (6:5) are used afterwards: 'the intention of man's heart is evil from his youth' (8:21). Even Noah, the only one who was righteous enough to be saved, is caught drunk and in a shameful state at the end of the story (9:21). Within the rescued family itself, arguments, cursing and violence resume. They repeat the sort of behaviour that provoked the flood.

But after the flood, God chooses a very different way of dealing with the same evil in people: he mercifully makes a covenant. There is something in the sacrifice that resolves the tension between God's concern for his creatures and the necessity of justice. Genesis does not tell us how the sacrifice works any more than it tells us why Abel's sacrifice was accepted while Cain's was not: it will take the rest of the Bible to unfold God's plan. Here, we see only that, in response to the sacrifice, God decides never to send another flood. Instead, he promises in a covenant to sustain all creation into the future, making our earthly habitat a stable place. The repeated covenantal commitments of 8:21 – 9:17 insist that the way opened by sacrifice is God's preferred option in dealing with the world.

So for the God who is love from eternity, the tension between his justice and salvation is found right in his own heart. Sin breaks the relationship between him and people, and, in love, he longs to restore us to that place of intimacy. Yet at the same time, his holiness demands justice. People have not changed since before the flood, and since 'None is righteous, no, not one' (Rom 3:10), all are deserving of a deluge every day. The pain arising from this tension as described in the flood story and his responses of sacrifice or judgement form the third and final element of the framework and find expression over and over again in the Bible.

Jesus Is the Pain in the Heart of God

In Jerusalem, just before the Passover at which he will be crucified, Jesus says:

> Woe to you, scribes and Pharisees, hypocrites! For you build
> the tombs of the prophets and decorate the monuments of the

righteous, saying, 'If we had lived in the days of our fathers, we would not have taken part with them in shedding the blood of the prophets.' Thus you witness against yourselves that you are sons of those who murdered the prophets. Fill up, then, the measure of your fathers. You serpents, you brood of vipers, how are you to escape being sentenced to hell? Therefore I send you prophets and wise men and scribes, some of whom you will kill and crucify, and some you will flog in your synagogues and persecute from town to town, so that on you may come all the righteous blood shed on earth, from the blood of innocent Abel to the blood of Zechariah the son of Barachiah, whom you murdered between the sanctuary and the altar. Truly, I say to you, all these things will come upon this generation.

O Jerusalem, Jerusalem, the city that kills the prophets and stones those who are sent to it! How often would I have gathered your children together as a hen gathers her brood under her wings, and you would not! See, your house is left to you desolate. For I tell you, you will not see me again, until you say, 'Blessed is he who comes in the name of the Lord' (Matt 23:29–39).

To Think About

How does Jesus' response to the violent human hearts of his day reflect God's response to the violent human hearts of the time of Noah?

Religions in the world in front of the text have also acknowledged and attempted to limit evil. The Qur'an recognizes both human and satanic evil and seeks to deal with them. In many surahs, God admonishes people for their disbelief, insolence, hardness of heart or idolatry, and encourages repentance and change. Through the prophets God warns people of the coming judgement: he *will* deal with evil. Indeed, the story of Noah that it relates is also about God judging human sin. Many Muslim people are aware of evil and seek to overcome it in their personal lives, families or societies. There is fervent debate about how best this struggle is to be fought: whether, as at one extreme, it is through violence or, at the other extreme, through contemplative piety – or somewhere in between.

A Well-Behaved Boy

We sat admiring the tiny picture, laughing at how little the baby looked, but how developed, too. Hadeeqa had just been for her first scan of her unborn baby. 'What do you hope for him?' I asked, after she'd put the photo away.

'I hope he'll be good and have good habits . . . not like his father,' she added sadly. I was familiar with the list of her husband's vices. She had confided in me that he drank, probably had affairs and lied.

'Oh, Hadeeqa, what a wonderful aspiration for your son; I really hope he'll be good and loving too.' Then I paused. 'How do you think you might help him keep on the right track?'

'As soon as he's old enough, I'm going to teach him the Qur'an.'

Hadeeqa is not alone in considering that reading the Qur'an will offer protection against evil. While she thought it would train her son's mind to stay away from evil thoughts, it is not uncommon to see Muslims soundlessly reciting parts of it to keep away evil spirits. Fighting evil and establishing good are very important tenets of Islam.

Genesis 1 – 11 presents a God who will not overlook any evil: he will either judge it or deal with it by sacrifice. So when we come to view Muslims in the 'world in front of the text', we can be sure that God will deal with any evil associated with them and with Islam – including evil directed towards Muslims by non-Muslims, evil in relationships between Muslims, as well as evil directed by Muslims towards non-Muslims. However, we will see from the Bible that God's preference is always to delay judgement and to offer salvation. It will help us understand God's responses if we stay sensitive to this tension when reading the Bible, recognizing that the tension is ultimately resolved only on the cross.

Genesis Framework: Conclusion and Summary

The world of the biblical authors was just such a world as described in Genesis 4 – 11. At different times and in different ways, people have continued to behave in the way they did right at the beginning, and God's responses remain the same. This chapter has introduced these patterns which run through the many different contexts of people in the Bible. Keeping this framework in mind offers a helpful guide for reading the text itself and for understanding all sorts of people, including Muslims.

- It is a world in which all sorts of people reach out to God through all sorts of sacrifices; and the biblical authors assume that God can and does speak to all sorts of people.
- It is a world in which much religion is linked with power. Gods are often linked with particular peoples and are seen as fighting for them.
- It is a world of persistent evil with which God deals. The tension between judgement and salvation as ways of dealing with it can be traced throughout the Bible.

This world is the world whose origins are described in Genesis 1 – 3, in which people have the capacity and need to reach out to God, as they are created in his image, but fallen. It is a world that Genesis presents through genealogies, in which all human beings are related to each other; but it is also a world in which we are placed in particular families and ethnic groups. Most importantly, it is a world to which God has committed himself in the covenant of the rainbow in Genesis 9.

2

Comparison with the Qur'an

In chapter 1, we examined the 'world of' the Genesis text and the 'world behind' the text, inviting you to consider how they relate to the world of Islam 'in front of' the text. In this chapter, we take the next step by reading the Qur'anic passages about the Genesis characters.

The previous chapter developed our framework for thinking biblically about Muslims as people with characteristics typical of all human beings. This chapter will help us to clarify the questions that need to be addressed in seeking to think biblically about Islam as a worldview and a way of life.

We will read the Qur'an, first, because it is the primary source of authority for, and pervades the thinking of, many Muslims. According to Kenneth Cragg, 'it is imperative . . . that the Christian strive to enter as fully as he may into the Qur'anic world, with the painstaking ambition to know it from within.'[1] This will be one way of accessing the Muslim thought-world we seek to understand in this book. Specifically, the passages we will study introduce the ways in which the Qur'an and its Muslim readers deal with our framework questions of seeking God, dangerous religion and dealing with evil.

Second, we will read the Qur'an so that we can put questions raised by one text to the other in order to discern the differences and similarities in theology. This will highlight areas of potential meeting and misunderstanding. Contrasts with the Qur'an will also highlight aspects of the Bible that we are liable to miss because of our familiarity with it.

There are other 'worlds in front of' Genesis 1 – 11 that are relevant to our study. There were many centuries between the writing of Genesis and the writing of the Qur'an, and, by Muhammad's time, many people had read Genesis in their own 'world in front of the text'. The Qur'an sometimes refers to Jewish and Christian readings, so in addition we will sometimes

1. K. Cragg, *The Call of the Minaret* (Oxford: Oxford University Press, 1956), 201.

look at how Jews and Christians before the time of Muhammad interpreted Genesis, and we will sometimes look at how the New Testament deals with the Genesis stories.

Cain and Abel

Cain and Abel, and Jesus

Jesus draws on the Cain and Abel story at least twice. On both occasions, Jesus is communicating to Pharisees, scribes and lawyers. First, he is crying woe upon them for participating in their fathers' persecution of the prophets since the beginning with Abel: 'the blood of all the prophets, shed from the foundation of the world, [will] be charged against this generation,' Jesus declares (Luke 11:50). He is placing them directly in Cain's tradition. So, the question arises, if these pious men are in Cain's line, who is *not* in Cain's line?

Aspects of the Genesis incident of the older brother turning against the younger make a surprising reappearance in Jesus' masterpiece parable of two brothers,[2] which Jesus also tells in the company of Pharisees (Luke 15:11–32). The character who parallels Cain is the older brother, hostile to the younger brother, 'angry' just as Cain was, and found in a field. Their position, aloof from God/the father signifies how little they share God's/their father's generous nature: they are jealous and unable to celebrate their brothers' lives and blessings.

Jesus' disciple John refers, right at the centre of his first epistle, to Cain, 'who was of the evil one and murdered his brother' (1 John 3:12), using him as a symbol of the evil in humanity. He then shockingly reminds his readers, in a paraphrase of his master's words, that 'Everyone who hates his brother is a murderer' (1 John 3:15). The New Testament casts all people as Cain.

The father in Luke 15 goes out to the angry one and 'entreats' him, just as God does in the Genesis incident, seeking fellowship with him. So though the hard truth is that we are all Cains, the wonder is that God keeps speaking to us. John expands on the hope there is even for those he had written about who are like Cain. He describes being 'born of God', being given new life with the capacity for love.[3]

---

2. J. Magonet, *A Rabbi's Bible* (London: SCM, 1991), 121.

3. 1 John 3:8–9, 14 says, 'The reason the Son of God appeared was to destroy the works of the devil. No one born of God makes a practice of sinning, for God's seed abides in him, and he cannot keep on sinning because he has been born of God . . . We know that we have passed out of death into life, because we love the brothers.'

To Think About

Does this reading of the Cain and Abel story, in the context of the New Testament, change the way you think about yourself in regard to Muslims now?

It can serve as a challenge to those who 'have always been with [the father]' but resent him extending grace to those they consider unworthy of it. In the context of your neighbourhoods, what do you feel about Muslims? Do you resent it when they are blessed? Would you prefer it if God did not go out to welcome them? Would you prefer not to celebrate with them in your congregation?

Jesus left the ending of his parable open: there is the possibility of the older brother choosing to rejoice with his father. John gives us hope of transformation. God can change hearts.

Cain and Abel in the Qur'an

Now we turn to look at how the Qur'an uses an apparently similar story to communicate ideas about God, humanity and creation:

> [Prophet], tell them the truth about the story of Adam's two sons: each of them offered a sacrifice, and it was accepted from one and not the other. One said, 'I will kill you,' but the other said, 'God only accepts the sacrifice of those who are mindful of Him. If you raise your hand to kill me, I will not raise mine to kill you. I fear God, the Lord of all worlds, and I would rather you were burdened with my sins as well as yours and became an inhabitant of the Fire: such is the evildoers' reward.' But his soul prompted him to kill his brother: he killed him and became one of the losers. God sent a raven to scratch up the ground and show him how to cover his brother's corpse and he said, 'Woe is me! Could I not have been like this raven and covered up my brother's body?' He became remorseful. On account of [his deed], We decreed to the Children of Israel that if anyone kills a person – unless in retribution for murder or spreading corruption in the land – it is as if he kills all mankind, while if any saves a life it is as if he saves the lives of all mankind. Our messengers came to them

with clear signs, but many of them continued to commit excesses in the land. Those who wage war against God and His Messenger and strive to spread corruption in the land should be punished by death, crucifixion, the amputation of an alternate hand and foot, or banishment from the land: a disgrace for them in this world, and then a terrible punishment in the Hereafter, unless they repent before you overpower them – in that case bear in mind that God is forgiving and merciful (Surah 5. 27–34).[4]

What questions did reading that story, at once familiar and strange, raise for you?

Perhaps you wondered where the differences come from. The traditional Islamic answer is found in the first line: '[Prophet], tell them the truth about the story of Adam's two sons . . .'[5] Muslims understand this to be the angel Gabriel speaking words from God to Muhammad: all the Qur'anic stories concerning people familiar to us from the Bible are considered by Muslims to be revelations from God and therefore definitive. For them, the Qur'anic accounts are the authoritative ones and tell 'the truth' about the biblical versions.

Different Muslims have different ways of dealing with the evident differences between the Bible and the Qur'an. For example, some say that the Bible has been corrupted, and that the Qur'an gives the corrected version; others say that the Qur'an is bringing out true lessons from the biblical stories and adding details by direct revelation from God; and some point out that the Qur'an assumes that the reader already knows the biblical stories, and they read the Bible in order to understand the Qur'an better. However, most Muslims will read the Qur'an by itself, with reference to Islamic commentaries and traditions, but without looking at the biblical versions. Anyone who wants to understand Muslim thinking will read the Qur'an in its own right and ask what Muslim scholars say about it. Readers will find that the Qur'an works differently from Genesis: it is a different kind of book. To understand any story in it, it needs to be understood on its own terms and in its own

---

4. M. A. S. Abdel Haleem, *The Qur'an: A New Translation by M. A. S. Abdel Haleem* (Oxford: Oxford University Press, 2008), Used with permission.
5. Ibid.

context. Only then can we develop fruitful dialogue between the qur'anic and biblical narratives.[6]

How might Christian readers understand the differences between the biblical and qur'anic versions of the story? Muslims would say that the extra details in the Qur'an come directly from God. However, some of them can also be found in the seventh century 'world behind the text'. Muhammad had a great deal of contact with Jewish people, and the Qur'an often refers to ideas that are in ancient Jewish commentary on the Genesis story. For example, the Jews asked how Abel was buried, and one answer they gave was that God sent a bird to scratch the ground and show Cain how to bury his brother.[7] As the Qur'an itself tells us, the laws about killing that follow the Cain and Abel story are also parallel to the Jewish commentary.[8] We will see in chapter 12 how the Jewish roots of the Qur'an can help us understand it from a biblical perspective.

It is important to note the context of the Cain and Abel story in the Qur'an. Surah 5 is one of the chronologically later surahs of the Qur'an, and much of it relates to times when Muhammad was facing opposition in Medina. According to many Muslim commentators, the Cain and Abel story was revealed following a foiled plot by Jews against Muhammad's life.[9] It fits with other major themes in Surah 5 that have just been introduced: Jewish covenant-breaking (5. 13–14) and Christian forgetfulness and blasphemy (5. 15, 19).

The two contexts of Muhammad's situation and of Surah 5 give the clue to what the Qur'an is doing with the story. Commentators draw parallels between Abel and Cain and Muhammad and his opponents, casting Muslims in the role of Abel and the older religions in the role of older brother Cain: the

---

6. Because the Qur'an is regarded as given by God, with no decisions about its presentation made by people, it is not appropriate to analyse the 'world behind the text' in order to discern authorial intention as we do with the Bible.

Because Muslim and Christian communities generally use different processes of applying their scriptures to their contemporary world, we will not study the texts from a reader-centred position but rather focus on what is actually written: aspects such as plot, character, dialogue, points of view and use of language.

References to many people in the Bible are found in different surahs of the Qur'an. These will be brought together and viewed as parts of the same story. This is in keeping with traditional methods of interpretation.

7. Midrash Tanhuma 1:10.

8. Mishnah: Sanhedrin 4:5.

9. See, for example, S. A. A. Maududi, *Tafhīm al-Qur'ān*, 1988–93, translated as *Towards Understanding the Qur'an* by Z. I. Ansari (Leicester: The Islamic Foundation, 1988–93), vols 1–4.

Jews and Christians are, they say, jealous of the Muslims. The story then functions as a warning for those opposed to Muhammad and as a reassurance for the faithful. It is more important as an illustration of the Qur'an's message than as a story in its own right: this is true of most of the stories in the Qur'an.

To Think About

This story is said to have been revealed after Jews plotted against Muhammad. Where do current conflicts actually reflect wrong Jewish and Christian responses to Muslims? We may want to dissociate Christianity from the imposition of suffering on innocent people as much as most Muslims want to dissociate Islam from terrorism; but we have to face the fact that the long history of Christian hostility towards Muslims has not gone away.

Do you perhaps have experience of Muslims expecting you as a Christian to oppose them because they interpret Christian history as antagonistic, making the relationship difficult even before you begin to talk?

In its context in Surah 5, the Cain and Abel story also functions as an introduction to a verse that is a very important basis for legislation: '...if anyone kills a person – unless in retribution for murder or spreading corruption in the land – it is as if he kills all mankind, while if any saves a life it is as if he saves the lives of all mankind' (Surah 5. 32).[10] This verse emphasizes the value of all human life, so is used as a basis for laws against murder. However, it also lists categories of killing that are not murder: retaliation for murder, and 'spreading corruption'; and the next verse goes on to specify the death penalty for those who 'wage war against God and His Messenger'.[11] We see that, in its qur'anic context, the Cain and Abel story speaks into the 'world behind the text' as it addresses the attack on Muhammad's life; but it also speaks into the 'world in front of the text', as the story of the murder that foreshadows all other murders.

---

10. M. A. S. Abdel Haleem, *The Qur'an: A New Translation by M. A. S. Abdel Haleem* (Oxford: Oxford University Press, 2008), Used with permission.
11. Ibid.

Surah 5. 32 is one of the verses most quoted by Muslims who are against such actions as 9/11. They emphasize the value of all human life and the classical laws that forbid the killing of non-combatants even during war. An attack on one person, they point out, is an attack on the whole human race. Other Muslims use this and the following verse to justify 'terrorism'. A nineteenth-century qur'anic interpreter who has influenced the 'Taliban' movement comments on this story that self-defence is legitimate for the community.[12] His comment is in keeping with the story's concern for the innocent person and punishment for the attacker. Moreover, Surah 5.32 is clear that some acts against Muhammad and his community are punishable by death. Putting all this together, we can understand why terrorist groups who consider that innocent Muslims have been attacked, often by those perceived to be Jews and Christians, can see these verses as supporting retaliatory attacks.

To Think About

Genesis 9:5–6 says, 'And for your lifeblood I will require a reckoning: from every beast I will require it and from man. From his fellow man I will require a reckoning for the life of man. Whoever sheds the blood of man, by man shall his blood be shed, for God made man in his own image.' How does this compare with Surah 5. 32–33?

Cain and Abel: Comparing the Stories

We now turn from the 'worlds behind' and 'in front of' the text, and its context in the Qur'an, to comparing the stories themselves. We begin by asking in what ways the Genesis and Qur'an stories are the same, and in what ways they are different.

---

12. S. A. Usmani, *Tafseer-e-Usmani*, 1991, translated as *The Noble Qur'an* by M. A. Ahmad (Lahore: Aalameen Publications, 1991). Usmani (1885–1949) was a student and spiritual successor of Sheikh-ul-Hind Maulana Mahmood Hassan, a teacher at the Deoband college, India, which was at the heart of the nineteenth-century revivalist movement. It was traditional in its interpretations of Islam, but stressed the need for personal sincerity and piety. It opposed popular overemphasis on the person of Muhammad and use of shrines, and was missionary but not political. Usmani completed his teacher's commentary on the Qur'an. The present 'Taliban' movement has arisen from the Deobandis.

At first reading, we note that the two versions deal with the same events. Both are about Adam's two sons and both present stories of primeval murder. Both portray rejected and accepted sacrifices, Cain's anger, a warning against wrongdoing, then the killing of a brother, loss and subsequent regret. Both emphasize the horror of fraternal killing by repeating the word 'brother'.

There is a shared teaching, then, that murder has been a mark of the human predicament from the very beginning, that it can occur within the closest of relationships, and that it is the most terrible of crimes. There is a shared understanding that it can arise out of jealousy and misdirected anger. Both stories also tell us that, from the beginning, humans have judged each other and responded unjustly towards each other.

To Think About

As we come to look at the differences in the texts, it is worth pausing to consider that it is inevitable that Muslims, Jews and Christians will disagree on some things, because Islam, Judaism and Christianity are not the same.

On what subjects do people of different religions disagree in your setting? Respect for truth will necessarily lead to discussion and challenge. But jealousy, injustice and violence need not follow.

Further consideration shows us many differences between the details of the two accounts. First, the Qur'an omits aspects of the Genesis version and adds some material that is not in Genesis. The Qur'an relates neither the story of Cain and Abel's births nor what happens to Cain and his descendants. It does not even tell us the names of the two brothers. Neither does it tell us anything about their sacrifices. However, it does have the story of how the murderer learned how to bury his brother, which reflects the Jewish comment that relates to legislation about the disposal of dead bodies.

These differences reflect the differences between qur'anic and biblical contexts and concerns that we have already noted. In the Bible, Cain and Abel find their place in the family history of human beginnings, while in the qur'anic account they illustrate some of the Qur'an's concerns. The biblical account does not tell us about legal matters, while the Qur'an, like the Jewish commentators, is concerned about the beginnings of the law. As we shall see, it is also typical of the Qur'an that it shows little interest in the sacrifices. This is a central concern of the Bible which, again and again, is omitted from qur'anic accounts of biblical characters.

Second, there are interesting differences in how the two accounts treat the motivations of the two brothers. The Qur'anic Cain has obviously wicked impulses: he determines to kill his brother and then, after the warning, it is his self (Arabic *nafs*) that tempts him. In Genesis, he becomes angry and is warned of 'sin crouching at the door'; but we are not told anything about what is going on in his mind when he kills his brother. The difference is more striking in the case of Abel. Genesis does not tell us anything that was in his mind, but the Qur'an gives him a long speech. He is as obviously good as his brother is obviously wicked. The implication is that he is pious because, as he says, 'God only accepts the sacrifice of those who are mindful of Him . . . I fear God, the Lord of all worlds' (vv. 27–28); and his speech shows that he is determined to do what is right, even if it means losing his life. Commentators discuss the meaning of verse 29: does it mean that Cain will be punished for Abel's sins as well as for his own? Maybe: no one is quite sure. But it certainly means that Abel will not risk God's punishment even if he would be within his rights to defend himself.

Third, there are important differences concerning who speaks and which characters are central. There are three characters in both stories: Cain, Abel and God. However, in one, the speaking characters are Cain and Abel; in the other, they are Cain and God. This indicates that the two versions of the story are communicating very different things. They may agree about the terrible nature of murder, but they offer different kinds of hope for murderous human beings.

In the Qur'anic version, Abel warns his brother, and the story itself stands as a warning that can be heeded. It gives its readers hope that human beings can avoid such violence. It also reassures them that murder will not go unpunished, and that God will vindicate the innocent.

The biblical version highlights a different hope. While the Qur'an focuses on justice for the innocent victim, the Bible focuses on God's interaction with the guilty perpetrator. Abel as victim is silent until 'his blood cries out'; and God does not seem to be concerned about protecting him. It is not Abel but God himself who warns Cain, offers him a way of acceptance, calls him to account after the murder and sentences him to exile rather than to the death he deserves. When Cain says that even this is too much, God listens and puts a mark of protection on him and promises to avenge him if anyone harms him.

Fourth, there are differences in the descriptions of the punishment given to Cain. In Genesis, Cain is exiled. From the warning in Genesis 2:17 – 'of the tree of the knowledge of good and evil you shall not eat, for in the day that you eat of it, you shall surely die' – one might have expected that he would have died. Indeed, Jewish commentators ask why he was not put to death, as Genesis 9:6 would require. Perhaps, they suggest, Cain did not know that his brother would die, as there had not yet been any deaths, so this was just manslaughter, for which exile was the punishment. Genesis 4 does not discuss this; we only realize that Cain gets less punishment than he appears to deserve. In the Qur'an, there are no details about what happens to Cain during the rest of his life on earth: rather, the emphasis is on his punishment in 'the Fire' after death. Genesis never deals with the question of what happens after death, and neither does most of the rest of the Old Testament. Many centuries later, however, this question is one of the Qur'an's greatest concerns. It has many descriptions of 'the Fire' and 'the Garden' that parallel what Christians usually call 'hell' and 'heaven'.

These similarities and differences can help us to see something of a worldview formed by the Qur'an:

- Like the Bible, the Qur'an recognizes *human beings as God's creation*. We are bound to worship God and we are answerable to him. There is a life after death, where *God will be our judge*, and where we will receive reward or punishment from him.
- Abel's speech and the murderer's punishment stand as *warnings against wrongdoing*. The implication is that people need these warnings, and that, through the Qur'an and through people like Abel, God has given us what we need. In the Qur'an, warnings come to ordinary people through prophets, and not directly from God.
- The Qur'an encourages the reader to *strive for innocence* to avoid Cain's fate. Hope is found in aspiring to be Abel.
- It encourages those with power to *legislate* to deter violence and promote virtue. As we have seen, the verses immediately following the story contain legislative material. They allow the death penalty for murder and for 'spreading corruption in the land', and list punishments for opposition to 'God and His Messenger'.
- In every case of violence, readers who take this account seriously will invest much in identifying the guilty and innocent parties,

since their fates are starkly different. Genesis' picture of Cain[13] would lead us to expect that people will tend to defend their own innocence and blame others. This is one among many stories in the Qur'an concerned with this *classification of the guilty and the innocent.*

- On the other hand, readers conscious of their own failings might become hopeless. Only the innocent are vindicated; there is *no hope here for the guilty.* Muslims have to look elsewhere in the Qur'an to find hope for those who struggle with sin.

Bible and Qur'an, Christians and Muslims – and most other people – are entirely agreed about the importance of human life, the danger of jealousy, the horror of murder and the fact that jealousy and murder can arise even within close families. Bible and Qur'an, Christians and Muslims, are entirely agreed that murder deserves the punishment of God, and that all human beings should seek his help to be like Abel, whose sacrifice was accepted, and not like Cain, who was rejected and wicked. The key questions, then, are, 'Why are so many people like Cain?' and, 'What can be done about it?' It is here that the Bible and the Qur'an differ.

Perhaps the most important aspect of the Genesis Cain and Abel story is that it does not permit us to do what Muslims do with the qur'anic version: it does not allow us to divide the world into guilty 'Cains' and innocent 'Abels'. A Muslim friend who read the biblical version for the first time confessed that she was unsettled that it made her feel sympathy for the murderer: 'I shouldn't feel sorry for him!' she said. She got the point: the New Testament would agree that we should not be like the murderer (1 John 3:12), but Genesis, particularly when read in the context of Luke 15, makes us recognize ourselves in Cain, however much we might want to be Abel.

From a New Testament perspective, we are like Cain not only if we actually commit murder, but also if we even have hostile thoughts about people (Matt 5:21–22):

> You have heard that it was said to those of old, 'You shall not murder; and whoever murders will be liable to judgement.' But I say to you that everyone who is angry with his brother will be liable to judgement; whoever insults his brother will be liable to the council; and whoever says, 'You fool!' will be liable to the hell of fire.

---

13. And of Adam and Eve in Gen 3:12–13.

That confirms the observation of the Muslim friend mentioned above: all of us can see something of ourselves in Cain. This is not surprising, because Genesis 4 is part of the account of the creation and fall of the whole world. These brothers are the first people to be born, and their story deepens the fall of humankind that was seen in the conflict, temptation and disobedience of Adam and Eve. Nonetheless, the story also continues to tell of God's mercy as well as his judgement. The pattern of creation and fall, judgement and mercy, will continue in the accounts of Noah, the nations and Babel, and is leading to the call of Abraham for the blessing of all humankind.

As we shall see below, the qur'anic Adam stories do not tell of a 'fall': instead, people are ignorant and forgetful, and liable to temptation from Satan. The qur'anic Cain and Abel story in its context of exhortation and legislation is in harmony with the Qur'an's teaching that people's primary need in life is for guidance. The Qur'an has patterns of creation and blessing, of judgement and mercy, but not of fall and salvation.

To Think About

Perhaps the most important thing about the Genesis Cain and Abel story is that it does not allow us to divide the world into guilty 'Cains' and innocent 'Abels'.

Read Genesis 4:1–16 again. What aspects of the Genesis story have been highlighted for you by the comparison with the Qur'an? How does it challenge your thinking about yourself, about your community, and about Muslims?

Babel

The Qur'an does not tell the Babel story. There is one verse that might refer to it: 'Those who went before them also schemed, but God attacked the very foundations of what they built. The roof fell down on them: punishment came on them from unimagined directions' (Surah 16. 26).[14]

---

14. M. A. S. Abdel Haleem, *The Qur'an: A New Translation by M. A. S. Abdel Haleem* (Oxford: Oxford University Press, 2008), Used with permission.

There is another verse about the origin of languages: 'Another of His signs is the creation of the heavens and earth, and the diversity of your languages and colours. There truly are signs in this for those who know' (Surah 30. 22).[15]

Together, these indicate that the Qur'an agrees with Genesis 11 that some people once built something and were judged for it, and that languages have their origins in the providence of God. Surah 16. 26 makes the point that the building is a plot – that it has to do with people working together. However, neither deals specifically with Genesis 11's concerns of 'dangerous religion' that propagates people, land and power, of the created-but-fallen state of the nations, or of the need to limit human cooperation. (We might also note that the first verse is about judgement and the second about blessing: we will see later that, while in the Bible, God often judges and blesses the same people, in the Qur'an the message of a prophet generally divides the people into those who will be judged and those who will be blessed.)

A qur'anic story that does deal with some of these issues is that of Abraham's encounter with the king in the land of his birth. This is referred to several times. In Surah 2. 258, Abraham presents a strong argument for monotheism to a powerful person who is thought to be that king. In 21. 68–70 and 37. 97–98, when Abraham demonstrates the foolishness of worshipping anyone other than the One God, the people punish him by throwing him into a fire from which God delivers him.[16] His opponents are then judged. All these references agree with the Genesis Babel story that it is foolish and useless to build any religion other than worship of the One Creator God, and that the powers used to propagate such religion will be judged.

It is interesting that Islamic tradition names the king who opposed Abraham and oversaw his punishment by fire as 'Nimrod', mentioned in Genesis 10:8-10 as a 'mighty hunter' and the king of Babel. This agrees with Jewish and Christian tradition and alerts us to the fact that, in Genesis 11, Abram with his father's family leaves the very land where the Babel tower was built, as Ur of the Chaldeans was a city in southern Babylonia.

Muslim stories of Abraham include anecdotes about Nimrod the king that echo some of the concerns of the Genesis Babel story. Perhaps the most graphic is the tale of how Nimrod tried not only to kill God's prophet but also

---

15. M. A. S. Abdel Haleem, *The Qur'an: A New Translation by M. A. S. Abdel Haleem* (Oxford: Oxford University Press, 2008), Used with permission.

16. As with the qur'anic additions to the Cain and Abel story, the stories of Abraham's arguments and of his being thrown into a fire can be found in pre-Islamic Jewish discussion of Gen 11:28, where 'Ur' means 'fire' in Hebrew. See *Genesis Rabbah* 38:13.

to kill God himself. He had a flying chariot made: a box with tall sticks rising from each corner. At the same time, he began rearing vulture chicks. Just when he was 'uncertain about how to proceed', Satan came and began to instruct him, advising him to tie a vulture starved of food to each lower corner and a chunk of raw meat to the top of each stick, just out of reach of the vulture. The vultures would fly up towards the meat, Satan explained, and carry the box, with Nimrod in it, towards the heavens. There, Satan recommended, Nimrod should 'snatch the empires from the God of Abraham straight away then establish his rule'. Nimrod did all that Satan had told him. At a great height, Nimrod shouted his challenge to God, and fired an arrow upwards. God had an angel catch the arrow, dip its head in the blood of a fish and drop it back down to Nimrod. Nimrod returned to earth boasting that he had killed God.[17]

Motifs we heard in the Genesis Babel account recur in this story. There is a challenge by the Babylonian Empire to the Creator God: 'I'm going to strike the God of the Heavens with an arrow and seize the kingdom of heaven from him.' Here again is the dangerous pride associated with political power.

We can hear mockery of another futile attempt to reach up physically to God when God sends a mosquito army to defeat Nimrod's army, which comprises 'the armies from east and west, from Rome, Turkey and India'. The chief, a blind lame insect, eats Nimrod's brain in grotesque fashion. There is also a hint at the confusion of languages that follows. On hearing Nimrod's boast, the Babylonians 'fainted from their happiness. After a moment, they all started talking at once, no one listening to each other'.[18]

However, where Genesis 11 presents Babel as something that affected the whole earth, Nimrod is a particular individual, strongly influenced by Satan, who represents a particular corrupt power. Genesis 11 may allude to the particular tower in Babylon, but the story is used as part of the history of the whole of humanity. In contrast, the Qur'anic Abraham stories are about one prophet's challenges to one people.

Thus we can read the Genesis story as diagnosing a general problem: we have argued that it signals the tendency towards territorial, ethnic and political religion in a fallen world, and that the rest of the Bible affirms the need to guard against such religion. In contrast, the Qur'an does not see this tendency as generally problematic. What is problematic is not the religion–

17. Maulana Khatr Hijazi, *Qiṣaṣ al-Anbiyā* (Lahore: Nashran-o-tajran kitab, 1978), 78–80.
18. Ibid.

power link but idolatry. An idolatrous leader is a problem: a leader who worships the One True God is not. On the contrary, Muhammad's political leadership lends as much weight to his prophethood as his message: indeed, the two cannot be separated in the thinking of most Muslims.

In short, where the Bible sees the triple link between people, power and land as potentially dangerous for all peoples, the Qur'an agrees that it is dangerous under a bad ruler but positive under a good ruler. Certainly, it sees some forms of religion as so dangerous that they have to be stopped, but not on the basis of their links to power: indeed, there are times when Muslims themselves are told to carry out the judgement on idolaters rather than wait for God's judgement to come – most famously in Surah 9. 5–14, where God tells the believers to kill the idolaters they encounter unless they remain loyal to a treaty with them: 'Fight them: God will punish them at your hands' (9. 14).[19]

Empire and Religion

'Within its walls, the lust of the eye and the lusts of the flesh have reigned and revelled to the full,' wrote the Reverend Midgeley John Jennings, of Delhi, the city in which he ministered as chaplain to the British from 1852.[20] Around this time, friendships between British officials and high-class Muslims were becoming rare, when earlier they had flourished. Increasingly, the British expressed disgust at Hindus and Muslims in India; Jennings was not alone in his views. They were also coming to believe the idea that God was rewarding England with an empire because of its religious efforts.

These attitudes, as well as the confiscation and demolition of some mosques, made it harder for the Mughal ruling class to cooperate with the British and strengthened the views of Muslims who had always opposed them. From among this latter group grew new strains of fundamentalist Islam opposed to both the liberal, Hindu-influenced court and to the British. One of the leaders of this school of thought, Sayyid Ahmad Barelvi, fought a jihād against them on the North West Frontier. Later, during the battle in Delhi in 1857, jihādis joined the fight against the British, many from well beyond the city. Not all were from a military background – many

---

19. M. A. S. Abdel Haleem, *The Qur'an: A New Translation by M. A. S. Abdel Haleem* (Oxford: Oxford University Press, 2008), Used with permission.
20. Quoted in William Dalrymple, *The Last Mughal: The Fall of a Dynasty, Delhi, 1857* (London: Bloomsbury, 2006), 58.

were just artisans, but devout. They came 'because they believed it was their duty to free what they regarded as the Dar-ul Islam from the rule of the hated kafirs'.[21]

To Think About

What kinds of 'power' did the various people in the above account have? What kinds of 'power' did they want? In what ways did they see power as linked with their religions?

Do you hear Christians and/or Muslims describe 'kingdoms' as 'good' or 'bad' today? What kinds of power do they think are right?

Noah

The Qur'an refers to Noah in many places.[22] Most of the references are brief, except for the entire story in Surah 11. 25–49, and the whole of Surah 71, which is called 'Noah'. The basic outline of the story can be found in Surah 7. 59–69:

> We sent Noah to his people. He said, 'My people, serve God: you have no god other than Him. I fear for you the punishment of a fearsome Day!' but the prominent leaders of his people said, 'We believe you are far astray.' He replied, 'My people, there is nothing astray about me! On the contrary, I am a messenger from the Lord of all the Worlds: I am delivering my Lord's messages to you and giving you sincere advice. I know things from God that you do not. Do you find it so strange that a message should come from your Lord – through a man in your midst – to warn you and make you aware of God so that you may be given mercy?' but they called him a liar. We saved him, and those who were with him, on the Ark and We drowned those who rejected Our revelations – they were wilfully blind.

---

21. Irfan Habib, 'The Coming of 1857', *Social Scientist* 26, no. 12 (January–April 1998): 8; quoted in Dalrymple, *The Last Mughal*, 264.
22. Surahs 3. 33; 4. 163; 6. 84; 7. 59–69; 9. 70; 10. 71; 11. 25–89; 17. 3; 21. 76; 23. 23; 25. 37; 26. 105; 29. 14; 37. 75; 51. 46; 54. 9; 69. 11.

To the people of 'Ad We sent their brother, Hud. He said, 'My people, serve God: you have no god other than Him. Will you not take heed?' but the disbelieving leaders of his people said, 'We believe you are a fool,' and 'We think you are a liar.' He said, 'My people, there is nothing foolish about me! On the contrary, I am a messenger from the Lord of all the Worlds: I am delivering my Lord's messages to you. I am your sincere and honest adviser. Do you find it so strange that a message should come from your Lord, through a man in your midst, to warn you? Remember how He made you heirs after Noah's people, and increased your stature: remember God's bounties, so that you may prosper.'[23]

Context

Again, we start by noting the context of this passage. It is the first of a series of brief accounts of prophets which includes Lot and the Qur'an's three non-biblical prophets: Noah is followed by Hud (7. 65–72), Salih (7. 73–79), Lot (7. 80–84) and Shua'ib (7. 85–93). Each story follows a similar pattern: God sends the prophet to a particular people; the prophet preaches monotheism and is opposed; the prophet persists, and so does the opposition; finally, God judges the opponents and saves the prophet and those who believed him. We can see, then, that the qur'anic Noah is the first example of a prophetic pattern that will be repeated throughout history. We also see a continuation of the division of humankind that we saw in the story of the first murder.

The passages that tell Noah's story are all in Meccan surahs, that is to say, in the context of Muhammad's struggles against opposition. Muhammad's knowledge of the stories was considered supernatural and seen as a sign that he had been directly inspired by God. They are part of his argument with those who reject his message, parallel to the arguments presented by the various prophets in Surah 7. Noah is presented as the same kind of prophet as Muhammad in many ways. His experiences parallel those of Muhammad in Mecca and are used to encourage and exhort Muhammad and the Muslims as well as to warn their opponents.

Noah has a message like Muhammad's message, telling them that they should worship only the One God, and pointing to God's forgiveness and

---

23. M. A. S. Abdel Haleem, *The Qur'an: A New Translation by M. A. S. Abdel Haleem* (Oxford: Oxford University Press, 2008), Used with permission.

blessing if people will only listen to and accept the message (71. 10ff.), and to his judgement if they refuse.

The qur'anic Noah's opposition is also similar to that experienced by Muhammad. The Qur'an offers details such as plots, accusations of madness or forgery and continued idolatry, all of which parallel what happened to Muhammad in Mecca. And, like Muhammad, the qur'anic Noah grieves over his people's disbelief. He prays for them, exhorts them, and pleads with God when he is rejected. Yusuf Ali, in his introduction to Surah 71, writes: 'The story of Noah's agony is almost a parable for the Holy Prophet's persecution in the Meccan period.'[24]

We see that the Qur'an's sacred history is about God sending messengers to call people back to the right way, to bless those who accept them, and to judge those who do not. God's promise that 'We will allow [others] to enjoy life for a time'[25] (11. 48) suggests that, until the judgement, all people will be able to enjoy creation, but Noah's story in the Qur'an is not one of a unique judgement followed by a universal promise. Rather, it is typical of God's interaction with people throughout the ages. Noah is one of many messengers throughout the generations who provoke a division between the blessed and the judged. It becomes clear that this is God's solution to the problem of evil. This pattern is repeated with other peoples at other times and in other places, notably in Mecca at the time of Muhammad.

Comparing the Biblical and Qur'anic Accounts

There are many obvious *similarities* between the biblical and qur'anic Noah stories. In fact, they are sufficiently similar for children's stories of the ark to be almost the same in the two faiths. As with the Cain and Abel story, the Bible and the Qur'an are agreed on the need to listen to and obey God, and that God will judge everyone. The Noah stories add the dimension of some people being spectacularly saved from the judgement, and also of God's direct guidance of human beings. In both, God speaks to Noah and Noah obeys: not only is God the creator and the judge, he is also one who speaks. These are very important points of agreement between Muslims and Christians. However, at every point we also find subtle *differences*. Sometimes, the Qur'an

---

24. A. Yusuf Ali, *The Holy Qur'an: Text, Translation and Commentary* (Jeddah: Islamic Education Centre, 1946).

25. M. A. S. Abdel Haleem, *The Qur'an: A New Translation by M. A. S. Abdel Haleem* (Oxford: Oxford University Press, 2008), Used with permission.

seems to be taking particular lessons from the Genesis story that are also discussed by Jews and Christians; other times, it tells a rather different story from the Bible.

There are *differences in the portrayals of Noah*. Most of the qur'anic account of Noah is taken up by what Noah *says*; in Genesis, he says nothing at all until he curses his son after the flood. The qur'anic Noah is essentially a prophet, with a message to preach. He speaks both day and night, and tradition has it that he persevered in his preaching for 950 years.[26] The Qur'an also details many of his prayers: for his son, for rescue, for forgiveness for his household and believers, and for judgement on unbelievers. In the New Testament, 2 Peter 2:5 can be interpreted to mean that Noah preached to his generation,[27] but in Genesis itself he is, like Abel, silent. He might have been a prophet in some sense, but this is certainly not his major role in the Bible.

In the Qur'an, Noah is the grieving prophet, saddened by the wickedness of his people (11. 36) and of his own son (11. 45). The Bible does not record the silent Noah as having such problems. Even 2 Peter 2:5-7, which describes the distress of Lot over the wickedness around him, does not mention anything of Noah's struggle. Genesis offers no clue to Noah's personality – not until the end of the story, when he gets drunk and angry and makes curses! He is simply someone who does what God tells him. On the other hand, his name links him with the grief of fallen creation. It brings hope into the genealogy of death in Genesis 5, where verses 28–29 describe him as one who 'out of the ground that the LORD has cursed . . . shall bring us relief from our work and from the painful toil of our hands'. The word 'relief' in Hebrew sounds like Noah's name, and the 'painful toil' has the same root as the word used to describe the pain in God's heart in 6:6. Noah's role is, somehow, to ease the sentence of Genesis 3:17. So the Noah stories point to *different ideas of prophethood* in the Qur'an and the Bible.

The two stories also point to *different ideas about God.* The Bible portrays not Noah but God as the one who is grieving over and angry at the wickedness of the people. The Qur'an tells us only what God *does*, and not what he thinks or feels. That different characters' emotions are described in each text shows the differences in points of view of each account. It seems as if the Qur'an

---

26. Usmani, *The Noble Qur'an*.

27. The phrase 'herald of righteousness' in 2 Pet 2:5 might mean this, but it might also mean that God's gracious choice of Noah heralded the possibility of righteousness and salvation for all. See, for example, M. Green, *2 Peter and Jude: An Introduction and Commentary* (Leicester: Inter-Varsity Press, 1968), 99–100.

presents a human perspective, while Genesis presents the divine perspective. This is interesting, because in the Qur'an the voice of God relates the stories, while in the Bible a narrator tells the stories.

So the Noah stories point to *different ideas of revelation* in the Qur'an and the Bible. There are differences in *what is revealed*. In particular, while the Bible tells us about the nature of God and gives us a glimpse of his 'heart', the Qur'an tells us what God says and what God does, but gives no glimpse of what he is like in himself. Many Muslims believe that God is so different from human beings that we can never know what he is like. The Qur'an may say that he is, for example, merciful; but God's mercy is different from people's mercy. God reveals not himself but his will.

There are also differences in *how revelation is given*. Muslims believe in a direct revelation of God's word by dictation from the angel Gabriel to Muhammad. Except for the first surah, the whole of the Qur'an is presented as God speaking.[28] The Bible, on the other hand, is obviously written by human beings, but Christians believe that they were guided by the Holy Spirit. They also believe that the main revelation of God is not in a book but in Jesus, the living Word of God.

There are *different motivations for judgement and salvation*. The flood in both Genesis and the Qur'an is God's response to human wickedness. However, the two accounts give us different views of the motivations behind the flood: one tells us God's motivation and the other tells us Noah's motivation. Genesis shows us the anger and pain that motivated God. The Qur'an shows us people's hostility to Noah and that his prayers were answered, first for his own rescue from those who rejected him, then for God to decide between him and his opponents, and finally for judgement on them.

The salvation of Noah in both Genesis and the Qur'an has to do with God's choice and Noah's obedience. The qur'anic Noah is saved because he is God's chosen prophet, described in a number of ways that indicate his qualifications: 'a faithful messenger' (26. 107); 'a thankful servant' (17. 3); the one bringing a 'clear warning' (11. 25; 71. 2).[29] He is also saved because he prays: Surahs 37. 75–76 and 21. 76–77 both record Noah's cry for help, followed immediately by deliverance. The flood is described as part of God's help for Noah in response to his prayers. Genesis introduces Noah in chapter

---

28. But note that some people think that the voice of the Qur'an represents the voice of the angel Gabriel dictating to Muhammad.

29. M. A. S. Abdel Haleem, *The Qur'an: A New Translation by M. A. S. Abdel Haleem* (Oxford: Oxford University Press, 2008), Used with permission.

6 by saying that he 'found favour [or grace] in the eyes of the LORD' (v. 8). He is then said to be 'righteous' and 'blameless' (v. 9), although what this means is not explained beyond saying that he 'walked with God'. The text simply refers to God's choice and Noah's nature, but does not say how the two are related. It is clear that the cause of the Genesis flood is not based on anything Noah thinks or says.

The scope of the flood's destruction is in keeping with the different motivations for it in the two accounts. The Qur'an portrays it as destroying those who rejected the prophet. The implication is that the flood was localized, since Noah is succeeded by further prophets. It is dealt with briefly and without any description of total destruction. Genesis, on the other hand, presents the flood as a universal catastrophe. That everybody and everything except those in the ark was destroyed is emphasized by repetition (6:11, 17; 7:21–23; 8:21; 9:15). We have already looked at how the flood reversed all of creation.

In the Qur'an, all who believed in the prophet were admitted into the ark, whether family members or not (11. 40). This already speaks of the importance of prophets in God's dealing with the world in the Qur'an. Since Noah had prayed that not one of the unbelievers should be saved, even the unbelieving of his own family perished in the flood. There is a heart-rending account of Noah's prayer for his unbelieving son:

> Noah called out to his Lord, saying, 'My Lord, my son was one of my family, though Your promise is true, and You are the most just of all judges.' God said, 'Noah, he was not one of your family. What he did was not right. Do not ask Me for things you know nothing about. I am warning you not to be foolish.' He said, 'My Lord, I take refuge with You from asking for things I know nothing about. If You do not forgive me, and have mercy on me, I shall be one of the losers' (11. 45–47).[30]

The qur'anic criterion for salvation was not, then, family, but accepting the prophet. In contrast, Genesis has only Noah's immediate family saved out of the entire human race, even though we are told nothing of their faith or character.

---

30. M. A. S. Abdel Haleem, *The Qur'an: A New Translation by M. A. S. Abdel Haleem* (Oxford: Oxford University Press, 2008), Used with permission.

The Basis of the Differences: Prophetic History or Covenantal History?

The Qur'an's view of sacred history is shaped around prophets. God works through a series of prophets connected by the unity of their message, and Noah is succeeded by messengers similar to himself. The Genesis story of Noah's successors has a very different focus: it is his family that is saved, and it is his family that matters. After the flood story, an outline of his descendants in the Table of Nations in Genesis 10 describes the relationships between extensive family networks but, again, is silent about these people's faith or deeds. None are prophets. There are no such genealogies in the Qur'an, although there are numerous lists of prophets.[31]

In the Bible, it seems from Genesis 4 – 11, God works through relationships and families. This is increasingly evident from the rest of Genesis and becomes the overriding narrative of the Old Testament. God calls Abraham and establishes his descendants, who then develop into the nation of Israel. God makes commitments to particular family groups (or tribes) and to the people who have joined them. Prominent among these is the story of God's call of David and the promises he makes to him and to his descendants. At each key stage, God makes a covenant, which will be the basis for the future of the family under God. It is these covenants that shape Old Testament history and become the basis of the New Testament view of history. Jesus is both the fulfilment of the previous covenants and the initiator of a new covenant which opens salvation for all peoples.

In Genesis, the covenant of chapter 9 is arguably the most important thing about the Noah story. The Qur'an also mentions a covenant 'taken from Noah' (33. 7),[32] but it does not describe it; it is simply mentioned among other covenants – those 'taken from' Abraham, Moses and Jesus, as from Muhammad. The commentators agree that these covenants are made with the prophets as individuals, charging each to carry out his mission with sincerity and to give an account of his trust. Surah 11. 48 mentions blessing for Noah's descendants, but the point of this verse is to show the division of Noah's descendants into two groups, one of which will receive blessings and the other, hell.

Reading Genesis after reading the Qur'an makes us realize again the significance of the Noahic covenant. It is all-encompassing: sharing the same

31. See, for example, Surahs 4. 163 and 6. 83–86.

32. M. A. S. Abdel Haleem, *The Qur'an: A New Translation by M. A. S. Abdel Haleem* (Oxford: Oxford University Press, 2008), Used with permission.

scale as the flood, filling a whole chapter and embracing all of life! Moreover, it is without conditions. The recognition in 8:21 that human beings are still wicked shows that the covenant is made not only with the righteous. The sad account of what Noah and his son did in the tent (9:20–27) immediately after the rainbow covenant seems to underline this point. It is God's commitment to the whole human race and to all life on earth.

The Basis of the Differences: Back to Adam

Why does the Qur'an tell the story of Noah in the way that it does? The most straightforward answer is that it is drawing out the aspects of the biblical story that relate to Noah as a typical prophet. Why are prophets given so much more importance in the Qur'an than in the Bible? Why does it have a prophetic history while the Bible has a covenantal history? The clue is in the question that underlies the biblical Noah story: what is the root of evil, and how does God respond to it?

The question is fundamental, and takes us to the even more basic question about how the Qur'an and the Bible view human beings and their relationship with God. We will deal with it by turning to the stories of the very first human beings. Here is the main qur'anic account:

> [Prophet], when your Lord told the angels, 'I am putting a successor on earth,' they said, 'How can You put someone there who will cause damage and bloodshed, when we celebrate Your praise and proclaim Your holiness?' but He said, 'I know things you do not.' He taught Adam all the names [of things], then He showed them to the angels and said, 'Tell me the names of these if you truly [think you can].' They said, 'May You be glorified! We have knowledge only of what You have taught us. You are the All Knowing and All Wise.' Then He said, 'Adam, tell them the names of these.' When he told them their names, God said, 'Did I not tell you that I know what is hidden in the heavens and the earth, and that I know what you reveal and what you conceal?'
>
> When We told the angels, 'Bow down before Adam,' they all bowed. But not Iblis, who refused and was arrogant: he was one of the disobedient. We said, 'Adam, live with your wife in this garden. Both of you eat freely there as you will, but do not go near this tree, or you will both become wrongdoers.' But Satan made them slip, and removed them from the state they were

in. We said, 'Get out, all of you! You are each other's enemy. On earth you will have a place to stay and livelihood for a time.' Then Adam received some words from his Lord and He accepted his repentance: He is the Ever Relenting, the Most Merciful. We said, 'Get out, all of you! But when guidance comes from Me, as it certainly will, there will be no fear for those who follow My guidance nor will they grieve – those who disbelieve and deny Our messages shall be the inhabitants of the Fire, and there they will remain' (2. 30–39).

    . . . We created you, We gave you shape, and then We said to the angels, 'Bow down before Adam,' and they did. But not Iblis: he was not one of those who bowed down. God said, 'What prevented you from bowing down as I commanded you?' and he said, 'I am better than him: You created me from fire and him from clay.' God said, 'Get down from here! This is no place for your arrogance. Get out! You are contemptible!' but Iblis said, 'Give me respite until the Day people are raised from the dead,' and God replied, 'You have respite.' And then Iblis said, 'Because You have put me in the wrong, I will lie in wait for them all on Your straight path: I will come at them – from their front and their back, from their right and their left – and You will find that most of them are ungrateful.' God said, 'Get out! You are disgraced and banished! I swear I shall fill Hell with you and all who follow you! But you and your wife, Adam, live in the Garden. Both of you eat whatever you like, but do not go near this tree or you will become wrongdoers.'

    Satan whispered to them so as to expose their nakedness, which had been hidden from them: he said, 'Your Lord only forbade you this tree to prevent you becoming angels or immortals,' and he swore to them, 'I am giving you sincere advice' – he lured them with lies. Their nakedness became exposed to them when they had eaten from the tree: they began to put together leaves from the Garden to cover themselves. Their Lord called to them, 'Did I not forbid you to approach that tree? Did I not warn you that Satan was your sworn enemy?' They replied, 'Our Lord, we have wronged our souls: if You do not forgive us and have mercy, we shall be lost.' He said, 'All of you get out! You are each other's enemies. On earth you will have a place to stay and livelihood – for a time.' He said, 'There you will live; there you will die; from there you will be brought out.'

Children of Adam, We have given you garments to cover your nakedness and as adornment for you; the garment of God-consciousness is the best of all garments – this is one of God's signs, so that people may take heed. Children of Adam, do not let Satan seduce you, as he did your parents, causing them to leave the Garden, stripping them of their garments to expose their nakedness to them: he and his forces can see you from where you cannot see them: We have made evil ones allies to those who do not believe (7. 11–27).[33]

The biblical and qur'anic Adam stories have the same shared basis that we have already seen in the stories of Cain and Abel, Noah and Babel: that there is one God who is the creator of the earth and of all human beings; that God speaks to human beings and they are answerable to him; and that obedience brings blessings and disobedience has negative consequences. These are very important agreements. However, you probably noticed some important differences that can explain some of the discrepancies we noted above between other biblical and qur'anic stories.

While Genesis 1:26 describes humans as *made in God's 'image'*, Surah 2. 30 describes Adam as *God's 'successor'*. The Arabic word is *khalīfah* and means literally, 'someone who stands in someone else's place'. The most common interpretation is that human beings are given responsibility in God's creation as stewards.[34] We are to care for creation by doing what he asks us to do. This is similar to the responsibility to have dominion over the earth (Gen 1:26) and to work the ground (2:5, 15).

Adam's first specific job in Genesis 2 is to name the animals. In the Qur'an, it is God who teaches Adam the names. This signals a subtle but important difference: is the major mark of *human knowledge* that it is produced by us, or that it is given to us? Putting the question another way, does being made 'in the image of God' mean that, just as God named the parts of creation

---

33. M. A. S. Abdel Haleem, *The Qur'an: A New Translation by M. A. S. Abdel Haleem* (Oxford: Oxford University Press, 2008), Used with permission.

34. As with many qur'anic terms, there is plenty of discussion among the commentators as to what the word means, and as to how far it refers to Adam and how far it refers to all humanity. Note that this term was also used of Muhammad's successors who led the Muslim people: the English 'caliph' comes from the Arabic *khalīfah*, the title used for the major Muslim rulers.

in Genesis 1, so human beings can name the animals for themselves rather than waiting for God to tell them what he has already decided? It seems that Genesis emphasizes human beings' likeness to God, whereas the Qur'an emphasizes human beings' difference from God.

A more obvious difference is that *the Qur'an introduces Satan and the angels.* From a historical point of view, this is not surprising. While such spiritual beings make remarkably few appearances in the Old Testament, there were many stories about them in New Testament times and many more by the time of Muhammad. In particular, some Jewish and Christian texts contained accounts with close parallels to the Qur'an.[35] However, the Qur'an retells these stories to make its own points. One of the points of the Adam stories is that they tell of the origins of human disobedience to God: unlike in Genesis 3, these lie not so much in the rebellion of the human heart as in the enmity of Satan and in human weakness and forgetfulness of God's commands.

As in Genesis, God warns Adam not to eat the fruit of a particular tree. Again, as in Genesis, Adam and Eve do eat, and God then calls them to account. However, *Adam and Eve's response* in the Qur'an is quite different from their response in Genesis. They do not try to hide, or excuse themselves or blame someone else; instead they repent and seek forgiveness.

Seeking forgiveness changes the whole direction of the story. *In Genesis, there are negative consequences* not only for Adam and Eve but also for the serpent and for all people and everything in creation: this is shown not only by the sentences of Genesis 3:14–19 but also by the exile from Eden. The garden in which they had first lived was on earth, and being locked out of it symbolizes that the earth has now changed. In contrast, the qur'anic garden was not on earth. God had planned to send them down to earth but, before he did so, the first temptation and disobedience took place. So 'sending down' Adam and Eve from the garden (2. 36; 7. 24) does not imply any drastic change. Rather, the story is about how Satan becomes the human beings' enemy, and is allowed to go 'down' to earth with them and tempt them.

What follows all this is also different in the two books. Genesis 4 – 11 diagnoses the human condition outside Eden as we have been studying in this and the previous chapter. This leads to God's plan of blessing the nations through Abraham and his descendants. In the Qur'an, meanwhile, Adam and Eve and all their descendants are told that God will send them messengers

---

35. *Genesis Rabbah* 8:5–10; *The Life of Adam and Eve* 12–16; and *2 Enoch* 29–32.

who will tell them how to live. God warns them to listen to those messengers instead of to Satan.

We can sum up the theological differences between the biblical and qur'anic stories by saying that the Qur'an does not see human beings as fallen. This accounts for why qur'anic sacred history is a history of prophethood. If the human problem is not that something has gone fundamentally wrong in our nature but that we are forgetful and weak, our greatest need is to be told and then reminded of what God wants of us, and we need to be warned of the consequences of going a different way. So, according to the Qur'an, God's great mercy to humankind is seen in sending prophets to give us what we need, and the greatest of these is the final prophet, Muhammad, who comes with the final message. Of course, the Qur'an recognizes that, as at the time of Noah, many people reject the messages and persist in their wickedness. Muslims recognize that, in practice, we need much more than guidance to change us, but they do not think of the persistent wickedness of many and the persistent short-falling of all in terms of a 'fall'.

There is an important underlying distinction here. The Qur'an and Muslim people do not think of human beings as sinless: they know very well that no one keeps God's laws perfectly. However, they see this as simply the way that we are: God made us in a natural state in which we know that he exists and is the Lord to whom we should answer.[36] We have not 'fallen' from that state, but that state is one of natural weakness and we learn to go astray. In contrast, Genesis tells us that we were made in an original state of relationship with God, and that the weak state in which we all now find ourselves is not how we were made. Therefore, something quite different from our 'fallen' state is possible. That something different is because we are 'made in the image of God', and it is pictured as 'walking with God' in the garden of Eden.

Digging deeper, we find an even more fundamental difference: Genesis tells us that human beings are, in some ways, like God. They are so like God that, were it not for their sin, they could walk and talk with God and even share in his creative work by, for example, naming the animals. In contrast, the Qur'an's insistence that 'no one is comparable to [God]' (Surah 112. 4)[37] leads most Muslims to insist that human beings are in no way like God.[38] This

---

36. See 7. 172, where all humanity acknowledges God before anyone is born.

37. M. A. S. Abdel Haleem, *The Qur'an: A New Translation by M. A. S. Abdel Haleem* (Oxford: Oxford University Press, 2008), Used with permission.

38. Of course, there are differences among Muslims on all these ideas, because Muslims are human beings. So, for example, Sufis seek a close relationship with God, and some do speak

links with the idea noted above: that we cannot really know what God is like, because any language we might use to speak of God has to mean something other than what it means when applied to human beings.

Thinking about Islam

As we move on to focus on biblical passages centred around the transfiguration, we will bear in mind the theological differences that have emerged from this study. They will help us to form the questions that we will take to the Bible in part 3 of this book.

Among these questions are:

1) How does the Qur'an relate to biblical revelation? This is closely linked with the question of what sort of person Muhammad was, and how we should think about him.

- The Qur'an clearly sees itself as continuous with the Bible. It intends to refer to the One God who created the world, and who is the God of Adam, Noah, Abraham and the other biblical characters, including John the Baptist and Jesus.

- Because it uses biblical stories, it contains much that agrees with biblical truth. However, it often chooses just one interpretation of a biblical story that removes some dimensions that are important for the overall understanding of the Bible as a whole and of the work of Jesus Christ in particular. For example, it keeps the judgement aspect of the flood, but omits the sacrifice.

- Muslims believe that the Qur'an can only be explained as a direct revelation from God. However, even the brief references to the historical context mentioned above suggest an alternative: that the Qur'an can be explained by reference to the life of Muhammad on the one hand and Jewish, Christian and other influences on the other.[39]

---

of themselves as becoming like God.

39. Some scholars think that the Qur'an did not reach its present form until long after the death of Muhammad, and that it is influenced by the development of the Islamic empire as well as by the life of Muhammad himself. For a selection of papers and relevant research on these ideas, see A. Neuwirth, N. Sinai and M. Marx, eds., *The Qur'an in Context: Historical and Literary Investigations into the Qur'anic Milieu* (Leiden: Brill, 2010). See also the Corpus Coranicum project, http://koran.bbaw.de/.

2) How do we understand the various aspects of Islam that we see around us that have developed from the foundations of the Qur'an and of the reported life of Muhammad?

- Because of the stress on the need for guidance, the question of what people should do became very important. Hence grew the shariah – a system that classifies all human actions on a scale from compulsory to unforgiveable.
- In the process, the example of Muhammad became of central importance.
- Seventh- and eighth-century Arabic culture spread and was considered to be universal.
- Empires became a means to implement shariah as a system of law and this culture.

3) How should we regard the variety of expressions of Islam? Is one or other of them a 'real' Islam? This takes us back to the human dimensions of what has developed. We have already emphasized that the first way of understanding Muslims we are in contact with is as human beings like everyone else. But we also need to recognize that qur'anic interpretation, the Hadith, Islamic law and poetry are also the products of human society. So we can expect to see:

- Aspects of Islam that represent genuine seeking after God. These might include Sufism on the one hand and forms of traditionalism that model everything on Muhammad on the other.
- Aspects of Islam driven by desire for power and territory. Babel is about the scattering of peoples: we should therefore not be surprised if there are many factions, disagreements and misunderstandings among Muslims, just as there are between Muslims and other people.
- Aspects of Islam that seek to identify and deal with evil; but also aspects of Islam which themselves reflect human evil.

To Think About

If you did the 'To think about' on page 10, read again the questions that were in your mind before you read this chapter.

Have any of them been answered? What new questions do you have as a result of reading this chapter?

Part 2

Transfiguration

Peter paused for breath and looked back down the way they'd just climbed. 'Good,' he thought, 'no one's following.' They'd made good progress, though: the river was now a silver ribbon below, and the last hamlets were far away and tiny. A sliver of the lake glinted on the horizon. It seemed like a lifetime since that water had been his entire world. And finally, people had disappeared. Last time they'd tried to get away together, tired after staying with strangers all over the place, preaching and healing, crowds had followed.

Now it was just him, James, John and Jesus. 'Behold, how good and pleasant it is when brothers dwell in unity,' they had quipped as the grass grew greener and fresher up the slopes; 'as pleasant as this mountain dew.'[1] But yes, it was good to be together, not sent off without Jesus this time, nor followed by five thousand!

The air was thinner up here and left them short of breath; they hardly spoke, simply following Jesus up the mountain. Peter kept trying to shake off the things Jesus had said the previous week about following him. Why that cross? It sounded like a bad dream now. But each footfall and each breath of his master seemed to confirm that he was soon going to suffer many things. The air was full of the bitter tang of alpine herbs. 'Not long till Passover,' Peter thought.

---

1. Ps 133:1, 3.

They grew tired. They had been so busy lately, and now, with the wind whipping round their heads, they were glad to finally stop on this summit, pull their cloaks around them, sit down and lean back. They'd pray in a minute . . .

Jesus, however, didn't sit down. His cloak flapped wildly in the wind as he stretched out his hands to pray. Peter grew dizzy; the distant lands below seemed to spin, with Jesus at the centre of them all. His heavy head dropped into sleep.

He didn't know how long he slept for, but when he tried to open his eyes they watered with the wind and the light. That light! He tried to open his eyes again, but could only squint. Jesus looked unutterably different, all the light of the sky reflecting off him. John and James had seen it too, for they were shielding their eyes as they watched.

It was no longer just the four of them now, either. Two men, gloriously bright, stood with Jesus, talking. 'When I go . . . fulfilling promises . . . Jerusalem . . .' The wind carried snatches of their conversation to Peter. He was a child again, hearing ancient men speak with wisdom full of Torah and prophecy that he could not grasp. Gathering up their robes, the two ancient men made to leave.

Peter scrambled to his feet. 'Wait!' He darted forward. 'Master, I'll make you some shelters.' He didn't know what to say and his voice sounded feeble, somehow insubstantial compared with theirs. 'It's . . . it's good to be here.'

Tendrils of mist crept around the mountain top and his voice trailed off. The air thickened with cloud until they were surrounded by its whiteness, blinding them. Fear gripped Peter; he wanted to shout out again, 'Get away from me, Lord, I am a sinful man.' He knew he might not be spared this time. But no sound came out.

And then, the voice: so full it seemed to fill the world, coming from right within this holy cloud: 'This is my son, whom I have chosen.' Every word was solid, true. 'Listen to him!'

Peter hardly dared hope that he still lived, but when he realized he still had breath in him, he summoned his courage to raise his head. He must have fallen flat on his face. He was alive – but only, he knew, by the grace of God.

He glanced up. There before them was Jesus, alone now, and ready to walk back down the mountain, back to where the people were.

The transfiguration is at the heart of all three Synoptic Gospels, and it is at the heart of our thinking in this book. In the Gospels, it is a turning point in the journey towards understanding who Jesus is, as Jesus turns towards his final journey to Jerusalem. The reader of the Gospels knows about John the Baptist and about Jesus' special birth, about his miracles, his teaching and his disciples. The question has just been raised, 'Is Jesus one of the prophets?' The disciples have discerned that he is someone special, and the word they use to describe him is 'Messiah'. Jesus agrees with the word, but, as soon as he starts to talk about his coming death, the disciples protest, as the Messiah, they think, must not die in the way he describes.

In this book we argue that Islam can be understood as reversing the transfiguration, and that Muslims are rather like the disciples at this stage: the Qur'an tells them about John the Baptist's birth and about Jesus' virgin birth, and a little about his teaching and his miracles. It sees Jesus as a prophet and calls him 'Messiah', but, at least as interpreted by most Muslims, it saves Jesus from dying on the cross.

So we will begin our study of the transfiguration by trying to get into the minds of the disciples and the first readers of the Gospels, digging down to 'the world behind the text' to consider what Peter, James and John might have learned from their experience and what the first readers of the Gospels might have understood. We will find many parallels with Islamic thinking on our journey.

We will look carefully at this story in its context in Luke's gospel, but we need first to think about what Moses and Elijah would have meant to people in the 'world behind the text' of the New Testament. So important were these figures in first-century Jewish thinking that they seem to have symbolized the whole Old Testament history, often called 'the Law and the Prophets'. Moses was the great law-giver, and Elijah was perhaps the greatest prophet who tried to get the people to obey the law. So the transfiguration tells us about Jesus' relationship to the law and to the prophets.

Like first-century Judaism, Islam has a central role for prophets and for laws, and it is by listening to them rather than to Jesus that Muslims effectively reverse the transfiguration. However, we need to discern the Bible's understandings of law and prophets – first, in order to learn what the transfiguration is teaching us and, second, to clarify what makes Jesus' voice distinctive so that we can really 'listen to him'. Then, third, we will be able to compare and contrast Islamic and biblical understandings.

There is a third Old Testament figure who would have been in the minds of the disciples at the transfiguration and of the first readers of Luke's gospel. The transfiguration takes place in the middle of a confused conversation about the possibility of Jesus being the Messiah. The transfiguration addresses what sort of Messiah he is and how he relates to the law and to the prophets. So, in order to understand 'the world behind' the transfiguration text, we need to study what the Jews of Jesus' time were expecting of the Messiah, the Son of David. We will therefore take time to look at Elijah, Moses, and the expectations of the Messiah before returning to study the transfiguration in its context in Luke.

As in our Genesis study, we will invite you to think about how the worlds of these biblical characters reflect Muslim societies in your own 'world in front of the text', and we will compare aspects of the biblical material with parallel Islamic material. We will then be ready to think more systematically about Muslims and about Islam.

3

Elijah

Why give so much space to Elijah? Although they appear in only a few chapters in the Old Testament, Elijah and his successor, Elisha, were so different from the other prophets and their stories raise so many questions that readers have always been fascinated by them. Christians, Jews and Muslims have continued to speculate about Elijah down the centuries.[1]

Ida's Story

It was through a study of Elijah with Islam in mind that I realized the importance of the transfiguration for 'thinking biblically about Islam'. I first chose not the whole story but the famous confrontation with the prophets of Baal in 1 Kings 18 as a focus, because I found it so uncomfortable. I had heard people using it to justify confrontational debates and even violence in relating to Muslims. All faiths other than Christianity, these people were saying, were like Baal worship: inimical to the Christian faith and to be strenuously denied. Christians were to keep right out of them, and only seek to rescue their adherents by preaching the gospel. I could see their point, but I'm not a person who enjoys confrontation and I couldn't see other faiths as totally negative. I had heard others using the story in an opposite way: they saw parallels between Elijah's confrontation of idolatry and Muhammad's confrontation of idolatry, and used the story to argue that Muhammad was like an Old Testament prophet. Again, I could see their point, but this time I was uneasy in the opposite direction: they seemed to be underestimating important differences between qur'anic and biblical ideas of prophethood. So I didn't like the story of Elijah and the prophets of Baal, and I

---

1. See the article 'Elijah' by Emil G. Hirsch et al., in *The Jewish Encyclopaedia*, 1906, JewishEncyclopedia.com, jewishencyclopedia.com/articles/5634-elijah.

certainly wouldn't have used it as my starting point in thinking about other faiths.

However, I claim to be someone who takes the authority of the Bible seriously. Indeed, I often say that I try to give it authority over both Christian tradition and my own reason. So, when there is an aspect of the Bible I don't like, I try to make it a principle to look at it carefully and to try to find out what God is saying to me through it. In the case of the Elijah story, I realized that it was referred to in the New Testament as well as in the Old Testament: while the Elijah–Elisha cycle in Kings appears to stand by itself and does not appear at all in Chronicles, it is central to the books of Kings, which I realized are classed as prophetic books in the Jewish tradition. So important is Elijah in Jewish thinking that even today Jews set a place for Elijah at the Passover table. So important was he in New Testament times that he was the one who appeared with Moses at the transfiguration. Elijah, then, mattered; and I decided to look carefully at his confrontation with the Baal prophets to find out what God would teach me. I am still learning!

In the light of this, we are going to study Elijah in some depth, with a particular focus on his confrontation with the prophets of Baal. The study will suggest ways of 'thinking biblically about Islam', but its main importance is to give insights into the 'world behind' the transfiguration narratives. For this reason, we concentrate on the incidents set on the three mountain tops – Carmel, Horeb/Sinai and finally Nebo – which converge at the transfiguration.

We will look at the 'world behind' the text, then at the place of the Elijah story within the biblical world of 1 and 2 Kings. As we go along, we will prompt you to ask yourself, 'How does this relate to the world in front of the text in which I meet Muslims?' We will then use our Genesis 1 – 11 framework as a basis for reading the Elijah story in the context of today's world.

The World behind the Text

Ahab the son of Omri did evil in the sight of the LORD, more than all who were before him. And as if it had been a light thing for him to walk in the sins of Jeroboam the son of Nebat, he took for his wife Jezebel the daughter of Ethbaal king of the Sidonians, and went and served Baal and worshipped him. He erected an

altar for Baal in the house of Baal, which he built in Samaria
(1 Kgs 16:30–32).

Elijah appears in the northern kingdom of Israel in the ninth century before
Christ. The scene is set in 1 Kings 16:21–34 with a short description of the
rise to power of Ahab's father, Omri, and then of Ahab himself. The focus
of the above passage is on religious concerns: on what was evil 'in the sight
of the LORD', and on the Baal worship that was established. However, this
is in the political context of economics, power and international relations.
We know quite a lot about both the religious and the political contexts from
archaeological findings as well as from within the Bible.

The Religious Context

The main 'evil' of Ahab was Baal worship, and it is this evil that Elijah
confronted throughout his ministry. Who was Baal, and why was serving him
so bad?

Baal was the god of weather and fertility. The name 'Baal' can be translated
as 'lord', and there seem to have been slightly different Baals in different
places. In the Holy Land, archaeologists have found evidence of Baal worship
such as platforms or 'high places', dated from the period of the Israelite and
Judean kingdoms.[2] There are also thousands of clay figurines of Baal's female
companion, Ashtoreth. She is normally naked, holding her breasts in her
hands.[3] Images of male Baal are also highly sexualized. Texts telling stories
about Baal and his fellow gods have also been found.

The book of the Bible that deals most directly with Baal worship is Hosea.
This is how Hosea describes what was involved:

> They sacrifice on the tops of the mountains
>   and burn offerings on the hills,
> under oak, poplar, and terebinth,
>   because their shade is good.
> Therefore your daughters play the whore,
>   and your brides commit adultery . . .
> for the men themselves go aside with prostitutes
>   and sacrifice with cult prostitutes (Hos 4:13–14).

---

2. John Bowker, *The Complete Bible Handbook: An Illustrated Companion* (London: Dorling
Kindersley, 1998), 99.

3. Negev, *Archaeological Encyclopedia of the Holy Land*, 45.

The sexual activity at the Baal altars was acting out the story of Baal and his consort, Ashtoreth. People believed that this would give them rain and good harvests: we could describe it as an acted prayer for fertility. However, it is not difficult to see how it could appeal to people's basic sex drive and would corrupt everyday life so that, as Hosea continues, 'When their drink is gone, they give themselves to whoring' (4:18). Sexual purity was very important in the Mosaic law; and sexual impurity was one of the things that God saw as an 'abomination' (see Lev 18 – 20). Baal worship, says Hosea, defiled Israel (5:3).

Worse than this, Baal worship was adultery and prostitution. God's command to Hosea to marry a prostitute was a picture of this. Israel is pictured as God's wife, who should practise steadfast love and faithfulness in her covenant relationship with the LORD. Instead, she runs after another lord, and her service of Baal so weakens her that she is unable to return. 'Their deeds do not permit them to return to their God. For the spirit of whoredom is within them, and they know not the LORD' (Hos 5:4). Israel's 'husband' had every right to be angry and repudiate her. The amazing fact was that God chose not to do this. Yes, he was angry, but he loved her so much that he was willing to take her back. This gives us a clue as to what the Elijah story is all about.

There is more. Baal worship, says Hosea, led to moral decline. Without 'faithfulness or steadfast love' and with 'no knowledge of God in the land' (Hos 4:1), all sorts of other sins abounded: 'there is swearing, lying, murder, stealing, and committing adultery; they break all bounds, and bloodshed follows bloodshed' (4:2). Later we are told, 'they deal falsely; the thief breaks in, and the bandits raid outside' (7:1). Elijah had to deal with some of these sins as well as with the worship of Baal.

Baal worship also led to God's judgement, and that judgement took an appropriate form. The people had to learn that it was not Baal but the LORD who had power over weather and fertility. In an agricultural society such as ancient Israel, people were utterly dependent on successful harvests. No doubt it was a huge temptation to pray to the god to whom the surrounding nations prayed for his blessing of rain in dry spells. However, because of the corruption that this worship brought, their prayers had the opposite effect:

> Therefore the land mourns,
>> and all who dwell in it languish,
> and also the beasts of the field
>> and the birds of the heavens,
>> and even the fish of the sea are taken away (4:3).

This is not just poetry. Under King Ahab's rule there was such a severe famine that the king and his servant Obadiah had to 'go through the land to all the springs of water and to all the valleys' for water and grass to save his horses and mules (1 Kgs 18:5–6).

The famine under Ahab came in fulfilment of Elijah's word that there would be 'neither dew nor rain' (1 Kgs 17:1). It made a striking point: not only God himself, but even the word of God's prophet, was still above the word of the weather and fertility god. Meanwhile, as evidence of the bountiful provision of God – and not Baal – ravens brought fresh meat to Elijah, royal fare directly from the table of the King in the heavens. Through Elijah, God also provided sustenance for the widow who lived in the original Baal-worship territory of Sidon. After the encounter on Mount Carmel, it is again God's prophet Elijah who warns that it *will* rain. Once again, Baal cannot provide food or rain.

When the Elephants Fight, the Grass Gets Trampled[4]

After Iraq invaded Kuwait in 1990, the United Nations imposed sanctions on Iraq. Formerly dependent on imports for food, Iraq was now banned from international trade. The Iraqi people began to suffer greatly, after a decade in which they had begun to experience improvement in their standard of living. Among other things, education collapsed, diseases spread and several hundred thousand children who would otherwise have reached their fifth birthday died.

In 1993, sanctions changed to a scheme whereby Iraq could trade oil for food. The limited trade quickly became riddled with corruption: contractors gained monopolies and grew rich off huge profits. The president, Saddam Hussein, built grand palaces for himself and his functionaries. Moreover, the grip of the police state grew stronger through the ration-card system used to regulate the imports, since everyone had to register to eat. It seems that Saddam manipulated the system, keeping drugs from hospitals, for example, in order to publicize the suffering from sanctions and so keep his people loyal to him in the face of a common enemy. According to Hans von Sponeck, the United Nations coordinator for humanitarian assistance in Iraq who resigned in protest in 2000, 'Local repression

---

4. African proverb.

and international sanctions became brothers-in-arms in their quest to punish the Iraqi people for something they had not done.'[5]

To Think About

This was a complicated set of circumstances in which war, international power politics, tyranny and greed led to intense suffering. How does this compare to the situation in 1 Kings 17?

Has poor leadership led to degradation of the land and/or increased hunger for the poor where you live?

In terms of our Genesis framework for understanding religion, we can see Baal worship as being an unacceptable attempt to reach out to God for several reasons. First, it was not directed to the One True God – 'For Israel has forgotten his Maker' (Hos 8:14) – and was directed to another deity altogether. Second, this type of worship was not worthy of that One True God, as it encouraged practices the Torah sees as wicked. Third, Baal worship was another incidence of a Babel-style linking of religion and power. Ahab's marriage to Jezebel was a political alliance and, as we shall see, Baal worshippers sought provision and political favour through their devotional practices. While these elements of Baal worship would make it abhorrent to God among any people group, among Israelites, the practices were scandalous because they violated Israel's covenant with the LORD.

Elijah confronts Baal worship not simply because it was 'someone else's religion' only practised by foreigners, but because it had crept into and warped Israel's own worship. Although 'no servant can serve two masters' (Luke 16:13), Israel was 'limping between two different opinions' (1 Kgs 18:21). The confrontation with the prophets of Baal is not a confrontation between Israelites who worshipped the One True God and foreigners who worshipped an idol: it was a confrontation of false worship within Israel.

---

5. David Rieff, 'Were Sanctions Right?', *New York Times Magazine*, 27 July 2003, 5, http://www.nytimes.com/2003/07/27/magazine/were-sanctions-right.html.

> **To Think About**
>
> Sometimes we think wrong religion is someone else's problem, only to realize we have aspects of it too. What might they be in your context?

The Historical Context

The archaeology and history of the Near East in ancient times give us a picture of the Omride dynasty to which Ahab belonged and which enjoyed a position of great political strength in the region. An inscription upon the stele of the king of Moab, for example, tells of how Ahab's father, Omri, conquered Moab. In 2 Kings 3:4 we find an indication of how rich that made him: the Moabites had to give Israel a regular tribute of 100,000 lambs and the wool of 100,000 rams. Omri was so rich that he was able to buy a hill at an enormous price and build a city there (1 Kgs 16:24). For the writer of 1 Kings, the most important thing about the new city was the terrible sin of Ahab in building a temple for Baal there (16:32); but archaeological findings indicate that Samaria was a glorious place, probably bigger than Jerusalem at that time.

The building of the Baal temple is linked to Ahab's marriage with Jezebel, which is yet another indicator of the power of the Omrides. Jezebel was the daughter of the king of Sidon, and the Sidonians only ever allied with those in the ascendency. Furthermore, fear of Israel's military power is probably the reason for the Syrian king, Ben-hadad, calling thirty-two allies to join him to attack Ahab (1 Kgs 20:1).[6]

The Elijah story is, then, situated at the height of the power of the northern kingdom of Israel. The story of Elijah himself is interrupted by accounts of battles, so the writer of Kings is clearly concerned with Israel's relationships with the surrounding nations as well as with what was going on within Israel.

Over the millennia of Old Testament history, Israel had many different experiences of nationhood, from her golden ages to the periods of war and exile. In the early days of monarchy, David had known that his power was given by God but was distinct from God's power. Israel had rejected Yahweh's monarchy and sought a political solution in the shape of a man from among them, and this man had overstepped his power by trying to take the role of priest as well as king (1 Sam 8 – 13). David showed that a king could both rule

---

6. C. Herzog and M. Gichon, *Battles of the Bible* (New York: Random House, 1978), 107.

Israel and accept the rule of God, and God made a covenant with him and his family. The royal family would be part of God's plan to bless both Israel and the nations.

The reign of David's son, Solomon, was the height of the power of the united kingdom. He ruled over many minority peoples and had cordial relationships with surrounding nations. Many non-Israelites were welcomed into Solomon's territory, including the queen of Sheba, who was greatly blessed by her visit. Israel was fulfilling her call to bring blessing to the nations![7] But there were also times of war, division and weakness in Israel, and terrible wars with the nations. Then there was exile and only a partial return to the Promised Land, so that, by the end of the Old Testament narrative, many of the Jews were living in foreign lands just as they had done in Egypt at the beginning of their story. The Old Testament deals with a huge range of situations in relation to power and in relation to the peoples who surrounded Israel.

During the time of Elijah's prophetic ministry, nearly everything was upside down. The visit of the queen of Sheba and her retinue during Solomon's glorious reign was a distant memory and now the kingdom was divided and there was another foreign queen in a rival palace. Queen Jezebel did not sit at the feet of Israel's anointed king and learn wisdom, but rather exerted a strong and destructive influence over her husband. Although the treasure from the temple had been borne away to Egypt, Ahab built his ivory palace (1 Kgs 22:39), revealing how far he had come from the days when David was embarrassed that he dwelt 'in a house of cedar, but the ark of God dwells in a tent' (2 Sam 7:2).

In another reversal of what God had done for Israel, during Ahab's reign the walls of Jericho were rebuilt (1 Kgs 16:34). Those fallen walls had been a symbol of God's power and grace in giving Israel conquest of Canaan under Joshua, who had expressly forbidden their restoration. Indeed, the curse Joshua had pronounced (Josh 6:26) on any who attempted to rebuild fell upon Hiel: his two sons died (1 Kgs 16:34). It was as if the conquest was being reversed as Israel, far from driving out the Canaanites, allowed their religious practices back in once again.

The society that God himself had ordered in the land that he had given was, in Elijah's days, reaching the depths of disorder. Things were so twisted

---

7. See, for example, Deut 24:17–22. For a discussion of the relationships of David and Solomon with non-Israelites, see Glaser, *The Bible and Other Faiths*, ch. 8.

that the king considered the prophet of God, Elijah, to be a 'troubler of Israel' (1 Kgs 18:17). Elijah spelled out the truth of the matter: 'I have not troubled Israel, but you have, and your father's house, because you have abandoned the commandments of the LORD and followed the Baals' (18:18). The king of Israel, who ought to have been leading the covenant community in the ways of the LORD, had done the very opposite and erected Baal altars and Asherah poles.

Baal worship had a strong political dimension in the time of the books of Kings, and this peaked under King Ahab. It was not the first time a king of the northern kingdom had adopted an alternative religion to strengthen his power. At the beginning of the split, King Jeroboam had sought to undermine Judah's influence and to strengthen his own with an alternative system of worship that he 'devised from his own heart' (1 Kgs 12:33), and which revolved around golden calves at a location far from Jerusalem, with his own priesthood and programme of festivals.

However, the verdict of 1 Kings (16:30) is that Ahab 'did evil in the sight of the LORD, more than all who were before him', largely because of his marriage with Jezebel, daughter of one of the supreme Baal-worshipping kings. We can see the temple to Baal in Samaria as a symbol of the link between religion and power: like the tower of Babel, it was a monument to the power that comes by using religion for imperial gain. When Elijah confronted the prophets of Baal, everyone would have understood that he was confronting not only a different spiritual orientation but also a political system. When he confronted Ahab and Jezebel after the incident of Naboth's vineyard, he was dealing with one of the unjust effects of the system on ordinary citizens.

Power through Marriage

That evening, the cathedral was festooned with lights. There was a marquee, the smell of roasting meats, the sound of laughter. 'How lovely,' I commented as we passed by, 'a church wedding for all to see.' It was at a time when the Christian minority normally kept a low profile. 'Well,' my friend explained, 'not exactly. The leader there has given his daughter to a Muslim to marry. Apparently he couldn't find a boy good enough from among us lot. She's a model, you see, with a huge salary, and they wanted someone rich for her.'

Prestige through Buildings

'A lot of people think that we are a small country, but we can accomplish great things.' This was part of the message to the world from HH Sheikh Hamad bin Khalifa Al-Thani, Emir of Qatar, on receiving the news that his country had been chosen to host the 2022 FIFA World Cup. He and his wife held the golden trophy between them as they celebrated what he described as a 'big achievement for all Arab countries'.[8]

Since that decision in Zurich 2010, construction of the ten stadiums has begun, the design of each one fantastically innovative. With foundations of some cut into the desert or, in one case, floating in a harbour, they will be breathtakingly beautiful.

Meanwhile, human rights campaigners have been observing these projects, where mostly South Asian low-wage migrant construction workers build under what they describe as 'appalling conditions', many of them risking their lives. In 2012 Human Rights Watch documented many cases in which employers were exploiting and abusing them.

In 2013, investigations by *The Guardian* newspaper in London found that forty-four Nepalese workers had died within three months, about half of them from heart failure or workplace accidents. But this was not the first time such findings had been reported: Human Rights Watch found that 191 Nepalese workers died in 2010; the Indian embassy in Qatar recorded 212 deaths in 2013 and around 700 deaths between 2010 and 2012.[9]

To Think About

What do you see in these stories of the conditions caused by the pursuit of power and prestige described in 1 Kings 16 – 17?

What do leaders in your community and in your country do to gain power? Have there been any marriages that are power alliances? Have there been any building projects that enhanced the prestige of leaders? Were they religious buildings?

---

8. 'Qatar 2022: Reactions', Fifa.com, 2 December 2010, http://www.fifa.com/worldcup/qatar2022/news/newsid=1344979/index.html.

9. 'Letter to SAARC on Improving Protections for Migrant Workers', Human Rights Watch, 17 December 2013, http://www.hrw.org/news/2013/12/17/letter-saarc-improving-protections-migrant-workers.

Elijah in the World of 1 and 2 Kings: The World of the Text

The books of Kings are structured around three accounts of building and destruction. The main account is about the temple in Jerusalem, which is built in 1 Kings 5 – 8 and destroyed in 2 Kings 25. Between the temple's building and destruction we can discern a chiastic structure in which the establishment of sacred buildings is mirrored by their destruction. The accounts of Elijah and Elisha are at the centre of the chiasmus.

    A Solomon builds the temple in Jerusalem (1 Kgs 5 – 8)

        B Jeroboam builds the altar with the golden calf at Bethel (1 Kgs 12:25–33)

            C Ahab builds the temple to Baal in Samaria (1 Kgs 16:33)

                D Elijah and Elisha

            C' Jehu destroys the house of Baal (2 Kgs 10:18–28)

        B' Josiah destroys the altar at Bethel (2 Kgs 23:15–20)

    A' Nebuchadnezzar destroys the Jerusalem temple (2 Kgs 25:8–17)

In the narrative of each building, there is a history of prophetic warnings and opportunities to repent. In each case, judgement is deferred because of God's faithfulness and patience but, eventually, it comes. The story of Elijah with the prophets of Baal comes within the central story of the building and destruction of the temple to Baal in Samaria. Through Elijah, God is warning Israel of the danger of judgement and offering her and her king an opportunity to repent.

The position of the Carmel story in the text indicates that it is not a general recipe for interfaith relations but a call to pure worship in Israel. The arch-pagan Jezebel is not even present during the confrontation. The central portion of the books of Kings tells Israel what repentance is about: it means choosing between Yahweh and any other god. Elijah makes this clear in his prayer: 'Answer me, O LORD, answer me, that this people may know that you, O LORD, are God, and that you have turned their hearts back' (1 Kgs 18:37).

The danger of judgement and the call to repentance can be seen throughout the Elijah story. Elijah appears suddenly with an announcement of judgement in the shape of the drought (1 Kgs 17:1), and the Carmel encounter is the climax of the story of that drought. Afterwards, Ahab and Jezebel seek to destroy the prophet, but Elijah runs away. God meets him and gives him a series of tasks that signal judgement on Ahab and on the whole Omride dynasty. He is to anoint Hazael, who will be the Syrian king who fights Ahab and Jezebel's son Jehoram (2 Kgs 8), and Jehu, who will kill Jezebel and all of Ahab's descendants (2 Kgs 9). He is also to appoint Elisha, who will ensure the preaching of the word of God and the preservation of a community of faith throughout.

Elijah anoints only Elisha, and appears again to confront Ahab and Jezebel about Naboth's vineyard (1 Kgs 21) and to confront Ahab's son about Baal worship (2 Kgs 1); he then travels with Elisha to meet the fiery chariot that is to take him to heaven (2 Kgs 2). Throughout the Elijah story, we see warnings of God's judgement, and we also see God actually judging people. The warnings and the judgements all offer opportunities for repentance. Some of the people seem to repent when they see the fire from God on Carmel, but their repentance does not appear to last, and neither Ahab nor Jezebel repent at all. Ahab finally repents when he hears the curse that results from the murder of Naboth, but he is too late to save anyone but himself from disaster (1 Kgs 21:27–29). Jezebel never repents. Through the Elijah story, we see Israel and her king missing opportunities to repent.

The story of Elijah is incomplete: the story of Elisha completes it. Elijah's ministry has not been fulfilled by the time God takes him up in the fiery chariot. He has not anointed Hazael and Jehu, the two instruments of God's judgement: it is Elisha who finishes this part of the job (2 Kgs 8:7–15; 9:1–13). We do not have space here to explore the stories of Elisha, but we will return to the idea that Elijah's ministry was unfinished, and we will see something of how the Gospels use aspects of Elisha as well as of Elijah in their presentation of Jesus.

The books of 1 and 2 Kings are concerned with the struggles over Israel's holiness in her internal worship and organization, as well as in her relationships with the nations and their gods. They also pick up the concerns of the linked[10] books of Samuel, which explore the problematic nature of kingship itself, seeing the very desire for a king as a response to political pressure and an attempt to be like the other nations (1 Sam 8). Here are some of the Samuel themes that can be seen in Elijah:

- The books of Samuel establish the sovereignty of God and his requirements for holiness through their accounts of Eli's family and the ark being captured by the Philistines. Elijah's encounter with the Baal prophets picks up similar themes.

---

10. 1 and 2 Samuel and 1 and 2 Kings were originally four parts of a single work.

- The books of Samuel explore the question of what a good king might be like, not least through their accounts of the family lives of Samuel, Saul and David. Elijah's ministry exposes arguably the worst king of Israel, including the weaknesses relating to his wife.
- The books of Samuel establish the importance of differentiating between the roles of political and religious leaders. The Elijah story indicates both the dangers of the wrong sort of religion influencing the king and the need for a separate prophetic role.
- The books of Samuel challenge human notions of power and demonstrate the importance of apparently insignificant people in God's purposes, not least through the story and song of the barren woman with which they start, and the story and song of the persecuted man with which they end.[11] Elijah appears without history or human backing and is persecuted by the royal family. At the same time, he is preserved by the ministry of a foreign widow, who miraculously receives back her son from the dead.

In sum, the Elijah story has a very significant place in the history of Israel. The Carmel encounter is a vivid challenge to Israel to be the holy people of God's calling; it is also part of a book that recognizes God's covenant faithfulness alongside Israel's failure and the sins of even the best of kings.

Using the Genesis 1 – 11 Framework to Read the Carmel Story

Although, as we have seen, the Carmel story is set in the northern kingdom of Israel in the ninth century BC, we can see in it the human condition diagnosed in Genesis 1 – 11. All the characters are made in the image of God but are fallen, and their religion displays seeking God by sacrifice, religion linked to power, and attempts to deal with evil. We can expect this diagnosis to apply to today's world, including today's Muslims and their relationships with Christians. This section uses our Genesis framework to read the Carmel story with its context in history and in Kings in mind, and invites you to think about how it can speak into your own situation.

---

11. Compare Hannah's song in 1 Sam 2:1–10 with David's song in 2 Sam 22. There is another song at the centre of Samuel – David's lament over Saul, with its repeated 'How the mighty have fallen!' (2 Sam 1:19, 25, 27). I am indebted to Carol Walker for pointing out this chiastic structure.

Two Sacrifices

The two altars on top of Mount Carmel open a new scene in the biblical drama about sacrifice. We have already seen that the first act outside Eden started with two sacrifices. One was acceptable; the other was not. Through the law, God established that sacrifice – but only the right sacrifice – is his appointed means of sustaining a relationship between himself and people infected by sin.

Right from the beginning, people have tried to reach God. That can be seen here in the encounter between Elijah and the prophets of Baal: there is no doubt that everyone in the drama is religious. In fact, aspects of their religious practice are outwardly similar. Elijah himself draws a parallel: 'Let two bulls be given to us, and let them choose one bull for themselves and cut it in pieces and lay it on the wood, but put no fire to it. And I will prepare the other bull and lay it on the wood and put no fire to it' (1 Kgs 18:23).

The main thing at stake, then, is on what terms God allows people to approach himself. The question is the same here as it was with the sacrifices of Cain and Abel. Which sacrifice is acceptable?

Elijah has confidence in the LORD that, despite any amount of religious fervour or advantage of the heat of the noon-day sun, nothing will be more powerful than a prayer to the 'God of Abraham, Isaac and Israel'. This is in contrast to the whipped-up emotion and man-made religiosity of the Baal prophets. Elijah asks that God will answer him, 'that this people may know that you, O LORD, are God, and that you have turned their hearts back' (18:37). God hears this prayer, so quiet in comparison with the noise made by the prophets of Baal, and sends down flames that set fire to water and stone. And so God shows himself. The people, all of them, acknowledge that the LORD is God.

Proclamations

A Hadith says that one should pray at first light, at the moment when one can first distinguish the white thread from the black. And so, in the grey light of pre-dawn, as the mountains emerge from the softly lit sky, there is a click and the air fills with static. An ancient man clears his sleep-filled voice and tells sleepers that God is great and prayer is better than sleep. Another click and a speaker transmits another sound: the early Hindu temple worship jangles the air with cymbals and chanting. The call to prayer rises and falls into it from moment to moment. Another click and the air is pulsing with electricity. Somewhere, an early morning preacher, whose voice is distorted by amplifiers, is punching the air and crying, 'Victory to Jesus!' When the temple music or the azan rises in a crescendo, he raises his voice, not to be outdone. 'He is exalted! He reigns on high! Alleluia!'

To Think About

What does your church worship have in common with local Muslim patterns of worship? What is it that distinguishes your worship? Do we feel the need to shout louder than everyone else? Do we try to compete in other ways? For example, do people want to make church buildings as impressive as nearby mosques, or do we worry when people build mosques that are taller than church towers?

People, Land and Power

As the building project of Babel revealed, religion can have a dangerous side. Like Babel religion, Baal religion was, for Ahab and the Israelites, a means of grasping power. As we have seen, Ahab's marriage with Jezebel increased Israel's power, and it was the marriage to Jezebel that led to Ahab's building the temple to Baal in Samaria (1 Kgs 16:31–33; 21:25–26). The ordinary Israelites might have worshipped Baal mainly to try to get good crops, but many would have done it to avoid persecution or to gain favour. We do not know very much about who the prophets of Baal and Asherah were – they could have been Sidonians or Israelites or both – but we do know that nearly a thousand of them ate meals at the royal table every day (18:19). Meanwhile, Jezebel had many of God's prophets killed. They found safety only in caves, existing on smuggled bread and water (18:4).

The king sought out Elijah, making communities swear he was not in their midst. Obadiah, a servant faithful to God, was afraid that, if he told Ahab he had spoken with Elijah, he would be killed. This was no doubt part of the quest for power. It has, after all, been typical of tyrants to take over religious institutions and persecute any who will not comply with their regime.

Living in Fear

On 4 January 2011, the Minister of the Punjab in Pakistan, Salman Taseer, was assassinated by his bodyguard, Malik Mumtaz Hussein

Qadri. On television, Mr Qadri said that Salman Taseer was a blasphemer, 'and this is the punishment for a blasphemer', referring to the shots he fired at close range. Taseer had appealed for the pardon of a young mother from the Christian community, Asia Bibi, who had been sentenced to death under the blasphemy law for allegedly insulting the Prophet Muhammad.[12]

Taseer's widow recalls being stunned when, at his funeral, almost no one from the government or his party turned up to show support. Little was said on the news analysis programmes that condemned the killing, and to this day, few lawyers are prepared to prosecute the bodyguard; far more would prefer to defend him. Meanwhile, in order to pacify the extremists, the government dropped plans to change the blasphemy law. However, according to Ali Hasan Dayan, of Human Rights Watch in Pakistan, the law 'was designed as an instrument of persecution; it's discriminatory and abusive'.[13]

Although most of those charged under this law are Muslims, campaigners say it is easily used against minorities: 'It is a hanging sword on the neck of all minorities, especially Christians,' says Shahzad Kamran, who ministers to prisoners. 'In our churches, homes and workplaces we feel fear,' he says.[14]

In such a climate, Shahbaz Bhatti, the Minister for Religious Minorities and a Catholic, predicted his own assassination, because he had also spoken against the blasphemy laws in the past and was prepared to do so again. And so, just two months after Salman Taseer's assassination, in the same city, he also was killed. For the extremists who carried out the murder, it was not an issue of politics, as plans to change the law had been dropped and Shahbaz himself had little power. It was all about ideology; it was enough that he had ever challenged the law.[15]

---

12. 'Punjab Governor Salman Taseer Assassinated in Islamabad', BBC News, 4 January 2011, http://www.bbc.co.uk/news/world-south-asia-12111831.

13. Orla Guerin, 'Pakistani Christian Asia Bibi "Has Price on Her Head"', BBC News, 7 December 2010, http://www.bbc.co.uk/news/world-south-asia-11930849.

14. Ibid.

15. Aamer Ahmed Khan, 'What Motives Led to Shahbaz Bhatti's Murder in Pakistan?', BBC News, 2 March 2011, http://www.bbc.co.uk/news/world-south-asia-12622080.

To Think About

In your country, are there people living in fear who have to keep a low profile? Are any Christians being persecuted? Are any Muslim groups being persecuted?

Do you know of people who have kept quiet about their own faith in situations like these, or who have even adopted another religion to stay out of trouble and look after themselves?

At Babel, we saw that power was linked with land. As Genesis 1 – 11 made clear, God has dominion over all the land, and humans should exercise power only under him. That is, perhaps, why 1 Kings describes Elijah's travels. God calls his prophet to travel now east of the Jordan, now north of Israel to Zarephath, now to the capital, now to the coast. He runs, with 'the hand of the LORD' on him, from Mount Carmel to Jezreel (18:46). It is a reminder that God is not bound by any political borders or geographic frontier, but can send his people wherever he wants them. Indeed, Ahab, searching for Elijah, had to send to every nation and kingdom to ask his whereabouts (18:10). Elijah moved so freely about the land that Obadiah's concern was that, after he had spoken to him, the Spirit of the LORD would carry him away 'I know not where' (18:12). Elijah demonstrates God's dominion over the territory by determining the place for the sacrifices to be performed and ordering the king to 'gather all Israel to me at Mount Carmel' (18:19).

Against this background, we can see how ugly was the royal couple's greed for land and power in the incident concerning Naboth's vineyard. They wanted another vegetable garden, and were prepared to have their neighbour killed to get it. Jezebel taunts her husband to prove his authority, asking, 'Do you now govern Israel?' and writes letters in his name (21:7–8). Hosea would suggest this is characteristic of a nation turned over to Baal worship:

> Gilead is a city of evildoers,
>> tracked with blood.
> As robbers lie in wait for a man,
>> so the priests band together;
> they murder on the way to Shechem;
>> they commit villainy.
> In the house of Israel I have seen a horrible thing;
>> Ephraim's whoredom is there; Israel is defiled (Hos 6:8–10).

God had left Ahab and Jezebel unpunished at Carmel, but now he sends Elijah on to the scene of this crime to bring down the curse that 'in the place where dogs licked up the blood of Naboth shall dogs lick your own blood' (21:19). The abuse of power, the drive to possess more, murder – these are things the Lord despises, along with lukewarm worship tainted by faith in other gods. In terms of the Genesis framework, the God of all the land gives land as a gift to people. Having a place, land, a home, is part of being human. It is not for anyone, not even royalty, to steal the land of another, as Ahab and Jezebel do here. 'Do not move an ancient landmark or enter the fields of the fatherless,' the proverb warns, 'for their Redeemer is strong; he will plead their cause against you' (Prov 23:10–11).

A House on the Hillside

It was a truly lovely spot – a house nestled between two grassy hills with a terrific view of the capital city in the valley below. Woodsmoke drifted up into the air, clear after the rain. But inside, the family was distraught. Never rich, now they were facing a crisis. First, the government had built a library below. No problem there, except that the roving eyes of visiting government officials had spied out this pleasant place, perfect for a weekend away. And now news had come that the family would have to move. The land, apparently, was needed for government residences. 'Pack your bags,' they had been told, 'and leave.'

To Think About

Do you see leaders greedy for power or territory in your area? Do you see instances of powerful people using their power for gain at the expense of the weak? What is God's response to this sort of thing in the Bible?

Dealing with Evil

We began to see from the Genesis story of Noah that God deals with evil either through *destruction* – in the case of Genesis 6 – 9, a flood – or through *sacrifice* by which judgement is averted. These two responses continue to be held in tension throughout the biblical narrative all the way to the cross. We can discern the tension in this section of Kings.

We see aspects of *judgement* as the confrontation of 1 Kings 18 reaches its climax in verses 38–39. Fire fell from heaven. Bull-meat, wood, dust, stone and even a pool of water burst into flame in front of people's faces to say, 'The LORD is God'. Then Elijah killed the prophets of Baal (v. 40). The people caught them, but Elijah himself slaughtered them. Why did he carry out such a bloodthirsty judgement when God had already showed himself? One might even ask whether he was right to do so. Up to this point, he says that what he has done has been according to God's word (v. 36). So is the slaughter of the Baal prophets also according to God's word? Or is it human vengeance, mirroring Jezebel's slaughter of Yahweh's prophets (v. 13)?

The text does not discuss the question, but comparison with Deuteronomy 13 suggests that Elijah was simply keeping the law. By the time of Jesus, Elijah is considered a model of pious zeal, together with Phinehas, who killed Zimri and Cozbi while the LORD himself was killing many Israelites during another encounter with Baal worship (Num 25). All this suggests that the purpose of this slaughter, like the earlier one before Israel entered Canaan, was restoration of Israel's holiness rather than stopping Jezebel's persecutions – although it achieved neither.

Hannah's Story: The Children's Idols

The children didn't want to write any more. Their little arms were tired of forming words from the story between two ruled lines. And I knew 'c-o-w' and 'g-o-a-t' did not mean anything to them, though they had plenty grazing around their homes. How could I bring the farmyard tale alive to them? They could parrot it to me well enough, but I wanted them to enjoy it.

'Please purchase 2 kg clay,' I wrote on the note to the school errand-boy. After lunch, the children returned to find a portion of clay on each of their desks. I showed them how to soften, twist and roll it, shape it into the forms of little animal bodies and attach four legs, a tail and a head with horns and ears. We began puppet theatre in the sand tray, all the animals lined up and pulling the giant turnip as in the story. How the children loved it! 'And they pulled and they pulled and they pulled . . .' we all chorused.

Sir Umar's form darkened the doorway. He was the administrator of the school and rarely entered the classroom. 'Ma'am Hannah, what have you done with this clay? Show me.' He tore a poorly formed figure of a cat from Naseeb's hand, half-buried in sand. He moved to the centre of the room and crushed the cat in his fist, smearing the clay over the palm of his hand. 'Children, do as I do!' he commanded. The children looked from him to me and back to him. Some copied him. 'These are idols. We will have no images like these in this school.'

'But, sir, it's just for their learning . . .'

He gathered up the figures and squashed them all.

On a much bigger, much more serious scale, world heritage sites have been destroyed in campaigns against idolatry. In March 2001 the world was shocked by images from Bamiyan, Afghanistan, showing the tallest Buddha statues in the world being blown up by the Taliban. The statues had stood for 1,700 years. 'They were the cultural heritage of Afghanistan,' admitted Wakil Ahmed Muttawakil, the Taliban foreign minister, arguing with the UN secretary's pleas for their preservation, 'but the part that contradicts our Islamic beliefs we would not like to have them any more' [sic]. And so, having failed to destroy them with anti-aircraft and tank fire, the defence minister supervised their destruction with a lorry-load of dynamite.[16]

To Think About

Some readers see in Elijah's stand against Baal worship similarities with Muhammad's campaign against idolatry. Have there been campaigns against idolatry in your area which have features of Elijah's campaign? In what ways are they different from Elijah's campaign?

Do you see differences in the ways in which Muslims confront idolatry and the ways in which Christians confront idolatry?

It is not uncommon in the Old Testament for evil within Israel to be dealt with by the death penalty: the sins of cursing one's parents and even of gathering fuel on the Sabbath could be punished by death (Lev 20:9; Num 15:32–36). It seems that anything that would lead Israel away from her role as God's people had to be removed from the community: this is certainly the principle behind the harsh judgements on idolatry and idolaters, and on the call for separation from the surrounding nations. Elijah's killing of

---

16. Ahmed Rashid, 'After 1,700 Years, Buddhas Fall to Taliban Dynamite', *The Telegraph*, 12 March 2012, http://www.telegraph.co.uk/news/worldnews/asia/afghanistan/1326063/After-1700-years-Buddhas-fall-to-Taliban-dynamite.html.

the prophets of Baal in 1 Kings 18, and his calling down fire on the Israelite messengers of the king who wanted to consult Baal in 2 Kings 1, makes sense in this context. Through the transfiguration, we will see how Jesus redirected and fulfilled Elijah's zeal for the holiness of God's people.

However, the 1 Kings 18 story does point to another possibility: as in the story of Noah, God prefers the way of acceptable *sacrifice*. He has made a covenant commitment to his people and he waits for them to repent. Elijah's encounter with the prophets of Baal has its place in God's dealings with evil in Israel, reminding them of God's covenant and showing them that he will accept a right sacrifice.

The pattern of the Noah story is seen most clearly in God's dealing with King Ahab. As God's choice of Noah follows his seeing the wickedness in the world (Gen 6:3-6), so the appearance of Elijah follows the description of how Ahab 'did evil in the sight of the LORD, more than all who were before him' (1 Kgs 16:30 – 17:1). Just as God sent a flood at the time of Noah, so he sent a famine at the time of Elijah. Just as God accepted Noah's sacrifice on Ararat, so he accepted Elijah's sacrifice on Carmel. Just as wickedness would continue after the flood (Gen 8:21), so Ahab's wickedness continued after Carmel. Indeed, as the words used to describe human wickedness before and after the flood are nearly the same (Gen 6:5; 8:21), so the words used to describe the wickedness of Ahab are very similar both before Elijah appears and after Elijah rebukes him for murdering Naboth (1 Kgs 16:30; 21:25).

The incident of Naboth's vineyard shows us that Ahab had not changed after the sacrifice on Carmel, and Elijah told him that his whole family would be judged; but the Noah pattern tells the reader that God is longing to have mercy on him. At last, Ahab realizes his condition and repents: 'He tore his clothes and put sackcloth on his flesh and fasted and lay in sackcloth, and went about dejectedly' (1 Kgs 21:27). In response, God tells Elijah that he 'will not bring the disaster in [Ahab's] days; but in his son's days [he] will bring the disaster upon his house' (21:29). It seems as if God has been waiting throughout for the slightest sign of repentance as an excuse for delaying judgement on his beloved people.

Ahab himself is killed in the battle in the next chapter (22:34–38) as his repentance has not taught him to listen to Micaiah's prophecy (22:19–20). However, his household is spared for about fourteen years after his own death. Judgement eventually falls twenty chapters later in 2 Kings 9, when the newly anointed king of Israel, Jehu, shoots Ahab's son Joram with an arrow (9:24) and has Jezebel thrown out of the palace window (9:33). Over the corpses, he quotes words of the curse pronounced for the crime against Naboth (9:26, 36–37).

Continuing to look at the Elijah story through the framework of religions in Genesis 1 – 11, we can see glimpses of *God's commitment to all people in the covenant with Noah* shining through. Centuries later, Jesus spoke of what God did for people from Israel's enemy territories (Luke 4:25–27). Among others, God cared for a widow from the kingdom of Ethbaal, Queen Jezebel's homeland, at a time when 'there were many widows in Israel . . . when the heavens were shut up three years and six months, and a great famine came over all the land' (4:25). Before we even begin to read about the challenge to the Baal prophets, we are invited to see God's heart for these enemies of Israel. 'Elijah was sent to none of [the widows in Israel] but only to Zarephath, in the land of Sidon, to a woman who was a widow' (v. 26).

This woman lived with her son in the north of Israel, in Zarephath, Sidon, where God told Elijah to go (1 Kgs 17:8). Elijah saw her there, depressed and famished, thinking of death as she scoured the land for enough wood to heat a single meal. There had been better times when Israel, blessed with good barley harvests, fed foreign widows, such as Ruth from Moab. But everything was upside down now.

Elijah came and introduced the purposes of God into her life by asking for a drink of water (17:10). This foreign widow became God's means of providing food for the prophet. First she saw God fill her container with wheat and her jug with oil every day, just as he had covered the land with manna before (vv. 14–15). Then she witnessed God answer Elijah's impossible prayer for the life of her son (v. 22). And so God changed from being the God of somebody else ('your God', v. 12) to the one whose word is 'truth' (v. 24). It was in *her* upstairs bedroom that God had first brought back life from the dead. God's priority for the Sidonians, as well as for the Israelites, was salvation.

Hannah's Story: Waiting on Widows

For a long time, I wondered why these women wait here. They have nothing to sell and are unprotected without their men around. In this downtown business district, they retreat into their all-covering shawls and keep their children close. Why do they sit here amid the hustle and bustle of young professionals grabbing a working lunch in a cheap-eat Afghan place?

What I hadn't realized was that after office hours, the diner does not simply close up and wait for tomorrow's influx of customers.

While it closes its till, waiters pile up takeaway meals in their arms to give to the refugee widows and their children who wait outside. They ask no questions, but put food into every outstretched hand.

To Think About

Who cares for the widows in your society? How does Christian care for the needy compare with Muslim care for the needy? What would it look like to care for needy people from 'enemy territory'?

In the Elijah story, we also discern *God's mercy for the other nations.* At the confrontation itself, it is important to note who was *not* slaughtered. The Sidonian people were not slaughtered, although they were the original Baal worshippers. We do not see the wicked Queen Jezebel's painted eyes and adorned head peering out of her tower in this encounter. God's curse on her was not for worshipping other gods herself but for her criminal activity against Naboth and for inciting her husband to worship Baal.

In his sermon that referenced the Sidonian widow, Jesus also spoke about Naaman from Syria, saying, 'there were many lepers in Israel in the time of the prophet Elisha, and none of them was cleansed, but only Naaman the Syrian' (Luke 4:27). Where the mention of a widow could have perhaps evoked pity in the synagogue congregation as Jesus spoke (though in practice it did not), talking about the leader of the Syrian army would certainly not have done so, because Naaman was the leader of the army of Israel's enemies. The people in the Nazareth synagogue were furious: they did not want to hear about God's concern for other nations, and especially not about God's concern for their enemies. However, it was Jesus, and not the synagogue members, who was in harmony with the overall treatment of the nations in the Old Testament. Almost all the judgement oracles against the nations are condemnation for injustice and what we might call war crimes; almost all the condemnations for wrong worship are addressed to Israel. God's whole purpose in choosing Israel was the salvation of the nations, and not their condemnation.

Between the Carmel story and the Naboth's vineyard story comes another encounter with 'the nations' in which another purpose of God is fulfilled: he has mercy on his people, and he gets glory through them. God's mercy to Ahab is in evidence in the miraculous victory against the Syrians led by their king, Ben-Hadad (1 Kgs 20). Ahab could never have defeated the Syrians alone. According to a historian of Israel's battles, he was 'cut off from the major part of his regular army'.[17] The people he mustered 'were like two little flocks of goats', while the Syrians 'filled the country' (20:27). But, because the Syrians had undermined God's glory in presuming he was only a territorial god of the hills and unable to rule the valleys (20:28), God allowed the people of Israel to defeat 100,000 of the Syrian foot soldiers. The city walls of Aphek fell on the 27,000 who remained. Where we would expect to read of God's judgement on Israel, we read of his mercy to them and of his judgement on the Syrians . . . and then of his judgement on Ahab (20:42). God's desire is for the salvation of all, but he will not put up with evil from anyone.

Sinai and Nebo: Covenant and Pain

On Carmel, we see Elijah bold and triumphant. In the very next chapter, we see him on Sinai, fearful and depressed. Later, near Nebo, we see him taken up to heaven, but outside the Promised Land and with his ministry unfinished. As we turn to study Sinai and Nebo, we will discern the final themes we met in the Genesis framework – the pain in God's heart and his covenant love. However, it will only be after the transfiguration, when Christ fulfils his ministry of zeal for God's name, that the intensity of the pain and the extent of the love will become clear.

After the drama on Mount Carmel, instead of being delighted at the worshipful response of those who saw the sacrifice turn to smoke, Elijah is depressed. He makes what was normally a six-day journey to Beersheba and then goes a further day's journey into the wilderness (1 Kgs 19:3–4). There, under a broom tree, he lies down and wants to die. And, although his fathers are never mentioned in the Bible and were not famous for anything, he moans, 'I am no better than my fathers' (19:4). For what Elijah has accomplished has not been enough to effect a change in people's hearts, turning them back to God in a lasting relationship. God's response to the sin before the flood was regret and pain, and it seems Elijah shares something of that in his own sense of dismay.

An angel of the LORD gives Elijah enough food for him to journey to the summit of Mount Sinai, here called Mount Horeb (19:7–8). It is a mountain that is already special in the historical memory of Israel as the place where Moses, and on one occasion, the whole of Israel, met with God. Elijah,

---

17. Herzog and Gichon, *Battles of the Bible*, 109.

like Moses before him, stays on Horeb, lodging in a cave (v. 9). There, he encounters the LORD and he expresses his broken heart: 'I have been very jealous for the LORD, the God of hosts. For the people of Israel have forsaken your covenant, thrown down your altars, and killed your prophets with the sword, and I, even I only, am left, and they seek my life, to take it away' (v. 10).

We have already seen that Baal worship is a breach of the covenant with God akin to a wife's betrayal of a loving husband. Through Hosea, though, God promises to remain faithful to his covenant bride. Here Elijah hints at the hope that God's covenant with Israel will continue to stand. Elijah had framed the confrontation in terms of the covenant by praying to the 'LORD, God of Abraham, Isaac, and Israel' (18:36), the one with whom the covenant was made and confirmed. There is also a subtle reminder of the Abrahamic covenant in the geography of Elijah's journey. He initially escaped to Beersheba, the first place Abraham acquired in fulfilment of God's promise to give him a land. Abraham dug a well and named it the 'well of oath' (Gen 21:22–31).

God's commitment to his covenant with Israel becomes clearer in his answer to Elijah. He has not entirely abandoned Israel, nor has everyone abandoned him. There are still 'seven thousand in Israel, all the knees that have not bowed to Baal, and every mouth that has not kissed him' (1 Kgs 19:18). Moreover, as God commissions Elijah to anoint the next kings of Israel and Syria and the next prophet, Elisha, he shows that his plans for Israel and the nations continue.

In our study of Genesis, we noticed that, since the first murder, the spectre of death has hung over the rest of history. Mournfully ringing out from chapter 5's genealogy is the repeated refrain 'and he died'. The one pause in the tolling of this funeral bell comes at Enoch's name, 'for God took him' (Gen 5:24). Being 'taken' by God and not dying raised the possibility that a way to avoid death was left open. But the pattern of death continued throughout the rest of the chapter and, indeed, the rest of history.

Elijah is another Enoch: he did not die. After his encounter with God at Sinai, he appears from time to time to announce God's judgements (1 Kgs 21:17–29; 2 Kgs 1; 2 Chr 21:12–15). In each case, we wonder where he has been in between his appearances; he appears 'out of the blue' in 1 Kings 17, and he continues to be a mysterious figure. But most mysterious of all is his departure from earth – a person who did not die in the midst of a book that records the sins of Israel which were leading them to judgement. As with Enoch, his mysterious departure once again raises the hope of life. Elisha saw 'chariots of fire and horses of fire [which] separated the two of them.

And Elijah went up by a whirlwind into heaven … And [Elisha] saw him no more' (2 Kgs 2:11–12). The Bible does not indicate the exact place where this occurred; only that it was across the Jordan (2:9), that is, outside the Promised Land. This is of great significance.

In Elijah's days, the people of Israel have been living in the Promised Land for generations, but with every page of their story in 1 and 2 Kings they get closer to losing the land, and they finally go into exile. We have noted that the stories of Elijah and Elisha are at the centre of these books. The departure of Elijah and his handing of his staff to Elisha is, in turn, at the centre of the Elijah–Elisha narrative. Significantly, Elijah's final journey is a retreat out of the land along the same route by which Joshua and the Israelites entered it. He starts from Gilgal (2 Kgs 2:1), the place where the Israelites established their distinct identity in their new land. (In this city, they were circumcised (Josh 5:8), the reproach of Egypt was rolled away (5:9), they celebrated the first Passover in Canaan (5:10) and at last replaced manna with 'the fruit of the land' (5:12). The two prophets go from Bethel to Jericho (2 Kgs 2:2, 4), the stronghold that God brought down for Joshua and the Israelites (Josh 6), and from there to the Jordan River. Elijah and Elisha cross the miraculously parted Jordan River in the opposite direction from that taken by Joshua (2 Kgs 2:8; Josh 3:14–17).

Outside the Promised Land, Elisha asks his spiritual 'father' for a double portion, not of land, as would be normal for the eldest son, but of his spirit (2 Kgs 2:9). Just as the Israelites had no land when they stood on this bank back in history, now Elijah has no portion in the land. He leaves the earth at the same place where Joshua's journey began with the LORD's words 'Moses my servant is dead' (Josh 1:2). This may suggest that Elijah's journey on earth finished at Mount Nebo itself, the place where Moses died.

Elijah's departure from the land suggests the departure of God's word and therefore of his presence. This is what the people deserve, and this is the danger they face. Elisha, carrying his master's staff, then retraces the journey again, back across the Jordan and into the land. His return announces that God has not entirely abandoned his people: he is giving them another chance to listen. This is yet another instance of what we have repeatedly observed: that God's preference is for salvation. He is always offering new opportunities for repentance.

The mysterious departure of Elijah leaves a longing that is felt throughout the Old Testament, a suggestion that things are unfinished. Indeed, the Old Testament ends with the prophecy that God will 'send you Elijah the prophet before the great and awesome day of the LORD comes' (Mal 4:4–5). This is immediately preceded by an exhortation to 'Remember the law of [God's] servant Moses': we will go on to think about Moses in our next chapter.

Ida's Story

I am so glad that I have put so much effort into studying Elijah. My journey towards this book on thinking biblically about Islam began with Elijah. Sitting in Northern Nigeria, as the journey draws to its close, I am thinking about Elijah again. The complex world of religion and power, of violence and corruption, and of repentance and hope that he encountered is so relevant to my students here!

The students' big concern is the dangerous mix of religion, power and violence that is represented by Boko Haram, which is destroying the lives and livelihoods of many Christians and also of many Muslims who dare to oppose it. 'Are they acting as Elijah did when he killed the prophets of Baal?' they ask. The Qur'an's short account of the Carmel confrontation says that those who opposed Elijah were punished, but it does not say how or when (Surah 37. 127). Other punishments recorded in this surah come directly from God (37. 82, 98, 136), but elsewhere in the Qur'an the Muslims are told to kill idolaters (Surah 9. 5). 'How do the Muslims decide when they should kill idolaters and when they should leave the judgement to God?' the students ask. I respond that this has long been an important question for Muslims, and that many good minds have been applied to it over the centuries. Almost all would say that Boko Haram has a very wrong answer.

The students then think about Christian responses to Boko Haram, and to the other acts of violence they have seen between Muslims and Christians; the violence has led to Muslim and Christian communities separating, and sometimes to Christians attacking Muslims. The acute question raised by the Carmel confrontation is, for the students, 'Was Elijah right to kill the prophets of Baal?' The text does not say that God told him to do so, they observe, but God did judge people by putting them to death in the Old Testament. I point out that killing the idolaters did not work. Israel was still idolatrous, and the king and queen did not repent at all: they just persecuted Elijah.

'We learn that Elijah made a terrible mistake,' says one student. 'Boko Haram cannot convince people of its brand of Islam by killing its enemies: people will just see how terrible they are. The state and the Christians are wrong if they think that they can solve any problems by killing Boko Haram. You cannot kill an ideology by killing people. But what is the alternative? That's the key question. How can we respond in Jesus' way?'

To Think About

Do you agree that 'Elijah made a terrible mistake'? Was he not just keeping the law of Moses (see Deut 13)?

How would you answer the questions, 'What is the alternative? How can we respond in Jesus' way?'

4

Moses and Mountains

In the last chapter, we saw Elijah in pain because of the ongoing evil among the people of God, and we ended with a note of longing for the fulfilment of God's own commitment to salvation. When we turn back to the transfiguration, we again find a world in which the Jewish people were suffering the pain of idolatrous foreign rule and were longing for promised salvation. There was therefore a strong expectation that God would act, and one of the expectations, based on Malachi 3:1 and 4:5–6, was that God's action would be preceded by the coming of Elijah. It is not, then, surprising that all the Gospels precede their account of Jesus' ministry with the appearance of John the Baptist, who would later be identified with Elijah. Neither is it surprising that, by the time of the transfiguration, people were wondering whether Jesus was Elijah, or that, at the transfiguration, Elijah appeared.

But what about Moses? Why was he there at the transfiguration? Elijah was an obvious person to appear with Jesus, but there had been no promise of Moses' coming back. However, Moses' death took place by the mysterious action of God, and 'no one knows the place of his burial' (Deut 34:6). There was plenty of speculation about exactly what had happened to him, and probably some expectation of his return.[1]

At the transfiguration, then, Jesus met two key leaders of Israel who had both experienced strange departures from earth. And what did they talk about? Jesus' own coming 'departure', or, as the Greek has it in Luke 9:31, his 'exodus'. That takes the reader to another reason for Moses' presence at the transfiguration. Moses was God's leader for Israel at the time of her exodus from Egypt, and the account of that exodus is centred on events on a mountain – on Mount Sinai, where Elijah would meet God, where Moses was

---

1. See A. W. Zwiep, *The Ascension of the Messiah in Jewish Lukan Christology* (Leiden: Brill, 1997), 64–70.

called in Exodus 3 and 4, and where Israel met God and received her laws in Exodus 19 through to Numbers 9.

The transfiguration, then, brings together two mountains and three 'exoduses': Mount Nebo, from which Moses and Elijah made their exoduses from life on earth, and Mount Sinai, which was so important in Israel's exodus from Egypt. The transfiguration points to a fourth exodus: the exodus that Jesus was to achieve on the cross.

There is a vast amount about Moses in the Bible, and we cannot study it all in this chapter. Instead, we will focus on the question raised at the beginning of our 'transfiguration' section: what might have been in the minds of the disciples and of the first readers of the Gospels as they tried to understand what the transfiguration was about? Matthew, Mark and Luke all set the scene for the transfiguration by describing Jesus leading his three disciples up a mountain, so we will do this by looking at the significance of the two mountains. First, we will consider both Nebo and Sinai as places of exodus. Second, we will consider the significance of Sinai as the place where people met God. We will then finish the chapter by looking at some Islamic thinking about Moses and about meeting God.[2]

Nebo and Sinai as Places of Exodus

Mount Nebo and the Exoduses of Moses and Elijah

Moses' departure was from Mount Nebo, looking across the river Jordan into the Promised Land, which he could never enter. As we saw in the previous chapter, it is significant that Elijah's departure was from a similar place, after he had left the Promised Land with Elisha. For Moses, too, the main significance of Mount Nebo was that it was outside the Promised Land. Deuteronomy, which records Moses' death, repeatedly states that he is not going to be permitted to enter the land, because of the Israelites' rebellion and his own disobedience at Meribah (Deut 32:48–52; cf. 3:23–27; 31:2; 34:4–6). Moses may have been a great prophet and the recipient of the law, but even he could neither keep the people from disobeying the law nor be perfectly holy himself.

---

2. Ida's colleague Elena Narinskaya was working on Moses as part of the 'Reading the Bible in the Context of Islam' project during the writing of this book. Discussions with her have enriched this chapter.

God's promise of the land remained, but the departure of Moses implied that the law could not get people into the Promised Land, just as the departure of Elijah implied that even the most zealous prophethood could not keep people in the Promised Land. Neither the law nor the prophets can satisfactorily deal with sin and produce a people sufficiently holy to remain in God's presence.

To Think About

Jesus' departure would be from outside the city of Jerusalem, but he would come back, risen from the dead, and then ascend to the right hand of God.

Compare Jesus' departure with Moses' and Elijah's departures. How does this help you to understand what Jesus achieved, and how he fulfilled all that Moses and Elijah tried to do?

Mount Sinai and the Exodus of Israel

Sinai is the most important mountain in the Old Testament. It is located in what is now called the Sinai Peninsula, and in the Bible is variously called 'Sinai', 'Horeb' or simply 'the mountain of God'. Almost a third of the chapters of the Pentateuch concern events at Sinai, first when Moses meets God at the burning bush in Exodus 3 and 4, and then when Israel camps at the foot of Sinai in Exodus 19. She stayed there for more than a year, and it is not until Numbers 10 that we read about her moving on.

The Sinai events beginning in Exodus 19 describe what a modern Jewish commentary calls 'the kernel and core of the nation's life, the Covenant by which all the tribes were united in allegiance to one God, the Covenant by which a priest-people was created, and a kingdom of God on earth inaugurated among the children of men'.[3] But, first, God had to rescue the people from their previous masters, the Egyptians. The Sinai story begins with the Passover, opening the way to the exodus.

God began the rescue of his people from Egypt with Moses. Exodus 1 and 2 tell us how God rescued and prepared this man; Exodus 3 tells us about his call, which took place on Sinai. Moses was doing his ordinary job

---

3. J. H. Hertz, ed., *The Pentateuch and Haftorahs* (London: Soncino, 1960), 290.

in what had been, until then, an ordinary place, when, suddenly, he saw a fire, and everything changed. Before Moses knew what was happening, he sensed that he was in the presence of something awesome. 'I will turn aside to see this great sight,' he said to himself (Exod 3:3). Immediately, God warned Moses not to come near in his ordinary clothing. He was on holy ground, and so he must remove his shoes. In his fear he hid his face; it was an utterly overpowering experience. Centuries later, the disciples would be similarly afraid as the cloud overshadowed them at the transfiguration (Luke 9:34).

Just as that little group on the Mount of Transfiguration would do, Moses heard the voice of God calling to him. After announcing that he is 'the God of Abraham, the God of Isaac, and the God of Jacob' (Exod 3:6), God described how intimately involved he was with his enslaved people: he *saw* their affliction, *heard* their cry, *knew* their suffering and *had come down* to deliver them (3:7–8). God revealed his plans to rescue his people and called Moses to be the one to go to Pharaoh and lead his people out of Egypt in the exodus. These verses echo down the ages as, time and again, God's people are suffering and long for rescue – for an exodus – from their difficulties. Elijah, for example, longed for escape as he ran from Jezebel (1 Kgs 19:4), and the Jews of Jesus' time longed for freedom from Roman rule.

Overwhelmed by the task God gave him, Moses asked how he could possibly carry it out. 'I will be with you' (Exod 3:12) was God's reply from out of the burning bush. God himself would be with Moses. The implication is that this work would be God's, and Moses was only his emissary. Towards the end of the meeting, Moses pointed out a problem: he was not a good speaker (4:10). God's response is similar to that in 3:12, and his solution is also similar: he would be with Moses' mouth (4:12). God was angry when Moses asked him to send someone else instead, but relented and said that he would send Aaron with Moses. It would not be until after Aaron had collaborated with the people in the worship of the golden calf that Moses would at last plead with God for *his* presence. By Exodus 33, Moses was no longer saying, 'Send someone else to come with me', but, in effect, 'LORD, if you don't come, we have no hope'.

The Qur'an is interested in the burning bush episode and tells the story in several places. It is an important beginning to its story of Moses' encounter with Pharaoh that is used to encourage Muhammad and the Muslims in their encounters with idolaters. The following passage is from the much-loved surah 'Ta Ha', which goes on to tell of Pharaoh's opposition to Moses and then of the Israelites' rebellion in the golden calf incident, and of God's judgement on both and his vindication of Moses and Aaron.[4] This surah served as an effective warning and call; reading it is said to have brought about the conversion to Islam of Umar, who had been so opposed to Muhammad that he had plotted to kill him, but who later became the second caliph. We invite you to think about it here, because it raises questions that can help us as we think about the significance of the transfiguration.

> Has the story of Moses come to you [Prophet]? He saw a fire and said to his people, 'Stay here – I can see a fire. Maybe I can bring you a flaming brand from it or find some guidance there.' When he came to the fire, he was summoned, 'Moses! I am your Lord. Take off your shoes: you are in the sacred valley of Tuwa. I have chosen you, so listen to what is being revealed. I am God; there is no god but Me. So worship Me and keep up the prayer so that you remember Me. The Hour is coming – though I choose to keep it hidden – for each soul to be rewarded for its labour. Do not let anyone who does not believe in it and follows his own desires distract you from it, and so bring you to ruin.'
>
> 'Moses, what is that in your right hand?' 'It is my staff,' he said, 'I lean on it; restrain my sheep with it; I also have other uses for it.' God said, 'Throw it down, Moses.' He threw it down and – lo and behold! – it became a fast-moving snake. He said, 'Pick it up without fear: We shall turn it back into its former state. Now place your hand under your armpit and it will come out white, though unharmed: that is another sign. We do this to show you some of Our greatest signs. Go to Pharaoh, for he has truly become a tyrant.' Moses said, 'Lord, lift up my heart and ease my task for me. Untie my tongue, so that they may understand my words, and give me a helper from my family, my brother Aaron – augment my strength through him. Let him share my task so that we can glorify You much and remember You often: You are always watching over us' (Surah 20. 9–35).[5]

The story is also told in Surah 27. 7–12:

---

4. The surah also tells of a strange figure called 'Samiri', who is responsible for the golden calf incident, and of Satan's tempting Adam and Eve.

5. M. A. S. Abdel Haleem, *The Qur'an: A New Translation by M. A. S. Abdel Haleem* (Oxford: Oxford University Press, 2008), Used with permission.

Moses said to his family, 'I have seen a fire. I will bring you news from there, or a burning stick for you to warm yourselves.' When he reached the fire, a voice called: 'Blessed is the person near this fire and those around it; may God be exalted, the Lord of the Worlds. Moses, I am God, the Mighty, the Wise. Throw down your staff,' but when he saw it moving like a snake, he turned and fled. 'Moses, do not be afraid! The messengers need have no fear in My presence, I am truly most forgiving and merciful to those who do wrong, and then replace their evil with good. Put your hand inside your cloak and it will come out white, but unharmed. These are among the nine signs that you will show Pharaoh and his people; they have really gone too far.'[6]

> **To Think About**
>
> What do these qur'anic passages say about God? What do they say about God's presence? What do they say about the exodus?
>
> How is this similar to and how is it different from Exodus 3 – 4? What important aspects of Exodus 3 – 4 does the Qur'an omit?[7]

Sinai: The Place Where the People Met with God

At the burning bush, Moses met God and received instructions about the exodus. After the exodus, the whole of Israel returned to Sinai to receive all that was needed to live as God's people:

- It was at Sinai that Moses was given details of how to make *sacrifices* that would be acceptable to God.
- It was at Sinai that Israel received the covenant that formed her as a people (Exod 19) and the laws that would be the basis for proper use of *power*.
- It was at Sinai that the Israelites fell into the *evil* of the golden calf, and that we see both God's judgement on them and his commitment to them in giving them a second chance.

---

6. A mid-Meccan surah. A later version is in Surah 28. 29–35, which is late-Meccan.
7. We will reflect further on the Qur'an's treatment of Moses in chapter 7.

In short, Sinai shows us God's plan for establishing a people who would show the fallen world what religion should be like. Where religion had gone wrong in ways we have seen in Genesis 4 – 11, this gave a different model concerning approaching God through sacrifice, concerning power for a people, and concerning how to deal with evil. Some Jews describe this by saying that Israel was called to re-make Eden in the Promised Land.

What would it take to re-make Eden outside Eden? What distinguished Eden from the space outside, and Genesis 2 from the chapters that follow? It was the presence of God. And so, what was it that would distinguish Israel from the other nations? Was it superior laws? A comparison of Israel's laws and the best extant example of contemporary law, the laws of Hammurabi,[8] shows a great deal of similarity. Israel's laws did give more respect to the poor, but the differences are quantitative rather than qualitative.

What would truly mark out the Israelites is that God himself would live among them: his presence would be with them in a very special way. So the most striking thing about the Exodus account of Sinai is that the people actually met God there. Sinai was the place of God's coming. The construction specifications of the tabernacle that fill the second half of Exodus are there to accommodate the remarkable fact that God's dwelling place was to be among the Israelites.

That was why Elijah walked 130 miles to Sinai for his meeting with God (1 Kgs 19). Elijah is the one person who is recorded as having gone there after the time of Moses. It is interesting that, while Mount Zion is often mentioned in the Old Testament, there is little explicit mention of Sinai outside the stories of Moses and Elijah: the meeting with God and the receiving of the law was a unique event, and Elijah's visit to the mountain stands out among the experiences of the prophets.

The single most important thing about Sinai is that this was the place where people met with God. The people were called to the mountain, and God came.

Exodus 19 describes his coming in graphic detail. The LORD announced to Moses that he would come to the people 'in a thick cloud, that [they] may hear when I speak with you' (19:9). The people had to take practical steps to keep themselves pure, ready for the coming of the Lord. God instructed

---

8. Hammurabi was a Babylonian ruler who lived in the eighteenth century BC. A stela (stone) inscribed with 282 of his laws is in the Louvre Museum in Paris. An English translation by L. W. King is available at 'The Code of Hammurabi', http://www.sacred-texts. com/ane/ham/index.htm.

Moses to 'set limits for the people all round, saying, "Take care not to go up into the mountain or touch the edge of it. Whoever touches the mountain shall be put to death"' (19:12). He warned them that his presence would be tangible – and dangerous. Indeed, when the moment of his arrival came, 'there were thunders and lightnings and a thick cloud on the mountain and a very loud trumpet blast' (v. 16). Terrified, the people gathered around the mountain, which 'trembled' and was 'wrapped in smoke because the LORD had descended on it in fire' (v. 18). God came down onto the peak and called Moses to ascend into this fearful place from which God spoke out to the assembled people below.

Philo the philosopher (c.20 BC–AD 50) and Josephus the historian (c.AD 37–100) can help us both to understand the importance of this event and to consider some of the sorts of questions people were asking about it at the time of the transfiguration.

The Event Was Seen as the Actual Coming of God

The idea that God came down on Sinai can be seen in a number of the Jewish writings around the time of Jesus. Even Josephus, who is more restrained about spiritual manifestations than other authors, speaks of Sinai as the place of the *parousia* (coming) of God (*Antiquities* 3:80). He acknowledges that this is an amazing thing, and seems to expect many of his readers to reject the idea, so he underlines the fact that the Israelites, too, were amazed at what happened:

> Of these happenings each of my readers may think as he will; for my part, I am constrained to relate them as they are recorded in the sacred books. As for the Hebrews, the sights that they saw and the din that struck their ears sorely disquieted them, for they were unaccustomed thereto; and the rumour current concerning this mountain, that here was the very resort of God (that is, the place where God came) deeply dismayed their minds.[9]

---

9. Josephus, *Antiquities of the Jews*, 3:80, trans. H. St J. Thackeray (Loeb Classical Library, 1930).

It Was Said That All the People (Not Just Moses) Heard the Words of God

Where Exodus tells us that there were loud noises, Josephus insists that all the Israelites heard the actual 'ten words' of the Ten Commandments. He is emphatic: 'All heard the voice which came from on high to the ears of all.'[10] The reason for this was, says Josephus, to make sure that God's words were not in any way spoiled through being transmitted by a human being. He even says that it is not permitted for Gentiles to write the exact words, presumably because they are so holy.[11]

Philo (*Decalogue* 9) agrees that all heard words spoken, and he discusses what was heard. It could not have been the actual voice of God, he says: this is a philosophical impossibility, because God cannot have a mouth and a larynx. Rather, God created an invisible sound: a miraculous voice which, like a trumpet, could be heard equally by all the people.

The Events on Sinai Were Miraculous

Here is a description from Philo that emphasizes the wonder of it all:

> And, moreover, as was natural, he filled the whole place with miraculous signs and works, with noises of thunder too great for the hearing to support, and with the most radiant brilliancy of flashes of lightning, and with the sound of an invisible trumpet extending to a great distance, and with the march of a cloud, which, like a pillar, had its foundation fixed firmly on the earth, but raised the rest of its body even to the height of heaven; and, last of all, by the impetuosity of a heavenly fire, which overshadowed everything around with a dense smoke. For it was fitting that, when the power of God came among them, none of the parts of the world should be quiet, but that everything should be put in motion to minister to his service . . . And a voice sounded forth from out of the midst of the fire which had flowed from heaven, a most marvellous and awful voice, the flame being endowed with articulate speech in a language familiar to the hearers, which

---

10. Idem, 3:90.

11. This seems to be Josephus' own emphasis: there is no evidence of any general prohibition of writing the Ten Commandments for Gentile readers.

expressed its words with such clearness and distinctness that the people seemed rather to be seeing than hearing it.[12]

Moses Was Glorious

Both Philo and Josephus present Moses as a very great person, perhaps because some of the pagan writers of their times criticized him.[13] For example, Josephus relates that even at the burning bush God told Moses that he would receive glory: 'The fire uttered a voice, and called to him by name, and spake words to him . . . and he foretold to him, that he should have glory and honour among men, by the blessing of God upon him' (*Antiquities* 2:12:1).

The glory is seen in the changed appearance of Moses when he came down from the mountain. Philo describes an inner change in Moses which could be seen through the shining of Moses' face:

> Before assuming that office, it was necessary for him to purify not only his soul but also his body, so that it should be connected with and defiled by no passion, but should be pure from everything which is of a mortal nature, from all meat and drink, and from all connection with women . . . He neglected all meat and drink for forty days together, evidently because he had more excellent food than that in those contemplations with which he was inspired from above from heaven, by which also he was improved in the first instance in his mind, and, secondly, in his body, through his soul, increasing in strength and health both of body and soul, so that those who saw him afterwards could not believe that he was the same person . . . He descended again forty days afterwards, being much more beautiful in his face than when he went up, so that those who saw him wondered and were amazed, and could no longer endure to look upon him with their eyes, inasmuch as his countenance shone like the light of the sun (*Life of Moses* 2:68–70).

---

12. *Decalogue* 11:44. Translation available online in *The Works of Philo Judaeus*, trans. C. D. Yonge (London, H. G. Bohn, 1854–90), www.earlyjewishwritings.com/text/philo/book26.html.

13. See the discussion in G. H. van Kooten, 'Why Did Paul Include an Exegesis of Moses' Shining Face (Exod 34) in 2 Cor 3?', in *The Significance of Sinai: Traditions about Sinai and Divine Revelation in Judaism and Christianity*, ed. George J. Brooke, H. Najman and L. Stuckenbruck (Themes in Biblical Narrative; Leiden: Brill, 2008), 149–82.

The encounters with God on Sinai, then, stand alongside the exodus as the defining events of Jewish identity. Moses was the greatest prophet and law-giver, and the events on Sinai served to assure the Jews of the truth of their religion during times when their monotheism was coming under severe criticism from the polytheistic peoples among whom they lived.

Sinai: More Encounters with God

The glory, the presence of God, the voice of God, the awe . . . all the people at the foot of Sinai were witnesses to all this. But some experienced more: just as Jesus would later choose three disciples to climb the Mount of Transfiguration with him, so Moses and selected others climbed Sinai and witnessed more glory.

Exodus records three occasions when Moses went to meet God on Sinai while Israel was camped at the foot of the mountain. In 19:20, he ascends alone into the glory, with all the people watching. In chapter 24, he ascends with Aaron, Aaron's two sons and the seventy elders of Israel for the covenant ceremony, and then returns with Joshua while Aaron and the others go back to the people. The final ascent is in chapter 34, when, after the disaster of the golden calf, he goes up again to plead with God. We can miss the continuity of the narrative because of all the laws and instructions recorded in Exodus: here is a re-telling that will help us to think about what was happening, starting in the middle of chapter 24.

> Moses, Aaron, Nadab, Abihu, Joshua and seventy elders had finished their meal. It had been a staggering experience and they could hardly believe that they had survived what had happened. They had been in the holy presence of God, but they had not died. They had seen God, but they had no words for what they had seen. He was indescribable, and all they could find words for was the place where he stood – and even then, the nearest they could get was to say that it was like the sky itself. The meal was to seal the covenant relationship that had just been explained to Moses.
>
> The time had come for Moses to ascend to receive the stone tablets on which God would carve the stipulations for his chosen community. Having gone a little way up, he took a moment to consider the best route towards the peak from which smoke poured forth. It seemed incredible that once, as a young man, he

had casually wandered onto this mountainside with his sheep. Back then, he had no idea that a surprise encounter with God here would lead to this. Curiosity had led him forward then, and God had to warn him to stay back. Now, he climbed with trepidation, his trembling legs unsteady on the narrow paths, his sweaty palms unable to grip grasses and rocks to pull himself up.

At last, the summit came into view as the mountainside swept upwards for the final ascent. Back in Egypt, Moses used to feel nervous approaching Pharaoh, crossing that great hall towards the throne. But now he felt faint as he came before the very presence of God. He did not need to be told to remove his shoes now; he came on bended knee, his head bowed low.

For forty days and nights Moses remained there, enveloped in cloud, alone with the LORD. The LORD told him all about the place where he would come to dwell among the people. It was to be a beautifully clean and holy place, perfectly scented and decorated. Bathed in the glorious light of his presence, the LORD described it in great detail. Moses grew excited that God was making a way, through a system of sacrifices and tabernacle regulations, to be present with the people. He couldn't wait to go back down and commission the joiners, weavers and metal workers.

Then the LORD said something in a tone that struck terror in Moses' heart. The people below had already built an altar and had already done their metal work – they had fashioned a golden calf. The LORD's anger burned hot – he even spoke of consuming them. Moses begged God to spare the people. He couldn't bear for the long history of the house of Jacob and the struggle to leave Egypt to end in this disaster. What would the Egyptians think about the LORD if he ended it all now? He was bold before the LORD as he spoke, and the LORD listened. He would spare them.

Nonetheless, it was with a heart heavier than the stone tablets he carried that Moses returned to the chaos below. How far short of God's holy standards his people had fallen! Dear Joshua joined him on the track down, and it was he who heard it first: people shouting. The two men fell quiet to listen. Moses discerned rhythm and a raucous melody. *'It is not the sound of shouting for victory, or the sound of the cry of defeat,'* he said, *'but the sound of singing that I hear.*[14] There was the clanging of cymbals and the beat of drums, all so coarse and vulgar after the majesty of God's voice speaking into the silence of the misty mountain. Moses became angry . . .

The cost of restoring order had been huge. Brothers had had to kill brothers and fathers had had to kill their sons. They had to dig three thousand graves for the fallen. Moses had pleaded to the LORD to forgive his people, but still the LORD had sent a plague. God had to deal with the evil.

Things were at last quiet in the camp again. The people stood solemnly whenever Moses went into the tent to meet with the LORD. Then into this sombre mood came the 'disastrous word'[15] which confirmed to them all that everything had changed: the LORD would not be going up with them to the land he had promised to give them; he would send an angel instead. The camp was devastated. The LORD had warned them that if he did go with them, he would 'consume' them, because they were so 'stiff-necked'. At his instruction they dressed themselves soberly; glittering jewellery seemed out of place at a time like this. There was nothing to rejoice in, nothing to be pleased about; it was a bleak prospect for them if God was not in their midst.

Moses could not rest. He could not think of moving forward without the LORD now. How immature he had been when he thought that Aaron would be a sufficient help to him with this task of leading the Israelites! He knew now that it was only the presence of the LORD with them that made them distinct and would allow them to survive among the much mightier nations surrounding them.

He went to speak with the LORD, to plead with him. *'If your presence will not go with me, do not bring us up from here,' Moses said. 'For how shall it be known that I have found favour in your sight, I and your people? Is it not in your going with us, so that we are distinct, I and your people, from every other people on the face of the earth?'*[16] The LORD relented: *'This very thing that you have*

---

14. Exod 32:18.
15. Exod 33:4.
16. Exod 33:15–16.

spoken I will do, for you have found favour in my sight, and I know you by name.[17]

Hope unfurled across Moses' vision of the future, colouring it with joy. His heart swelled, tender with relief and big with gratitude. 'If only I could reach out and touch him who is filling our future with glory,' he thought. 'Oh, to rest my eyes on the face of kindness itself! 'Please,' he heard himself stammer aloud, 'show me your glory.' The wind caused Moses' coat to flap wildly about him like something desperate.

He heard the LORD declare wonderful things about himself, but then came the answer: 'You cannot see my face, for man shall not see me and live.'[18] He directed him to look over to an outcrop of rock where, the next day, between giant boulders that dwarfed Moses, the LORD would hide him as he passed by.

Moses rose long before sunrise the next day, while the camp slept. The solid black of the rock of Sinai blocked out a whole swathe of the starry sky. Moses strained every muscle to climb it again. Breathless, his chest stinging and his head throbbing, he knew that, when the sun rose, he would experience glory. When at last he attained the cleft in the rock, he crumpled to the ground, panting, trying to steady himself.

But then he found he could not stand up. Great weight bore down upon him: the weight of thunder clouds, of earthquakes, of oceans. And in the weight was glory, and in the glory, the voice of God. 'The LORD, the LORD, a God merciful and gracious . . .'[19]

After it all, his lungs able to expand again, Moses still did not rise to his feet. Reverence kept him low, in the dust, his head bowed. God loved salvation: truly he was committed to these people if, after all their rebellion, he was still willing to keep the covenant with them.

After the days Moses spent on the mountain, forty in all, it became clear that sin had left its mark on the community and things would not go on as they had before. When Moses returned, the Israelites had to shield their eyes: his face was too bright to

---

17. Exod 33:17.
18. Exod 33:20.
19. Exod 34:6.

behold, 'because he had been talking with God'.[20] From then on, Moses had to veil his face in order to speak to his people. Aaron, his sons Abihu and Nadab, and the seventy elders realized that they would never be able to see God again. And God's voice would ring out only in the memories of the people of Israel, for sin had veiled them from the fullness of God's presence.

If we read 1 Kings 19 with this story in mind, we immediately see how Elijah's experience parallels Moses' experience. We can then read the transfiguration account with these parallels in mind. Both Moses and Elijah had awesome experiences of wind and fire and of hearing the voice of God, but there is more:

- Moses had just led his people across the Red Sea and out of Egypt; Elijah had come from the wilderness near Beersheba, where he had escaped, having run from Mount Carmel to Jezreel. Both had been miraculously fed.
- They both arrived saddened by their people's unfaithfulness to God. In Exodus 33 – 34, Moses had just seen the same families he had led out of slavery bowing down to the golden calf. Elijah had just confronted 450 prophets of Baal, and he felt that he alone was left as one who was 'jealous for the LORD, the God of hosts' (1 Kgs 19:10).
- Both had meted out terrible judgement: Moses had seen three thousand killed by the Levites (Exod 32:25–28) and Elijah had supervised the killing of the prophets of Baal (1 Kgs 18:40).

In their meetings, God reassured both men of his continued presence with them. In response to Moses' pleas, 'O Lord, please let the Lord go in the midst of us' (Exod 34:9), God proclaimed a covenant with the people (34:10). At a time when Elijah felt utterly alone, God spoke to him and recommissioned him. In neither case was the people's sin to be the end of God's dealings with them after all. When the LORD 'passed by' Elijah, he experienced winds so strong that they 'tore the mountains and broke in pieces the rocks' (1 Kgs 19:11); this was followed by an earthquake, fire, and finally, God's voice in the silence (19:12–13). At the transfiguration much later, the disciples would once again be awestruck as God descended in cloud just as he had upon Moses.

---

20. Exod 34:29.

Sinai: The Place Where the Moses of the Qur'an Does Not See God

We appointed thirty nights for Moses, then added ten more: the term set by his Lord was completed in forty nights. Moses said to his brother Aaron, 'Take my place among my people: act rightly and do not follow the way of those who spread corruption.' When Moses came for the appointment, and his Lord spoke to him, he said, 'My Lord, show Yourself to me: let me see You!' He said, 'You will never see Me, but look at that mountain: if it remains standing firm, you will see Me,' and when his Lord revealed Himself to the mountain, He made it crumble: Moses fell down unconscious. When he recovered, he said, 'Glory be to You! To You I turn in repentance! I am the first to believe!' He said, 'Moses, I have raised you above other people by [giving you] My messages and speaking to you: hold on to what I have given you; be one of those who give thanks' (Surah 7. 142–144).[21]

This is the Qur'an's most detailed account of Moses' experience on Sinai.[22] It refers to the incident in Exodus 33:17 – 34:9 in which Moses asks to see God's glory and is told that he can see only God's back. In Exodus, this occurs after the golden calf incident, and it is part of God's response to Moses after he has sought reassurance that God's presence will go with them. In the Qur'an, this takes place before Moses goes down the mountain and finds the people with the golden calf. The Qur'an does not have him going back up the mountain.

To Think About

What are the main questions that this qur'anic story addresses? How is it similar to the Exodus story, and how is it different?

What might the differences imply about biblical and qur'anic views of the nature of God, and of how he relates to human beings?

---

21. M. A. S. Abdel Haleem, *The Qur'an: A New Translation by M. A. S. Abdel Haleem* (Oxford: Oxford University Press, 2008), Used with permission.

22. Other references occur at 2. 51; 2. 63; 19. 52 (which could refer to the burning bush); 20. 83 (a brief reference that this was where Moses was while the people were making the golden calf. The Qur'an gives lots of attention to the golden calf incident).

From all the material about the presence of God on Sinai, the Qur'an chooses only the incident that says that Moses cannot see God. For the Qur'an, even wanting to see God is a problem. In Surah 2. 55, it is evidence of the Israelites' unbelief that they say to Moses, 'we will not believe you until we see God face to face'.[23] Far from hesitating to go up the mountain, as in Exodus, the Israelites want to see God. But far from their seeing God, the verse in the Qur'an goes on, 'thunderbolts struck you'.

The idea that people might see God, 'him who is invisible' (Heb 11:27), has also been problematic for Jewish and Christian readers. The New Testament says several times that God is invisible or cannot be seen (Col 1:15; 1 Tim 1:17; Heb 11:27). The Septuagint translators were so concerned about this that they translated Exodus 24:10–11 as 'they saw the place where the God of Israel stood' rather than 'they saw the God of Israel'. Some of the rabbis also interpreted the 'seeing God' of Moses, Aaron, Nadab, Abihu and the seventy elders in Exodus 24:10–11 as negative: Nadab and Abihu, they say, looked at God greedily, while Moses bowed his head, as in Exodus 3:6. Nadab and Abihu's deaths, which are referred to repeatedly (Lev 10:1–2; 16:1; Num 3:4; 26:61), were not only a punishment for the sin of using their censers to offer 'unauthorized fire before the LORD' (Lev 10:1): they were also a delayed punishment for their presumption on Sinai, which God had deferred because he did not want to detract from the joyful sealing of the covenant.[24] In other words, ignoring God's regulations on incense-burning was typical of their presumption, which was first manifested on Sinai.

The problem with seeing God has two different elements. One is that 'seeing God' is impossible, because it is not in the nature of God that human beings should see him. The other is that wanting to behold God is presumptuous, because human beings are not worthy of looking at him. The Qur'an combines these two problems so that the mountains will fall down before a human being can see God, and Moses has to repent of his request. Exodus identifies quite a different problem that could also be read into the qur'anic account: God is holy, and human beings are not. It is because of sin that human beings cannot survive seeing God.

---

23. M. A. S. Abdel Haleem, *The Qur'an: A New Translation by M. A. S. Abdel Haleem* (Oxford: Oxford University Press, 2008), Used with permission.

24. Midrash Rabbah Leviticus 15:24, which says that the seventy elders were also killed at the time of the judgement by fire in Num 11:1 – for the same sin of presumption on Sinai – hence, says the midrash, the appointment of seventy new elders in Num 11:16–25.

With these questions in mind, let us go back to Exodus and ask again what can be 'seen' of God. In chapters 19–20, the first meeting with God, it is emphasized that God 'came down' on the mountain (19:18, 20), and the physical manifestations of his presence are graphically described. It is, then, clear that God was actually there on the mountain in a very special way, and that his presence was signalled by many things that the people could see, hear and smell. Philo, in the passage quoted above, even suggests that the voice of God was so strong that it could be seen. This is in explanation of Exodus 19:19:

> And a voice sounded forth from out of the midst of the fire which had flowed from heaven, a most marvellous and awful voice, the flame being endowed with articulate speech in a language familiar to the hearers, which expressed its words with such clearness and distinctness that the people seemed rather to be seeing than hearing it. And the law testifies to the accuracy of my statement, where it is written, 'And all the people beheld the voice most evidently.' For the truth is that the voice of men is calculated to be heard; but that of God to be really and truly seen. Why is this? Because all that God says are not words, but actions which the eyes determine on before the ears (*Decalogue* IX:46–47).

It is Exodus 24, the second meeting with God, that gave rise to the Jewish questions about whether God could be seen, and what that might mean. However, the chapter itself offers few clues, simply stating that the people 'saw' God. It is chapters 33–34, Moses' final ascent of the mountain, that is a closer parallel to the qur'anic story and deals with the question of what aspects of God can be seen with human eyes.

God promises Moses that his *panim* will go with the Israelites (33:14). The word means, literally, 'face', but because someone's face represents their character and nearness, it is more often translated 'presence'. In 33:18 this is not what Moses asks to see, but rather his *kavod* – his glory. In the presence of God, hearing his voice and being reassured of God's commitment to him personally and to the Israelites (v. 17), Moses still wants more. 'Please show me your glory,' he asks, wanting to see God with his physical eyes, for though the *panim* of God is there, Moses cannot see it. 'I will make all my goodness pass before you,' God responds to Moses (v. 19), but he prohibits him from seeing his *panim*. What Moses sees, apart from the cloud, we are not told. Rather, we are told what he hears about the character of Yahweh (34:6–8).

It seems that what matters is not what is physically visible but the fact that, as previously, Yahweh is there: 'The LORD descended in the cloud' (v. 5). But to add weight to the reality of God's presence, the writer adds, 'and [the LORD] stood with him there'. The revelation of God's goodness is not, then, in what Moses perceives with his eyes, but in the words of grace and love in verses 6–7: 'The LORD, the LORD, a God merciful and gracious, slow to anger, and abounding in steadfast love and faithfulness, keeping steadfast love for thousands, forgiving iniquity and transgression and sin, but who will by no means clear the guilty, visiting the iniquity of the fathers on the children and the children's children, to the third and the fourth generation.' This is sufficient for Moses, who then bows down and worships (v. 8).

So, in Exodus, what remains beyond doubt is the goodness of God revealed in his words and the reality of his presence with his people. However, the degree to which he makes himself visible is less clear: something can be seen and something cannot be seen, but seeing him is dangerous. After all, he does not say to Moses, 'a person cannot see me because it is impossible' but 'a person cannot see me and live' (33:20). His very presence is dangerous unless humans are properly prepared to meet him. So he gives regulations for the tabernacle, the priesthood and the sacrifices in order that he can come among them. God is to be present among his people, but his holiness and purity cannot tolerate their sinfulness and impurity.

Seeing God in the Qur'an

Returning to the Qur'an, we find that most Muslims agree that the story of Moses wanting to see God in Surah 7. 143 implies that God is invisible by nature, and that this is in agreement with Surah 6. 103, which states, 'No vision can take Him in.'[25] It is therefore presumptuous even to wish to see him. There are some things in existence that are seen, and there are some that are unseen, and God is among the latter (see also Surah 59. 22).

However, the Qur'an does speak of believers looking at God in the hereafter: 'On that Day there will be radiant faces, looking towards their Lord'

25. M. A. S. Abdel Haleem, *The Qur'an: A New Translation by M. A. S. Abdel Haleem* (Oxford: Oxford University Press, 2008), Used with permission.

(Surah 75. 22–23).[26] The commentator Ibn Kathir[27] says that this means 'they will see Him with their very eyes', and he quotes Hadith as proof, including:

> Some people said, 'O messenger of Allāh! Will we see our Lord on the day of judgement?' The prophet said, 'Are you harmed by seeing the sun and the moon when there are no clouds beneath them?' They replied, 'No'. The prophet said, 'Then you will surely see your Lord like that.'

'Seeing God' then becomes the aim and the longing of many Muslims, and turning towards Mecca to pray is seen as turning towards God. Some, particularly those from the Sufi tradition, hope also to 'see God' in this life. They understand this in various ways. It can be a metaphor for spiritual understanding, it can mean 'seeing God' in his creation, or it can mean a personal experience of seeing God's light. A Sufi website describes it as realization of God that can be attained through realization of the self:

> The path to experiencing the Divine Presence starts within. It is said that one who realizes oneself realizes the Lord. God is present but individuals cannot see the Almighty because curtains of ignorance veil their eyes and rust encases their hearts The average person is ego-centred. Only after he or she has polished the heart and purified the self will the curtains lift, the rust fall away, and the eyes become able to see God.[28]

The Presence of God

In Exodus, the question of seeing God is closely linked with the fact of his presence: his presence is primary; the question of what can be seen is secondary. This is so not only on Sinai: the presence of God is of central importance throughout the Bible. Sinai is only the place where he comes to dwell among the Israelites.

God's presence is evident throughout the life of Moses, starting with God's announcement at the burning bush, 'I have come down' (3:8). The

---

26. M. A. S. Abdel Haleem, *The Qur'an: A New Translation by M. A. S. Abdel Haleem* (Oxford: Oxford University Press, 2008), Used with permission.

27. Ibn Kathir (died AD 1373) is popular among some orthodox Sunni Muslims. The quotation below is from his commentary on Surah 75. 22–23. The whole commentary is available in English online at www.qtafsir.com.

28. 'Sufism', The School of Sufi Teaching, Singapore, http://singapore.sufischool.org/.

rest of Exodus prepares for God's glory to come to dwell in the tabernacle in 40:34. God's presence then continues to be important in the life of Joshua, Moses' successor. The first time God speaks to Joshua after Moses' death, he reassures him: 'Just as I was with Moses, so I will be with you' (Josh 1:5). God repeats his promise as he commissions Joshua for the task ahead (Josh 1:9). Throughout the Old Testament, the tabernacle, the priesthood and the temple revolve around the presence of God.[29]

The Old Testament history of the LORD's presence with his people leads into the New Testament, which relates how 'the Word became flesh and dwelt among us' (John 1:14). The presence of God came in Jesus Christ and through the Holy Spirit. The history of God among us concludes with the final triumph in Revelation 21:3: 'Behold, the dwelling place of God is with man . . .'

So we could say that the whole Bible is about how God fulfils his desire to live among human beings.

Because the presence of God determines the direction of the biblical narrative, an important question for our thinking about the similarities and differences between Christianity and Islam is, 'What does the qur'anic account tell us about God's presence?' God's fulfilling his desire to live among us can be a strange idea to Muslims, not only because the Qur'an never describes God as 'coming' to us, but also because it never tells us what God desires. On the contrary, most Muslim scholars insist that human beings cannot know what God feels; God is so different from us that we cannot talk about him 'feeling'.

However, the Qur'an does speak of God being everywhere, and of his nearness. For example:

> [Prophet], if My servants ask you about Me, I am near. I respond to those who call Me, so let them respond to Me, and believe in Me, so that they may be guided (2. 186).[30]

> We created man – We know what his soul whispers to him: We are closer to him than his jugular vein . . . (50. 16).[31]

The Qur'an also implies longing for God through the use of a term which, in the Bible, expresses the presence of God: the 'Face of God'. (See also

---

29. A good summary of the idea of the presence of God on Sinai, and the questions raised by it, can be found in J. Goldingay, *Old Testament Theology, Vol. 1: Israel's Gospel* (Downers Grove: IVP/Paternoster, 2003), 378–407.

30. M. A. S. Abdel Haleem, *The Qur'an: A New Translation by M. A. S. Abdel Haleem* (Oxford: Oxford University Press, 2008), Used with permission.

31. Ibid.

p. 169). It is God's Face to which people turn when they pray, God's Face that is sought through right actions, a desire for God's Face that keeps the believer faithful, and God's Face that will remain when everything else has passed away. For example:[32]

> The East and the West belong to God: wherever you turn, there is His Face. God is all pervading and all knowing (2. 115).
>
> . . . who remain steadfast through their desire for the face of their Lord . . . (13. 22).
>
> So give their due to the near relative, the needy, and the wayfarer – that is best for those whose goal is God's approval [literally 'face']: these are the ones who will prosper. Whatever you lend out in usury to gain value through other people's wealth will not increase in God's eyes, but whatever you give in charity, in your desire for God's approval, will earn multiple rewards (30. 38–39).[33]
>
> Everyone on earth perishes; all that remains is the Face of your Lord, full of majesty, bestowing honour (55. 26–27).

These passages are interpreted differently by different groups of Muslims – philosophers, Shi'ites, mainstream Sunnis and Sufis – and each group thinks that the others are in danger of blasphemy. For example, it is common among Sunnis to think that God's 'nearness' is mainly about his knowledge of us, and that his 'face' is one of the many anthropomorphisms that mean something different when applied to God than when applied to human beings. The idea that God has a 'face', then, means that he is watching us at all times. 'Seeking his face' means 'seeking his pleasure' by carrying out all our religious obligations. Some Shi'ites add the idea that God's 'face' is seen in Muhammad, his family and the imams. Sufis may seek an experience of actually seeing God's face, while recognizing that they will not fully 'see God', whatever that may mean, until after death.

Whatever the disagreements, there is a very important common concern: the Qur'an calls people to seek God's 'face', and people respond by doing that.

---

32. M. A. S. Abdel Haleem, *The Qur'an: A New Translation by M. A. S. Abdel Haleem* (Oxford: Oxford University Press, 2008), Used with permission.

33. The Qur'an translation by M. A. S. Abdel Haleem, which is used in this book, sometimes avoids translating the Arabic *wajh* by 'face' when it refers to God – for example, in Surah 2. 272; 92. 20. Where he does use 'face', he often adds a footnote to explain the anthropomorphism – for example, in Surah 2. 115; 55. 26.

There is a seeking and a longing for God that should be the mark of every faithful Muslim. There is a famous Hadith that defines the perfection of faith[34] as 'that you worship God as if you see Him, and if you do not see Him, He nevertheless sees you'. Right worship means being aware that God is here, whether he is seen or not.

God is, then, according to the Qur'an and to Islamic thinking, both high above his creation and present everywhere. The philosophical concept is that he is transcendent, but also omnipresent. The Bible would agree: God is transcendent, as seen in Isaiah 57:15: 'For thus says the One who is high and lifted up, who inhabits eternity, whose name is Holy: "I dwell in the high and holy place."' He is also omnipresent, as seen, for example, in Psalm 139:7–12.

So, is there any real difference here between the Qur'an and the Bible? We think that there is. First, while the Qur'an sometimes says that God is 'near', it never speaks of God's 'coming' to people – whether on Sinai or anywhere else. God's declaration in Isaiah 57:15, which as we just saw speaks of God's transcendence, then goes on to say that God dwells 'also with him who is of a contrite and lowly spirit'. This is just one example of the Bible's use of language about God coming to people and living among them, which is a theme that continues into his coming in Jesus and in the Holy Spirit, and his presence in the church.

Second, the Bible has a strong sense of the possibility of God's absence, which, whenever it arises, brings terrible anguish. Think of Cain crying out, 'My punishment is greater than I can bear. Behold, you have driven me today away from the ground, and from your face I shall be hidden' (Gen 4:13–14). When God told the Israelites that he would send an angel before them but not go with them himself, 'lest I consume you on the way, for you are a stiff-necked people' (Exod 33:3), they received it as a 'disastrous word' (33:4). Unlike Cain, they did not face wandering as fugitives, for this angel would be leading them to 'a land flowing with milk and honey' (33:3); yet even in this good place, the absence of God is a cause for deep mourning. Years later, after the Israelites had been living in the land of Israel for generations, the Philistines captured the ark of God and took it outside the Promised Land (1 Sam 4:11; 5:1). This news was so devastating that it killed Eli, a long-standing priest and judge (4:18). At the same time, the midwives of his daughter-in-law tried to encourage her, telling her that she had borne a son, after she heard the news

---

34. The Arabic word is *ihsān*.

of the loss of her husband and the ark. But she would not be comforted. She named her son 'No glory', Ichabod, and died (4:19–22).

The desperate question, 'My God, my God, why have you forsaken me? Why are you so far from saving me?' (Ps 22:1) gives witness to the horror of God's absence from a person's life. This is the corollary of the delightful experience of his presence. The fact that God can forsake someone emphasizes that when he talks about being present with them, he really *has* come, and really *is* there with them. However, the possibility of God's absence is not a theme in the Qur'an, where God is so transcendent that he is everywhere and knows everything about all of us: his absence is impossible. The Bible has similar ideas of God's omniscience and omnipresence, but the possibility of absence adds a different kind of 'presence' that human beings experience as his coming to us.

The qur'anic story of Moses' request to see God points, then, to a fundamental difference between the Qur'an's view of God and the Bible's view of God. In the former, the mountains will fall down before even a great prophet can see God's glory. Even here, however, there are some hints of the presence of God: the Qur'an does not completely remove the presence of God from the Moses story – at the burning bush, God insists, 'I am God' (Surahs 20. 14; 27. 9; 28. 30), and 27. 10 is translated by Haleem as, 'The messengers need have no fear in my Presence.'[35] Neither is the idea of God's coming completely absent from Islamic tradition. There are some Hadith in which Muhammad speaks of God as 'coming down' during the last nights of Ramadan. Muslim scholars ask what this means: in what sense does God 'come'? Is it just that his blessings are more accessible, or is there more?

Perhaps the best way of beginning to understand what Muslims might mean by seeking God is the concept of 'nearness'. For mainstream Sunnis, God's nearness is part of the blessing that people seek when they do extra night prayers. Two well-known Hadith explain:

> The closest that a slave comes to his Lord is during the middle of the latter portion of the night. If you can be among those who remember Allāh the Exalted One at that time, then do so (At-Tirmidhi).
>
> Our Lord, the Blessed, the Superior, comes every night down on the nearest Heaven to us when the last third of the night

---

35. M. A. S. Abdel Haleem, *The Qur'an: A New Translation by M. A. S. Abdel Haleem* (Oxford: Oxford University Press, 2008), Used with permission.

remains, saying: 'Is there anyone to invoke Me, so that I may respond to invocation? Is there anyone to ask Me, so that I may grant him his request? Is there anyone seeking My forgiveness, so that I may forgive him?' (Ṣaḥīḥ Al-Bukhāri 19:14).

For Sufis, 'nearness' is something to be sought after, although few can achieve it. The Sufi manuals tell the believer how to climb the ladder of faith and practice to reach a knowledge and vision of God. This is sometimes described as 'unveiling': the believer needs to remove various veils of ignorance and self in order to perceive God. 'Nearness' to God can be achieved through obedience, through knowledge, through conquering one's 'self', through love of God and through fear of God. It is not so much a matter of God coming near to the believer as of the believer realizing God's closeness to his world. There are degrees of closeness to God, and Sufi writers generally agree that only the very special 'friends of God' can achieve the highest degree of closeness. In that highest degree, they can lose awareness of themselves, so that their state is best described as 'silence'.[36]

So, then, what is the difference between Islamic ideas of God's nearness and biblical ideas of God's presence? What is the difference between a God who comes and can be 'absent', and a God who does not come but is nevertheless everywhere? As we have already noted, the Bible does see God as seeing and upholding all things, so, in that sense, he has no need to 'come' and cannot be 'absent'. So what can his 'coming' and his 'absence' mean? Here are some suggestions:

- The Islamic focus is on how human beings can realize the presence of God that is everywhere; the biblical focus is on God's making himself known to people.
- 'Nearness' is about God's knowledge of us; 'coming' is about our getting to know God.
- Getting 'near' to God is something that we have to do; 'coming' is what God does, on his own initiative.
- Omnipresence refers to what God *is*: it is his very nature to be everywhere. 'Coming' refers to what God *does*, that is, to his actions in space and in time.

---

36. There is a helpful summary of the teachings of several Sufi writers in M. Ruston, 'Approaches to Proximity and Distance in Early Sufism', in *Mystics Quarterly*, 2007:1–25. Available at www.jstor.org.

To Think About

With a Muslim friend, discuss the Exodus accounts of people meeting God at Sinai. How does your friend understand the Qur'an's call to 'seek the Face of God'?

What are the similarities and differences that you can discern between the biblical and qur'anic views of God? How do these relate to the similarities and differences between biblical and qur'anic views of human beings that we explored in chapter 2?

Coming back to the Bible, what, then, is happening on Sinai? The answer is simply that God is giving Israel his presence; the giving of the law was secondary. For over a year, while Israel camped at the foot of Sinai, the LORD gave instructions to the people about the design and dedication of the tabernacle. Then, his glory that had blazed on the mountain came down, entered the tabernacle and dwelt there (Exod 40:34–38). From within the tabernacle, the LORD spoke to Moses, giving him the laws about ritual, about purification and about the behaviour required by his holiness, as recorded in Leviticus. He organized the people for their journey, with his instructions recorded in the first part of Numbers. It is not Moses but God who is the main actor throughout. Where in the Qur'an the story is about Moses receiving the law, the thrust of the story in Exodus is that Israel received God's presence. The law details the conditions needed for the presence to continue to dwell among them. The law is part of the gift, not the gift itself. The golden calf incident and its aftermath make it clear that God is even more concerned to be present than is Israel to have him with her.

There is a Jewish idea that Sinai is the place of God's marriage with Israel:[37] the bride comes to the mountain, the Bridegroom comes to meet her, and then takes her with him towards the Promised Land. However, the bride's holiness must match that of the holy Bridegroom. And so, the bride must be purified and kept faithful to her Bridegroom. This is what the law is for: she is often told that the ordinances are to keep her holy and free from idolatry because she belongs to Yahweh (e.g. Lev 25:55; 17:6–7; 18:30; 19:27–34; 20:26). In this context, we can understand why the golden calf incident was

---

37. For references to Israel as God's bride, see Isa 54:5–6; 62:4–5; Ezek 16.

so devastating: the bride was defiling herself in the middle of her wedding ceremony! The tabernacle, the sacrifices and the priesthood were given in order to deal with her sinfulness; that is, they were for keeping the purity and the fellowship in the marriage.

From the ceremony at Sinai, Israel went with God; she did not have to return to Sinai to find his presence. When Israel was established in the Promised Land, God permitted her to have a temple to replace the tabernacle, and everyone would come there to meet him. So why, we wonder, did Elijah have to go back to Sinai for his commissioning? It is unlikely that it was because he came from the northern kingdom and would have been unwelcome in the Jerusalem temple; surely all Israel would have come to Jerusalem for feasts. Was it an indication, like his going outside Israel for his departure, that Israel was losing God's presence? Certainly, the exile outside the Promised Land was linked with the loss of God's presence. This forms a large part of the message of Ezekiel.

The presence was what was needed to rebuild Eden. What had been lost was not just the *place*, but the *presence* of God: God 'walking with' human beings in love. What would restore that? The fallen pattern of Genesis 4 – 11 would have to be put right:

- Israel needed right sacrifices: the laws given through Moses at Sinai give all the necessary instructions.
- Israel was to be a right people, under the rule of God, in the land given by God: at Sinai, God is calling and forming that people.
- Evil was to be dealt with: the golden calf incident underlines the ongoing need for this at the heart of it all. Hence the purity regulations, and the *need* for the right sacrifices: this fulfils the conditions for the presence of God by dealing with the evil of the people.

By New Testament times, it was evident that Israel was a very long way from seeing Eden rebuilt. Some had returned to the land, but it was hardly 'theirs'. They were under foreign rule, and the glory of God's presence, which the Jews call 'the shekinah', had not returned to the temple. And what about the sacrifices? Were they 'right'? At the heart of Jewish faith, in the temple, there were people waiting for things to improve; Luke tells us about some of them at the beginning of his gospel. John the Baptist's father praised God because he had 'visited and redeemed his people' (Luke 1:68); Simeon was 'waiting for the consolation of Israel' and 'the Lord's Christ' (2:25–26); and Anna was waiting for 'the redemption of Jerusalem' (2:38). Luke's gospel builds towards the question of how these expectations are met in Jesus.

5

Messiah

The Promised Mahdi: the Deliverer of the Whole of Mankind[1] is the title of a book about the 'hidden Imam' – the twelfth Shi'ite leader who disappeared from the earth in AD 940, and who is expected to return. When he comes, he will govern the earth according to the Qur'an and the pattern of Muhammad, and 'the doors of favours and goodness will be opened from the sky for all people. The lifetimes will last long. People will wholly live in welfare . . . full security will exist.'

To Think About

What makes people long for a deliverer?

We are now ready to return to the big question in the disciples' minds at the transfiguration: 'What does it mean that Jesus is the Messiah?' They (and the first readers of the Gospels) would probably have been discussing how he was like and unlike the other prophets, including Moses and Elijah, and, following the feeding of the five thousand, Elisha too (2 Kgs 4:42–44). But what sort of Messiah could this be, one who was expecting to be rejected by his own Jewish people and then be killed and rise again? What exactly did he mean by calling himself 'the Son of Man'? And who, then, was John the Baptist, who had already been killed and whom Herod feared had risen again?

In order to understand how the transfiguration begins to answer these questions, we need first to explore the messianic expectations of the 'world

---

1. M. Qummi, *The Promised Mahdi: the Deliverer of the Whole of Mankind* (Isfahan: Amir-Ul-Mu'mineen Library, 2008). The quotation is from page H.

behind the text', of the first-century Jews. We can then go on to explore some of the expectations that are presented within the 'world of the text' of the Gospels.

We will end this chapter by thinking about expectations in our 'world in front of the text'. The world today is surprisingly similar to that 'behind' the Gospels: it is full of tensions, and it is also full of longing and expectation, especially among Muslims. This chapter is very important for our project of 'thinking biblically about Islam' for two reasons. First, the mirror of the text helps us to think about our longing world, and, second, our own longings and the longings that people express today help us to understand the expectations in the 'world behind' the transfiguration.

Behind the Text of the Gospels: The Plight and the Hope

Exploring first-century Jewish expectations is not an easy task: the writings of the time give some information, but they vary greatly, so scholars have reported conflicting ideas of what people were expecting. The obvious conclusion is that, while people were expecting something to happen, they were by no means in agreement about what it might be. They were certainly expecting God to act on their behalf, and that he would send someone – or several people – to bring them the victory and freedom that was promised in Isaiah and the other prophets. However, there was a variety of ideas about just who might come and how this person would reflect the previous prophets and kings. All these expectations were strongly affected by the political tensions of the time.

The land of Israel was under Roman rule. During the exile, the prophets had predicted a glorious return to the Promised Land followed by a reign of peace and righteousness. There had indeed been a return but it had been partial, and the intervening years had been turbulent, with the Jews sometimes ruling themselves but more often being ruled by foreign powers. There had been no recognized prophets from God for centuries, and the Jews themselves were divided into religious and political factions. There had been a glorious revolution under the Maccabees,[2] but that was long past. There was a local, non-Roman king, but the Herodian dynasty was only part-Jewish, and the kings were notoriously unjust and often violent. Saddest of

---

2. The feast of Hanukkah still celebrates the liberation of the temple under Judas Maccabeus in 164 BC.

all, the prophets had predicted a rebuilding of the temple and a return of the presence of God: the temple had been rebuilt, but there had been no signs of the return of God's presence.

When Solomon dedicated the first temple, God's 'shekinah' glory came down with fire and filled the whole place (2 Chr 7:1–3). When the second temple was dedicated, there was no 'shekinah': instead of God coming to be present among his people, we read about Ezra coming to teach the law (Ezra 6:13 – 7:10). Herod the Great had built his new temple (known as the 'Second Temple') in the fifteenth or eighteenth year of his reign (i.e. 22 or 19 BC[3]), but there was still no 'shekinah' there. Even now, Jewish tradition tells us that, since the time of Ezra, the study of the law has replaced the temple sacrifices, and the 'shekinah' will not return to Israel until the coming of the Messiah.

It is not surprising, then, that first-century Jews were still hoping for God to fulfil his promises to them. They expected freedom to govern themselves in their Promised Land, God's presence in their temple and the sort of peace described in, for example, Isaiah 11:6–9.[4] It is also not surprising that their hopes followed our Genesis 4 – 11 pattern, and so displayed the tension between God's plan in creation and human fallenness:

- They hoped for right sacrifices. The peak of the disaster against which the Maccabees fought was the desecration of the temple under the Greek ruler Antiochus Epiphanes in 169 BC, and one of the most important matters to Jewish people thereafter was that they should be free to offer right sacrifices in the temple.
- They wanted power for their people in their land. On the one hand, this was a right desire for the fulfilment of God's promises; but, on the other hand, they expected to have political power, and that meant taking power over their enemies. Many hated the Roman occupiers; there were tensions between people who cooperated with the Romans, people who resisted them and people who went to the desert to keep away from them; and there were religiously driven violent uprisings from time to time.
- They wanted to get rid of the evil in their land. On the one hand, this was a right desire for justice and righteousness. On the other hand, many saw the evil in other people rather than in themselves,

---

3. Negev, *Archaeological Encyclopedia of the Holy Land*, 372.

4. N. T. Wright helpfully describes this hope as a hope for full return from exile. See his *The New Testament and the People of God* (London: SPCK, 1992).

and some focused so hard on keeping the letter of the law that they missed important aspects of love and inner purity.

Who Was Expected?

The expectation was, as we have said, that God would fulfil his promises; but people expected that he would use human beings to do so. However, there was no single idea of whom he would use and how.[5] There was an idea of a coming Messiah, but the word 'Messiah' is not used of an expected figure in the Old Testament, and it is only occasionally used like that in the other writings that we have from before Jesus' time. Rather, there was a variety of different ideas.

First, there were hopes that God would send prophets again. In fact, although there had been no prophets whose work was seen as scripture for centuries, there were a number of people who were regarded as prophets in a lesser sense, so it is difficult to discover exactly what people were waiting for. On the basis of Deuteronomy 18:18, some people had a specific expectation of 'a prophet like Moses', but this does not seem to have been widespread except among the Samaritans. It is not surprising, then, that the people saw John the Baptist and Jesus as prophets, but were not sure exactly what that might mean.

Next, there were hopes for a king. 'Messiah' means 'anointed': it was the title given to the kings of Israel. As David had been promised that his dynasty would never end (2 Sam 7), there was an expectation that God would re-establish a Davidic kingdom. At the exile, the Davidic kingdom came to an end: after the exile, it was never re-established. There had been various attempts to re-establish Jewish rule, but never a clearly Jewish kingdom. The Herodian dynasty was certainly not seen as the fulfilment of God's promises.

So people were longing for a proper king who would free Israel, fight their battles and rule justly. These are the ideas most likely to have been in the disciples' minds when just before the transfiguration they ventured the opinion that Jesus was the Messiah. It is not surprising that Jesus told them to keep quiet about it: such a Messiah would have been a threat to Roman rule, and would have been quickly executed. Jesus did not want that to happen until the right time.

---

5. A great deal of recent scholarship explores the various expectations. This section largely follows the analysis of N. T. Wright in his *Jesus and the Victory of God* (London: SPCK, 1996), where full references can be found.

Did anyone expect 'the Son of Man'? This was the way Jesus described himself most frequently, so we might expect there to have been an expectation of a 'Son of Man' among the Jews of Jesus' time. However, a careful study of the Gospels indicates that this is not a title that other people gave to Jesus. The only time it is used by anyone other than Jesus himself is in John 12:34, when the people are trying to work out what Jesus means by it. The most obvious allusion is to the 'Son of Man' in Daniel 7.[6] That 'Son of Man' is closely associated with God's ultimate judgement, victory and reign; that is, with God's kingdom. It is not surprising, then, that there are writings that associate this 'Son of Man' with the expected king, and it is very likely that people would have thought about Daniel 7 when Jesus talked about 'the kingdom of God'.

Elijah and the Coming of God

Perhaps the most important expectations for our study of the transfiguration are those relating to Elijah. As we have seen, Elijah seems to have been the one person whose coming was definitely expected. It was clearly stated in Malachi 3:1 and 4:5–6 that Elijah would come as a forerunner. But this was not a forerunner to a 'Messiah': it was a forerunner to the presence and judgement of God; and the coming of God is something that was repeatedly announced by the Old Testament prophets, often linked with the idea that God would reign in Zion (e.g. Ps 96:12–13; 98:8–9; Isa 24:23; 25:9–10; 35:3–10; 40:1–11; 59:15–21; Ezek 43:1–7; Zech 2:4–12; 8:2–3; 14:1–16).

We begin to understand the discussion in Luke 9:18–20 better. If Elijah was to come, then maybe John the Baptist was Elijah. But if John the Baptist was Elijah, when was God coming? And who was Jesus? On the other hand, maybe Jesus was Elijah. But if Jesus was Elijah, who was John the Baptist? And what had all this to do with the hope of a king and with Jesus' preaching about the kingdom of God? With such questions in mind, we turn to consider the ministry of John the Baptist, keeping our focus on Luke's gospel.

---

6. N. T. Wright argues that this was one of the main passages that Jesus saw himself as fulfilling.

In the Text of the Gospels: Elijah and John the Baptist

> The people were filled with expectation, and all were questioning
> in their hearts . . . (Luke 3:15).

How do the Gospels themselves deal with the Jewish expectations of their
time? They see the events that they record as both fulfilling and correcting
the expectations. Their main focus is on Jesus; and we will look at him in our
next chapter. However, they also deal with the expectation of Elijah, and they
do that through their accounts of John the Baptist.

Matthew starts his gospel with a genealogy and with a series of events
that fulfil specific Old Testament prophecies, so building the expectation
that Jesus is the culmination of the history and purpose of Israel. However,
Matthew does not explain what the Jewish people were expecting: perhaps he
assumes that his readers know about that. Mark jumps into history with the
announcement of good news about Jesus, and then the sudden appearance of
John the Baptist: we are left to guess what the people of the time might have
been thinking. It is Luke who gives us a picture of a Jewish people waiting and
hoping, in his first chapters. It is Luke who sets the political scene, with the
corrupt half-Jewish king Herod (1:5) ruling under the Roman Empire and
subject to its control (2:1–2; 3:1–2). It is he, too, who gives us a glimpse of the
ordinary people involved.

The picture begins in the temple, with priests and people worshipping
God as they await his deliverance (1:5–10). We are introduced to a righteous
priest and his wife, and taken with him to the greatest privilege of his career.
He is chosen to go into the holy place to offer incense. As he goes in, all the
people are outside, waiting and praying. We are reminded of Moses going
into the tent while the people waited outside.

What did the people expect as they waited for Zechariah? Probably not
very much: the priests had been carrying out their duties for a long time
since the last spectacular response from God. Yet there would have been a
hope that God would accept the offering and that, one day, God would act,
someone would come, and the 'shekinah' would return. This is a picture of
faithful Israel, with a righteous priest, following the law of their Lord.

Unlike Matthew and Mark, Luke continues to mention the crowds of
ordinary people who wait and wonder as the amazing events unfold (1:21–
22, 58–66; 2:3, 38; 3:7, 10, 15, 21). He introduces us to some of them in
more detail:

- There are those who, like Simeon and Anna, have dedicated themselves to waiting for the deliverer, and who believe that they will see him in their own lifetime (2:25–38).
- There are those who, like Zechariah and Elizabeth, are longing for a personal need to be met (1:5–7).
- There are those who, like Mary, are planning for a normal family life (2:27).
- There are those who, like the shepherds, are simply getting on with their work (2:8).

The longings and expectations are expressed in three songs, all of which are used in the daily morning and evening worship of many Christians. They are all songs that rejoice that now, at last, the expectations of Israel are being fulfilled.

Simeon's song (2:29–32) recognizes Jesus as the fulfilment of the longing for salvation and light for all peoples and for glory for Israel. Mary's song (1:46–55), too, sees God's fulfilment of his promises to Israel in the expectation of Jesus: specifically, it looks forward to the overturning of power structures and the blessing of oppressed people. Both Simeon and Mary rejoice in their personal roles as God's servants: the coming of Jesus is the meaning of their own lives as well as the fulfilment of God's promises to Israel and God's blessing for the world.

To Think About

Read Luke 1:46–55 and 2:29–32. In what ways do these songs express the longings of the Jewish people of Jesus' time? In what ways to they express the personal longings of Mary and of Simeon?

Between Mary's song and Simeon's song comes a passage that even more explicitly describes God's promises and Israel's hope. This is Zechariah's song in Luke 1:68–79; and it is not a response to the coming of Jesus, but a response to the birth of John the Baptist. Like Simeon's song and Mary's song, it is a song of praise, because it sees that, at last, God is acting on the promises that he made so long ago. Luke describes the song as a 'prophecy': in it, Zechariah sees far beyond his son John to God's ultimate purposes.

Thinking about Zechariah's Song

> *Blessed be the Lord God of Israel,*
> *for he has visited and redeemed his people . . .*

God visited his people and redeemed them from slavery in Egypt at the time of Moses. Now he is doing it again!

> *. . . and has raised up a horn of salvation for us*
> *in the house of his servant David . . .*

God saved Israel from her enemies through David, and promised to establish a king on David's throne. Now he is doing it!

> *. . . as he spoke by the mouth of his holy prophets from of old,*
> *that we should be saved from our enemies*
> *and from the hand of all who hate us;*

God sent prophets to tell Israel what he planned to do. Now he is doing it!

> *to show the mercy promised to our fathers*
> *and to remember his holy covenant,*
> *the oath that he swore to our father Abraham . . .*

God made a covenant with Abraham. Now he is keeping it!

> *. . . to grant us*
> *that we, being delivered from the hand of our enemies,*
> *might serve him without fear,*
> *in holiness and righteousness before him all our days.*

And what was the point of all this? It was that Israel should serve her Lord in holiness and righteousness. The problem was that she had enemies, and those enemies needed to be conquered. So Zechariah prophesied, and so it turned out; but, as Luke goes on to show, the enemies who stopped Israel being righteous were not the Romans!

The song then turns to speak of his son, John:

> *And you, child, will be called the prophet of the Most High;*
> *for you will go before the Lord to prepare his ways,*
> *to give knowledge of salvation to his people*
> *in the forgiveness of their sins,*
> *because of the tender mercy of our God,*
> *whereby the sunrise shall visit us from on high*
> *to give light to those who sit in darkness and in the shadow*
> *of death,*
> *to guide our feet into the way of peace.*

Zechariah recognizes John as the forerunner of the coming of God mentioned in Malachi 3:1 and 4:5–6. His song reminds us, too, of Isaiah's descriptions of God's deliverance (9:3; 40:3; 42:6–7).

Luke's first two chapters, then, build up a picture of a waiting people whose expectations are, finally, about to be fulfilled. As they began in the temple with Zechariah's presentation of incense, so they finish in the temple with the presentation of Jesus. As Zechariah's presentation was accompanied by something extraordinary, so Jesus' presentation was accompanied by something extraordinary. In 2:40, we read, 'The child [Jesus] grew and became strong, filled with wisdom. And the favour of God was upon him.'

Luke has set his scene: what will happen next? There will be two more preliminary scenes before we get to Jesus' genealogy and the beginning of his ministry.

Scene 1 is the ordinary piety of Jesus' family: their regular Passover visit to the temple. The return of God to his temple was expected; but what would it be like? Would there be the 'shekinah' of his glory? Would he bring victory for the Jews? What would happen? Here, in Luke 2:41–51, people are amazed and astonished (2:47–48), but it is not at any visible glory or angelic appearance or military might, but at a child. And this is not a prince who threatens the power of Rome, but a child who asks questions of the Jewish religious teachers. In Luke's gospel, Jesus will not enter the temple again until he cleanses it in 19:45–46.

Scene 2 is the appearance of John the Baptist. John does not appear in the temple, but in the desert. Luke once again paints the political context, this time including the Jewish leadership as well as the Roman rulers (3:1–2). The expectation rises as we hear that the word of God comes to John (3:2). What will that word be? A word of redemption and of salvation from enemies, as expected in Zechariah's song? The first words of John the Baptist are, 'You brood of vipers!' (3:7); and this is addressed not to the Roman occupiers but to the Jews who have come to hear him.

To Think About

A child who questions the religious leaders . . . a forerunner who calls the Jews 'vipers' . . .

How do these scenes in the lives of Jesus (Luke 2:41–51) and John the Baptist (3:1–20) fit with the expectations of Zechariah's song (1:68–79)?

John the Baptist

Since John the Baptist is linked with Elijah, and since both John and Elijah are important in Luke's lead-up to the transfiguration, we will take time to look at him further.

In Matthew and Mark, John the Baptist appears suddenly, without warning and with no details of his parentage. In both, he is the voice in the desert telling people to prepare for God's coming that was prophesied by Isaiah (Isa 40:3). The reader can immediately see parallels with Elijah, who also appeared without warning or details of parentage (1 Kgs 17:1), who spent time in the desert (1 Kgs 17:2–6; 19:1–6), who called Israel to repentance (1 Kgs 17 – 19) and who was to prepare the way for God's coming (Mal 3:1; 4:5). In their accounts of the transfiguration, Matthew explicitly identifies John the Baptist with Elijah (Matt 17:10–13; see also Matt 11:14) and Mark records Jesus' saying that Elijah has come and been ill-treated (Mark 9:11–13). Both gospels are clear that expectations of the return of Elijah have been fulfilled in the events that they record.

Luke handles the question of Elijah in a different way. He does not record the conversation about Elijah immediately following the transfiguration: instead, in the angel's message about John's birth, he refers to the prophecy of Malachi 4:6: '. . . he will be great before the Lord. And he must not drink wine or strong drink, and he will be filled with the Holy Spirit, even from his mother's womb. And he will turn many of the children of Israel to the Lord their God, and he will go before him in the spirit and power of Elijah, to turn the hearts of the fathers to the children, and the disobedient to the wisdom of the just, to make ready for the Lord a people prepared' (Luke 1:15–17). So readers of Luke's gospel are expected to look out for 'the spirit and power of Elijah' in John. In particular:

- John will share Elijah's abstemious lifestyle. As we read on, we also find that John, like Elijah, spent much time living simply in the desert.
- John goes first into Jordan, from where Elijah had been borne away in a whirlwind, suggesting continuity with his ministry.
- John will share the power of the Holy Spirit that Elijah knew. We do not see such spectacular events as the raising of the widow's son or the fire from heaven in John's ministry; but we do see the power of authoritative preaching.
- John, like Elijah, will call Israel to repentance. Indeed, this is to be John's main function, as can be seen both from Zechariah's prophetic song about his son (Luke 1:76–79) and from Luke's description of his ministry (3:3–20).

Elijah was, by New Testament times, seen as a paradigm of prophetic zeal and was a hugely important figure in Jewish thinking. Some remembered Elijah as one who challenged the rich and ministered to the poor. Some saw him as a return of Phinehas, the other paradigm of zeal. While Israel was in the wilderness, Phinehas had killed Zimri, an Israelite who took Cozbi, a Midianite woman, into his tent at a time when such relationships led Israel to worship Baal of Peor. God put an end to the plague he sent in his wrath because Phinehas 'was jealous with my jealousy among them, so that I did not consume the people of Israel in my jealousy'[7] (Num 25:11). Some even interpreted the 'covenant of peace' that God made with him (Num 25:12) as meaning he did not die at that stage but reappeared as Elijah. Elijah had also defeated and killed the idolatrous prophets of Baal in his zeal for the LORD, so both had averted God's anger from Israel.

John the Baptist's zeal was like Elijah's zeal in some ways and unlike it in others. Like Elijah, he was uncompromising in his opposition to Israel's sin. Unlike Elijah, he killed no one. However, also unlike Elijah, he did not run away from an angry queen. We never read of Elijah meeting Jezebel or of him rebuking Ahab for marrying her; but we do read of John the Baptist rebuking Herod for his marriage and getting put into prison for it. He then meets the queen – or, rather, his head is brought to her on a plate (Matt 14:3–12; Mark 6:17–28; Luke 3:19–20). So, unlike Elijah, John the Baptist died: his zeal led him to his own death. Yet he prepared the way for the coming of God, and people's hearts were changed as a result of his ministry. In confronting evil

---

7. The word translated 'jealous' could also be translated 'zealous'.

even to the point of death and in seeing real repentance in Jewish people, John completed and fulfilled Elijah's zeal. And he did it in a very different way from the 'zealots', who directed their zeal towards opposing and fighting Roman rule rather than towards confronting sin.

In the Gospels, however, the link between Elijah and John the Baptist is mainly important because Elijah was to come before the return of God to his temple and to his people. That is, John's link with Jesus is more important than his link with Elijah. This is most stressed in John's gospel, where John the Baptist is so insistent on getting people to look at Jesus that he will not even identify himself with Elijah. He is only the voice who prepares the way for someone much greater, and he sends his followers to follow Jesus (John 1:19–36).

John the Baptist is also an important figure in the Qur'an. Like the Gospels, the Qur'an provokes questions about how he relates to Jesus. The main accounts, in Surahs 19. 2–15 and 3. 38–41, tell the story of his birth, and are followed by the story of Jesus' birth.[8] They have many parallels to Luke's account. In Surah 3, the stories are preceded by a story of the birth of Mary and her growing up under the guardianship of Zechariah and receiving miraculous food from God (3. 35–38),[9] which makes it all the clearer that John and Jesus are linked. The way that the stories are told emphasizes this, as, for example, the angelic messages to Zechariah and to Mary announcing the births of John and of Jesus are very similar (3. 39 and 3. 45). However, it is not very clear why Jesus and John are linked or how the work of John relates to the work of Jesus. Here are the only two verses that describe John's ministry:

> The angels called out to [Zechariah], while he stood praying in the sanctuary, 'God gives you news of John, confirming a Word from God. He will be noble and chaste, a prophet, one of the righteous' (3. 39).[10]

> [We said], 'John, hold on to the Scripture firmly.' While he was still a boy, We granted him wisdom, tenderness from Us, and

---

8. The other references are Surah 6. 85, where he appears in a list of other prophets, and 21. 89–90, which mentions Zechariah's prayer for a son and God's answer to it.

9. This story is not found in the Bible. It reflects early Christian tradition such as that found in the *Protoevangelium of James*, available in translation at http://www.earlychristianwritings.com/infancyjames.html.

10. M. A. S. Abdel Haleem, *The Qur'an: A New Translation by M. A. S. Abdel Haleem* (Oxford: Oxford University Press, 2008), Used with permission.

purity. He was devout, kind to his parents, not domineering or rebellious. Peace was on him the day he was born, the day he died, and it will be on him the day he is raised to life again (19. 12–14).[11]

It was John's job to be a prophet who would 'hold on to the Scripture'. This is usually interpreted as confirming and teaching the Torah which the Jews already had. His pure and gentle character is emphasized, but what about his relationship to Jesus? Many Muslims see that as being described in the phrase 'confirming a Word from God' in Surah 3.39, because, just a few verses later, Jesus is called 'a Word from [God]' (3. 45).[12] The idea is that John confirmed the truth of that Word by, for example, telling the Jews that Jesus was their Messiah.

In short, the Qur'an's treatment of John the Baptist fits into its picture of God sending a series of prophets who confirm each other's messages. John is unusual because he affirms not only the Torah that came long before him, but also Jesus who comes so soon after him. The Qur'an raises its own questions and expectations through the miraculous events surrounding the births of Mary, John and Jesus, but it does not paint a picture of the Jews waiting for their Messiah. In contrast, all the Gospels use the story of John the Baptist to build up the reader's expectations about Jesus. Luke tells us about John's own expectations and questions as, from prison, John asks Jesus, 'Are you the one who is to come?' and Jesus responds with miraculous healings (Luke 7:18–23).

There is a detail in the qur'anic account of John that is particularly significant for Shi'ah Muslims: he received God's wisdom when he was still a child. They link this with the qur'anic story of Jesus speaking from his cradle (Surah 3. 45–46; 19. 29–31), and then with their belief in the coming deliverer, the Imam Mahdi – the 'hidden' twelfth leader in the succession from Muhammad who will return one day to bring justice. He was only five years old when he disappeared, and some Sunnis argue that a child could not be an imam. Shi'ites then point to the examples of Jesus and of John the Baptist, who both became prophets when they were very young.

Our thinking about John the Baptist has brought us from the world of expectations in the text to today's world of expectations in front of the text.

---

11. M. A. S. Abdel Haleem, *The Qur'an: A New Translation by M. A. S. Abdel Haleem* (Oxford: Oxford University Press, 2008), Used with permission.

12. Ibid.

In Front of the Text of the Gospels: Approaching the Transfiguration with Islam in Mind

'What makes people long for a deliverer?' we asked at the beginning of this chapter. The obvious answer is that they are experiencing something from which they need to be delivered.

In our world today, millions of people are experiencing injustice, violence, poverty and grief, and are living in fear of what might happen to them and to their families. They feel in danger, and they want safety – when Zechariah spoke of God saving his people from their enemies (Luke 1:71), he was probably not thinking of a spiritual salvation from sin, but of finding safety from the threat of human enemies, and that is what many people need. It is not surprising that, as at the time of Jesus, many of them are longing for a deliverer: both Muslims and Christians turn to expectations of people who will come in the last days. The expectations are important because they give both hope and meaning.

The promise of a deliverer gives hope. When the world around us falls apart, we feel powerless and in danger. So we long for safety and for the ability to control our circumstances. Both Christians and Muslims know that their ultimate safety depends on God, and that it is, in the end, God who controls everything. However, in many cases, people's worlds have fallen apart as the result of something that human beings have done, and they naturally want to put things right. They are likely to be angry as well as hurt, and to want revenge. The coming deliverers are expected to bring justice by punishing oppressors, and to bring security by establishing justice and peace for believers.

Security and justice are closely linked: without correction of the injustice that has caused the chaos and suffering, what hope is there of security? The big question is, 'Who will bring that justice?' In particular, what is the role of human beings in bringing justice while they are waiting for the deliverer? Some people think that they should just get on with their lives and trust that God will eventually act; some think that they can hasten the coming of the deliverer by the way that they live or by calling other people to faith; and some think that they should fight for justice and deliverance and that, by doing this, they are fighting God's enemies on his behalf. This was true at the time of Jesus, and it is true of both Muslims and Christians in today's world.

The promise of a deliverer gives meaning. When the world falls apart around us, one of the worst feelings is that nothing seems to mean anything any more. Everything feels confusing and pointless. So, when terrible things happen to us, we try to make sense of them, and we need hope that it is worth going on with life and with God. So we ask whether God knows about the horrors and the injustices, why he lets them happen, and whether he is doing anything about them. Our difficulties might make sense if they are part of his purposes for his world.

Along with expectations of deliverers, both Muslims and Christians have beliefs about the last days; and both have apocalyptic writings – that is, writings about the end of the world that interpret current events as part of the end of times. Such writings arise at times in history when people are oppressed and under attack. For example, Christians interpreted the Arab conquests of the seventh and eighth centuries as part of the pattern of history leading to the end times.[13] It gave them a way of finding meaning in the shocking situation of a Christian empire being taken over by Muslims. If this had been prophesied, it meant that God knew all about it and had it under control, and that their oppression meant something as part of his plans.

Some Christians today try to make sense of 9/11 and of all the news they hear of violence in Muslim areas in a similar way, seeing current events as part of the 'last days' predicted in the books of Daniel and Revelation. This is particularly seen in the United States, which was the direct target of the 9/11 attack. Typically, popular apocalyptic books see Islam as the Antichrist and the Middle East as the place where the last battles are being fought.[14] The expectations of God's final acts of judgement may give people security and meaning in a puzzling world; but the apocalyptic imagery can lead to even more fear of Islam and of Muslims, and to active hostility.

Much of the discussion appears on the Internet. Some is calm and thoughtful, but some seems designed to produce polarization, anger and fear. For example, one site has a talk in a moderate, winsome style that makes careful references to history and to predictions in the book of Daniel to show that 'the king of the south' (Dan 11) is Islam. It describes how, since the break-up of the Roman Empire, there has been conflict with Islam, and says that

---

13. See R. Hoyland, *Seeing Islam as Others Saw It: A Survey and Evaluation of Christian, Jewish and Zoroastrian Writing on Early Islam* (Princeton: Darwin Press, 1997), ch. 8; and pp. 231–232 of this book.

14. Popular Christian books include J. Smith, *Islam: The Cloak of the Antichrist* (USA: WinePress, 2011); J. Richardson, *The Islamic Antichrist* (Los Angeles: WND Books, 2015). R .G. Kyle, *Apocalyptic Fever: End-Time Prophecies in Modern America* (Eugene: Cascade Books, 2012) gives an overview, including discussions of non-Christian apocalyptic ideas.

'now we're entering into the third and final conflict'.[15] Another site, neither moderate nor winsome, links the kingdom of the north to Turkey, 'the tenth Islamic nation'. Here, Daniel's fourth kingdom is, apparently, Islam, 'Satan's religion'. The writer interweaves this interpretation with statistics about the Islamization of Europe ('Go into any school in Germany, France or Spain and you will see only Muslim children')[16] and the page concludes with an alarming article about 'Muslim neighbourhoods . . . mushrooming in every city across Europe'.[17]

Many of these Western writers are responding to frightening reports about Muslims that they see in the media, and not to things that they have experienced themselves. Hopes for deliverance are likely to be different in situations where people experience the violence more directly, whether on a personal, communal or national level. No doubt everyone reading this will be able to think of plenty of examples of places where people are suffering dreadfully today, and where people are trying to piece together their lives in the aftermath of atrocities. This is the way the world is: as we saw in our study of Noah in chapter 1, even the flood did not wash away human violence.

Human responses to violence are also part of 'the way the world is'. To 'think biblically' about them, we can turn to the Psalms, with their expressions of anger, grief and despair, and their expectations of deliverance. Some respond to terrible situations on a personal level, and some to those on a national level. Some psalms, such as Psalm 137, express despair and a desire for revenge; some, such as Psalm 60, express hope that God will help to conquer the enemies; and some, such as Psalm 22, move on to expressing a glorious future hope.

---

15. Tim Roosenberg, 'Islam and Christianity Daniel 11 Seminar', Sealing Time Ministries, http://www.sealingtime.com/resources/featured-speakers/tim-roosenberg/islam-and-christianity-daniel-11-seminar-tim-roosenberg.html; accessed October 2014.

16. 'Islam Is the Prophesied Beast System (Revelation Chapters 13–18)', Apocalypse Prophesied 2008–2015, http://www.apocalypse2008-2015.com/Beast_System-Islam.html; accessed October 2014.

17. Geert Wilders, 'Who Lost Europe?', Apocalypse Prophesied 2008–2015, http://www.apocalypse2008-2015.com/Beast_System-Islam.html; accessed October 2014.

> **To Think About**
>
> Where do you see agony, despair, vengeance and hope in yourself and in the world around you today?
>
> Read Psalms 137, 60 and 22. In what ways can the promise of a deliverer help people who are feeling the emotions expressed in those psalms?

Many of the people who experience terrible things in today's world are Muslims. Some have experienced violence from non-Muslims, some have experienced violence from Muslims, and many are still reacting to violence experienced by their parents, grandparents or earlier generations. This is so not only in places where there is war and terror: it can also happen in England.

His Grandfather Was Kicked to Death

Why did Mahmoud try to bomb a police station? His family had plenty of problems, but no one had ever done anything violent. They were horrified.

But . . . seventeen years earlier, just before Mahmoud's birth, something terrible had happened. The evening prayer was over, and Mahmoud's grandfather was coming home from the mosque. A group of white lads thought it would be fun to attack him. They pushed him to the ground and kicked him. One of them kept kicking . . . and kicking . . . and kicking . . . Someone called an ambulance but, by the time it got there, it was too late. By the next morning, Mahmoud's grandfather was dead.

This was the first fatal racist attack in that area, but it was, sadly, not surprising that it happened. The Muslim community had only arrived there in the past few years. People like Mahmoud's father had limited English and were ready to get to know the local English people, and there were some English people who tried to get to know them. But there were others who resented the arrival of foreigners and who could not understand them or the changes that they saw in their home. There had been an increasing amount of racial abuse, and tension had been rising. Many of the Muslims, especially the women, were afraid of the local white youth. And many of the local white youth were unemployed, had no hope of finding a job, and could not understand why the local authorities were spending money on helping new immigrants.

> **To Think About**
>
> Where do you see the need of hope for deliverance and justice in this story? How might that need have affected Mahmoud?
>
> Imagine Mahmoud watching a news report of British troops involved in war in a Muslim country. What questions and fears might that raise for him?

If some Western Christians turn to apocalyptic ideas in order to make sense of turmoil in the world, it is not surprising that some Muslims also turn to apocalyptic ideas. Just as there is a range of ideas about the end of the world among Christians, so there is also a range of ideas about the end of the world among Muslims. It is generally expected that an evil and unjust figure called the *dajjāl* (usually translated 'Antichrist') will arise in the Middle East, and that Jesus the Messiah will return to defeat him and his armies. However, Sunni and Shi'ite expectations are very different.

Shi'ite Expectations[18]

Central to Shi'ite expectations is the return of the 'hidden' Imam Mahdi. Shi'ites believe that Ali, Muhammad's cousin, should have succeeded Muhammad; but there were three other caliphs before he became leader of the Muslim people. After Ali, Shi'ites believe that the succession should have been through Ali's son, Hussain, and then his descendants; but Hussain and most of his family were killed at the Battle of Karbala (AD 680), and, from then on, others ruled the majority of Muslims. Following Hussain, there came a series of 'Imams' who were recognized as the legitimate Shi'ite leaders, and it is the twelfth of these who disappeared and whose return is expected by the majority group of Shi'ites.

Ever since Karbala, Shi'ites have sought 'restoration of justice'. This means that the longing for Imam Mahdi is built on the desire to put right past injustice as well as to see future justice. The prayer quoted below has a long passage that mourns over the martyrdom of Hussain and his family before it goes on to pray for the coming of Imam Mahdi. The past as well as the future mirrors the believer's own pain.

---

18. There are different Shi'ite groups who accept different imams. Here, we deal only with the majority group, known as the 'Twelvers' because they accept twelve imams.

Like the first-century Jews, Shi'ites long for justice in political terms. Like first-century Jews, they have often lived under what they have seen as illegitimate rule. Like first-century Jews, Shi'ites look to the past as well as to the future for examples of oppression and deliverance. Like first-century Jews, they are expecting someone to come and deliver them. They base their expectations partly on their scriptures, but partly on other traditions; and they adapt the expectations to the cultural and political contexts of their own times.

Longings and expectations are in the heart of Shi'ite Islam. An ancient prayer, called 'The Supplication of Lamentation', is recited by many pious people every Friday. It expresses longing for Imam Mahdi thus:

> It breaks my heart (when) I look at all that has been created, but cannot see you, nor hear a whisper about your whereabouts, nor any secret communication! It is disheartening to know that you are attending to and watching over the disorder and confusion, and I, in the thick of violent turmoil, am far away, unable to give report of injustice. I eagerly long for you who are out of sight, but have not forsaken us. I eagerly long for you who have departed and are invisible, but are not far from us . . .
>
> Already the period of expectation has lasted too long! When shall we receive our share from you and have our minds set at rest? For we have fixed our eyes upon you and strive with perseverance. When shall we be happy, and see your beautiful form and fine aspect? Groups of cheerful willing disciplined helpers, in great numbers, gathering around you to carry out one work after the other! You fulfilling (every promise) and giving joy, heart and confidence (to the faithful); filling the earth with justice; making your enemies follow the law and accept the revolution; taking the wind out of the haughty and the boastful, and those who knew but denied the truth; breaking the back of the proud and the arrogant; uprooting the roots of the unjust; and we-singing [sic] the praise of Allāh, the Lord of the worlds.

The prayer then calls on God to unite the believers with the Mahdi:

> O my Allāh! You disperse the clouds of sorrows and hardships. Unto You we turn to ask for help against the enemy; for You (alone) help and guide.

Show them the face of their Leader. O the Mightiest Almighty. Allow him to put an end to evil and corruption, and satisfy his Love (for the faithful) and dislike (for the sinners).

O my Allāh! Set up truth, destroy falsehood, show the right path to Thy friends, humiliate Thy enemies, and do it without interruption, (through him). O my Allāh! Unite us with him.

Let us be friends with his ancestors. Give us courage to disperse those who oppose and try to prevent him, and make them stay in their shame and disgrace for ever.

Help us to discharge the duties made incumbent upon us by him, and make every effort to obey him, keep from that which is declared unlawful by him, rely upon him to get his approval.

Let us be with him when he makes peace, and frees mankind from fear, gives currency to love are kindness [*sic*], brings bliss and happiness, spreads good and virtue, so that we may do our best to promote his cause through Thy mercy, and win victory for Thee.[19]

To Think About

What similarities and what differences do you see in the longings expressed in this prayer and the longings expressed in Mary's song (Luke 1:46–55) and Simeon's song (Luke 2:29–32)?

Sunni Expectations

Many Sunnis, too, expect 'the Mahdi', but this is not a returning imam. The word *mahdi* means 'guided one', and it is used in several ways. There is an expectation that 'the Mahdi' will appear as a righteous leader in the last days, but there have also been several historical figures who have been called *mahdi*. In addition, there is a common belief that God will send a *mujaddid* (renewer), who will reform Islam at the beginning of each Islamic century, so

---

19. Edited extracts from the translation at http://www.qul.org.au/library/duas-supplications/410-dua-nudba-the-supplication-of-lamentation; accessed June 2015.

there can be discussions as to whether a particular person is the Mahdi or a *mujaddid*.[20]

Another hope expressed by some Sunnis is for a caliph to rule the Islamic people. This is not so much a future hope as a desire to return to past glory – to the time of the 'rightly guided caliphs' who ruled the Muslims after the death of Muhammad, and to the many times in history when there have been powerful Muslim rulers.

Together with the coming of Jesus the Messiah to defeat the *dajjāl*, all these expectations bring hope to Muslims who feel that the world has gone wrong. All are associated with the restoration of both power and justice for Muslims and for Islam, and all depend on the appearance of particular figures sent by God.

The Mahdi, the Messiah and the caliphs are clearly different figures, but it is by no means clear how they might relate to each other. The Mahdi and the Messiah will come in the last days, but will there be a new caliph before they appear? Or will the Mahdi be a caliph? Are the Mahdi and the Messiah two different figures, or might they be the same person? If they are different, what will be their different roles? Reading the history of Muslim views of the end times[21] is a bit like reading the sources on first-century Jewish messianic expectations: it is clear that people have been expecting God to act, to bring victory to his people and justice to the world, and to do so through sending particular figures. Beyond that, different people put the evidence together in different ways; and the expectations affect different people in different ways.

For many Muslims, as for many Christians, what will happen in the last days is an interesting question, but one that does not affect their lives very much today. For others, it makes a big difference. We finish this chapter with three examples that illustrate how expectations can give meaning to people in extremely difficult situations.

---

20. Different Muslims identify different people as *mujaddid* in different centuries. The present century AH began in 1979, the year of the Iranian revolution, so some Shi'ites see Ayatollah Khomeini as this century's *mujaddid*. Sunnis are likely to say that there can be several *mujaddid*s, and to suggest people who have affected their own community.

21. For a thorough analysis, see M. Cook, *Studies in Muslim Apocalyptic* (Princeton: Darwin Press, 2002).

A Sufi View: Expectations Mean That We Can Wait in Peace

A Sufi leader summarizes his expectations thus:

> As believers of the traditions, we believe in a saviour who will come first, before Jesus Christ. We have in our traditions his name, which is Muhammad d'ul Mahdi.
>
> He is coming, but his arrival will be after a great war. It will be the fight of the big powers with each other.
>
> And in that war the saviour will come like a divine hand from heavens to the earth and stop the war.
>
> After a short time a tyrant will appear, well known through traditions as the Anti-Christ. When Jesus Christ was on earth he never touched a sword, but now he is coming as a saviour. In his time all technology will be finished.
>
> His sword can reach any point to where He sends it. It is a miraculous sword, a heavenly sword. His Lord gave it to Him. He will save the people from the hands of the Anti-Christ.[22]

For this Sufi teacher, the coming of the Mahdi means that Muslims have no need to fight now. Rather, they should keep away from all disorder, in case they get drawn into it. When the Mahdi comes, he will bring the punishment that the violent people deserve, and the believers will be unharmed.

A Shi'ite View: Expectations Give Meaning to Suffering

During the Iran–Iraq War (1980–1988), Iranian soldiers were seeking meaning and solace in the figure of Imam Mahdi in the tragic face of atrocities, especially when faced with Saddam Hussein's chemical attacks.

Here are some excerpts from Iranian soldiers' martyrdom testaments, taken from a weblog dedicated to 'those who await the return of Imam Mahdi'.[23] These soldiers were all killed in the war and their testaments have been published by the Foundation for Martyrs and Affairs of Self-Sacrificers.

> I know that one day Imam Mahdi (peace be upon him) will come. Let us be his helpers, not out of duty and because of fear of punishment, but lovingly, let us sacrifice our lives for his and for his speedy return.

---

22. Sheikh Nazim Adil al-Haqqani, leader of the Naqshbandi Sufi order, 'The Coming of the Mystery Imam al-Mahdi', http://khidr.org/al-mahdi.htm; accessed June 2015.

23. See http://montazerane12.persianblog.ir/post/116/. The excerpts have been translated from Persian by Shirin Shafaie. 'Pbuh' stands for 'Peace be upon him'.

Imam Mahdi (pbuh) is the saviour of all mankind. He is the hope for the oppressed. He is the only living being on earth most loved by God. Keep praying so that God will hasten his return and bring light to our eyes and lives.

Peace and greetings to the flag bearer of Islam and deliverer of justice, his holiness Imam Mahdi (pbuh). God I pray to you to show his presence to me, even if briefly, so that my heart is strengthened in these hours of agony and grief, so that my only wish comes true. I pray for martyrdom so that I can meet my Imam.

I go [will be martyred] so that I can prove that I am Muslim and a lover of Mahdi (pbuh). Mother, tell everyone that your tulip [i.e. her son, the author] was also in love, in love with Imam Mahdi (pbuh). Tell everyone that I could not bear his absence any more, that I yearn for him day and night and prayed all the time for his return. Now I am going to be martyred and meet him at last. He will return and bring love and justice with him. Mother, tell the bullets and grenades to tear my flesh and throw my blood everywhere, maybe my blood will hasten my lord's return.[24]

For these Shi'ite soldiers, the expected Imam Mahdi does not only make sense of dying in a terrible war. It also gives a goal for life.

A Militant View: An Apocalyptic Division of the World

As some American Christians see Islam as the antichrist, some Middle Eastern Muslim writers see Israel as the *dajjāl*, with Western states as the *dajjāl*'s helper.[25] One writer expects a Muslim conquest of Jerusalem, in which half of the Jews in Israel will be killed, followed by the Mahdi coming from Afghanistan and killing the remaining Jews. After this, the *dajjāl* will lead the European Union against the Mahdi: the Mahdi will win, and will conquer all of Europe and the Vatican. The *dajjāl* will intensify his fight against the Muslims, until Jesus returns to lead the Muslims in a final cleansing of

---

24. This soldier, like many others, died before getting married. In Persian, he would be called a *nakam*, i.e. a male virgin who dies.

25. The material in this example is based on 'The Figure of the Antichrist', D. Cook, *Contemporary Muslim Apocalyptic Literature* (New York: Syracuse University Press, 2005), ch. 9. There is a long tradition that the *dajjāl* will be Jewish.

Jerusalem and end of the Jews. This writer uses the Bible as well as the Qur'an and Hadith. For example:

> In the twelfth chapter of the book of revelation there is mention of the struggle between the Zionist-Crusader beast,[26] which rule the earth in its entirety, on one side, and the Islamic community, which is bringing forth in suffering with the birth pains [on the other]. Those [Zionist-Crusaders] wish to stop the birth or kill the expected child after its birth before it can grow and strengthen. The expected child is the Islamic revival or the Mahdi, and with him the Islamic youth foundation and the Afghan fighting army, because together they are a tool and basis for the establishment of the rightly guided Islamic caliphate a second time.[27]

We can compare this with those Christian writers who see the seventh horn of the beast as being Islam, which is hostile to Jews and to Christians.[28] Both Christian and Muslim writers see eventual victory for 'their' side. The point here is not to ask who, if anyone, is right about what the images in Revelation may stand for, but that we see how both Muslims and Christians make sense of current international tensions by seeing them as predicted in the Scriptures. Both want to believe that God is on their side, and that he will soon send a deliverer to conquer all their enemies. They are reacting to the same set of historical events, but looking at them from very different perspectives.

Ida's Story: Maybe We Are All the Same

When I started to think about Muslim expectations of deliverers, I asked my colleague, Dr Shirin Shafaie, to help me find Shi'ite writings about Imam Mahdi. Together, we discussed some of the ideas in this chapter, and thought about the question with which it starts: what makes people long for a deliverer? Shirin made this observation:

> 'People yearn for justice and deliverance regardless of their specific faith or religion. However, their messianic traditions develop in accordance with the cultural and religious material and persona that are available to them. At heart, Shi'ahs, Sunnis,

---

26. That is, the Jewish state and the Western powers that support it.

27. B. M. Abdallah, *Zilzāl al-arḍ al-'aẓīm fī al-Qur'ān al-Karīm wa-al-sunnah wa-al-Injīl wa-al-'Ahd al-Qadīm* (Cairo: n.p.,1991), 414; cited in Cook, *Contemporary Muslim Apocalyptic Literature*, 198.

28. For example, Smith, *Islam: The Cloak of the Antichrist*, 123–133.

Christians and Jews seem to be yearning for the same kind of justice, and due to similar situations (human condition in the world), even if expressed in different or even oppositional terms.'

To Think About

Read again Zechariah's song in Luke 1:68–79 and Simeon's song in Luke 2:29–32.

How do these songs give meaning to life and to death? In what ways do they express longings and expectations similar to those of the Christians in your community?

Where can you see in these songs, and in yourself, longings and expectations that are similar to those expressed by Muslims in today's world?

How has this chapter helped you to understand the hopes that would have been in the minds of the first readers of Luke's gospel when, just before the transfiguration, they read, 'I tell you truly, there are some standing here who will not taste death until they see the kingdom of God' (Luke 9:27)?

6

Jesus

For we did not follow cleverly devised myths when we made known to you the power and coming of our Lord Jesus Christ, but we were eyewitnesses of his majesty. For when he received honour and glory from God the Father, and the voice was borne to him by the Majestic Glory, 'This is my beloved Son, with whom I am well pleased', we ourselves heard this very voice borne from heaven, for we were with him on the holy mountain (2 Pet 1:16–18).

Right at the centre of each Synoptic Gospel, the transfiguration gives the disciples – and us – a glimpse of the answer to the question that the Gospels are written to answer: *who is Jesus?* Luke prepares his readers for this through the first half of his ninth chapter. We have just read about a series of spectacular miracles: Jesus has stilled a storm, cast out a legion of demons, healed an unclean woman through a touch in the crowd, and raised a dead girl (Luke 8:22–56). So we come to Luke 9, and move towards the Mount of Transfiguration.

Preparing to Go Up the Mountain

Preparing with the Disciples in Mind

The disciples were first-century Jews whose understanding of the world was based on the prophets like Moses and Elijah; and they lived in the world of longing and expectancy that we explored in the last chapter. We can imagine the longings and expectations in their minds. We can imagine their search for hope and meaning in the midst of the Roman occupation. Perhaps there was a disciple who saw the Romans as the apocalyptic enemy to be fought. Perhaps there was a disciple who believed that God's promises meant that fighting was unnecessary. Perhaps there was a disciple who lamented the sins of Israel every day. Perhaps there was a disciple who was hoping to lay down his life for the freedom of the Jewish people. What hopes might the miracles of Luke 8 have stirred in them!

To Think About

Imagine that you are with the disciples, and share their longings and expectations. Read slowly through Luke 9:1–37. What makes you hopeful? What makes you excited? What puzzles you?

Preparing with Muslims in Mind

Muslim readers are not likely to find Luke 8 very surprising, because the Qur'an tells them that Jesus healed people and raised the dead. It does not record him stilling a storm, but it does have him making birds out of clay and then breathing life into them so that they fly away (Surah 3. 49; 5. 110). However, it insists that Jesus did all this by God's permission, which implies that he did not have power and authority in himself. The Qur'an then gives its own answers to the question, 'Who is Jesus?'

> In God's eyes Jesus is just like Adam: He created him from dust and said to him, 'Be', and he was (Surah 3. 59).[1]

> The Messiah, Jesus, son of Mary, was nothing more than a messenger of God, His word, conveyed to Mary, a spirit from Him (Surah 4. 171).[2]

Muslims see these answers as putting Jesus on the same level as all the other prophets. However, the titles of Messiah, Word and Spirit are unique to Jesus; the virgin birth that leads to the idea that Jesus is like Adam also makes him special; and no other prophet is said to have performed such miracles. The Qur'an raises questions about Jesus at the same time as it gives answers about him.

---

1. M. A. S. Abdel Haleem, *The Qur'an: A New Translation by M. A. S. Abdel Haleem* (Oxford: Oxford University Press, 2008), Used with permission.
2. Ibid.

> **To Think About**
>
> Ask a Muslim friend what they know about Jesus' miracles. What do they think of the miracles recorded in Luke 8:22–56?

Luke 8 might fit the qur'anic view of Jesus' miracles, but Luke 9 challenges it. In verses 1–6, Jesus gives the disciples authority to heal and to cast out demons. If Jesus can give authority to others, he has authority in himself, and is not just doing miracles 'by the permission of God'. Muslim readers will understand why Herod was so puzzled (Luke 9:7–9): he could cope with the idea of a healer, but he was amazed at someone who had the authority to give others healing power. Herod was the king, so he knew what authority was about. He knew that only someone who has authority in himself can give others authority. Who is this Jesus?

Verses 10–17 tell the story of the feeding of the five thousand. The Qur'an tells us that Jesus asked God to send a table of food from heaven at the request of his disciples (Surah 5. 112–115), and that God sent it. The feeding of the five thousand could be the event to which the Qur'an refers;[3] but the food does not come down from heaven. The bread and the fish are multiplied in Jesus' own hands. Who is this man?

Verses 18–22 raise the question about Jesus' identity, and the disciples give very Islamic answers. Jesus asks, 'Who do the crowds say that I am?' Any Muslim crowd would have the same answer as the first-century Jewish crowd: Jesus was one of the prophets. Jesus then asks, 'Who do you say that I am?' The Qur'an would agree with Peter's answer: Jesus was the Messiah. When Jesus says that he is going to die on the cross (vv. 21–22), most Muslims would answer like Peter in Matthew 16:22. God would not let his Messiah die at the hands of his enemies. However, the call to the disciples to be ready to die for their faith is something that Muslims can understand. They agree that Jesus was such an obedient servant of God that he was willing to die if God willed that for him; and they agree that believers should be prepared for martyrdom if necessary.

For Muslim readers, as for the disciples and the first Gospel readers, the events recorded in Luke 9:1–37 raise the questions, 'Who is Jesus? What

---

3. It is also possible that it refers to the Last Supper and hence to Holy Communion.

does it mean that he is the Messiah?' The transfiguration gives the Gospels' answers; and they are different from the answers that Islam gives.

Looking at the Structure of the Passage

Each of the Synoptic Gospels sets the transfiguration at the centre of a much longer passage; and all have similar incidents arranged in a similar order. Here it is, set out as a chiasmus:

> **A** Who is Jesus? (Luke 9:18–20 / Matt 16:13–16 / Mark 8:27–30): Peter's confession that he is the Messiah (Luke 9:20b / Matt 16:16 / Mark 8:29)
>> **B** Jesus predicts his sufferings (Luke 9:21–22 / Matt 16:21 / Mark 8:31); the call to all to 'take up the cross' (Luke 9:23–26 / Matt 16:24 / Mark 8:34–38)
>>> **C** No one here will die before seeing the kingdom of God (Luke 9:27 / Matt 16:28 / Mark 9:1)
>>>> **D** Transfiguration (Luke 9:28–36 / Matt 17:1–8 / Mark 9:2–8)
>>> **C'** The healing of the boy with the unclean spirit (Luke 9:37–43 / Matt 17:14–18 / Mark 9:17–27)
>> **B'** Jesus predicts his sufferings (Luke 9:44–45 / Matt 17:22–23 / Mark 9:31)
> **A'** Who is the greatest? (Luke 9:46–48 / Matt 18:1–5[4] / Mark 9:33–37)

Section A sets the question about Jesus. In the quiet that falls after all the well-fed people have left, the disciples come close to Jesus. He asks them who the crowds say that he is. Apparently, they think that he is Elijah or another prophet. 'But who do you say that I am?' Jesus asks next. The question that the transfiguration is about to answer is the one that Jesus himself raises: who is he? We can imagine the tension as the disciples look at each other, and Peter voices the wonderful answer that they have all been hoping for: 'The Christ [Messiah] of God' (Luke 9:20). He is not just a prophet, but the expected King! But what does this mean?

Section B explores the question about Jesus in view of Peter's answer. What do we expect to come after this affirmation that Jesus is the one for

---

4. Matthew inserts the story of the temple tax before introducing this question, and when he gets to this question he deals with it differently (Matt 17:24 – 18:5). However, it is the same question!

whom everyone has been waiting? Will he now lead them to free Israel? No wonder the disciples are shocked when the next thing is Jesus telling them not only that he will suffer, but also that they will have to suffer if they follow him! What *he* means by 'Messiah' is obviously different from what *they* mean by 'Messiah', which is not surprising in view of what we know of the Jewish expectations of the time. They have the right title for Jesus, but they still don't really know who he is. The transfiguration can be seen as God's own visual explanation.

Section C prepares the disciples for what is coming. Jesus reminds them of the coming of 'the Son of Man' in Daniel 7, and tells them that some will see 'the Son of Man coming in his kingdom' (Matt 16:28), 'the kingdom of God . . . come with power' (Mark 9:1) or 'the kingdom of God' (Luke 9:27). Contrary to what Christians often suppose, it sounds as if the coming kingdom and power are imminent: something is going to happen that the disciples themselves are going to see.[5]

What they see next is the transfiguration (D), followed by the healing of a boy with an unclean spirit (C'). The structure of the passage as we have analysed it above puts the healing story in a parallel position to Jesus' announcement of the coming kingdom. This suggests that the healing is part of the answer to the question 'Who is Jesus?'

We are now prepared to look at the transfiguration itself and to see how it answers this question in actions, in words, and in the way that it deals with Elijah and Moses. We will also begin to explore the implications of the different answers that are found in Islam.

The Mountain and the Glory: The Answer in Actions

The transfiguration is a picture of who Jesus is. We will try to explain it, but an explanation can never replace a picture. The best way to appreciate a picture is to spend time looking at it, and we encourage you, reader, to spend time contemplating the transfiguration story, keeping in mind all that you have learned about Elijah, about Moses, about mountains and about messianic expectations.

The disciples who were present did not really understand it until later (and they did understand it later – see 2 Peter 1:16–18), but Jesus understood

---

5. For an argument that not only this but all of Jesus' 'apocalyptic' teaching can be seen as referring to his first coming and to the fall of Jerusalem in AD 70, see Wright, *Jesus and the Victory of God*.

it, and the disciples must have begun to realize that he was even more special than they had thought. They would have seen the dazzling light, the cloud, the voice of God – all of which would have reminded them of Moses and Elijah's experiences on Mount Sinai, the place of the awesome presence of God. Following our studies in the last two chapters, we can see the implication that, above all, *the transfiguration is about the coming of God.* This Messiah brings not political freedom, but something much greater.

Commentators puzzle over the fact that Elijah was not expected as the forerunner of the Messiah, but as the forerunner of God (see chapter 5). The Gospels, they suppose, present him as the forerunner of the Messiah, and not as the forerunner of God. The transfiguration can solve their problem: it points us to the fact that the coming of the Messiah *is* the coming of God. It gives us a glimpse of the incarnation: the Messiah is not merely a king or a prophet, but God with us.

What Moses and Elijah see on Sinai is described as the glory of God; so another way of looking at the transfiguration is seeing it as a glimpse of that glory breaking through into the everyday world. Commentators discuss whether it is a preview of Jesus' resurrection and ascension, and how far it is also a preview of the resurrection glory for which all believers can hope. Some suggest that this is not only a preview of things to come, but a revelation of what actually *is*: it strips back the veils of time and human perception and shows the watching disciples the reality of Jesus. In Jesus, they have the glory of God among them. The transfiguration grants to those who were there and to those who read about it the experience of what John 1:1–18 says in words: 'And the Word became flesh and dwelt among us, and we have seen his glory, glory as of the only Son from the Father, full of grace and truth' (v. 14).

Christians have understood this from the earliest times. There is an ancient tradition of seeing the Holy Trinity as present at the transfiguration: the voice of the Father, the glory of the Son, and the Holy Spirit as the bright cloud.[6] Icons show Jesus on the mountain surrounded by an oval which represents the cloud and therefore the Holy Spirit. On the oval can be seen overlapping triangles, which represent the voice of God. The painters are

---

6. For example, Origen (died AD 254) in M. Simonetti, ed., *Matthew 14 – 28* (Ancient Christian Commentary on Scripture: New Testament vol. 1b; Downers Grove: IVP Academic, 2002), 55; and St Ambrose (died AD 397) in A. A. Just, ed., *Luke* (Ancient Christian Commentary on Scripture: New Testament vol. 3; Downers Grove: IVP Academic, 2003), 161.

bringing to our attention what Peter, James and John were surely meant to glimpse on that mountain: God was there.

Icon of the Transfiguration by Theophanes the Greek, early 15th century tempera on wood, located in the Tretyakov Gallery in Moscow.

Luke's gospel does not quite leave the glory of the transfiguration behind when Jesus comes down the mountain. Just before, in 9:26 (section C), Jesus spoke of his coming in glory. Afterwards, in verse 43 (section C'), people got to see something of this glory in the healing of the boy with the unclean spirit. People 'were astonished at the majesty of God' (9:42). All the Synoptic Gospels show us that Jesus as Messiah is the anointed King, and that his dominion is over the demonic forces which human beings themselves cannot master. Luke emphasizes that the actions of Jesus here proclaim the presence of God.

Islam denies this aspect of the transfiguration. As we began to see in our thinking about Moses, in Islamic thinking, God is simply too transcendent to come in this way. The incarnation is impossible and Jesus remains just a man.

A Shi'ite website quotes the following words:

> Allāh cannot be described as incarnate, for that would mean the combination of the self-existing with what is not self-existing and that is impossible.
>
> Allāh does not have a child or a wife for it has been proved that He is not in need of anyone else. Further all that is besides Him is not Self-Existing. Then how can a non-self-existing being become self-existing? The Holy Qur'an says: There is not anything like Him. Jesus is like Adam. Allāh created him from clay.[7]

However, that does not stop Muslims longing for God's presence.

The Face of God

'O God! O God! O God! We ask that Thou wilt turn away our faces from any other goal than Thyself and grant us to gaze towards Thy noble face until we see Thee in everything.' (A Muslim prayer[8])

'What do your people believe about the "face of God"?' I asked my Sufi friend. 'We want to see it!' she answered. She explained that she and other Sufis like her think that they can see the face of God if they look at their pir's (Sufi leader's) face, then remember it and meditate on it.

---

7. 'Non-incarnation' and 'Absolute': articles by Shaykh Tusi (385–460 AH) on 'Monotheism', 'Tenets of Islam', http://www.al-islam.org/gallery/kids/Books/tenets/monotheism.htm; accessed October 2014.

8. Prayer from the prayer manual of Muhammad Uthmanal-Mirghani (died 1853), quoted in C. Padwick, *Muslim Devotions*, 2nd ed. (Oxford: Oneworld, 1996), 62.

To Think About

Do you want to see the face of God? What does it mean to you that God has actually come to live among human beings in Jesus? How does this study of the transfiguration help you to pray for your Muslim friends?

'This is My Son': The Answer in Words

Personally answering the question of who Jesus is comes God's voice from heaven: 'This is my Son, my Chosen One' (Luke 9:35). This is the climax of the transfiguration story, given similarly in the other accounts: 'This is my beloved Son with whom I am well pleased' (Matt 17:5); 'This is my beloved Son' (Mark 9:7). All three continue, 'Listen to him!' As the title 'Son of God' is considered so objectionable by Muslims, it is worth taking some time here to think about what it means and what it does not mean.

Most importantly, it does *not* mean what the Qur'an fears that it might mean. The Qur'an's use of words is a clue. In Arabic, there are two words for 'son'. *Walad* has a root meaning of physical birth, and is used only of a person's physical son. *Ibn* is often used for a physical son, but can also be used metaphorically, even in the Qur'an (Surah 2. 215). The Qur'an has some very strong denials that God can have a son, and contains strong condemnations of people who call Jesus 'Son of God':

> Say, 'He is God the One, God the eternal. He begot no one nor was He begotten. No one is comparable to Him' (Surah 112. 1–4).[9]

> . . . it would not befit God to have a child. He is far above that: when He decrees something, He says only, 'Be,' and it is (19. 35).[10]

> The disbelievers say, 'The Lord of Mercy has offspring.' How terrible is this thing you assert: it almost causes the heavens to be torn apart, the earth to split asunder, the mountains to crumble to pieces, that they attribute offspring to the Lord of Mercy. It does not befit the Lord of Mercy [to have offspring] (19. 88–92).[11]

---

9. M. A. S. Abdel Haleem, *The Qur'an: A New Translation by M. A. S. Abdel Haleem* (Oxford: Oxford University Press, 2008), Used with permission.
10. Ibid.
11. Ibid.

People of the Book, do not go to excess in your religion, and do not say anything about God except the truth: the Messiah, Jesus, son of Mary, was nothing more than a messenger of God, His word, directed to Mary, a spirit from Him. So believe in God and His messengers and do not speak of a 'Trinity' – stop [this], that is better for you – God is only one God, He is far above having a son, everything in the heavens and earth belongs to Him and He is the best one to trust (4. 171).[12]

It is important that all these verses use the words related to *walad* and not *ibn*. The only place where *ibn* is used in a denial about Jesus is in Surah 9. 30: 'The Jews said, "Ezra is the son of God," and the Christians said, "The Messiah is the son of God": they said this with their own mouths, repeating what earlier disbelievers had said. May God confound them! How far astray they have been led!'[13]

We can see that the Qur'an's major concern is that people should not suppose that God could have had sexual relations of some kind with Mary and so have physically fathered a son. This sort of idea would have been equally repugnant to the New Testament writers, and should be so to all Christians.

What, then, *does* the New Testament mean when it calls Jesus God's Son? The disciples at the transfiguration and the first gospel readers would probably have understood it as another way of describing the Messiah, God's anointed one. In 2 Samuel 7:12–16, God makes a promise regarding David's son, who will build the temple: 'I will be to him a father, and he shall be to me a son. When he commits iniquity, I will discipline him with the rod of men . . . but my steadfast love will not depart from him' (vv. 14–15). This would apply not only to Solomon, but to a line of kings descended from David; and this kingdom, like God's love, would last for ever. It was on this promise that the expectation of the Messiah was built. From then on, the king was from time to time called God's son (e.g. Ps 2:7; 89:26–27). 'Son of God' is therefore a Davidic kingly title, and Jesus is a very special Davidic king.

Here at the transfiguration (as at Jesus' baptism), the heavenly voice tells the disciples that Jesus is the son who is, like Solomon, chosen and beloved. It tells us one more important thing: God is pleased with him. Solomon did wrong and had to be disciplined, and so did all the kings after him. Jesus is

---

12. M. A. S. Abdel Haleem, *The Qur'an: A New Translation by M. A. S. Abdel Haleem* (Oxford: Oxford University Press, 2008), Used with permission.
13. Ibid.

the only anointed king who does not have to be disciplined, because he does only what pleases his Father.

God had another 'son' in Old Testament writings: Israel. For example, Matthew 2:15 quotes Hosea 11:1: 'Out of Egypt I called my son.' Hosea is speaking of Israel and referring to the exodus. He is doubtless thinking of what God said to Moses in Exodus 4:22–23: 'Then you shall say to Pharaoh, "Thus says the LORD, Israel is my firstborn son, and I say to you, 'Let my son go that he may serve me.' If you refuse to let him go, behold, I will kill your firstborn son."'

Jesus as the pleasing 'Son of God' is, then, not only the king who needs no discipline, but also the representative of Israel. The Hosea 11 passage goes on to bewail Israel's sin and to affirm God's love for his son despite his sin (Hos 11:8): 'How can I give you up, O Ephraim? How can I hand you over, O Israel? How can I make you like Admah? How can I treat you like Zeboiim? My heart recoils within me; my compassion grows warm and tender.' Again, Jesus is the son who pleases God and has no sin. Peter, James and John probably did not think of this idea of Jesus' sonship at the time of the transfiguration, but it was certainly understood by the time Matthew wrote his gospel.

As we can see from Acts and the Epistles, the title 'Son' gained more meaning after the resurrection, as the early Christians reflected on all that they knew and had experienced of Jesus. Hebrews explains who the Son is in terms that reflect the insights in John 1:1–18: 'You, Lord, laid the foundation of the earth in the beginning, and the heavens are the work of your hands' (Heb 1:10). Jesus did not become the Son of God when he was conceived in Mary's womb or when he was born in Bethlehem. Rather, he has always been the Son of God, as he has always been the Word of God, and that Son has come to us. We are back again to God's presence among us in Jesus, and to the transfiguration as a glimpse of his glory.

This is important and needs explaining to Muslim friends. Jesus is not called 'Son of God' because he had no human father. He has been 'Son of God' from eternity: 'You loved me before the foundation of the world,' Jesus says to his Father (John 17:24). It is because he was already the Son of God that he came into this world through a virgin birth.

Muslims reverse the transfiguration by rejecting the message of the divine voice: 'This is my Son.' This is a huge loss for them. It means that they lose the meaning of the title 'Messiah'; the Qur'an would agree with Peter and call Jesus 'Messiah', but it gives no clue as to what this name means. They also lose the story of Jesus' fulfilment of all for which Israel was called; the Qur'an speaks of the prophets sent to Israel, but not of God's plan of blessing all the nations and bringing salvation through his chosen people. Finally, the Qur'an is right in its denial that Jesus is God's physical son, but its emphasis on this usually means that Muslims and Christians waste a lot of time discussing how a human being can be God. That is the wrong question; the right question is how the eternal Word and Son of God could come to us as a human being. Muslims have lost the divinity of Jesus.

Ida's Story

I was thrilled when my Muslim friend started to read Luke's gospel. I so wanted her to get to know Jesus! But she had only been reading a short time when she threw the book down and said, 'This is a bad book! I can't read it!' 'Why?' I asked. She pointed to Luke 1:35. The words 'Son of God' reminded her of Qur'an 19:88–92 (quoted above). I tried to explain that the word for 'son' in the Qur'an implied a physical union between God and Mary, and that that was just as horrifying to me as it was to her, and that Luke didn't mean that at all; but nothing I said could persuade her to pick up the gospel again.

How can Muslims who have such a strong objection to the phrase 'Son of God' be introduced to Jesus? Some Christians have recommended changing the phrase to words that imply sonship, but do not actually say 'son' – for example, 'God's uniquely beloved one' – in translations for Islamic contexts. There has been a huge debate about this, and I have been part of a review panel to try to settle the question.[14] I have had in my mind both my friend's reaction to Luke's gospel and Luke's account of the transfiguration: 'This is my . . .: listen to him!' Jesus, says God, is in a different category from Moses or Elijah.

The review panel decided that the Greek *huios*, usually translated into English as 'son', should always be translated by a word or words that have the direct meaning 'son'. They also suggested that, if necessary, an adjective might be added, such as 'eternal Son', which would help the reader to understand that Jesus has been God's Son from the beginning. They recommended using explanatory footnotes.

---

14. The World Evangelical Alliance's panel on the translation of divine filial language. The panel's report (April 2013) can be found at http://www.worldea.org/images/wimg/files/2013_0429-Final%20Report%20of%20the%20WEA%20Independent%20Bible%20Translation%20Review%20Panel.pdf.

Some translators have chosen to use the Arabic *ibn* even in non-Arabic languages. Others have chosen an unusual word – for example, an old word that is seldom used, or a word that applies only to a king's son – to make the point that Jesus' sonship is different from ordinary human sonship.

To Think About

What word is used to translate huios in Luke 1:35 in your language? Are there other words that mean 'son' in that language? If you had the job of explaining the verse for Muslims in a footnote, what might you write?

Moses and Elijah: The Answer about the Prophets

'The commentators might not understand why Peter wanted to make huts for Moses and Elijah and Jesus, but we can,' said a Sufi friend. 'Our people are always building places for holy people, especially around their tombs, and they had no tomb for either Moses or Elijah. We want to keep the presence of those holy people, and to visit them to get their blessing.'

There are other things that could have been in Peter's mind. Perhaps he was practising the important Jewish virtue of hospitality, saying, 'It is a good thing that you brought us so that we can make places for you and your visitors to stay in.' Perhaps he simply thought that this was a wonderful event, and he wanted to make it last longer. The Gospels tell us that Peter himself did not know what he was saying. However, since all the Synoptic Gospels record it, it must be significant. Peter's words symbolize the mistaken idea that Jesus is basically the same as Moses and Elijah. In response, God glorifies and affirms his Son, while the law-giver and the zealous prophet recede from view. What, then, does the transfiguration tell us about how Jesus relates to Moses and the law, and to Elijah and the prophets?[15]

---

15. For a detailed discussion of how the Gospels present Jesus as being in the line of the various Old Testament prophets, and of how that relates to the expectations of the Jews of his time, see Wright, *Jesus and the Victory of God*, ch. 5.

Moses: The Prophet Who Gives the Law

Matthew is the Synoptic Gospel which most clearly presents Jesus as fulfilling the ministry of Moses – as the 'prophet like Moses' of Deuteronomy 18:18. Luke only mentions Moses by name in the transfiguration, but he has already put the idea of Moses into the mind of the reader. It is Herod who first asks the question, 'Who is Jesus?' and who asks whether he might be John the Baptist, Elijah or one of the previous prophets (Luke 9:7–9). The phrase 'one of the prophets of old' would immediately suggest that Jesus might be 'the prophet like Moses' who was to come. It is significant that Luke next tells of the feeding of the five thousand. As becomes very clear in John's gospel (John 6:31–33), Jesus' miraculous gift of bread to hungry people reminded everyone of the miraculous gift of manna to hungry people through Moses. While Herod asks specifically whether Jesus is Elijah, it is this miracle that raises the question of whether Jesus might be Moses.

In Matthew, Jesus is often presented more explicitly as the second Moses. Moses was born in Egypt and escaped with his life when Pharaoh ordered the killing of baby boys. In Matthew 2, Jesus is taken to Egypt as an infant in order to escape from Herod's slaughter of baby boys. Like Moses, Jesus is prepared in the wilderness for his ministry, and he deals with the temptations by quoting the laws of Moses in Deuteronomy (Deut 8:3; 6:16, 13). One of the temptations is to make bread in the wilderness – just as God gave manna to the Jews under Moses' leadership. Just as Moses went up a mountain to receive the law, so Jesus then goes up a mountain to teach his own interpretation of Moses' law (Matt 5 – 7).

So it is not surprising that Matthew's account of the transfiguration emphasizes the parallels with Moses' ascents of Sinai in Exodus 19 – 34. Though they appear subtle, these different emphases in Matthew and Luke are real and noteworthy. The very word *metamorphothe*, 'transfigured', used by Matthew but not by Luke, would have reminded Matthew's Jewish readers of Moses. Philo, in his *Life of Moses*, not only describes Moses' shining appearance on Sinai in detail (14:70), but also uses the word 'transfigured' to describe what happened to Moses at the burning bush (he was 'transfigured into a prophet' *Life of Moses* 1:57), and what happened to him at the end of his life:

> And some time afterwards, when he was about to depart from hence to heaven, to take up his abode there, and leaving this mortal life to become immortal, having been summoned by

the Father, *who now transfigured him*, having previously been a double being, composed of soul and body, into the nature of a single body, transforming him wholly and entirely into a most sun-like mind . . . (*Life of Moses* 51: 288, emphasis added).

The 'six days' of Matthew 17:1 (compared with the 'about eight days' of Luke 9:28) remind the reader of that part of Exodus when Moses and Joshua had gone up Sinai, leaving Aaron and Hur to wait at the foot of the mountain with the Israelites: 'Moses went up on the mountain, and the cloud covered the mountain. The glory of the LORD dwelt on Mount Sinai, and the cloud covered it for six days. And on the seventh day he called to Moses out of the midst of the cloud' (Exod 24:15–16).

We then find that Matthew's gaze is on Jesus' shining face and clothes, the brightness of the cloud and the fear of the watching disciples, reminding him of the brightness and the cloud around Moses and the awesome sights seen by the watching Israelites. But here it is Jesus, and not Moses, who has the shining face. Moses just 'appears', and is not alone, but rather shares the honour with another prophet, Elijah. Matthew does not even make Luke's observation that Moses and Elijah appear 'in glory' (Luke 9:31). And this time, Moses does not come down the mountain with the law and a shining face: he disappears, and it is Jesus who comes down the mountain to confront the faithlessness of his people.

The message is clear: Jesus is not only different from Moses, he is also greater than Moses. There seems to be a sense in which Jesus has replaced him. The key question is, in what sense does Jesus replace Moses? What aspects of the Mosaic law does he fulfil? And how do followers of Jesus now deal with the law? These are questions that are thoroughly explored in the New Testament, particularly in Romans, Galatians and Hebrews; and they have been discussed by Christian theologians ever since. We will not go into detail here, but note that these are very important questions when thinking about Islam, and we will pick them up when we look at Islam as a religion of the shariah in part 3.

> ## To Think About
>
> I have not checked the validity of the ways and wonts of
>   Islamic law
>
> Except this, that the denier of love is an infidel and a heathen.
>
> (Muhammad Iqbal[16])
>
> When Matthew's gospel refers to Moses again it is in the context of Jesus'
> discussions with the religious leaders about the Mosaic law – about the
> purpose of the divorce laws in 19:3–9, and about how the scribes and
> Pharisees misinterpret the law and practise it wrongly in chapter 23.
> Clearly, such questions are still important, even after the transfiguration
>
> What does Matthew 19:3–9 say is the purpose of particular laws about how
> we relate to people? How can we follow that purpose as followers of Jesus?
>
> According to Matthew 23, what was wrong with the scribes' and
> Pharisees' treatment of the law? How can followers of Jesus treat the law
> rightly rather than ignoring it?
>
> Would your Muslim friends agree with what Pakistan's most famous
> poet, Muhammad Iqbal, says about the purpose of the law (quoted
> above)? What do they think of the way in which their religious leaders
> treat the shariah law today?

Elijah: The Zealous Prophet Who Confronts Law-Breaking

Luke is the gospel that has the most references and allusions to Elijah. There
are also allusions to Elisha: we noted that the Elijah story is not complete
without the Elisha story, so it is not surprising that both are referred to in
Luke. The Elijah–Elisha theme is explicit in the very important passage
in Luke 4:16–29 that we considered earlier in this book. Let us consider it
again as we ask, 'What is the transfiguration saying about how Jesus relates
to Elijah?'

Jesus has just returned to Nazareth after the wilderness temptations,
and he announces his ministry. He begins by reading a passage from Isaiah

---

16. From part 2 of *Zabūr-i-'Ajam* in *Kulliyat-i-Iqbal* (Lahore: Iqbal Academy, 1990), 410–11.
Quoted in *Iqbal Quarterly* 6, nos 3–4 (2006).

(61:1–2) which is about the end-time salvation of Zion; but just before the tender verse of comfort for Zion begins – '. . . to grant to those who mourn in Zion – to give them a beautiful headdress instead of ashes, the oil of gladness instead of mourning . . .' – Jesus rolls up the scroll and sits down. With everyone staring at him, he declares the fulfilment of the passage. He refers to Elijah and Elisha, deliberately choosing one incident from each of their lives. Both incidents concern miraculous healings of non-Israelites – in fact, of people who were Israel's enemies. The widow of Zarephath lived in the land of the Baal worshippers who were soon to be destroyed on Carmel, and Naaman was not only a Syrian but actually the commander of the army that had defeated Israel. The people react with the first attempt to kill Jesus recorded in Luke's gospel, and 'all in the synagogue were filled with wrath' (4:28).

This passage must have both excited and challenged Luke's first readers, and must have raised for them the question, 'Who is this Jesus?' The Isaiah passage suggests that he is the Messiah, but the references to Elijah and Elisha suggest that he is also going to follow the pattern of their ministries. At the same time, there is something very different here. Most obviously, there is a shift from the focus on ministry to Israel towards a concern for people of other nations, which would have been very good news for Luke's largely Gentile readers. But there is also a question about what sort of Messiah this might be. There is no mention of the judgement or the battles linked with the Elijah and Elisha stories: there is only mention of people who were healed, and both of those were Israel's enemies.

The idea that Jesus is like Elijah and Elisha, but also not like them, continues throughout Luke. For example, Elijah and Elisha are, with Moses, the miracle-working prophets, and some of Jesus' miracles recall their miracles. In Luke, the raising of the widow of Nain's son (7:11–17) mirrors Elijah's raising of a widow's son (1 Kgs 17:17–24); indeed, the phrase 'the dead man sat up and began to speak, and Jesus gave him to his mother' (Luke 7:15) uses the exact words of the Septuagint translation of 1 Kings 17:23. The feeding of the five thousand in Luke 9:10–17 mirrors Elisha's feeding miracle of 2 Kings 4:42–44. However, although Jesus announces judgement and calls for repentance as did Elijah, he neither competes with nor destroys his opponents. He is indeed like Elijah in his challenge to the powerful and in his ministry to the poor, but his zeal is directed differently. So it is not surprising that people continue to ask about Elijah as they consider Jesus all the way to the cross and even as he dies: some spectators expected Elijah to appear as the sky darkened that afternoon (Mark 15:36). Their words were deeper than they realized, for Jesus did fulfil Elijah's ministry by going all the way to the cross.

Luke 9, the chapter which has the transfiguration at its centre, includes many allusions to Elijah. We have seen how the first part of the chapter raises the question of how Jesus relates to Elijah. The transfiguration itself shows that Jesus is greater than Elijah and different from Elijah. In chapter 13, we will see how the rest of the chapter shows how Jesus transforms Elijah's zeal, especially in verses 51–56, when he rebukes the disciples for suggesting that they should bring down fire from heaven on the Samaritans. Elijah is the only prophet who literally called down fire from heaven, and it was Samaritans who were destroyed by it (2 Kgs 1). If Jesus is like Moses in bringing heavenly bread, he is like Elijah in bringing heavenly fire only inasmuch as the second part of Luke's writing tells of a different kind of heavenly fire, 'tongues as of fire', which come upon the disciples at Pentecost (Acts 2:3). This is not a fire that brings destruction, but a fire that brings the power of the gospel to save three thousand people in one day.

The question here is, 'How did Jesus deal with evil?' Elijah was dealing with the evil of idolatry in Israel, while the disciples were dealing with the evil of rejecting Jesus. Elijah's zealous monotheism destroyed some of the idolaters, but it did not end idolatry. Jesus had not come to destroy people's lives, but to save them (Luke 9:55, margin).

To Think About

During his lifetime, people said that Jesus was Elijah or another one of the prophets. What did they mean?

'Jesus is my prophet,' said a Muslim friend. What did she mean?

We have said that Islam reverses the transfiguration and so takes us 'back' to Elijah and to Moses, and makes Jesus a prophet like them. Prophets are so important in Islam that they merit a whole chapter: we will explore what the Qur'an does with Elijah and with Moses in chapter 7.

Talking about the Exodus: Elijah, Moses and the Cross

In Matthew and Mark, the transfiguration follows a major disagreement between Peter and Jesus. Peter rejected the idea that Jesus would be shamefully rejected and killed. We can hear the heavenly voice settling the argument: it is Jesus, and not Peter, who is right about his coming death: 'Listen to him!' Luke does not tell us about Peter's disagreement, but he does tell us what Jesus was discussing with Moses and Elijah on the mountain: his departure, or 'exodus'. This is Luke's way of linking the transfiguration with Jesus' death on the cross. The cross features in sections B and B' of the transfiguration chiasmus, and Luke brings it into the central passage in this way.

We can, perhaps, imagine the discussion. We can imagine Moses and Elijah remembering their previous encounters with God's glory on Mount Sinai: Moses, agonizing over Israel's adultery with the golden calf at the very time when he was receiving instructions about the tabernacle, and begging God to continue with them; and Elijah, despairing over Israel's adultery with Baal and his own inability to make any difference. We can then imagine the conversation about 'departures'. 'I had to leave the earth without ever getting into the Promised Land,' says Moses. 'All my attempts to get Israel to keep the law failed, and I couldn't even keep it well enough myself to merit getting into the land. No wonder God turned down my offer of giving myself to be punished so that Israel could be forgiven [Exod 32:31–34]. I realize now that I just was not good enough.'

'You might have been disappointed if you had gone into the Promised Land,' says Elijah. 'I lived there, but the people were so sinful that God gave them a famine rather than the "milk and honey" that you were expecting. I had to go all the way to Sidon to get a good meal. In the end, I had to leave the land for my departure – going right back along the route that Joshua took when our people entered the land in the first place. All the miracles that God gave to me and to my pupil, Elisha, couldn't prevent the slide into sin that ended in exile.'

And what about Jesus? What did he tell them? The context of the conversations with the disciples gives the clue. His departure would be a shameful death caused by the leaders of the nation that had so disappointed Moses and Elijah; but that would not be the end, because he would be raised from death (Luke 9:22, 44; B and B'). He was the one who would fulfil all that Moses and Elijah longed for, by dealing with the problem that had beset Israel from the beginning: sin.

It is human sin that hinders God's presence among us; so, if the transfiguration is about the coming of God, it must also be about holiness and about dealing with evil. The heavenly voice assures us that Jesus is the one who pleases God: he alone has the goodness, the purity, the holiness to deal not only with the evil that beset Israel, but also with the evil that besets all the rest of the human race. In Genesis 6:6, we saw God responding to evil in pain: now, evil is to be dealt with on the cross.

Moses and Elijah go back to where they came from, and Jesus takes his disciples back down the mountain, where they immediately see a sight that illustrates Israel's plight. Luke focuses on this, while Matthew and Mark focus on the disciples' inability to deal with it. Israel is, we remember, God's son, but that son so often acts in a crazy way: he turns away from his father and runs after other gods; or he tries so hard to keep his father's law that he ends up by missing the most important parts; or he tears himself apart with sects and arguments. No wonder, as Jesus looks at the demon-possessed boy and hears the father's plea for his only son, that he, like Moses and Elijah, agonizes over his people: 'O faithless and twisted generation, how long am I to be with you and bear with you?' (Luke 9:41). The disciples are powerless to do anything, but Jesus can do what is needed. He rebukes the demon, heals the boy and gives him back to his father.

This is what Jesus will accomplish through his departure. He will deal with the powers of evil, he will restore people to their right minds, and he will present them to the heavenly Father. No wonder that the Father is pleased with him! No wonder that the people, even if they did not yet understand all this, were 'astonished at the majesty of God'!

To Think About

> For you have not come to what may be touched, a blazing fire and darkness and gloom and a tempest and the sound of a trumpet and a voice whose words made the hearers beg that no further messages be spoken to them. For they could not endure the order that was given, 'If even a beast touches the mountain, it shall be stoned.' Indeed, so terrifying was the sight that Moses said, I tremble with fear. But you have come to Mount Zion and to the city of the living God, the heavenly Jerusalem, and to innumerable angels in festal gathering, and to the assembly of the firstborn who are enrolled in heaven, and to God, the judge of all, and to the spirits of the righteous made perfect, and to Jesus, the mediator of a new covenant, and to the sprinkled blood that speaks a better word than the blood of Abel (Heb 12:18–24).

In what ways does the transfiguration point to how God will deal with the aspects of fallen human nature shown in the Cain and Abel story that we explored in chapter 1?

What implications does this have for your relationships with Muslims in your area?

Part 3

Islam

Ida (twenty years old, having read one book on Islam): Doesn't your faith teach that God is very high up and separate from us?

Fatimah (thoughtfully): Well, yes, I suppose that is what they teach us in religion lessons. But I know different, because I pray.

The transfiguration has pointed to Jesus as the presence of God, the face of God, the pain in the heart of God and, therefore, the one through whom all peoples can find salvation. This raises acute questions for the Christian trying to think about Islam. If Jesus is all this, they ask, what more could we need other than to understand, accept, preach and live this good news? What could any later 'prophet' who denied all this be but a false prophet? How could a religion be anything but false if it leads away from the transfiguration towards the perception of the Messiah as a great prophet who could not be permitted to suffer? And not only a false religion, but disastrous too, as it cuts out the cross and resurrection? Islam cuts salvation out of salvation history – and, in doing so, denies the fall and the need for salvation.

One of the main problems in 'thinking biblically about Islam' is that Muhammad lived so long after the completion of the Bible. This means, first, that the Bible says nothing directly about Islam; but then neither does it say anything directly about British politics, about the United Nations or about the computer which has been used to write this book, but there are still ways of applying biblical ideas to those areas of life. The second aspect of the problem is more serious: it is that Islam claims both that *it is* the faith of the Bible and that God has sent another revelation. Our study of the transfiguration has brought us to the point where we can recognize that, from a biblical point of view, another revelation is simply unnecessary. More than that, our study has highlighted how different Jesus and his work is from that of the other prophets – and the Qur'an removes those differences.

Can our studies, then, take us any further than lamenting the loss of Jesus in Islamic thinking? Can we develop any more positive a view of Muhammad than simply as a false prophet? Can we see good things in the Qur'an, in the shariah and in Muslim peoples? What might be *biblical* views of Islam as we see it in today's world? In this section, we will not attempt to answer these questions from the whole Bible, but to ask what we can learn from the Bible study that we have done so far. We hope that others will continue to examine the questions using all the other parts of the Bible.

Why do these questions matter? Why might we look for more positive assessments of a religion that cuts out the heart of the New Testament? There are three major reasons: first, quite simply, because we need to speak the truth; and there is much in Islam that agrees with parts of the Bible. We must not 'bear false witness against [our] neighbour' (Exod 20:16). This leads us to the second reason: we are not thinking about an abstract system, but about our neighbours in this world. Islam is the faith of many human beings, and Islam as we see it today has been developed by human beings over the centuries. As we have seen from our Genesis studies, although those human beings are fallen, they are also made in the image of God, so we can expect to find some truth in what they say and some good things in what they do. Third, we are called to relate to all peoples and to seek the salvation of all (2 Tim 2:10): therefore we need, practically, to seek both areas in which we can relate to Muslims and starting points for explaining the gospel.

7

Elijah and Moses in the Qur'an

The first two parts of this book gave two bases for biblical thinking about Islam. Part 1 explored the religious nature of human beings from Genesis 1 – 11. Muslims are human beings, which means that they are made in the image of God as well as being fallen. They are likely to seek God as well as to fight and kill (Gen 4), and to be struggling to deal with evil (Gen 6 – 9). We, as well as they, are fellows in the line of death of Genesis 5, but also in God's blessing of the peoples in Genesis 10. We, as well as they, are liable to use religion to build power for ourselves and our people (Gen 11). This means that we must not fall into the temptation of thinking 'Muslims = bad, Christians = good'. Our redemption in Christ should make a difference, but the unredeemed are still made in the image of God, and the redeemed still struggle with the results of the fall. Thus, in our thinking, we will try to remember that Christian thinkers and communities often get things wrong, and that Muslim thinkers and communities are likely to get some things right.

So far, we have separated 'thinking about Muslims' and 'thinking about Islam': it is now time to bring the two together. We cannot think about Islam without thinking about Muslims, because Islam is not a detached system of beliefs but a worldview and way of life developed by Muslim people. Muhammad was a human being; the first Muslims who recorded the Qur'an and the traditions about Muhammad were human beings; the caliphs who led the early conquests were human beings; the thinkers who developed Islamic philosophy, theology and law were human beings; and the variety of Islam that we see today represents centuries of human life, thought and action. In short, we can expect to find aspects of Islam that are in agreement with the Bible as well as aspects of Islam that are in disagreement with the Bible, not only because of the Qur'an's intent to build on the previous books, but also because the Muslims who have developed Islam are human beings.

Part 2 explored the transfiguration, suggesting that Islam effectively reverses all that the transfiguration symbolizes. It removes the cross to which the transfiguration points; it removes the sonship announced by the voice from heaven; it puts Jesus on a level with prophets like Moses and Elijah; and it puts the law and prophethood at the heart of its view of sacred history. In Islamic thinking, it is not Jesus who is the completion of God's revelation, but Muhammad. He is both a zealous prophet of monotheism like Elijah and a prophet like Moses who brings the law and establishes a people.

The transfiguration points to differences between the ways in which Islam and the Gospels see the fulfilment of all that Moses and Elijah stand for. However, it is important to recognize that the transfiguration does not reduce Moses and Elijah in stature or in significance. They may not be as great as Jesus, but they are great enough to appear with Jesus in glory. Insofar as Islam takes us back to Moses and Elijah, then, it takes us back to something good. Some Christians have so focused on God's grace in Christ that they have dismissed the law and the prophets as irrelevant; and some focus so much on the New Testament that they scarcely know the stories of Moses and Elijah, let alone the details of the Torah. The Qur'an sees itself as a reminder and a warning (Surah 6. 19, 51), and thinking about Islam can helpfully remind Christians of forgotten aspects of Moses and Elijah.

In chapter 3, for example, we saw how the Elijah story can warn us of straying from our calling as Christians: we need the warnings of the prophets. Later in part 3, our reflection on shariah will remind us of the importance of law for all humankind. Focus on the New Testament has led some Christians into individualism and others into separating themselves from political life: our reflection on the Muslim concept of *ummah* will remind us of the importance of community in the Bible as a whole, and of the resources offered by the Old Testament for dealing with political tensions.

However, it is not so simple as that outline may suggest: Islam does not simply take us back to the Old Testament. Moses and Elijah and all that they stand for were used in a particular situation and provided the basis for something that was different from qur'anic faith – as can be seen from the fact that it found its fulfilment in the transfiguration. Since then, Islam has developed to the maturity and variety we see today, with some of the best human minds being applied to it.

The Qur'an's versions of the Moses and Elijah stories may include much that is similar to the Bible's versions, but they also have huge omissions. Not surprisingly, the things that are omitted include the aspects of Moses and

Elijah that are fulfilled in the incarnation, death and resurrection of Jesus Christ. Every time we find something in Islamic thinking that agrees with the Bible, we will find that it is in a context that, from a Christian point of view, omits something very important. That is the tension in thinking biblically about Islam.

At the end of part 1, we studied some of the key similarities and differences between Muslim and Christian views of humanity by comparing the biblical and qur'anic stories of Adam and Eve, Cain and Abel, Noah, and Babel. We saw that the views of humanity are linked to ideas of what God is like, so it is not surprising that they affect ideas of how God acts in his world. In this chapter, we will look briefly at what is included and what is omitted in the qur'anic stories of Elijah and Moses as compared with the biblical stories. We will then be ready to think specifically about the Qur'an, about Muhammad, and about the political and legal dimensions of Islam.

Elijah

Elijah is mentioned in only two places in the Qur'an. In Surah 6. 85, he is simply mentioned by his Arabic name, Ilyas, in a list of other prophets. His story is told, very briefly, in the middle of Surah 37. Again, he is one in a list of prophets, but in this surah each name is accompanied by a short account of incidents from the prophet's life. Each prophet is then praised and blessed. Noah, Abraham, Isaac, Moses and Aaron, Lot, Elijah and then Jonah each in turn warn people who reject their messages. Here is the passage about Elijah:

> Elijah too was one of the messengers. He said to his people, 'Have you no fear of God? How can you invoke Baal and forsake the Most Gracious Creator, God, your Lord and the Lord of your forefathers?' but they rejected him. They will be brought to punishment as a consequence; not so the true servants of God. We let him be praised by succeeding generations: 'Peace be to Elijah!' This is how We reward those who do good: truly he was one of Our faithful servants (Surah 37. 123–132).[1]

This material clearly relates to the Kings account of Elijah. It offers a summary of what it sees to be the main points and omits all the details. It is interesting that the focus is similar to the one we found from our biblical

---

1. M. A. S. Abdel Haleem, *The Qur'an: A New Translation by M. A. S. Abdel Haleem* (Oxford: Oxford University Press, 2008), Used with permission.

study in chapter 3: the story is about God's dealings with Israel's idolatry, rather than about the peoples who had Baal as their god; and it is about Israel's response. There were some 'true servants of God', but most of Israel rejected Elijah's message and would, eventually, be judged. We saw that the power encounter on Carmel brought the Israelites to their knees, but that, except for the preserved seven thousand, the repentance was only temporary. It seems to have made little long-term impression on Ahab and to have but fuelled the hostility of Jezebel. The bow drawn 'at random' that struck Ahab (1 Kgs 22:34) and the horses trampling on Jezebel's corpse (2 Kgs 9:33) are graphic reminders that God's judgements on the royal house of Omri and on the people of Israel were only deferred rather than averted. However, here the qur'anic story ends, and we read that God 'let him be praised by succeeding generations . . . Peace be to Elias [Elijah]' (Surah 37. 129–30).[2]

The short qur'anic account underlines some important aspects of the biblical Elijah story. It affirms the zeal that confronts idolatry, the warnings of God's judgement and the call to Israel to repent. The Qur'an has a very clear conception of good and evil. Throughout, the hope is that the wicked will be brought to belief and obedience through its warnings and guidance. These are the channels it describes of God's mercy to human beings. In that sense, it can be seen as bringing a similar message to that of Elijah and to that of his successor, John the Baptist. Does that mean, then, that the Qur'an can function, as did John the Baptist, to prepare people to hear the gospel of Jesus Christ? Experience suggests not only that it can, but also that it sometimes does lead Muslims to long for the assurance of forgiveness that the gospel brings.

However, the qur'anic story omits much that points to Jesus and to the need for him. There is no mention of Elijah's flight from Jezebel, of his depression, of his meeting with God at Sinai, of the strange end to his life or of his return to earth. First, fearful and depressed, the biblical Elijah shows himself to be weak and wavering in faith. This underlines how great is the need for the redemption of all people, if even prophets like him depend on it. In Islamic thinking, the prophets are preserved from major sin, and it is highly unlikely that a prophet would run away frightened. This omission reflects the fact that few Muslims see the need for redemption. Second, Elijah's meeting with God reveals God not only as one who sends prophets, but also as one

---

2. M. A. S. Abdel Haleem, *The Qur'an: A New Translation by M. A. S. Abdel Haleem* (Oxford: Oxford University Press, 2008), Used with permission.

who comes to the world himself. In Islamic thinking, however, God is not the kind of being who could 'come' in this way. This omission points to the fact that Islam denies even the possibility of the incarnation.

Finally, Elijah's departure from the earth without dying and his prophesied return creates a sense of expectation in the Bible for him to come and prepare the way for the coming of God in the Messiah. Although there are Islamic traditions that reflect the idea of Elijah as a mysterious being who did not die,[3] Islamic thinking does not link Elijah to the Messiah. It does not see Jesus as the one who fulfils and completes all previous revelation, and it certainly does not see him as God come among us. In short, the Qur'an omits most of the aspects of the biblical Elijah story that prefigure the transfiguration.

Moses

The Qur'an gives more space to Moses than to any other prophet. Aspects of his story are used to illustrate its argument again and again. There is far too much material for us to survey in this book: all we can do is to note what the Qur'an includes and what it omits. What it does include is remarkably similar to what is found in the biblical stories:

- Moses' birth, his mother's floating him in a basket on the Nile, his upbringing in the royal household and his being nursed by his mother (Surahs 20. 38–40; 28. 7–13)
- The killing of the Egyptian, flight into the desert and becoming a shepherd (28. 14–28; 26. 19–21)
- His call and the burning bush (19. 51–53; 20. 9–56; 27. 7–14; 28. 29–35)
- Moses and Aaron confronting Pharaoh, the plagues, and the drowning of the Egyptians (7. 103–137; 10. 75–92; 11. 96–99; 17. 101–103; 20. 42–79; 23. 45–49; 25. 35–36; 26. 10–69; 28. 36–42; 40. 23–46; 43. 45–56; 51. 38–40; 79. 15–26)
- The exodus from Egypt (7. 138–141; 10. 90; 26. 52–65)
- Receiving the law on the mountain (2. 63–71; 7. 142–147)
- Receiving the Torah (2. 53; 11. 110; 23. 49; 28. 43–46; 53. 36; 87. 19)

---

3. Some traditional stories identify Elijah with Idris, who apparently did not die but was taken up to heaven, and who is usually thought to be the biblical Enoch (see Surahs 19. 56–57; 21. 85). Others say that Elijah was also Khidr, the mysterious figure who met Moses in Surah 18. 60–82. See Roberto Tottoli, 'Elijah', *Encyclopaedia of the Qur'an*, ed. Jane Dammen McAuliffe (Georgetown University, Washington DC: Brill Online, 2014).

- The golden calf (2. 51–54; 7. 148–156; 20. 83–97)
- The seventy elders (7. 155–156)
- The Israelites' rebellions in the wilderness, and manna in the desert (2. 55–61; 7. 160; 20. 80–82)

Not only is there more about Moses than about any other prophet, but also these stories about Moses are closer to the parallel biblical stories than are most of the qur'anic stories about other biblical characters. The only major incident recorded in the Qur'an that is not in the Bible is the story of Moses' mystical journey with a person whom Muslims call Khidr, whom some identify as Elijah (Surah 18. 60–82).

However, there are different emphases. Most striking is the fact that more space is given to Moses' interaction with Pharaoh and the Egyptians than to his interaction with the Israelites. You may have noticed this when you were asked in chapter 4 to think about the Qur'an's story of the burning bush, comparing it with Exodus 3; it totally omits the LORD saying, 'I have surely seen the affliction of my people who are in Egypt and have heard their cry because of their taskmasters. I know their sufferings, and I have come down to deliver them out of the hand of the Egyptians and to bring them up out of that land to a good and broad land . . .' (Exod 3:7–8). The rescue of the Israelites is mentioned, but the focus is the judgement of the Egyptians, about which there are several passages. When the Qur'an does deal with Moses as the leader of the Israelites, he is mostly confronting them over the golden calf and their rebellions in the wilderness.

If we compare this to the life of Muhammad, we can see that the Qur'an emphasizes aspects of Moses' life that are parallel to aspects of Muhammad's life – for example, the confrontation with idolatry and with the idolatrous leaders, the leading of the people out of a place of insecurity, the formation of a people under a new law and the struggle with Jewish people who did not obey him. If we then ask what purpose the stories of Moses serve in the Qur'an, we can see that they encourage Muhammad and the Muslims, and warn the pagans and the Jews of the time. We can also see that the Qur'an presents Muhammad not only as the final prophet (we will consider this idea further in chapter 9), but also as a prophet like Moses; and the amount of space given to Moses in the Qur'an suggests that Muhammad is seen to be more like Moses than like other previous prophets. Muslims often apply the prediction of a 'prophet like Moses' in Deuteronomy 18:18 to Muhammad. Christians see Jesus as the fulfilment of this prophecy, not least because of

Acts 3:18–22. Muslim apologists point out that there are many ways in which Muhammad is more like Moses than Jesus is.

> Since, [*sic*] this prophesy [*sic*] is made already in the presence of the Israelites, a blessing before the birth of Moses, that means then that the reference to brethren here would be the closest kin to the Israelites. The closest kin to the Israelites are the descendants of the other son, Ishmael, the Ishmaelites . . .
>
> If one examines carefully . . . we find that Muhammad and Moses are very very similar in their lives and in all of these points Jesus is different. That includes the natural birth of both Moses and Muhammad but not so in the case of Jesus. They both had a normal family life with having children and that is not known in the case of Jesus. The fact that both of them died of natural causes and we know that according to the Qur'an and the Bible the end of Jesus' mission on earth is clouded with some mystery. Also, in the case of Moses and Muhammad, they both received a code of law, a complete code of law; Jesus' teaching was essentially spiritual and he said so himself when he said that he did not come to destroy the law but came to fulfil them [*sic*]. Moses and Muhammad both faced their enemies in hot pursuit and they both have moral as well as physical victory over their enemies. We don't have these parallels in the life of Jesus. Moses and Muhammad were both prophets, judges and statesmen; they succeeded or God gave them the life and the possibility to achieve in their objectives, not only in the spiritual sense but also in establishing a state and control over the state according to the commands of God. That is not a parallel in the case of Jesus.
>
> The Torah was revealed to Moses in Mount Sinai and was all written down during his lifetime, so was the Qur'an revealed to prophet Muhammad and this is not so in the case of the teachings of Jesus where records were written much after that. In all of these points, like I said, these and more relate obviously that the closest prophet that came after Moses that was like unto him with the same greatness and the same impact and the same nature of the message and life was not really prophet Jesus, even though we recognize his prophethood and his authority and all,

but was really pertaining to prophet Muhammad may peace be upon them all.[4]

We have to agree that there are some ways in which Muhammad was more like Moses than Jesus was. However, this is only true if we limit ourselves to looking at what the Qur'an includes of the Moses story. When we ask what it omits, we see that there are very important parts of the biblical Moses story that were indeed fulfilled in Jesus and that make any further prophet unnecessary.

There are three key areas of the Bible's account of Moses which the Qur'an scarcely mentions. First, although the Qur'an sees Moses as a prophet who received a book from God, it tells us very little about the laws that were in the book. In several places it mentions the seriousness of breaking the Sabbath (Surah 2. 65; 7. 163–166; 16. 124), and there are commandments in the Qur'an that are similar to those in Exodus (e.g. Surah 17. 22–39), but most of the details are missing. Second, there is hardly anything about the tabernacle, the priesthood or the sacrifices, which take up such a large proportion of Exodus, Leviticus, Numbers and Deuteronomy. There is only a hint of the sacrificial system in Surah 2. 67–71, where the people argue with Moses about God's commandment to sacrifice a heifer. Third, although the Qur'an speaks of covenants between God and Israel, they are simply agreements that people should acknowledge God and keep his laws: the word 'covenant' conveys little of the biblical idea of the promises of God that underpin his people's story (we explore this further in chapter 12).

As in the case of Elijah, these differences can be understood in relation to the transfiguration. First, as the Qur'an is silent about the details of the Mosaic law, it leaves us to hear its message that it is replacing the Torah of Moses rather than fulfilling it. In Islamic thinking, many laws can change according to circumstance, and Muslims generally see the Gospel[5] of Jesus as superseding the Torah of Moses, and the Qur'an and Sunnah of Muhammad

4. Dr Jamal Badawi, 'Muhammad the Last Messenger of Allāh – Muhammad and the Abrahamic Tree IV: Moses' Prophecy', in answer to the question 'Are There Any Other Prophesies [sic] of Prophet Muhammad May Peace Be Upon Him in What Is Commonly Referred to as the Torah?', http://jamalbadawi.org/index.php?option=com_content&view=article&id=211:124-muhammad-the-last-messenger-of-allah-muhammad-a-the-abrahamic-tree-iv-moses-prophecy&catid=25:volume-12-muhammad-the-last-messenger-of-allah&Itemid=13; accessed October 2014.

5. The Arabic word translated 'Gospel' is injīl. In the Qur'an, this appears to be a book which God gave to Jesus, just as the Qur'an is a book which God gave to Muhammad and the Torah is a book which God gave to Moses.

as superseding both. Where the transfiguration points to Jesus fulfilling the law, Muslims see Jesus as continuing the law and Muhammad as bringing a final law.

Second, the tabernacle, which symbolizes the presence of God with Israel, is never constructed in the Qur'an; there are no priests to go in and no sacrifices to be offered to enable a holy God to live among sinful human beings. The empty space left shows one of the basic differences between the Qur'an and the Bible that we have seen already. In Islamic thinking, God does not dwell among human beings, so there is no tabernacle. The separation between God and human beings is not due to his holiness but his transcendence, so it cannot be overcome through sacrifices. The presence of God in Jesus seen at the transfiguration is, then, impossible, and the cross to which the transfiguration points is unnecessary.

Third, the Mosaic covenant determines the direction of biblical history by commissioning Israel for her role in bringing salvation to the nations. It can only be understood in the context of the covenants with Noah, Abraham and David that are all part of God's commitment to his fallen world and that lead, eventually, to the new covenant in Jesus. The different idea of covenant in the Qur'an is consistent with the qur'anic view of sacred history as a cycle of God sending prophets with guidance. In such a context, Jesus is just one of many prophets, rather than the climax and the focus of all sacred history. In short, the Qur'an omits or minimizes the aspects of the Moses story that have to do with the presence of God and his commitment to redemption, and lays instead the foundation for the eventual replacement of Moses by Muhammad.

To Think About

As a Christian, you might regret, or even be angry about, the fact that the Qur'an omits many of the ideas that are fulfilled in Jesus. But do you and your Christian community tend to omit some of the other aspects of the biblical Moses and Elijah stories?

Do you perhaps focus so much on the grace of God in Jesus Christ that you forget the demands of God's laws? What is the difference between seeing Moses and Elijah fulfilled through the transfiguration and forgetting them altogether?

8

Thinking about the Qur'an

'How does the Qur'an relate to biblical revelation?' we asked at the end of chapter 2. As we have seen, the tension is that, on the one hand, the Qur'an refers to biblical characters and agrees with the Bible on many ideas, while, on the other hand, it tells a story that ends with the prophethood of Muhammad rather than with the cross and resurrection of Jesus. The qur'anic Elijah and Moses stories are good examples of this. So, should we see the Qur'an as building on biblical revelation or destroying it, and as a source of truth or a source of error? Or should we try to keep the tension by rejoicing in any truth we find but refuting error? More importantly, what role does the Qur'an have, and can it have, in drawing Muslims into relationship with Jesus?

We begin this section by listening to Ali, a believer in Jesus from Muslim background.

Ali's Comments

'I think of the Bible as the sun: the source of light. The symbol of Islam is the crescent moon, and that is how I think of the Qur'an. The crescent reflects the light of the sun. It is only a small part of the light, but it is enough to make people want more light, and to be glad to see the sun. When the sun comes out, the moon is still there, but you don't notice it.

'The Qur'an can be a bridge to the Bible. We can talk about the parts of the Qur'an that reflect biblical truth, especially about Jesus. We can also study the Qur'an so that we can better understand our Muslim friends. I often use the Qur'an in my preaching.'

I ask, 'What about the dark part of the crescent moon?' Ali laughs. 'We don't worry about that,' he says. 'Talking with Muslims, we want to focus on the light – what we need is more light! For our own thinking, we understand the Qur'an as a book that originates in a particular time and place. No, we don't think that it comes from

Satan, although we do know people who use parts of it for black magic. But we also know Hindus who do black magic. We hear that Christians in some places get involved in black magic too: do they use the Bible for that?'

The Qur'an stands at the centre of Islam as its communication from God. It is the Qur'an that is the authority for all Muslims and the primary basis for both law and belief; and it is the Qur'an that was the basis for Muhammad's claim to prophethood and that continues to be the basis of Islam's claim to truth.

The Qur'an itself bears evidence of these claims:

The Qur'an Sees Itself as a Self-Authenticating Miracle

Surah 29. 49 claims, '. . . [this Qur'an] is a revelation that is clear to the hearts of those endowed with knowledge. No one refuses to acknowledge Our revelations but the evildoers.'[1] That is, the Qur'an claims that its divine origin is obvious, and only deliberately evil people will refuse to recognize it. Muslims often quote Surah 2. 23–24 to show that no human being could have produced the Qur'an: 'If you have doubts about the revelation We have sent down to Our servant, then produce a single sura like it – enlist whatever supporters you have other than God – if you truly [think you can]. If you cannot do this – and you never will – then beware of the Fire prepared for the disbelievers, whose fuel is men and stones.'[2] The Qur'an's style as well as its content, these verses imply, prove to the honest reader that it must have come from God.

The Qur'an Sees Itself as Confirmed By and Confirming Previous Scriptures

A well-known passage about the nature of the Qur'an begins thus: 'God: there is no god but Him, the Ever Living, the Ever Watchful. Step by step, He has sent the Scripture down to you [Prophet] with the Truth, confirming what went before: He sent down the Torah and the Gospel earlier as a guide for people and He has sent down the distinction [between right and wrong]'

---

1. M. A. S. Abdel Haleem, *The Qur'an: A New Translation by M. A. S. Abdel Haleem* (Oxford: Oxford University Press, 2008), Used with permission.
2. Ibid.

(Surah 3. 2–4).[3] It continues, '. . . it is He who has sent this Scripture down to you [Prophet]' (3. 7a).[4] The Qur'an sees its relationship with the Bible as working two ways: the Qur'an affirms that the law and the gospel are true, and its continuity with the law and the gospel show that it, in turn, is true. This is a theme in the passages of the Qur'an that call the Jews to accept Muhammad's message – for example, in Surah 2. 40–41, 87–89, 91, 97, 101.

The Qur'an, therefore, Presents Itself as Proof of Muhammad's Prophethood

If the Qur'an is from God, then Muhammad must be a messenger from God. Again and again, the Qur'an's knowledge of biblical stories and ideas is used as evidence of this. For example, its story of Joseph is introduced thus: 'We tell you [Prophet] the best of stories in revealing this Qur'an to you. Before this you were one of those who knew nothing about them' (Surah 12. 3).[5] The Joseph story is followed by these words:

> This account is part of what was beyond your knowledge [Muhammad]. We revealed it to you: you were not present with Joseph's brothers when they made their treacherous plans. However eagerly you may want them to, most men will not believe. You ask no reward from them for this: it is a reminder for all people and there are many signs in the heavens and the earth that they pass by and give no heed to – most of them will only believe in God while also joining others with Him. Are they so sure that an overwhelming punishment from God will not fall on them, or that the Last Hour will not come upon them suddenly when they least expect it? Say, 'This is my way: based on clear evidence, I, and all who follow me, call [people] to God – glory be to God! – I do not join others with Him' (Surah 12. 102–108).[6]

These verses imply that Muhammad has received this story directly from God: on this basis, people are called to accept him and follow him.

---

3. M. A. S. Abdel Haleem, *The Qur'an: A New Translation by M. A. S. Abdel Haleem* (Oxford: Oxford University Press, 2008), Used with permission.

4. Ibid.

5. Ibid.

6. Ibid.

The first claim, that the Qur'an is miraculous, has three parts. The first part is largely subjective: it invites us – including the readers and writers of this book – to read it and to see whether it authenticates itself to us. Do we perceive its form as unique? Do we find it totally coherent (lacking in contradictions)? Are we overwhelmed by its beauty? Do we hear God's voice through it? We will leave it up to our readers to respond to this part.

The second part of the claim is about the perfection of the language and form of the Qur'an. Most of us will not have sufficient Arabic language to judge such literary claims, so we might see this claim as itself a problem: why would God give us his revelation in a form whose truth could only be assessed by people from a particular language group? Why should Persian, Turkish, Chinese or English speakers have to depend on the opinions of Arabic speakers on a supremely important matter?

There is a further problem: the form of the Qur'an may be unique, but how far does its form fit in with the form of biblical literature? This relates to the question of how the scripture came into being: the Qur'an refers to itself as directly dictated by God. Muslims believe that it was dictated to Muhammad by the angel Gabriel, bit by bit over a period of twenty-three years. There are some parts of the Bible that are presented as the direct word of God – for example, some of the laws given to Moses, and parts of the prophetic books. However, most of the Bible is evidently written by human beings. For example, Luke tells us very clearly that his writing is based on his own research (Luke 1:1–4) and a large amount of the New Testament is composed of letters written from one human being to others. Even the prophetic books that are nearly all oracles from God are introduced with the words of humans (e.g. Joel 1:1; Mic 1:1), and it is likely that many oracles are God-given ideas put into the prophets' own words. Christians believe that this came about under the inspiration of the Holy Spirit, so the Bible is truly the word of God; but the idea of how God speaks is different in the Bible from that in the Qur'an.[7] The form of the Qur'an has some similarities with some of the prophetic books, but it is very different from the form of the Bible as a whole. A 'biblical' assessment of the Qur'an, then, asks not only, 'Does this agree with what the Bible says?' but also, 'Does this fit with the way that God speaks in and through the Bible?'

7. See also I. Glaser, 'Towards a Mutual Understanding of Christian and Islamic Concepts of Revelation', in *Themelios* 7.3 (April 1982): 16–22, available at http://www.medievalchurch.org.uk/pdf/islamic-revelation_glaser.pdf.

The final part of this first claim can be tested historically: is the content of the Qur'an miraculous, or could Muhammad have produced it himself? Non-Muslim scholars have long found possible sources of qur'anic material in seventh-century Arabia and its surroundings, and there is currently a revival of academic interest in the Qur'an as a historical document, which suggests that the Qur'an did not reach its present form until some time after the death of Muhammad.[8] We do not have space to explore this here, but we can say that current scholarship indicates that there is no need to appeal to miraculous revelation in order to explain any of the information in the Qur'an.[9]

The second claim, that the Qur'an confirms and is confirmed by the Torah, the Psalms and the Gospels, needs careful consideration in a book on thinking biblically about Islam. We could even see this whole book as, on one level, a response to this claim. The Qur'an itself is telling us as Christians to 'judge by our Book' (see Surah 5. 46–47).[10]

In our readings of the qur'anic stories of Adam and Eve, Cain and Abel, Noah, Moses and Elijah, we have already seen many ways in which the Qur'an affirms biblical material. It affirms the importance of the history of Israel and of many of the key characters involved in that history. It affirms many aspects of the relationship between God and his creation as revealed in the Bible. However, it also omits some very important aspects of each story, and tells each story in its own way and for its own purposes. The net result is a worldview that is significantly different from that of the Bible and that displays what we have described as a reversal of the transfiguration.

The crucial question for Christians is, of course, *how the Qur'an treats Jesus*. The answer is that it treats Jesus as part of a pattern of prophecy that reaches its peak with Muhammad. It is usually possible to argue that it is not the Qur'an itself but Muslim interpretations of the Qur'an that contradict the Bible's teaching about Jesus – for example, the Qur'an's denials of Jesus'

---

8. This agrees to some extent with traditional Muslim understandings about the history of the collection of the Qur'an. See A. von Denffer, *'Ulūm Al-Qur'ān: Introduction to the Sciences of the Qur'ān*, 2nd ed. (Leicester: The Islamic Foundation, 2005), ch. 2. For a more critical, non-Muslim account of the development of the Qur'an, see K. Small, *Holy Books Have a History: Textual Histories of the New Testament and the Qur'an* (Kansas City: Avant, 2009).

9. For an introduction to the development of the Qur'an in its historical context, see M. Cook, *The Koran: A Very Short Introduction* (Oxford: Oxford University Press, 2000), part 4; or A. Rippin, ed., *The Blackwell Companion to the Qur'an* (Oxford: Blackwell, 2006), chs 12 and 13.

10. M. A. S. Abdel Haleem, *The Qur'an: A New Translation by M. A. S. Abdel Haleem* (Oxford: Oxford University Press, 2008), Used with permission.

sonship can be seen as denials of a physical fatherhood of God rather than of Jesus' eternal relationship in the Trinity – but the overall effect of the Qur'an tends to lead to a rejection of both the incarnation and the atonement.

Putting all this together, we have to say that the Qur'an's claims to be continuous with the Bible are only partly correct. There are fundamental aspects of the Bible's message that it does *not* confirm, and some that it contradicts. In short, if we think biblically, the Qur'an cannot be a final revelation from God.

However, this is all negative; can we see the Qur'an more positively? Is Ali right in seeing it as 'the crescent moon', reflecting some of the light of the Bible? This would fit in with one of the Qur'an's ways of describing itself: as reminding people of what they should already know. With the 'reminding' goes a warning: there will be judgement if people do not listen. For example,

> By the Qur'an with its reminding[11] . . . I ask no reward from you
> for this, nor do I claim to be what I am not: this is only a warning
> for all people (Surah 38. 1, 86–87; see also 21. 10; 43. 44).[12]

There is a question here: what is it that people knew before, and have forgotten? One interpretation is that God told all people of his lordship before they were created, and that all human beings are born submitted to him.[13] They need reminding of what they knew when they were born. But, for Jews and Christians, a different reminder seems to be needed. Jews and Christians have their books, and the Qur'an reminds them to pay attention to what God has given them:

> . . . but why do they [the Jews] come to you [Muhammad] for
> judgement when they have the Torah with God's judgement, and
> even then still turn away? These are not believers. We revealed
> the Torah with guidance and light, and the prophets, who had
> submitted to God, judged according to it for the Jews . . . those
> who do not judge according to what God has sent down are
> rejecting [God's teachings] . . . We sent Jesus, son of Mary, in their

---

11. The word translated 'reminding' and 'warning' is the same in these two verses: *dhikr*. Dhikr is an important aspect of worship for many Muslims, as they spend time 'remembering' God, by, for example, reciting his names. It is sometimes translated 'admonition', 'explanation' or 'honour', as these are all implications of its being a reminder.
12. M. A. S. Abdel Haleem, *The Qur'an: A New Translation by M. A. S. Abdel Haleem* (Oxford: Oxford University Press, 2008), Used with permission.
13. This idea is based on Surah 7. 172.

footsteps, to confirm the Torah that had been sent before him: We gave him the Gospel with guidance, light, and confirmation of the Torah already revealed – a guide and lesson for those who take heed of God. So let the followers of the Gospel judge according to what God has sent down in it (Surah 5. 43–44, 46–47; see also vv. 65–68).[14]

Clearly, the Qur'an sees itself as reminding people of what they should know from the Bible.

A Qur'anic Prayer

The following surah is recited several times whenever a Muslim performs the ritual prayer. People sometimes compare this to the way in which Christians use the Lord's Prayer:

In the name of God, the Lord of Mercy, the Giver of Mercy! Praise belongs to God, Lord of the Worlds, the Lord of Mercy, the Giver of Mercy, Master of the Day of Judgement. It is You we worship; it is You we ask for help. Guide us to the straight path: the path of those You have blessed, those who incur no anger and who have not gone astray (Surah 1).[15]

To Think About

Can we rejoice in the truths that we find in the Qur'an? For example, can we be glad that it calls people to worship their creator?

Could we think of the Qur'an as a reminder to us to listen to the Bible? It actually tells Jews and Christians to pay attention to their books. Have any of the comparisons with the Qur'an in this book reminded you of aspects of the Bible that you had forgotten or not noticed?

There is a more important question than how we should judge the Qur'an. The crucial question is about Jesus: can we see the Qur'an as a book that can

---

14. M. A. S. Abdel Haleem, *The Qur'an: A New Translation by M. A. S. Abdel Haleem* (Oxford: Oxford University Press, 2008), Used with permission.
15. Ibid.

point people to Jesus as Lord? We know that Muslims often use the Qur'an to deny some of the central biblical truths about Jesus, but the Qur'an does also say things about Jesus that agree with the Gospels.

We have said that Islam has the effect of reversing the transfiguration: that is devastating from a New Testament perspective. However, it also means that the qur'anic material on Jesus can be read as consistent with the Gospels up to the transfiguration. Here, we look at that material from a slightly different perspective, asking, 'Can the Qur'an, then, lead Muslims to consider the questions addressed by the transfiguration, and hence to listen to the Gospels' answer to them?'

Here is what Ali says about his own experience:

Ali's Story

I first met with my 'friend, mentor and guide' on a hot and humid day in my relative's house. The relative told me, 'Today I will introduce you to a religious leader of Islam.' At first sight it seemed to me that he was totally different from any other religious teacher of Islam. When he talked with us that time I realized that he was a great scholar of Islam. He frequently recited some relevant verses in Arabic from the Qur'an with a good Arabic accent. He was trying to prove that Isa al-Masīḥ (Jesus the Messiah) is the only way to come to God. He said that Isa al-Masīḥ came from above. The Qur'an also states that Allāh cast his spirit to the womb of Mary and Mary became pregnant and gave birth to Isa. So Mary is like a pot, she is nothing more; Isa is the main object because he came from above, that is, from heaven. So he knows everything of invisible matter (Surah 3. 39). He made a way to come to God, the only way. He told us that the Qur'an proves this fact. So like the people of Berea (Acts 17:11), with an open mind I brought the Qur'an to him and he showed us the evidence to back up his claim. We asked several questions and he gave us good answers, and we were all very pleased and satisfied as we listened to his answers!

When we returned in the evening, a gentle breeze was blowing and cuckoos were singing in the orchard. He told us that he liked cuckoos because they are migratory birds. He told us that we too are like birds as this is our temporary home. The Hadith says that the believer in the world is like a traveller in a foreign country, an idea which is also affirmed in the Bible; we are foreigners, strangers and refugees, temporary residents in the world (1 Pet 2:11). Our real home is in heaven!

> Next time, as an enquirer, I met with him in a rented room with other believers. We were all attentively listening to a foreigner, who was teaching in our own language. He taught us about *logos*, a concept from John's gospel. At first when I heard that Jesus and God were the same person, it was very new to me, but the missionary explained this basic doctrine so clearly that the confusion was soon removed. He taught us that the Greek word *logos* is *kalam* in Arabic. Together, the foreigner and my mentor proved that Isa al-Masīḥ is the only way and that he is the Word of God – *kalimatu Allāh* (as in Surah 3. 45) – and after that I became a believer. This is how I discovered al-Masīḥ.

The qur'anic Jesus is one of the prophets, but he is unique in several ways. He is born of a virgin: the story told in Surah 19. 2–23 and Surah 3. 38–50 has many similarities with Luke chapters 1 and 2. He teaches, he heals and he performs miracles: Surah 3. 49 gives the outline although few of the details. He is sinless (implied in Surah 19. 19), and he shows the way to which Muslims pray to be guided in Surah 1 (Surah 19. 36). Most remarkable from a biblical perspective are his titles of 'word' and 'spirit' (Surah 4. 171). All this can make the reader ask, 'Who is this man? He seems special; how does he fit in among the other prophets?'

The special nature of Jesus in the Qur'an is summed up in his title 'Messiah'. The Qur'an uses the term frequently, and it seems to be something more than a name, but there are no explanations about what it means. For example, in Surah 4. 157, the Jews say, 'We killed the Messiah, Jesus, son of Mary, the Messenger of God',[16] which implies that 'the Messiah' was a title in its own right and that they recognized Jesus as the person to whom that title belonged. The qur'anic commentaries give many suggestions as to what the word means,[17] but there is no agreement among them. The disciples before the transfiguration knew that the Messiah was Israel's promised king and were asking, 'Is Jesus really the Messiah?' The reader of the Qur'an knows that Jesus is indeed the Messiah, but will be wondering what 'Messiah' means.

Before the transfiguration the disciples were shocked at the idea that the Messiah would be crucified. 'This shall never happen to you,' exclaimed

---

16. M. A. S. Abdel Haleem, *The Qur'an: A New Translation by M. A. S. Abdel Haleem* (Oxford: Oxford University Press, 2008), Used with permission.

17. For the range of possibilities, see Neal Robinson, 'Jesus', *Encyclopaedia of the Qur'an*. A common idea is that 'Messiah' is a nickname derived from a root meaning 'wiping', so it could refer to Jesus' healing, or it could mean that he was somehow anointed.

Peter on hearing that Jesus would suffer and be killed (Matt 16:22). So are the disciples right, or is Jesus? And why should he die? These are some of the questions brought to the transfiguration story. The Qur'an also raises questions about Jesus' death. Three verses seem to speak of his death:

> [Jesus as a baby] said: 'I am a servant of God. He has granted me the Scripture; made me a prophet; made me blessed wherever I may be. He commanded me to pray, to give alms as long as I live, to cherish my mother. He did not make me domineering or graceless. Peace was on me the day I was born, and will be on me the day I die and the day I am raised to life again' (Surah 19. 30–33).[18]

> God said, 'Jesus, I will take you back and raise you up to Me: I will purify you of the disbelievers. To the Day of Resurrection I will make those who follow you superior to those who disbelieved' (Surah 3. 55).[19]

> [In the future, when God asks Jesus about his teaching, Jesus will say], 'I was a witness over them during my time among them. Ever since You took my soul, You alone have been the watcher over them: You are witness to all things' (Surah 5. 117).[20]

However, a better-known verse follows immediately after the Jews' boast of killing him in Surah 4:

> [The People of the Book] disbelieved and uttered a terrible slander against Mary, and said, 'We have killed the Messiah, Jesus, son of Mary, the Messenger of God.' (They did not kill him, nor did they crucify him, though it was made to appear like that to them; those that disagreed about him are full of doubt, with no knowledge to follow, only supposition: they certainly did not kill him – God raised him up to Himself . . .) (Surah 4. 157).[21]

Most Muslims understand this verse as teaching that Jesus did not die, but that God took him straight to paradise and let someone else die in his

18. M. A. S. Abdel Haleem, *The Qur'an: A New Translation by M. A. S. Abdel Haleem* (Oxford: Oxford University Press, 2008), Used with permission.
19. Ibid.
20. Ibid.
21. Ibid.

place. The verses about Jesus dying refer, they say, to what will happen when he comes again at the end of history.

Commentators see the difficulty in this interpretation; for example, why would God let such a deception be believed for six hundred years? Also, if God can make someone look like Jesus, how can we ever be sure that a person we are seeing is really who we think they are? Furthermore, Christian writers sometimes point out that, in the Arabic, it is not clear who was 'full of doubt' about what. It might mean that people were confused about the meaning of Jesus' death rather than about the fact of the death. Anyway, they say, the verse does not state that *Jesus did not die*, but only that *the Jews did not kill him* – and the New Testament actually agrees with this: on the one hand, the Jews did not have the authority to put him to death so had to get the Romans to do it; on the other hand, what happened was not so much because the Jews wanted it, but because God wanted it and because Jesus chose to accept it. On both counts, the Jews' boast of verse 157 is challenged.[22] All this can make the reader ask, 'So, did Jesus die on the cross or not? If so, why? And why do Christians think that it matters so much?'

Many Muslims are not sufficiently familiar with the Qur'an to know what it says about Jesus, and many read it assuming that it teaches that Jesus is just like the other prophets and that he did not die. Many do not think much about Jesus at all; but, when they do, and when they go to the Qur'an to find out about him, it can lead them to the questions that the transfiguration answers. It can even take them further:

- The Qur'an takes readers further into the gospel story when it agrees that the Jewish leaders wanted to crucify Jesus. This can point its readers towards the terrible rejection of God's Messiah into which human hearts can fall.

- The Qur'an takes readers further into eschatology by hinting that Jesus will return as judge, and Muslim tradition agrees. He is a witness about his followers (4. 159), and eminent in the next world as well as this world (3. 45), so most Muslims believe that he will come again before the world ends and will, among other things, judge the Christians.

---

22. For a discussion of the Muslim commentary on the crucifixion, see T. Lawson, *Crucifixion and the Qur'an: A Study in the History of Muslim Thought* (Oxford: Oneworld, 2009). For a Christian discussion, see C. Moucarry, *Faith to Faith: Christianity and Islam in Dialogue* (Leicester: IVP, 2001), ch. 10.

- The Qur'an reveals something special about the ministry of Jesus. Surah 57. 27 indicates that the followers of Jesus would have changed hearts: 'We gave [Jesus] the Gospel, and put compassion and mercy into the hearts of his followers.' Of no other prophet is anything like this said.

- Read carefully, the Qur'an can even take Muslims and Christians who are reading together further into discussions about the Trinity and about the divinity of Jesus. Usually, of course, it takes Muslims into direct denials of those key Christian doctrines, but it does have the potential to lead to better understanding. This is because the Qur'an can be understood as denying heresy rather than the truth of the Trinity. It rebukes those who say, 'God is the Messiah, the Son of Mary' (5. 17, 72) and that 'God is the third of three' (5. 73). It instructs people, '. . . do not say, "Three" . . . God is only one God' (4. 171).[23] We can agree with the Qur'an on those points: we do not say that 'God is Jesus', but that 'Jesus is God'; neither do we say that 'God is the third of three'; and we do not say 'there are three gods', but that 'the One God is Trinity'. Discussion of these qur'anic denials can be a way into explaining our faith to Muslim friends.

So, then, what should Christians do with the Qur'an? Where should they shelve it? How should they use it? Should they put it in a place of honour, or should they banish it, burn it or leave it to gather dust? Should they read it furtively, critically, and hide it behind better books? Is it World Literature (Arabian section) or somewhere nearer our Christian collections?

One way of thinking biblically about this is to consider how the Bible treats literature from outside the covenant community.

On the one hand, the Old Testament often rejects the beliefs of the nations surrounding Israel. On the other hand, some of the key Old Testament characters studied their literature. At the very least, this implies that Christians have no need to fear books from other religions. Before Moses began approaching the throne of Pharaoh, he was schooled in Egyptian thought. Before Daniel took his seat at the centre of Babylonian power, he took a course on the 'literature and language of the Chaldeans' (Dan 1:4), which would undoubtedly have been based on Babylonian religion. When

---

23. 'Do not say "Three"' is a literal translation. Abdul Haleem, in the translation of the Qur'an used in this book, follows the common Muslim understanding of the verse and translates it, 'Do not speak of a "Trinity"'.

his kingdom hosted many minority peoples and foreign visitors, Solomon prayed that God would hear them in the house of prayer for the nations. He also prayed for wisdom. God answered this prayer by bestowing upon him a discerning mind and through Solomon's 'weighing and studying and arranging many proverbs with great care' (Eccl 12:9). And so it is that the wisdom literature attributed to Solomon includes much material from beyond Israel. His study of it blessed both Israel and the nations that Solomon had prayed for. Symbols, sayings, structures and songs of surrounding cultures, and even of other religions, are found woven into the Bible.[24]

In the New Testament, too, there is both rejection of some non-Jewish religion and use of some non-Jewish writings. On the one hand, new believers at Ephesus burned their magic books (Acts 19:19): on the other hand, Paul used pagan literature in his preaching (Acts 17:28). The example of Paul, like those of Moses, Daniel and Solomon, suggests that study of the Qur'an might be important and fruitful. At the very least, it can open ways for Christians to communicate with Muslims as well as helping them to understand Islamic thought.

However, as Ali noted (see pages 197–198 above), there are some people who use parts of the Qur'an for 'black magic', and that can be very dangerous. Ali is happy to read the Qur'an and to use it to point Muslims to Jesus, but some Muslim background believers have had bad experiences and find reading the Qur'an oppressive. They may need prayer for deliverance from the spiritual influences of magic. It is important to recognize that the Qur'an in itself is not a book of magic, and that it speaks strongly against magic practices[25]. In our thinking about the Qur'an, we need to distinguish between what it is and how people use it. Like so many other books, even the Bible, it can be used for good or for evil, for peace or for violence, to seek truth or to propagate falsehood. The key question for Christians is not how we should categorize the Qur'an, but whether we can use it for good, for peace and for truth.

Ida's Story: All Truth Is God's Truth

In the days when I was a physics student, the big challenges to Christianity were not Islam and secularism, but communism and

---

24. Obvious examples from outside the Wisdom Literature include Hosea's use of Baal imagery and the allusions to Babylonian images in Ezekiel's visions of God. See also Ida's *The Bible and Other Faiths*, ch. 8.

25. It describes magic as the evil work of devils (2. 101–102) and contains prayers for God's protection from the evil of magic and Satan (Surahs 113 and 114).

so-called 'scientific' thought. Christian students wondered how they should think about those competing ideas. I suppose that we were a bit afraid of them.

One idea above all others freed me from fear and has, ever since, helped me to study. The French philosopher, Simone Weil, thinking about Jesus as the Truth, says, 'If one turns aside from him to go towards the truth, one will not go far before walking into his arms.'[26] I realized that if I look for truth as honestly as I can, I need never be afraid that it will take me away from Jesus. Truth will always lead me towards him.

A few years later, a book came out with a title that sums this up: *All Truth Is God's Truth*.[27] The writer argues that both the Bible and the early Christians believed that all truth has its origin in God, 'that all truth is God's truth no matter where it is found.' (p 14)

He also argues that most human thinking is a mixture, so that we should not suppose that a system of thought must be wholly true or wholly false:

'A position may be true to some extent and in some regards and false in others. Sometimes a student will ask of a given assertion, 'Is that right or not?' To which I answer, 'Yes,' and go on to explain what may be right about it and what may be wrong. Blanket judgements must give way to careful and critical discernment.' (p 67).

It is this kind of thinking that has enabled me to study the Qur'an, and that makes me appreciate Ali's idea that the Qur'an is like the crescent moon. I can be glad that it reflects some of the truth of the Bible, and, at the same time, be sad that it rejects or distorts other aspects of that truth.

To Think About

What have you learned from the studies of the Qur'an in this book?

In what ways have they helped you to understand Muslim people? In what ways have they equipped you to share the gospel?

---

26. Simone Weil, *Waiting on God: The Essence of Her Thought* (London: Fontana, 1959), 36.

27. Arthur F. Holmes, *All Truth Is God's Truth*, first British edition (Leicester: IVP, 1979).

9

Thinking about Muhammad

Be Careful with Muhammad! is the title of a book written by Ida's colleague Shabbir Akhtar. It explains to non-Muslim readers why Muslims were so offended by Salman Rushdie's portrayal of their beloved prophet in his book *The Satanic Verses*, published in 1988.[1] Since that time, there have been several highly publicized incidents when Muslims have reacted violently to what they have seen as dishonour to Muhammad;[2] and people have become very careful in what they say about him.

In this chapter, we will be very careful to say what we believe to be true. We want to honour Muhammad as we would honour any human being made in the image of God, and we want to appreciate all that is good about him. However, if thinking biblically leads us to the conclusion that the Qur'an is not what it claims to be, and if the Qur'an is the proof of Muhammad's prophetic claims, then we have to conclude that Muhammad is not the carrier of God's final revelation that Muslims believe him to be. But what, then, is he? How can our studies of Genesis and the transfiguration help us to think about him?

Ali's Ideas

Muslims believe that Muhammad came to bring a shariah. Did he come to bring salvation? No! That is what Jesus came to bring. When people hear about Jesus and start to follow him, then, little by little, they stop thinking about Muhammad and the law he brought.

We say Muhammad was a reformer and a great charismatic leader, and we can talk about the good things that he did as well

---

1. Akhtar's book is *Be Careful with Muhammad! The Salman Rushdie Affair* (London: Bellew Publishing, 1989). Rushdie's book is *The Satanic Verses* (New York: Viking, 1988).

2. The best known are the controversies about cartoons of Muhammad in Denmark (2005) and in France (2014).

as the things that, from a biblical perspective, were good only for his time or even that were wrong. But we want to be friends with people, not their enemies, so we never dishonour him. It does not really matter what they think of Muhammad, or what new believers in Jesus think of Muhammad: what matters is what they think of Jesus!

Eventually, as people grow in their faith in Jesus and read the Bible, they think that Muhammad was not a prophet at all, even though he preached a lot of good things. They read in the New Testament about false teachers and about the 'antichrist' who says that Jesus is not the Son of God, and realize that Muhammad is one of the people whose teaching has prevented people from hearing the gospel and has resulted in a denial of Jesus' Sonship.

Christians disagree as to how they should view Muhammad. At one end of the spectrum, some have seen him as a genuine prophet of some kind, perhaps one especially for the Arabs. At the other end of the spectrum, some have seen him as thoroughly wicked. One of the reasons for this range of opinions is the range of different Christian experiences of Islam. For example, in medieval Spain, a story was circulated about Muhammad's body being eaten by dogs.[3] This was in the context of the recent Muslim conquest of Spain, when some Christians were anxious to make sure that their fellow believers should not leave Christ to follow Muhammad. But there is another reason why it is very difficult for Christians to agree on what they think of Muhammad: it is difficult to be sure of what Muhammad was like and what he really did and thought.

To begin with, Muslims vary in their opinions of him. While all believe that he was God's messenger who received the Qur'an directly from God, different Muslims emphasize different aspects of his life, and see his status in different ways.

- Some emphasize the nobility of his personal relationships, his gentleness and his forbearance.
- Some emphasize his political and military leadership.
- While Sunnis see him and his example as final, Shi'ites accept the example and teaching of his successors.

---

3. This can be found in a horrible *History of Muhammad*, written c.850, that mocks Muhammad and accuses him of all sorts of sins. A translation by K. B. Wolf is in O. R. Constable, ed., *Medieval Iberia: Readings from Christian, Muslim, and Jewish Sources* (Philadelphia: University of Pennsylvania Press, 1997).

- Some are emphatic that he was a human being just like everyone else, while others insist that prophets are in a different category from the rest of us.
- Some have such a high view of him that they sing hymns to him and claim that he was pre-existent, the light of the world and the one who will intercede for his people on the day of judgement.

Scholars, meanwhile, question the historicity of the traditional Islamic texts about him, further compounding the difficulty of understanding what he was really like.

- The Hadith were not collected until at least two hundred years after Muhammad's time. The collectors are said to have applied rigorous tests to each Hadith, checking both the chain of transmission and the consistency of the content with other Hadith and with the Qur'an. Muslim scholars grade the Hadith, some of which are 'strong': that is, they are confident that they are from Muhammad. Others are 'weak' and not so certain, and therefore not so authoritative.[4] Nevertheless, some non-Muslim scholars think that very few of them relate to Muhammad himself, most having developed to cater to the needs of the growing Islamic empires. Today, many Muslims are re-examining the Hadith, and some reject many of them.[5]
- The Sirah, the traditional accounts of Muhammad's life, were collected earlier than the Hadith. The best known, Ibn Ishaq's *Sīrat rasūl ullāh*,[6] dates from the mid-eighth century, about 120 years after the death of Muhammad. However, it has many elements that non-Muslim scholars see as mythical.
- Probably the best historical document on the life of Muhammad is the Qur'an itself. Again, non-Muslim scholars vary in how far they think that the Qur'an represents exactly what came from Muhammad's lips. Some think that it is substantially what he recited; others think that much of it dates from the decades after

---

4. For a thorough study of the nature of Hadith, see D. Brown, *Rethinking Tradition in Modern Islamic Thought* (Cambridge: Cambridge University Press, 1996).

5. See, for example, Fatima Mernissi's discussion of which Hadith are valid for thinking about gender issues in her *Women and Islam: An Historical and Theological Enquiry* (Oxford: Blackwell, 1991), chs 2–4.

6. Translated by A. Guillaume as *The Life of Muhammad* (Oxford: Oxford University Press, 1955).

Muhammad.[7] Most, however, would agree that it mainly represents what Muhammad taught.

Given that our aim is to think about Islam, we need to think about the Muhammad in whom Muslims believe: the final prophet, the example to be followed, and a figure who is greatly honoured and to whom devotion is given. However, as Ali implies, we also need to think about what we make of Muhammad as a human being who lived at a particular time and in a particular place. We will begin by using our Genesis framework to think about Muhammad as a person of his time, taking the traditional Islamic sources as the main evidence for his life. We will then reflect on Islamic beliefs about him and their effect of reversing the transfiguration.

Muhammad as a Person of His Time: Using the Genesis 1 – 11 'Mirror'

The framework from Genesis we established in part 1 helps us to think about Muhammad as a human being. As with all people, we can be certain that he was created in the image of God but that he also shared the sinfulness that followed the fall. We can therefore expect to see in Muhammad the characteristics of the fallen religious world of Genesis 4 – 11.

First, it would only be normal for him to have sought relationship with God, just as Cain and Abel did in offering sacrifices. Not every religious act is necessarily pleasing to God, and we cannot know how God perceived Muhammad's personal attempts to relate to him. But we do know, from God's conversation with Cain, that he continues to communicate even with those whose efforts are not pleasing to him. God has communicated in all sorts of ways to all sorts of people. So, however we view Muhammad, we can assume that at some stage and in some way, God spoke to him.

Next, Muhammad was concerned to deal with evil. His response was, in many ways, in line with God's response to evil in Genesis 6: he saw it as hateful and warned sinful people of the coming judgement. His Sunnah pattern of life and the qur'anic message he communicated show that he burned with zeal against wickedness and idolatry; he had an acute sense of evil. He and his followers ever since have tirelessly preached against it and tried to regulate it through the shariah.

---

7. For an introduction to the development of the Qur'an in its historical context, see Cook, *The Koran: A Very Short Introduction*, part 4; or Rippin, *The Blackwell Companion to the Qur'an*, chs 12 and 13.

The flood story gives an early indication of two different responses to evil: those of judgement and of atoning sacrifice whereby judgement is averted and mercy given. Muhammad knew of both justice and mercy – the qur'anic message he bore is full of them. However, his message barely hints at the crucial link between sacrifice and mercy. Instead, he deals with sin differently: by admonishing communities to submit to the will of God. He and the qur'anic prophets before him saw ignorance, weakness and stubbornness to be the causes of all wickedness. They perceived their hearers as either believers or unbelievers, good or bad. Muhammad became the judge and arbiter over his followers as he began to establish the oasis settlements of Yathrib as his city, Madinat al-Nabi. To believers who were under attack, authority was given to fight against the faithless and wicked (Surah 22. 39–41). The Muslim community developed, then, the responsibility of executing God's justice on earth.[8]

That takes us to the third part of the Genesis framework: the use of religion to propagate the dangerous triangle of people, power and land seen in the Babel story. As is well known, Muhammad's prophetic role was not only to bring a message from God but also to establish a community, which meant that he increasingly took on the role of a social, political and military leader. The journey from Mecca to Medina, which marks 'Year One' of the Islamic Calendar – that is, AD 622 – signalled the start of his political leadership, as he arbitrated between rival tribes in Medina and became the clan leader of the community of his followers. Because the community was based on faith rather than on tribal loyalty, it had to be organized according to new principles. As the leader of the new group, Muhammad was also, according to the understanding of the time, the protector of it, so he became a military leader. Eventually, he had sufficient support to return to Mecca, to deal with the idolatry there, and to lay the basis for the wider Islamic conquests that would rapidly follow his death.

This is the aspect of Muhammad that Christians find most difficult, tending to compare him with Jesus, who refused political power and went to the cross. When Jesus entered Jerusalem, lauded with palm leaves and hosannas, he came not to overthrow the political authorities, but to die at their hands and open the gates to the kingdom of heaven, which is 'not of this world'. We think of the way in which religious and political roles were

---

8. For an analysis of the progression in the Qur'an from preaching against evil to fighting against evil people, see D. Marshall, *God, Muhammad and the Unbelievers* (Richmond: Curzon Press, 1999).

separated in the Old Testament, as the kings and the priests were not permitted to perform each other's roles, and we see biblical accounts of kings tempted by power and getting tangled in a web linking land, religion, politics or people groups. Muhammad, say many Christians, acted as a religious figure when he was in Mecca, but, when he moved to Medina and developed political power, he went badly astray. Even within Islam today, there are people who suggest that it is appropriate for Muslims in today's world to focus on the example of Muhammad while he was at Mecca, rather than on what happened after the move to Medina.[9]

Most Muslims, however, see the rule in Medina and the final conquest of Mecca as intrinsic parts of Muhammad's prophetic ministry. They point out the need for society to be properly regulated, and see the measure of justice that Muhammad brought to seventh-century Arabia. And, indeed, the society that he established seems to have been more egalitarian than the society of the surrounding tribes, not least in the way that it treated women and vulnerable people. It also seems that his battles were fought along fairer principles. There were instances when he adopted conciliatory measures with enemies and he was relatively merciful to traitors. It is, these Muslims say, very important that religion should regulate the whole of life, and not just the spiritual parts of it.

How should we deal with this contrast between Muhammad and Jesus? First, from our study of the transfiguration, we saw that Islam avoids the cross, so we should not be surprised to find that Muhammad followed quite a different model than Jesus in his dealings with power. This is part of the fundamental difference between Islam and Christianity. However, we also saw that the Moses–Elijah model is not in itself wrong. The laws by which Moses established the Jewish community and laid the foundations for the conquest of the Promised Land were good, and it was God's plan to establish a people with authority to rule a land. Indeed, that is how he created humanity: to have authority in the land which he gave them. Even the Babel story does not teach that ethnicity, territory and authority are wrong in themselves, especially when it is read alongside the Table of Nations in Genesis 10. Rather, it tells us that the triangle linking them is dangerous, because people tend to put themselves at the centre rather than living under God.

---

9. The idea is proposed by Mahmud Muhammad Taha, *The Second Message of Islam*, trans. Abdullah al-Naim (New York: Syracuse University Press, 1987). Contemporary writers who explore this idea include Farid Esack (South Africa) and Omid Safi (USA).

So we can say that Muhammad's development of power was not wrong in itself: we can also appreciate the Muslim view of the importance of exercising power under the authority of God's laws. However, there are still the crucial questions of what happens when we do not keep God's laws and of what the human predicament really is; and there is always the temptation to take power for ourselves, our people and our place. We will explore this further in the next chapter, where we consider how we might think biblically about the power dimensions of Islam.

Using Genesis as a mirror in which to see the capacities for good or evil of the human heart and God's responses to it, we have, then, seen Muhammad as a religious man who fits into the Bible's picture of the world. The power dimension of his life, as every other dimension, reflects something of God's image in what he created as well as demonstrating the results of the fall. One way of discerning this is to continue to look in the 'mirror' of the Bible and find other people whose lives parallel that of Muhammad. To do this faithfully, we will need to read the biblical records at the three different levels we have developed in this book: first ensuring that we appreciate the historical context in the 'world behind the text', then seeing how they are portrayed by the writer in the 'world of the text', and only then making parallels with Muhammad or anyone else in 'the world in front of the text'. Here are some places in which we might 'see' Muhammad:

- There is some continuity between Muhammad and some of the *Old Testament prophets*. As a prophet like Elijah, preaching monotheism and higher ethical standards in an idolatrous and unjust generation, Muhammad delivered a positive message, but, in the light of the New Testament, it was of limited value without the hope of redemption. This would suggest that Muhammad can be viewed as a reformer who preached in accordance with much of the previous prophetic teaching.
- It has been traditional for Christians to see Muhammad as *a preacher to the Ishmaelites*. On the one hand, this idea is based on the biblical grounds that some of the Arabs were descended from Ishmael.[10] On the other hand, Muslims see Ishmael as the ancestor of Muhammad, a legitimate son of Abraham who was involved in building the Kaaba with him.[11] As there is no biblical

---

10. See Maalouf, *Arabs in the Shadow of Israel*.
11. This is based on Surah 2. 125–129.

warrant for accepting this Islamic view, many Christians would be wary of identifying Muslims with Ishmaelites. However, there are some helpful parallels. Ishmael was a descendant of Abraham who worshipped the God of Israel, but his descendants (like those of Esau, who was also ancestor to some of the people in the Arabian Peninsula) were not the covenant community. Both Ishmael and Esau enjoyed some of God's blessings. God made them 'fruitful' so that they multiplied to become great nations, but they were without the covenant promises. They, like all the other peoples, needed all that God would do through Israel, and they were often at enmity with Israel. We might view Muhammad as having brought an important message to these peoples, but, as we have seen, it was a message that stopped short of leading them to redemption.

- We might also see parallels between Muhammad and some of the *kings of Israel*. Jeroboam established the northern kingdom as a rival to the Davidic kingdom of Judah, setting up Samaria as an alternative to Jerusalem and his own forms of worship outside the ordained temple. Similarly, Muhammad changed the direction of worship from Jerusalem to Mecca and established a religious power block that was a rival to the Christian empires of his time. The fusion of political and religious spheres can also be seen in Saul, the first king of Israel. He overstepped his responsibilities and brought sacrifices to the altar: the result was judgement and the loss of his kingdom (1 Sam 15). We will reflect further on the question of religion and power in the next chapter; here we note that judgement for any overstepping on the part of Muhammad is in God's hands.

- Aspects of the military prowess of Muhammad might be seen in *Nebuchadnezzar and Cyrus*. They both acknowledged the God of Israel and were used as his instruments. This allows for the possibility that Muhammad may also have been used by God for particular purposes.

- Turning to the New Testament, we find a preacher whose early career offers a parallel to Muhammad as a preacher. 'Competent in the Scriptures . . . instructed in the way of the Lord . . . fervent in spirit', *Apollos* was a powerful speaker with many followers (Acts 18:24–25). To the extent that he was informed, he 'taught accurately' about Christ. Muhammad's revelation also included much of the

Old Testament and some details of the life of Christ. However, Apollos' understanding was limited, for he 'knew only the baptism of John' (18:25), which suggests that he lacked knowledge of the death and resurrection of Jesus and of the outpouring of the Holy Spirit. The message Muhammad delivered was likewise lacking in its understanding of Jesus and of the Holy Spirit, although it adds specific denials about his divinity. The response of one believing couple was simply to draw aside Apollos the gifted orator, and explain God's plan 'more accurately' (v. 26). The brothers then 'encouraged him' and asked for him to be welcomed by the disciples. Some Christians have suggested that the Qur'an's denials about Jesus and the Trinity refer to heresies rather than to orthodox doctrine,[12] and have wondered what would have happened if someone had accurately explained the gospel to Muhammad.

All these offer ways of thinking about the historical person of Muhammad as a human being of his time; we can be both positive and negative, because he was made in the image of God but was fallen. However, we do not need to stand in judgement over him, partly because of our limited knowledge of him, and partly because it is God's job to do that. As we move on to see what Muslims have made of him, and, in particular, how that affects their views of Jesus, the challenges to the gospel become sharper, and we need to make some judgements.

Muhammad in Islamic Thinking: Reversing the Transfiguration

Muhammad, lord of both worlds, lord of both species,
Lord of both assemblages – Arabs and all others.

He is the one whose meaning and form were perfected,
And then the Originator of souls chose him as the beloved.

Incomparable, his beauty has no peer –
The essence of beauty itself is in his nature.

Leave aside what the Christians have claimed for their prophet –
Then praise him as you like, but do so wisely.

Ascribe to his essence what you wish of honour,

---

12. See, for example, G. Parrinder, *Jesus in the Qur'an* (Oxford: Oneworld, 1965), ch. 14.

Attribute to his exalted status what you will of greatness!

Truly, the Messenger of God's bounty
Cannot be overstated by two lips and a tongue.

If a miracle could equal his stature in magnitude,
The mere mention of his name would revive decaying bones.

The extent of what we know of him is this: He is a man,
And yet, without exception, he is the best of God's creation.

All of the signs brought by the noble prophets before him
Came to them through his light alone.

He is the bounteous sun and they her orbiting planets –
She reveals their lights for humanity in the darkness of night –

Until finally his light dawned on the horizon,
And his radiant guidance suffused the world and brought life to
    countless civilisation.

What excellence lies in the birth of a prophet adorned with such
    character!
Beauty itself shines forth from his smiling face!

Exquisite as a lily, illustrious as a full moon,
Magnanimous as the ocean, persistent as time.

Due to his majesty, even when alone,
He seemed surrounded by military might and cohorts of
    courtiers.

It is as if precious pearls, locked in their shells,
Poured from the treasury of his sweet mouth and smile.

As if, face to face with the sun,
Minds were forced to blink at the mere sight of him.

No perfume is as sweet as the ground that holds his bones –
What Paradise awaits the one who breathes its scent or brushes
    lips against its soil!

(From a famous Sufi poem)[13]

---

13. Al-Busiri, *Qaṣida al-Burda* or *The Poem of the Cloak* (13th century). This is a selection of stanzas from the translation by Hamza Yusuf at http://syedsalman.buzznet.com/user/journal/60429/blessed-burdah-poem-cloak-noble/; accessed October 2014.

To Think About

What is your reaction to this praise given to Muhammad?

How do the Muslims you know think and feel about Muhammad?

We turn now from the historical figure of Muhammad to Muslims' views of him. What should we think about their beliefs in him as the *final prophet*, as an *example* to be followed, as a figure who is *greatly honoured*, as the *first leader of the ummah* (Muslim people), and as someone to whom *devotion* is given?

On the one hand, our consideration of the Qur'an has already led us to say that we cannot accept Muhammad as 'the *final prophet*'. On the other hand, we have seen that his ministry paralleled that of some of the Old Testament prophets, and, in particular, of Moses and of Elijah: that is, Muhammad takes us back to a pre-transfiguration view of the prophets. Muhammad can be seen as modelling himself on Moses and Elijah, and we can see positive aspects to this. However, in Islamic thinking his ministry does not just take us back to a time before the transfiguration, because it happened long afterwards. Effectively, it removes all that is signified by the transfiguration and establishes the new Moses–Elijah figure as the final prophet.

Muhammad then becomes not only the preacher of a monotheistic message, but also the embodiment of that message and an *example* to be followed. His example becomes, along with the Qur'an, the basis for shariah law, which we will consider in chapter 11 below. There is much about Muhammad's life that accords with biblical ways of living. For example, he was concerned about social justice, about making provision for orphans and widows, about ethical conduct in war, and about honesty in speech and conduct. From a Christian perspective, the problem is that most Muslims see him as an example to be followed in the details of life, and not just in principle. If Muhammad was a person of his time, then, however good his example might have been in that time and place, it is unlikely to be good for all times and places. Further, there are aspects of Muhammad's life that, when compared with New Testament teaching and with the life of Jesus, were wrong: an obvious example is his polygamy.

As the prophet who brought the message on which Muslims base their lives, and as the example they wish to follow, it is not surprising that Muhammad is *greatly honoured* by Muslims. Islam grew in a society where honour was important, and Muslim cultures today generally see the honour of family and community as a central plank of society. Leaders in particular are to be honoured; and honouring the leader also honours the family or community which he leads. So Muslims honour Muhammad not only in their individual thinking but also in set words and actions. For example, people recite, in Arabic, *ṣalā allāhu 'alayhi wa āhlihi wa salim* ('peace and blessings be upon him and his family') after mentioning Muhammad's name, and try to copy his actions in everything they do. From a Christian perspective, the problem is that Muslims can therefore be very sensitive to anything they perceive to be dishonouring Muhammad.

At a social and political level, sensitivity about Muhammad's honour can be due to his role as *the founder of the Muslim ummah*. As its first leader and its model, Muhammad's honour is also the honour of his community. The honour of Islam and the honour of Muslim people worldwide are therefore bound up in the honour of Muhammad.

At the personal level, the honouring of Muhammad raises the question of how far a Christian can or should use honorific titles for Muhammad. Muhammad is not the only person on whom Muslims call down blessings: all prophets may have their names followed by *'alayhi salām* ('peace be upon him'), and most Muslims give prophets an honorific title in everyday speech. For example, they would not simply say 'Moses' but 'the prophet Moses', or (on the Indian subcontinent) *hazrat*[14] Moses. From a biblical perspective, we can use honorific titles for the prophets, and especially for Jesus, but what about Muhammad? We are told to honour all people, and particularly political authorities (1 Pet 2:17; Rom 13:1–7), so we can honour Muhammad as a human being and acknowledge his role as a leader and reformer; but can we find a way of talking about him that does not also imply that we accept him as a prophet or that we admire everything that he did? The answer will depend on the particular Muslims to whom we are speaking. Some have no problem with non-Muslims simply calling him 'Muhammad'. Some are at ease with us calling him 'your prophet'. Some Christians are happy to say, 'peace be upon him' – but it is wise to find out what Muslims understand by this.

---

14. This is a title of honour and respect. It is an Arabic word which literally means 'Presence'.

Is It 'Just Being Polite'?

My Urdu teacher insisted that I learn to pronounce *ṣalā allāhu 'alayhi wa āhlihi wa salim* properly, and that I say it every time that I read 'Muhammad' or any word that referred to him. 'It's just being polite,' she said; so I did what she asked. Then, bit by bit, she told me what Muhammad meant to her, and why this formula was so important. She wanted me to join in her prayers for Muhammad and even to Muhammad. I eventually told her that I could not do that, so we came to an agreement. I would read the word 'Muhammad' and would then pause, and she would recite the blessing.

To Discuss with Muslim Friends

Do the Muslims you know recite this blessing after the name of Muhammad? What do they mean by it? How do they feel about the way you speak about Muhammad?

Many Muslims, like the Urdu teacher, go beyond 'honouring' Muhammad to what we might call *devotion* – as can be seen, for example, in the poem at the beginning of this section. They sing hymns to him, revere his tomb and his relics, and even pray to him. Among Sufis, whole nights can be spent in singing in his honour. Some go so far as to speak of him as the pre-existent light, whose light lightens all the prophets. Among Shi'ites, the honour and devotion extend to his family and descendants. We may wonder how such a position can be given to someone who, historically, was simply a human being and never claimed to be more than that – and many Muslims would agree and say that this sort of devotion is wrong.

At both ends of the Islamic spectrum, people would say that the other end is not properly Muslim: they accuse each other either of not honouring Muhammad or of *shirk* (associating someone with God). But, from a Christian perspective, there is a bigger problem: the position that is given to Muhammad is that which, we believe, is the position properly occupied by Jesus. On the one hand, we might say that devotion to Muhammad represents the desire of the human heart for Jesus; on the other hand, we will be jealous for the honour of Jesus, and sad that devotion to a Muhammad who effectively takes the place of Jesus often gets in the way of people looking at Jesus at all.

We can sum this up by saying that, in much Islamic thinking, the transfiguration and all that it signifies is *replaced* by Muhammad, as the Qur'an would later replace the Bible and Mecca would replace Jerusalem. This is vividly illustrated in the story of Muhammad's own trip to Jerusalem, which can be seen as an Islamic parallel to the transfiguration. Just as the transfiguration deals with the question 'How does Jesus relate to the other prophets?' so this story answers the question 'How does Muhammad relate to the other prophets?'

The event is called 'the night journey' (*mi'rāj*), and is said to have occurred in the year preceding the *hijrah* to Medina. The story is based on a single, hard-to-understand verse in the Qur'an which, interestingly, is followed by a verse which parallels Muhammad with Moses:

> Glory to Him who made His servant travel by night from the sacred place of worship to the furthest place of worship, whose surroundings We have blessed, to show him some of Our signs: He alone is the All Hearing, the All Seeing. We also gave Moses the Scripture, and made it a guide for the Children of Israel (Surah 17. 1–2).[15]

The 'sacred place of worship' (*Al-masjid al-harām*) is taken to be the Kaaba at Mecca, and the 'furthest place of worship' (*Al-masjid al-aqsa*) to be the site of the temple in Jerusalem. Some commentators see the trip as a dream, but most Muslims believe that this was a literal journey. The story is told in the Hadith.[16]

The *Mi'rāj*

The prophet recounted how, one night by the Kaaba, an angel came to him, opened up his body and, cleansing his heart with sacred Zamzam water, filled him with wisdom. He was given a white animal named Buraq, sized between a donkey and a mule, to ride. In one stride it could reach the horizon. Gabriel then took him through the heavens, ascending from the lowest to the highest. At each level, Gabriel called out for the gate to be opened. From there, the prophets

---

15. M. A. S. Abdel Haleem, *The Qur'an: A New Translation by M. A. S. Abdel Haleem* (Oxford: Oxford University Press, 2008), Used with permission.

16. There are numerous Hadith and stories about the *mi'rāj* from which the following account is taken. One of the most important is *Sahih Muslim*, Book 1, No. 309, at www.usc. edu/org/cmje/religious-texts/hadith/muslim/001-smt.php. Other quotations are from *Ṣaḥīḥ Bukhāri* and *Sahih Muslim I*, both available on www.sunnah.com.

called down to enquire who it was and who was with the angel. 'Has he been sent for?' they all asked on hearing it was Muhammad. 'Yes,' Gabriel announced. Accordingly, the gates were thrown open.

'Welcome unto him! His is a blessed arrival,' each prophet declared, starting with Adam; then, in the second heaven, Jesus and John the Baptist; Joseph in the third; Idris (Enoch), Aaron and Moses in the following heavens; culminating with Abraham in the seventh heaven, reclining against the House of Allāh (Bayt al-Ma'mūr). They welcomed him and prayed for his welfare. In the heavens higher than Adam's, the prophets called Muhammad 'brother and righteous prophet'. In some accounts, Moses wept when he saw Muhammad. 'On being asked why he was weeping, he said, "O Lord! Followers of this youth who was sent after me will enter Paradise in greater number than my followers."'

In the seventh heaven, Muhammad was shown wonderful sights. Seventy thousand angels entered Bayt al-Ma'mūr, and he was told that a host of seventy thousand more visited each new day. There was a tree with massive fruit and leaves as big as elephant ears from whose roots flowed the Nile, the Euphrates and two more hidden rivers. Gabriel brought to Muhammad two cups, one of wine and the other of milk. When he chose the milk, Gabriel was pleased and remarked, 'This is the Islamic religion which you and your followers are following.'

Allāh then instructed Muhammad that he and his followers were to pray fifty times a day. When Muhammad returned to Moses and told him this, Moses urged him to go back and seek a reduction. 'Your followers cannot bear fifty prayers a day, and by Allāh, I have tested people before you, and I have tried my level best with Bani Israel [the Sons of Israel] (in vain). Go back to your Lord and ask for reduction to lessen your followers' burden.' And so, Muhammad returned to Allāh and asked for a lessening of this 'burden'. Allāh reduced the number bit by bit, until they settled at five prayers a day. One Hadith writer includes Allāh's explanation: 'There are five prayers every day and night, O Muhammad, each being credited as ten, so that makes fifty prayers.' Although Moses continued to urge Muhammad to return and ask that his followers might pray even fewer than five times, at this point Muhammad replied, 'I have requested so much of my Lord that I feel ashamed, but I am satisfied now and surrender to Allāh's Order.'

Many stories have arisen around these accounts, emphasizing the supernatural nature of the event. They glorify Muhammad, but do so in a different way from that by which the transfiguration glorifies Jesus. Perhaps the greatest contrast is that Muhammad makes a journey up into the heavens to speak with God, while the transfiguration has the voice of God coming down to speak, not only to Jesus, but also to the watching disciples on earth. Similarly, Muhammad has to go to the heavens to meet the other prophets, while Moses and Elijah come down to earth to speak with Jesus.

Wherever we can see similarities between the transfiguration and the *mi'rāj*, we also see differences:

- Both are travel stories of journeys to mountains, but Jesus' journey is an ordinary one: a hike up an ordinary hill with only a few disciples for company. Muhammad's is an extraordinary journey, a miraculous one, to the holy of holies in Jerusalem in the company of angels.

- Both glorify the central character, but while Muhammad is given glory through being 'sent for' to receive a revelation in the highest heaven, Jesus shines with the glory of God come down and is honoured by the voice of God heard on earth.

- Both cases include revelation, but while it is Muhammad who receives revelation about the prayers, it is Jesus' disciples who receive revelation about the nature of Jesus.

- Both show how the central character relates to the prophets. Muhammad, ascending to the highest heaven, is seen as superior to all the other prophets, and the *mi'rāj* is, after the Qur'an, the one 'miracle' from the life of Muhammad that is universally recognized (even if some think it was a dream, and some believe stories of his other miracles). The transfiguration, by contrast, does not present Jesus simply as greater than Moses and Elijah, but as different from them.

- Both record interactions between the central character and the former prophets. In the *mi'rāj*, the prophets acknowledge Muhammad and pray for his welfare. At the transfiguration, Peter has just shown concern for Jesus' welfare, but Jesus stays determined to go to the cross. While Moses discusses the daily prayers with Muhammad, it is about the 'departure' on the cross that he and Elijah talk with Jesus.

- Both mark the beginning of the next season of their ministries. Muhammad comes down with the five daily prayers and goes on to lead the *hijrah* (which also means 'exodus' and 'departure') to Medina and, eventually, the triumphant return to Mecca. Jesus comes down to heal the demon-possessed boy and 'set[s] his face to go to Jerusalem' (Luke 9:51), towards the cross and resurrection.

It is the replacement of Jesus by Muhammad that leads to the most negative Christian thinking about him. However open we may be to trying to understand him as a human being in history, we always come face to face with what Muslims have made of him and of his teaching. If this Muhammad effectively replaces Jesus, he must surely be, from a biblical perspective, a false prophet or a false messiah. If, in that replacement, he denies the divinity of Jesus and all that goes with it, he functions as what is called, in 1 John 2:18–27, 'an antichrist'. Insofar as an antichrist 'denies the Father and the Son' (1 John 2:22), Muhammad (among others – for, according to this passage, many are to come) can be said to be one.

On the other hand, Muhammad does not easily fit some other aspects of the 'antichrist' description. An antichrist denies that Jesus is the Messiah (1 John 2:22): the Qur'an frequently gives Jesus the title 'Messiah', although it never suggests what the title means. The 'antichrists' in 1 John were people who had been part of the church: there is no evidence of Muhammad ever having identified himself as a Christian, even though he saw his message as continuing from Judaism and Christianity. Historically, he seems to have identified with Jewish belief and practice, and then to have parted from that as he changed the *Qiblah* (direction of prayer) from Jerusalem to Mecca. (This gives an important clue for thinking about Islam which we will pick up again in chapter 12.)

What is, perhaps, more important than how we label Muhammad is what the implications of our labels might be for the way we think about Islam and treat Muslims. If we see him as an 'antichrist', should that lead us to anger and hostility, and to a view of Islam as a sign of the end times, with Muslim communities perhaps as threats to our security to be fought by military means? We will explore this question further in part 4. Here, we think briefly about the context of the 'antichrist' passage in 1 John. It is important to note that John's response to the 'antichrists' is not to attack them but to call believers back to the true news of Christ they have already heard, which they must allow to 'abide' in themselves. Here, the antichrists' coming is seen as no cause for panic and dread, for no call to arms nor bristling hostility, but simply firmer faith: the antichrists were just one part of a world 'in the power of the evil one' but in which Christians could know they were under God's protection (5:18–19). Muhammad's claims were and still are a challenge to Christians, but not a unique one, and they in no way require a desertion of the love, righteousness, discernment and faith in Jesus that overcomes the world. 'Let what you heard from the beginning abide in you,' wrote John (1 John 2:24). Can we respond to these aspects of Muhammad, his message and his followers with this quiet confidence in the truth?

The issue becomes acute as we take it beyond questions of personal and communal belief and into the realms of politics and law, as we will see in the next chapters. But, first, we consider how one Christian leader talked about Muhammad to a powerful Muslim ruler. One of the earliest accounts that we have of a dialogue between a Muslim and a Christian is that of the Nestorian Patriarch Timothy's answers to the questioning of the powerful Caliph Al-Mamun over two days in Baghdad in AD 781. At that time, Al-Mamun's son, Harun Ar-Rashid, was fighting against the Byzantines. The situation must have been tense: Timothy was not only defending the gospel, but determining also the treatment of his whole Christian community. There is in his defence a great deal of interesting discussion about many aspects of the Christian faith, but what interests us here is how, in this potentially explosive situation, Timothy handled questions about Muhammad.

During the first day's discussion, Timothy explained why he did not believe that the Bible predicted the coming of Muhammad, why he would not accept that Muhammad was the 'prophet like Moses' of Deuteronomy 18:18, and why the only 'final prophet' predicted in Scripture was Elijah. On the second day, after a brief discussion about the book of Gospels that Timothy had brought at the caliph's request, the caliph launched the debate with the crucial question, 'What do you think of Muhammad?' Here is Timothy's initial answer:

> Muhammad is worthy of all praise, by all reasonable people, O my Sovereign. He walked in the path of the prophets, and trod in the track of the lovers of God. All the prophets taught the doctrine of one God, and since Muhammad taught the doctrine of the unity of God, he walked, therefore, in the path of the prophets. Further, all the prophets drove men away from bad works, and brought them nearer to good works, and since Muhammad drove his people away from bad works and brought them nearer to the good ones, he walked, therefore, in the path of the prophets. Again, all

the prophets separated men from idolatry and polytheism, and attached them to God and to His cult, and since Muhammad separated his people from idolatry and polytheism, and attached them to the cult and the knowledge of one God, beside whom there is no other God, it is obvious that he walked in the path of the prophets. Finally Muhammad taught about God, His Word and His Spirit, and since all the prophets had prophesied about God, His Word and His Spirit, Muhammad walked, therefore, in the path of all the prophets.[17]

Timothy would go on to talk about the Trinity in terms of God, his Word and his Spirit later that day.

To Think About

'He walked in the path of the prophets.' What do you think Timothy meant by this? Could you use it as a beginning to a discussion with a Muslim who asked, 'What do you think of Muhammad?' in your context?

---

17. This translation is by A. Mingana and can be found at 'Timothy I, Apology for Christianity (1928)', http://www.tertullian.org/fathers/timothy_i_apology_01_text.htm; accessed October 2014.

10

Thinking about the *Ummah*: Community, Power and Violence

Moses was, under God, a political leader. Like Muhammad, he formed a people under a law. His political power was God-ordained, and it differed in important ways from the political power of the surrounding nations and from the political powers regularly seen throughout history. *Elijah* challenged the political powers of his day because they were corrupt. Like Muhammad, his challenge was first towards their religious idolatry and then towards their selfish and unjust abuses of their power. *Jesus* inaugurated a powerful kingdom, but it was a different kind of kingdom from that of the Romans or even of the Jews. Unlike Muhammad, he refused to become a political leader. How, then, shall we 'think biblically' about a religion that returns to a model of law and of political power?

As we saw in chapter 5, people in tense situations often find hope and meaning in expectations of the end of the world, and it is popular in some Christian circles today to think about increasing Islamic political power in apocalyptic terms, identifying some of the images in both Old and New Testament writings with Muslims.

This sort of thinking is not new: it dates back to the earliest Islamic conquests when, for example, Pseudo-Methodius, writing in the Byzantine Empire at the end of the seventh century, described the period of the dominance of 'the Sons of Ishmael' as 'the chastisement that is to come before the Anti-christ is revealed'. He expressed his hope that, after the period of ease and pride for the Muslim 'tyrants', 'the king of the Greeks will go out against them in great wrath . . . and will cast desolation and destruction in the desert of Yathrib [Medina] and in the habitation of their fathers'.[1] One might ask whether today's Internet-based theologians are any less likely to be mistaken than were the writers of the seventh century.

However, as we start to think about manifestations of Islam that frighten many people (Muslims as well as non-Muslims), the message of the apocalyptic writings remains important in thinking biblically about Islam. We may or may not be in the 'end times', but, whatever our views on this, if we focus on what may and may not be the fulfilment of prophecy, we are in danger of missing an important dimension of biblical thinking. The Bible's apocalyptic pictures are not intended to make people afraid – quite the opposite: they are intended to enable people to live faithfully and joyfully, knowing that God is in control of all the clashing powers.

For example, the book of Daniel deals with a situation in which the Jews were a captive minority living under a powerful and often corrupt empire. The apocalyptic imagery of Daniel 7 – 12 gives an assurance of God's supremacy over history that is as much needed today as it was then. It is such an assurance that underpins the sorts of lives that were lived by Daniel and his three friends, which set an example for God's people in a place of weakness of effective godly witness to political powers. The problem is that apocalyptic thinking can draw people's focus in quite a different direction: away from the glorious vision of God's strength for limiting evil and for enabling us to be faithful witnesses, towards a threatening image of the whole of Islam as an enemy, embodied as one of the beasts.

Sadly, some Muslim groups do act in such beastly ways. At the time of writing, a militant group fighting across the Middle East announced the formation of 'the Islamic State', to be headed by a caliph. A colleague who studies Islamic law and history agrees with the many Muslims who say that this declaration is 'nonsense' – that this cannot be seen as a legitimate state or a legitimate caliph from the perspective of any school of Islamic law.[2] However, it claims to be based on the Qur'an and the Hadith. The declaration of the caliphate begins thus:

---

1. Ch. 13, 'The Apocalypse of Pseudo-Methodius', tr. in Paul Alexander, *The Byzantine Apocalyptic Tradition* (Berkeley: University of California Press, 1985), 36–51. Here he is referring to 2 Thess 2:3, rendering the word usually translated 'rebellion' as 'chastisement'.

2. For Muslims explaining why the 'Islamic State' is not properly Islamic, see, for example, 'Haqiqah: What Is the Truth Behind ISIS?', http://imamsonline.com/blog/haqiqah-what-is-the-truth-behind-isis/; and 'Open Letter to Al-Baghdadi', http://www.lettertobaghdadi.com/.

Praise be to Allāh, the Mighty and Strong. And may peace and blessings be upon the one sent with the sword as a mercy to all creation . . .

Allāh (the Exalted) said: 'Allāh has promised those who have believed among you and done righteous deeds that He will surely grant them succession [to authority] upon the earth just as He granted it to those before them and that He will surely establish for them their religion which He has preferred for them and that He will surely substitute for them, after their fear, security, [for] they worship Me, not associating anything with Me. But whoever disbelieves after that – then those are the defiantly disobedient' (An-Nūr [Surah 24]. 55).

Succession [caliphate], establishment, and safety – a promise from Allāh reserved for the Muslims, but with a condition. {They worship me [Allāh] and do not associate anything with me} [An-Nūr: 55] . . . only after this condition is met will the promise be fulfilled. For by fulfilling this condition comes the ability to build, reform, remove oppression, spread justice, and bring about safety and tranquillity. Only by meeting this condition, will there be the succession [caliphate], which Allāh informed the angels about.[3]

Without this condition being met, authority becomes nothing more than kingship, dominance and rule, accompanied with destruction, corruption, oppression, subjugation, fear, and the decadence of the human being and his descent to the level of animals. That is the reality of succession, which Allāh created us for. It is not simply kingship, subjugation, dominance, and rule. Rather, succession is to utilize all that for the purpose of compelling the people to do what the Shariʿah (Allāh's law) requires of them concerning their interests in the hereafter and worldly life, which can only be achieved by carrying out the command of Allāh, establishing His religion, and referring to His law for judgment.

---

3. This is an interpretation of God's declaration to the angels that he would put a caliph on the earth in Surah 2. 30.

This succession . . . is the purpose for which Allāh sent His messengers and revealed His scriptures, and for which the swords of jihād were unsheathed.

Indeed, Allāh (the Exalted) honored the *ummah* (nation) of Muhammad and blessed them. He made them the best *ummah* of all peoples.[4]

To Think About

Where do you see the themes of expectation discussed in chapter 5 (e.g. themes of hope, safety, meaning, deliverance, justice and the fulfilment of God's promises) in this passage?

What can you see here that might be attractive to young Muslims who feel that the world is a dangerous place for them and for their people?

Before the final paragraph of the 'Declaration of the Islamic State' comes this poem:

We took it forcibly at the point of a blade.
  We brought it back conquered and compelled.
We established it in defiance of many.
  And the people's necks were violently struck,
With bombings, explosions, and destruction,
  And soldiers that do not see hardship as being difficult,
And lions that are thirsty in battle,
  Having greedily drunk the blood of kufr [unbelievers].
Our khilāfah has indeed returned with certainty
  And likewise our state, becoming a firm structure.
And the breasts of the believers have been healed,
  While the hearts of kufr have been filled with terror.

---

4. 'Declaration of the Islamic State', June 2014, https://ia902505.us.archive.org/28/items/poa_25984/EN.pdf.

> **To Think About**
>
> Is your heart 'filled with terror' as you read this? What other feelings and thoughts does it raise for you? As a Christian, what would you want to say to the person who wrote this?

This declaration is an interesting starting point for our thinking about the power dimension of Islam, not because it represents a standard Islamic view – it does not – but because it represents what many Christians fear that Islam is 'really like'. It uses many Islamic concepts to produce a fearful version of Babel-religion, using religion to take power for a particular group in a particular area. While there are many Christians and other minorities who are suffering in the present conflict in that area, most of the people who are suffering are Muslims on all sides of the fighting. That increases people's sense of danger, which, in turn, increases the need for apocalyptic expectations.

One of the main concepts that underlies the declaration is that of Muslims as an *ummah*. The Arabic word *ummah* is usually translated 'people'. Muslims have a theoretical idea of the Muslim *ummah* as the worldwide community of Muslims, who are to be treated as brothers: at its best, this produces strong, caring communities that include people from many different backgrounds.

In practice, however, there have been different groups claiming to be the true Muslims from very early in Islamic history, but there have usually been one or two political leaders who have had the title 'caliph' and have been widely recognized as leaders of the *ummah*.[5] Today, as we have frequently noted, there continues to be a variety of claims to true Islamic identity, and there is also a huge variation, not only in how Islamic law is interpreted, but also in how far it is incorporated into the laws of Muslim-majority countries. The last caliph was the leader of the Ottoman Empire, which ended in 1922, and, since then, some Muslims have felt that there needed to be a new caliphate in order to re-establish Islamic rule. Others point out that Muslims are not sufficiently united to form a caliphate, that power structures have changed since the times of the Islamic empires, that large numbers of Muslims live happily under non-Muslim rule, and even that non-Muslim countries are often safer places for Muslims than are Muslim-majority countries; and most agree that the so-called 'Islamic State' currently being established does not at

---

5. For a good overview, see A. Silverstein, *Islamic History: A Very Short Introduction* (Oxford: Oxford University Press, 2010), or D. Brown, *A New Introduction to Islam* (Chichester: Wiley-Blackwell, 2009), Part 2.

all satisfy the conditions for a legitimate caliphate. However, it is clear that, at root, Islam has an essential link between faith and power: this originated in the life of Muhammad himself. Before we ask how our biblical studies can help us to think about all this, let us listen again to Ali:

Ali's Comments

We need to see the concept of *ummah* in historical perspective. We need to know about the expansion of Islamic rule and the spread of Islamic religion so that we can see what was and is meant by the word. In my view, the *ummah* concept did not really become important until after the period of Ummayad rule [AD 661–750, based in Damascus]. The kings were not so strong, and the *ummah* concept was a way of affirming identity and exerting control over a growing and very diverse empire.

When I think about Muhammad's concept of *ummah*, I see that he saw Abraham as the father of the *ummah*, so I ask whether it might include Jews and Christians – the 'People of the Book'. Of course, Muslim thinkers now exclude Jews and Christians, and we see some problems arising. Some people are going back to the idea of a caliphate and trying to establish their version of Islamic rule. There's a big problem with the dar-ul-islam / dar-ul-harb mentality: the idea that the world is divided into the 'House of Islam' and the 'House of War'. That doesn't leave much room for our community of believers in Jesus from Muslim backgrounds. Our local communities tolerate us – we have some problems with, for example, finding burial space, but they don't eject us from the community. The new wave of Islamists are not so tolerant. They killed my spiritual 'father' and we don't know what they will do next.

There's a difference between ideals and reality. Sometimes, I think that the main function of the ideal of the Muslim *ummah* is to hide the reality of disunity. For example, in practice, there are at least two different *ummah*s: Sunni and Shi'ite. Like the church, the true *ummah* – the international community of believers – is invisible. It's the visible manifestation of the *ummah* that is – or at least should be – different from the visible manifestation of the church, because it's linked with political power. It's the visible *ummah*, not the invisible one, that can cause problems.

Next to the denials about Jesus, the 'power' dimension of Islam is its most difficult aspect from a Christian point of view. As we start our biblical reflection on this aspect, it is important to remember that it is not specific to

Islam. Ali starts his reflection on the *ummah* by considering how the concept grew in its historical human situation. He has experienced how the idea that Muslims should have political control can make life difficult for a non-Muslim minority, but he has also seen his community finding ways to tolerate converts. He has experienced loss due to 'Islamists' who act somewhat as 'the Islamic State' recommends, but he speaks without bitterness, knowing that they also cause trouble for many Muslims and for other minorities. He notes the difference between theory and practice: the problem is not so much the system as sinfulness.

All this fits our Genesis framework. We can see in the *ummah* something of the image of God, in the ideal of a diverse but loving and united brotherhood; we can also see the Cain-and-Abel-like actuality of division and violence within it. We can see people really seeking God, even sacrificing lives – on the one hand, thinking that they are pleasing God by killing Ali's 'spiritual father', and, on the other hand, as 'martyrs', sacrificing their own lives as they kill to further their Islamic cause. We can see the joining of power and religion that our study of the Babel story in chapter 1 shows is to be expected in a fallen world. We can see people trying to deal with what they see as evil.

The *ummah* is a very attractive ideal that reflects not only what the Bible sees as God's intention for his creation but also the ideal of what Israel ought to be, the ideal of what the church ought to be, and the reality of the redeemed community of worshippers in heaven. However, our Genesis framework points to two problems. First, human beings are fallen, and so, when we build 'our' communities, we tend to exclude others – the *ummah* can then break into factions, and develop hostility towards competing *ummah*s either within the faith or outside it. Second, from the time of Muhammad's move to Medina, it has been assumed that, ideally, this *ummah* should be in a position of power – that is, the rulers should be Muslim, ruling in accordance with Islamic law. When combined with the problem of fallen human nature, this has the potential of producing the triumphalist hatred and violence exhibited in the Islamic State declaration.

Power is not wrong in itself: when God created human beings, he gave them authority to rule in the place where he put them. When he established the people of Israel, he also raised up leaders and judges and, eventually, kings. Yes, Israel's demand for a king showed lack of faith in God (1 Sam 8), so we can see that kingship is a danger; but God himself established the kingship and he undertook to use it for his glory and for the blessing of not only Israel but also the nations. There were good kings who ruled under God, as well as bad kings who rebelled against him. In sum, authority in society is necessary; but, in our fallen world, it can also go very wrong, especially when it joins forces with religion. We should expect to see the same patterns in Muslims as in other people; and we will need to beware of falling into the same patterns ourselves.

So, is there anything uniquely violent about bids for power in Islam as represented by the caliphate declaration? Are they any different from, for example, the Spanish Inquisition, the aggressive imposition of communist rule under Mao or Stalin, the violent attempt at an 'Aryan' takeover under Hitler, or the violence that is being perpetrated by a variety of non-Muslim states at this very moment?

The most obvious answer is that, because Islam has linked faith and power from the beginning, people easily find aspects of it that justify them taking power for their particular group in their particular place. It readily lends itself as a plank for building the 'dangerous triangle'. In classical Islamic thinking, shariah law carefully regulates power so that the conduct of war and of government is as just as possible. However, there is also room for the abuse of violence and of power that can be based on appeals to the Qur'an and the Hadith. After all, the Qur'an and Hadith do urge fighting in the establishment of Islam; the questions are, under what conditions should Muslims fight? For what purpose and in what ways? And, perhaps most importantly, who has the authority to declare a war a 'jihād', a venture that strives in the way of God?[6] Most Muslims would say that the self-declared caliphate of 'the Islamic State' has answered these questions wrongly; but if even a few Muslims think they have them right, it is dangerous.

However, there is a further answer that arises from our Genesis study which relates to the question of how we deal with evil. We saw in the Noah story the two alternatives of flood and sacrifice: of judgement that destroys the evildoers with the evil, or of finding a way to cleanse both evil and evildoers. Jesus, we said, is the acceptable sacrifice to which Noah's sacrifice and all the other acceptable sacrifices point. Jesus' own sacrifice on the cross is the way that he responded to the evil perpetrated by his enemies; and it offers the model and the incentive for his followers to love their enemies, as he commanded (Matt 5:44).

Islam, as we have seen, takes out that sacrifice as it effectively rewrites the transfiguration and replaces the centrality of Christ, facing the cross,

---

6. For a helpful account of the history of Islamic views of *jihād*, see D. Cook, *Understanding Jihad* (Berkeley: University of California Press, 2005).

with Muhammad and all he stands for. Logically, then, we are left with the 'flood' alternative of dealing with evil. That is, evil should be punished and, if necessary, the evildoers should be removed.

Of course, it is not so simple as this. The Qur'an has a strong emphasis on God's mercy as well as on God's judgement, so most Muslims see mercy as very important. They know that they (and everyone else) need forgiveness, and they hope for the mercy of God. At a personal level, many expect that all who acknowledge the unity of God and the prophethood of Muhammad will eventually get to paradise. However, there is much uncertainty as to how far their more serious sins can be forgiven, and little hope of forgiveness for unbelievers.[7] At this level, there is, according to the oft-quoted qur'anic verse, 'no compulsion in religion' (Surah 2. 256):[8] judgement for evil will be carried out by God.

At the society level, too, mercy and forgiveness are important, as we will see in the next chapter, on shariah. The legal system deals with evil and it frequently recommends mercy. However, it often uses severe punishment, including capital punishment for certain offences. Islamic law also deals with international relations and with war. This is not surprising, since it developed through times when Islamic rule was expanding and warfare was normal. There are strong traditions of mercy towards enemies who accept Islamic rule, but, in the Qur'an itself, there is also the tradition of killing those who do not (Surah 9: 5–15). There is much discussion among Muslims as to whether, how and under what circumstances enemies of Islam should be killed today.[9] However, the principle of dealing with some evils by killing the perpetrators is there, and can feed the 'dangerous triangle'.

Dealing with evil through punishment – even capital punishment – is not, according to the Bible, necessarily wrong – indeed, it might sometimes be right, as is shown by many of the laws given to Moses[10] and by the punishment

---

7. See C. Moucarry, *The Search for Forgiveness: Pardon and Punishment in Islam and Christianity* (Nottingham: IVP, 2004) for a detailed discussion of these questions.

8. M. A. S. Abdel Haleem, *The Qur'an: A New Translation by M. A. S. Abdel Haleem* (Oxford: Oxford University Press, 2008), Used with permission.

9. At one extreme, people hear it as a call to kill people they see as enemies of Islam. At the other extreme, people say that these verses were only for use in that context, and have no relevance for today except, perhaps, as a metaphor for non-physical struggles against evil. In the middle, there are discussions about how and when warfare is required that are quite similar to Christian discussions about 'just wars'. For a helpful overview of the range of Muslim understandings of struggle, see D. Cook, *Understanding Jihad* (Berkeley: University of California Press, 2005).

10. For example, Deut 13; 21:18–21; 22:13–22.

meted out to the prophets of Baal by Elijah (1 Kgs 18:40). Similarly, dealing with a whole nation's evil through warfare is not necessarily wrong, and might be right: we find biblical records both of God using Israel as his instrument of judgement, as in the conquests of Joshua, and of God using other nations as his instruments for judging Israel, as in the exile. The completion of Elijah's ministry of challenging Baal worship and the Omride dynasty is a particularly vivid example of dealing with evil through destruction: Jehu (whom Elijah was told to anoint, but who was eventually anointed by Elisha) had all the seventy sons of Ahab and all the Baal worshippers slaughtered, and this is seen as obedience to God (2 Kgs 10 – 11).

It is important to note that the biblical material about such judgements is all in the Old Testament – in the era before the transfiguration. We recall that, in the story of Noah, God committed himself to the way of sacrifice that would mean that the world would not be destroyed. The transfiguration leads on to the cross, and the challenge for the Christian is then to re-read the Old Testament judgements with that in mind. How should taking the alternative way of the cross form our responses to criminal and national evil, and to violence? We will take up this question in our final chapter.

The point here is that we can find, in the biblical mirror, many instances of people like the fighters for the current 'Islamic State' or those who fight under other banners of Islam (or indeed any other banner) who seek to deal with evil through violence. This does not make their fighting right, but it does help us to understand it. We can see it as people trying to deal with evil, and thinking that they are doing this on God's behalf. The problems are that they might be quite wrong about whom they see as 'evil', and that, in fighting, they can themselves do much evil. What is needed is the cleansing of evil in the human heart: the taking out of the 'log' in our own eyes before we try to correct anyone else (Matt 7:3).

It is also important to recognize that most Muslims, like most other human beings, dislike violence. This was evident even in qur'anic times, as the Qur'an had to urge people to fight on a particular occasion when they evidently did not want to do so: 'Believers, why, when it is said to you, "Go and fight in God's way," do you feel weighed down to the ground? Do you prefer this world to the life to come? . . . If you do not go out and fight, God will punish you severely and put others in your place . . .' (Surah 9. 38–39).[11]

---

11. M. A. S. Abdel Haleem, *The Qur'an: A New Translation by M. A. S. Abdel Haleem* (Oxford: Oxford University Press, 2008), Used with permission.

The Pew Research Center published the results of a survey of attitudes to terrorism and to al-Qaeda just a few days after the 'Islamic State' published its caliphate announcement. It indicated great anxieties about the rise of terrorism throughout the Middle East, and that the vast majority of people have negative views of groups like al-Qaeda. As the following tables show, increasing concern about terrorism has been accompanied by increasing disapproval of 'suicide bombing'.[12]

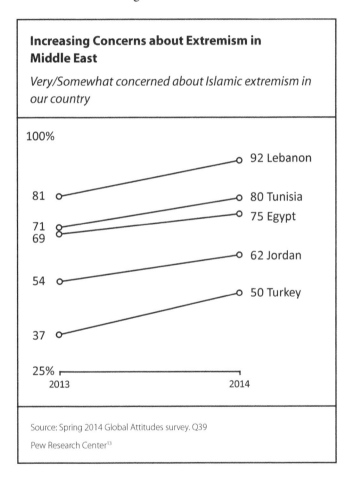

Increasing Concerns about Extremism in Middle East

Very/Somewhat concerned about Islamic extremism in our country

Source: Spring 2014 Global Attitudes survey. Q39

Pew Research Center[13]

---

12. 'Concerns about Islamic Extremism on the Rise in Middle East', Pew Research, 1 July 2014, http://www.pewglobal.org/2014/07/01/concerns-about-islamic-extremism-on-the-rise-in-middle-east/.

13. Adapted from Spring 2014 Global Attitudes Survey. Q39. Pew Research Center, Washington DC. http://www.pewglobal.org/2014/07/01/concerns-about-islamic-extremism-on-the-rise-in-middle-east/pg-2014-07-01-islamic-extremism-01/

Levels of Support for Suicide Bombing over Time

Suicide bombings can be often/sometimes justified against civilian targets in order to defend Islam from its enemies

Muslims in...	2002	2004	2005	2006	2007	2008	2009	2010	2011	2013	2014
	%	%	%	%	%	%	%	%	%	%	%
Palest. ter.	-	-	-	-	70	-	68	-	68	62	46
Lebanon	74	-	39	-	34	32	38	39	35	33	29
Egypt	-	-	-	28	8	13	15	20	28	25	24
Turkey	13	15	14	17	16	3	4	6	7	16	18
Jordan	43	-	57	29	23	25	12	20	13	12	15
Tunisia	-	-	-	-	-	-	-	-	-	12	5
Bangladesh	-	-	-	-	-	-	-	-	-	-	47
Malaysia	-	-	-	-	26	-	-	-	-	27	18
Indonesia	-	-	15	10	10	11	13	15	10	6	9
Pakistan	33	41	25	14	9	5	5	8	5	3	3
Tanzania	18	-	-	-	11	12	-	-	-	-	26
Nigeria	-	-	-	-	-	-	-	34	-	8	19
Senegal	-	-	-	-	-	-	-	-	-	18	15
Israel	-	-	-	-	-	-	7	-	20	7	16

Note: Asked of Muslims only.

Question wording: "Some people think that suicide bombing and other forms of violence against civilian targets are justified in order to defend Islam from its enemies. Other people believe that, no matter what the reason, this kind of violence is never justified. Do you personally feel that this kind of violence is often justified to defend Islam, sometimes justified, rarely justified, or never justified?"

Source: Spring 2014 Global Attitudes survey. Q100.

Pew Research Center[14]

14. Adapted from Spring 2014 Global Attitudes Survey. Q39. Pew Research Center, Washington DC. http://www.pewglobal.org/2014/07/01/concerns-about-islamic-extremism-on-the-rise-in-middle-east/pg-2014-07-01-islamic-extremism-11/

It is interesting to compare the level of support for 'suicide bombing' in Muslim countries with the level of support for air strikes on Syria in the USA:

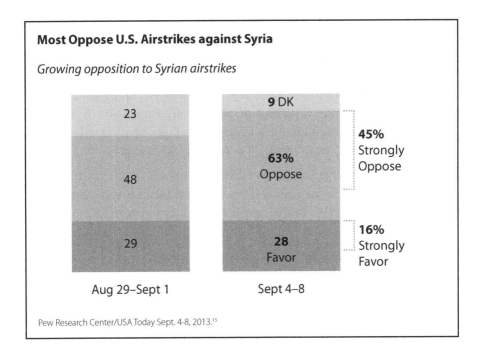

Most Oppose U.S. Airstrikes against Syria

Growing opposition to Syrian airstrikes

9 DK

23

45%
Strongly
Oppose

63%
Oppose

48

16%
Strongly
Favor

29

28
Favor

Aug 29–Sept 1   Sept 4–8

Pew Research Center/USA Today Sept. 4-8, 2013.[15]

Although considering suicide bombing permissible for people under threat is not quite equivalent to considering that a strong country should fight a war, we can at least see that human beings in the USA and in the Middle East share a desire for peace, and that similar proportions favour violence as a way towards peace. Further, opinions on the subject vary: they depend at least as much on the political situation as on any theory about how war and religion relate. This would seem to confirm the view that violence carried out by Muslims should be viewed, theologically, as part of the fallen human condition in general rather than as a result of Islam.

And what about Christianity? Does the gospel make people less inclined to fight? Sometimes it does, but a 2006 survey indicated that a greater percentage of American evangelical Christians than of other Americans considered military methods the best way of countering terrorism:

---

15. Adapted from Pew Research Center/USA TODAY Sept. 4-8, 2013. http://www.people-press.org/2013/09/09/opposition-to-syrian-airstrikes-surges/9-9-13-1-1/

Evangelical Christians tend to believe a strong military is important in the fight against terrorism. Asked whether the Bush administration should put more emphasis on military or diplomatic and economic methods, about half of evangelicals (51%) say military methods, slightly more than Republicans overall (44%) and much more than Democrats (19%). But nearly as many evangelicals (44%) say the administration should put greater emphasis on diplomacy, compared to 52 percent of Republicans and 77 percent of Democrats. Americans overall favor greater emphasis on diplomatic and economic methods rather than military means, 67 percent to 28 percent.[16]

Evidently, there are human patterns in desires for peace and in seeing war as a good way towards achieving peace; and it seems that strong religious views can incline people towards fighting. The question is, how do we fight?

Two Christian Responses to Violence

An Iranian Believer Thinks about War

Let the high praises of God be in their throats
    and two-edged swords in their hands . . .
    This is honour for all his godly ones (Ps. 149:6, 9).

A couple of weeks ago I was reading this Psalm and suddenly, in a strange way verse 6 caught my attention. What is the connection between worship and war? Can violence coexist with romance, namely loving God? It seems that the Psalmist is persuading his readers to have them both. Moreover, the last verse of the Psalm also says that 'this is honor for all his godly ones' (verse 9)'. So the Psalm creates a mood of expectancy that his readers will have the same belief and act accordingly. Therefore what is the connection between the Sword and the Word?

I believe the overall teaching of the Bible especially in the New Testament is against violence and this is very clear in the teaching of our Lord Jesus Christ. However, there is a type of violence which is

---

16. 'WPO Poll Analysis: American Evangelicals Are Divided on International Policy', 2 October 2006, World Public Opinon.org, http://www.worldpublicopinion.org/pipa/articles/brunitedstatescanadara/270.php?nid=&id=&pnt=270.

not only justifiable but also necessary. This violence is not targeted outward but inward. It is not against the evil outside of us but inside of us. It is a self-inflicted violence against our moral compromises and spiritual laziness. And this war is not finished until we 'bind the dark spiritual realms within and chain their nobles with fetters of iron' (verse 8). If we want to be the real worshippers of the true God we can not [sic] do it without the sword. We can not [sic] be the faithful servants of God without first using this sword against ourselves and then and just then we will be honored to be called 'his godly ones'. Many times in our lives our praise lacks the focus or sharpness that our God deserves. This happens sometimes because we easily forget that our fight is first and foremost taking place inside of us. If we stop taking the sword we become just a shadow of what God really wants us to be. We do things without having belief in them because we know we have already lost the battle. We become professionals in the eyes of people but losers in the eyes of God and ourselves. Dear brothers and sisters, let us consciously take the sword against our inner world of evil, let us accept though painfully this self-inflicted violence, namely what the Bible defines as 'repentance' on a daily basis and then think about serving our Lord. May [we be genuine] worshippers who have not forgotten [our] swords.[17]

A Western Christian Magazine Calls Believers to Care for Persecuted Brothers and Sisters

It is unfortunate that just at the time when Muslims worldwide are committing themselves to the concept of the umma with renewed vigour, many Christians have largely lost sight of the Biblical doctrine of the Church. This teaching explains what it means for believers to live as the people of God, not least in relation to a hostile world . . .

Christians in Muslim-majority contexts . . . desperately need a robust and supportive Christian community to sustain them against the power of the Muslim umma.[18]

---

17. Afshin Latifzadeh, 'The Sword and the Praise (Psalm 149:6)', Pars Theological Centre, http://www.parstheology.com/message-of-the-week/the-sword-and-the-praise-psalm-1496/; accessed October 2014. Used with his permission.

18. Anonymous, 'What Does the Bible Say about the Church?', *Barnabas Aid*, July–August 2012.

To Think About

What is the difference between the Muslim *ummah* and the Christian church?

What sorts of power and what sorts of weakness do you see in the Muslim *ummah* in your area?

Should Christians be 'against the power of the Muslim *ummah*'?

In what ways does the Iranian believer's article explain 'what it means for believers to live as the people of God'?

11

Thinking about *Shari'ah*

Ali's Comments

Shari'ah? We don't need it. What do I mean by that? Well, we don't need it for salvation. That's the most important thing. We can compare it to the Mosaic law, and see good things in it, but law is not what saves us.

Of course, we have to live with it in our society. Mostly, that's not a problem. A lot of what is called 'shariah' is our culture, and we can live in our culture as Christians can live in any culture. In the end, we try to test shariah by the Bible. Most of it is acceptable. For example, we should not commit adultery, we can use our right hands for 'clean' tasks, and we can eat ḥalāl food. Some of it is unacceptable. For example, we cannot say the *shahāda* (the statement of witness that 'there is no God but God and Muhammad is the prophet of God') any more. In teaching new believers, we sometimes use the story of Naaman in 2 Kings 5 to encourage them if they feel that they have to compromise their worship. But we also use the story of Daniel to show them how he and his friends were able to both live within the Babylonian religious culture and be faithful to Yahweh.

There are some tensions when it comes to interpretation and enforcement of the shariah. It's not a single system, and it's not even very systematic. There are different schools of thought, and a lot depends on local interpretations. In our country, I say that we might have shariah law in the towns, but we have *maulana* (religious leader) law in the villages. Whatever the local *maulana* decides goes; and there is a very effective way of enforcing it. Anyone who goes outside the *maulana*'s law can be punished by exclusion. The rest of the village stops talking to them or doing business with them. Of course, it's different when people come to the towns, and there is no strong community.

There are specific aspects of shariah law that are, from a Christian perspective, a problem. Prominent among them are the laws on apostasy, family, war and the treatment of minorities. Biblical reflection on these – and on the many other areas covered by shariah – would need a whole book for each subject. To understand them we would need to take into account the long human history through which these laws have developed, their origins in the Qur'an and in the life of Muhammad, and their actual practice in today's world.

This chapter is not going to focus on such problems, but to explore the ideas of shariah and of law as a whole, using specific laws as illustrations. The word 'shariah' does not mean 'law', but 'path' or 'way', and Muslims believe that it is the path revealed by God that shows them how he wants them to live. It is based on the Qur'an and on the example of Muhammad, and has developed over the centuries through the agreement of Muslim scholars and the application of sophisticated legal thinking. There are four major 'schools of law' in Sunni Islam, and, within these, there is much variation of thinking.[1] *Shari'ah* deals with the whole of life, giving guidance about everything from worship to international relations, and from personal hygiene to criminal law.

Law is very important in the Bible, and the laws in the Torah also cover all aspects of life – from worship to international relations, and from personal hygiene to criminal law. The work of Moses may have been fulfilled in Jesus, but the law that God gave him had a vital part in the formation of Israel and has a very important part in helping Christians to think about how God wants them to live in the world even today. This is because law is part of God's way of dealing with evil. Our study of the Noah stories showed the alternatives of flood and sacrifice; but God's choice of the way of sacrifice is followed immediately by laws that are added to the original creation blessings (Gen 9). These laws are particularly to do with dealing with the ongoing violence that will be part of the human condition throughout time. Like the confusion of languages at Babel, the laws will limit the effects of evil in the world.

Moses received many positive laws, telling the people how to worship God and how to love and serve human beings: that is, one of the functions of the Mosaic law is to show people how to be good. This is a major function of shariah – it calls people to do good things. Moses also received negative laws, telling people what they should not do: that is, one of the functions of

---

1. The four schools are Hanfi, Maliki, Shafi'i and Hanbali. For a helpful introduction, see Brown, *A New Introduction to Islam*, ch. 10.

the Mosaic law is to forbid evil. Forbidding evil is another major function of shariah; and there is a great deal of agreement between shariah and Mosaic law about what is good and what is evil. Wholehearted worship of God is good; idolatry is evil. Honouring parents is good; rebelling against them is evil. Faithfulness in marriage is good; adultery is evil. Honesty is good; lying, cheating and stealing are evil. Loving your neighbour is good; murder is evil . . . and so on.

The question then arises as to what happens when people do the evil rather than the good; and both the Mosaic law and shariah deal with this too. Both specify the punishments for murder, adultery, rape and disobedience, and even give instructions on how to judge people's guilt in these offences. Evil is to be dealt with not only by informing people through laws and through God bringing punishment or forgiveness, but also by punishment meted out by human beings. And this is where problems can arise, because the way in which evil was dealt with in the historical situations of seventh-century Arabia or of the ancient Near East might not be appropriate today. The death penalty for sexual immorality (Lev 20:10–21) or for disobedience to parents (Deut 21:18–21) that is laid down in the Mosaic law would horrify most twenty-first-century people. The idea that a rapist should marry his victim (Deut 22:28–29) might have been the most just solution for the welfare of the woman in the ancient patriarchal society, but it could be the most unjust solution in a twenty-first-century society. Jews and Christians as well as Muslims have had to work hard to see how the ancient laws on dealing with evil should be used in new times and places.

For Christians, the whole idea of law has been transformed through Jesus, and through the knowledge of his acceptable sacrifice which emphasizes the love of God for all humankind. For Muslims, the option of sacrifice has been removed. In its place are the example of Muhammad and the emphasis on God's mercy. Thus shariah has often developed by comparing current situations with those at the time of Muhammad, and by carefully balancing justice and mercy. For example,

- The Torah requires stoning for adultery for both the man and the woman (Lev 20:10), but Jesus' dealing with the woman caught in adultery (John 8:1–12) offers the alternative of forgiveness. Adultery is considered a sin by Christians, but is not now treated as a crime to be punished by law.
- The Qur'an does not require the death penalty for adultery: it has verses that say, first, that women offenders should be put under

house arrest (4. 15); second, that any pair committing sexual sin should be punished unless they repent (4. 16); and, third, that both the man and the woman should be beaten with 100 lashes (24. 2). A Nigerian, writing on shariah, quotes these verses,[2] but then goes on to a Hadith which says: 'For unmarried persons (guilty of fornication), the punishment is 100 lashes and an exile for one year. For married adulterers, it is 100 lashes and stoning to death.' The questions he then discusses are, first, whether married adulterers need the lashing, or whether the stoning is sufficient; second, what qualifies a person for stoning (the offender must be sane, a Muslim, married, over the age of puberty and free); and, third, how judgement and punishment should be carried out. He emphasizes the need for indisputable proof of guilt (four eyewitness are required) and says that the harsh punishment is an important deterrent. However, the writer also acknowledges that there are some scholars who reject stoning for adultery, as the Qur'an itself does not command it. There is much current debate among Muslims about all this, and about how the adultery laws relate to God's mercy. For example, some ask whether the harsh punishment in this life means that the offender will be forgiven for the sin after death. Some Muslims go on to point out that it is not the Qur'an but the Bible that requires stoning for adultery.

To Think About

What do the Muslims in your area do to punish sexual sin? What does your Christian community do? Why does Jesus make such a difference to the way the law deals with evil?

Shari'ah law is, of course, varied, as are other aspects of Islamic practice. There is variety among the Sunni law schools, among the Shi'ite groups, and among people trying to apply the law to today's issues. However, there is a common idea that the law covers all human actions, and the way that it deals with them is by classifying them: most simply, into actions that are permitted

---

2. A. R. Doi, *Shari'ah: The Islamic Law* (London: Ta Ha, 1984), 237–40.

(*halāl*) or forbidden (*harām*). Within this broad classification, there are different ways of classifying *halāl* actions as compulsory, recommended or neutral, and *harām* actions as discouraged, forbidden or unforgiveable. The underlying idea is that human beings are not in need of redemption but of guidance. Linked with this is the idea that God does not reveal himself but his will.

In contrast, God's revelation of himself is central to the Bible: our study of the transfiguration, with its glory, dazzling light and heavenly voice, made that very clear. Meanwhile, the Genesis study showed us that our world is fallen. Therefore, the Islamic understanding of the context of shariah as what God reveals and what we most need, contradicts our reading of the Bible. Where Genesis leads Jews and Christians alike to believe that something has changed in human nature following Adam's sin,[3] Muslims believe that all human beings are born in a state of *fitrah* – as God created us – and then learn and choose to worship God or not. Hence, any evil promptings within us are simply due to the way that God made us, and what we need is to learn to listen to his guidance rather than to the devil or any other voices within us or outside us.

Theologically, this is at the root of some of the problems raised by the specific problem areas mentioned at the beginning of this chapter. For example, some men want more than one wife at a time. Christians would see this as a wrong desire born of their fallen human nature, but Muslims would see it as part of their created nature and therefore not wrong in itself. So shariah law regulates polygamy to make sure that, should a man have multiple wives, he treats them fairly. Christians, while recognizing that polygamy was practised by some of the Old Testament figures, take Jesus Christ's teaching about God's plan in creation as normative (Matt 19:4–6). As with his teaching about divorce, they recognize that any law that allows for anything other than lifelong one man–one woman marriage is taking into account 'hardness of heart' (Matt 19:8).

The fundamental difference here is that Christians, on the basis of the Bible, are called to lead redeemed lives that reflect the good state in which Adam was created: the call of Jesus is to perfection (Matt 5:20). Muslims are called to lead regulated lives that listen to the voice of God rather than to the evil voices within and without.

---

3. A Jewish way of understanding this is that the evil inclination, which tempts us to do wrong, was outside human beings before, as symbolized by the serpent. Since Adam, we have all had the evil inclination as well as the good inclination within us.

Yet, one might ask, how far does this difference really go? Muslims might reject the idea of redemption, but does that mean that Christians should reject the idea of regulation? If we are fallen, our instinctive ideas of 'right and wrong' might be wrong: we need God's guidance. If Jesus himself recognized the law as dealing with 'hardness of heart', should we not also recognize the need that all human beings have of that law? However much evangelism is done, there will always be people in every society who remain unredeemed. And however mature a redeemed person may be, there will be aspects of their character that tend towards sin until the end of this life. Once again, we see that what was there before the transfiguration was good. Israel needed the law and the prophets, and so do we. We need more than the law, but not less than the law. The presence of Muslims can be a reminder of that.

An implication of all this is that with our ears tuned to the themes of the Bible, the ideal of shariah should not strike us as discordant. It is limited, in that it cannot save people – and Muslims themselves recognize that they cannot keep it perfectly but must hope for God's mercy. There are aspects of it that, especially when applied according to the letter of ancient formulations, contradict New Testament ethics – and Muslims themselves struggle with interpretations and applications. However, the idea of law resounds through much of the Bible. In particular, it permeated the world in which Jesus was born. So, one of the key ways of learning to respond to Islam as a follower of Jesus and his apostles is by seeing, in the pages of the New Testament, how they responded to the Jewish laws of their time.

Jesus' example teaches us that different people think differently about law, and have different needs. He knew how to treat each segment of Jewish society: the Pharisees tithing their mint and coriander, the Sadducees hand-in-glove with the people in power, the Zealots with their violent activism and the crowds of people just pursuing their daily lives.[4] The whole range of human responses to divine law can be seen in the 'world behind' the New Testament, and that whole range can also be seen among Muslim responses to shariah today. This is because responding to the law in different ways is basic to the human condition: we need and desire a legal system, rebel against it, find injustices within it and argue about it. We finish this chapter by inviting you to think about two very different sorts of legal discussions.

---

4. Glaser, *The Bible and Other Faiths*, 211, reflects on how we might see different trends within Islam in each of these expressions of Judaism.

Legal Discussion 1: Jesus, Muhammad and Inheritance Laws

'Concerning your children, God commands you that a son should have the equivalent share of two daughters. If there are only daughters, two or more should share two-thirds of the inheritance, if one, she should have half. Parents inherit a sixth each if the deceased leaves children; if he leaves no children and his parents are his sole heirs, his mother has a third, unless he has brothers, in which case she has a sixth. [In all cases, the distribution comes] after payment of any bequests or debts. You cannot know which of your parents or your children is more beneficial to you: this is a law from God, and He is all knowing, all wise' (Surah 4. 11).[5]

This is a verse from a passage in the Qur'an that gives detailed rules for the allocation of inheritance (Surah 4. 5–13). The verses are said to have been given to Muhammad on two occasions: on one, a dying man was asking for guidance on how to allocate his wealth; on the other, a woman was asking for justice for her daughters who had been left without any inheritance. Muhammad responded with detailed instructions which Muslims believe came directly from God.

Here is Jesus dealing with a similar question:

Someone in the crowd said to [Jesus], 'Teacher, tell my brother to divide the inheritance with me.' But he said to him, 'Man, who made me a judge or arbitrator over you?' And he said to them, 'Take care, and be on your guard against all covetousness, for one's life does not consist in the abundance of one's possessions' (Luke 12:13–15).

To Think About

Why did Jesus refuse to give instructions about how to divide the inheritance? Read on in Luke 12: what do you learn about human and divine responsibility in making such decisions? How does this help you to think about shariah? How does it help you to think about the inheritance laws in your country?

---

5. M. A. S. Abdel Haleem, *The Qur'an: A New Translation by M. A. S. Abdel Haleem* (Oxford: Oxford University Press, 2008), Used with permission.

Legal Discussion 2: Music and Dancing

Billi has saved up to hire fairy lights and a sofa to put in her garden. 'I've never had a party before,' she squeals as she watches teenage neighbours clamber over walls to rig up the lighting. 'There's going to be heaps of food just like we had in the city, and music and Pepsi!'

Billi didn't always live in one room in an annexe off the madrasah. She comes from an upper-class neighbourhood in the country's cultural capital and, although poor now, she still has immaculate taste and sophisticated manners. She has planted flowers outside her house and, with hard work, makes every surface inside gleam. She should have had an engagement party far more lavish than this one that she's throwing for a girl she fosters. But the death of her parents left her alone in the world and easily taken advantage of. The parents of her betrothed quietly annulled the agreement. For twenty years she has made her living by sewing, seeking refuge with neighbours, and suffering, like the woman who touched the hem of Jesus' garment, with a haemorrhage.

Charitably, the madrasah teacher, Baji, took her in, allowing her to stay. The wonder of Billi is her tender heart. Through the struggle of her life, she has remained as cheerful as a child. In every conversation, even with coarse people, her words are sweet. And here, this evening, she is pouring out love for this girl to whom she owes nothing.

'Come and sing for us, sir – please!' she begs a gentleman passing by, who is renowned for his deep and gentle voice. She laughs and claps as he begins, 'Tonight, tonight was the night someone came, into my arms he ran. Don't ask me his name.' For a moment she is transported back to a more glamorous past when she could dream about romance. 'We have a singer for tonight!' She rejoices and returns to her tray of spiced mince to continue shaping kebabs for later. Presently a caterer comes in and takes payment for a vat of luxury pink tea she has ordered.

Soon the party begins. Billi has invited all the women from her street to come and celebrate with her young friend. We all twinkle under the fairy lights as we start dancing. Another neighbour rigs up a CD player and cranks up the volume. Billi looks on, enrapt. 'I have never celebrated anything before,' she whispers. Soon the little yard is whirling.

All at once, the door to her yard opens. We have all been keeping our eye on the door lest a man should come in and observe us relaxed and dancing. But this is no man: Baji, head to toe in black, tall as a pillar, stands disapproving in the doorway. 'Turn the music off,' someone hisses. There is a click and then silence, broken only by the jingle of jewellery as we bring our dance to a sudden standstill.

Baji, a sarcastic smile cutting across her face, tells Billi to turn the music back on. Billi, innocent and submissive, says, 'OK, Baji,' but when the beat begins again no one dances and Billi quickly senses it is not appropriate and fades it out.

'Who danced?' asks Baji, walking around the circle, looking into the eyes of each woman one by one. 'WHO DANCED?' We all hang our heads in shame. One chubby girl – the star of the show, in fact – lies. 'I didn't.'

'You know that music is forbidden. You know how Shaitaan uses it. The Prophet, peace be upon him, never listened to it. Neither should we.' Realizing that the party is over, we cover our heads and sit down to listen to her teach. Billi turns off the fairy lights and switches on the tube light instead; everyone's face goes suddenly white and the yard seems to grow cold and hard. 'Me – I never listen to music. If it's on in a shop, I leave. I will not let my girls watch telly. I will not attend weddings if I know there'll be music.'

Someone offers her a chair, the only one. She sits down and, no men being present, lifts her veil. 'This is what obedience means, friends.' She looks around at each one of us. A note of sadness creeps into her voice. 'My own sisters invited me to their weddings. I did not attend a single one.'

Next morning, I go round to Billi's to thank her for the party and to see if she needs any help clearing up. She is utterly exhausted, frail as she is. 'I wish I could have afforded a bigger gift. I saw such beautiful things in the market. I would love to have got them wrapped up for her.'

Baji meets me on the way out. 'You – you're a Christian. What did you think of the party? Was Billi right to do that?'

To Think About

What would you say? What might Jesus say to Billi? And to Baji?

12

Thinking about Islam

After all this, we are ready to ask, 'How might we think biblically about Islam as a whole?' Do we dismiss it, as do some Christians, as a false system with which we should have nothing to do? Do we fight it, as do some, as a satanic and idolatrous system against which we should wage spiritual warfare? Do we accept it, as do yet others, as a way in which large numbers of human beings worship God? Do we fear it, as a powerful threat to our world and our ways of life? Do we attend to it, as a call to repentance to peoples who have turned away from Christ? Do we watch it, seeing it as playing a role in an apocalyptic vision of the last days? Do we study it, seeking to understand our enemies . . . or seeking to love our neighbours? Do we see in it falsehood that keeps people from Christ, or truth that points them to him?

For those readers who have jumped straight to this section, we repeat here that 'Islam' is very varied, and that Muslims are human beings forming nearly a quarter of the world's population. The idea developed in part 1 of this book is that, biblically, we should see Muslims primarily as human beings. Islam is, therefore, part of the created but fallen world with which the Bible deals. Within that world there are people seeking God through religious acts, people fighting about what is acceptable to God, people falling into 'dangerous', power-based religion, and people struggling with problems of suffering, justice and evil. These ideas provide a way of seeing that the whole Bible is as relevant to the world of Muslims as it is to the world of any other human beings. They lead us to expect that we will find all aspects of humanity as we look at Islam, and that there might be occasions when any or even all of the above responses might be appropriate. There can be no single answer to how we should think about Islam.

However, we want to suggest an answer that picks up a number of clues from our study so far and that can be used as a basis for discerning how to think about the various facets of Islam: that we think of Islam as having grown from Jewish roots.

- This makes sense *theologically*, since the Qur'an clearly intends to refer to the God of Abraham, Isaac and Jacob. Islam is in agreement with present-day Judaism that God is Creator and Judge, and that he is merciful to all human beings. It also agrees with present-day Judaism in its denials of the Trinity, the divinity of Christ and the atonement. The question 'How far can we say that Muslims and Christians worship the same God?' is, therefore, closely parallel to the question, 'How far can we say that Jews and Christians worship the same God?'

- It makes sense *historically*, because the Qur'an builds on Jewish thinking and Muhammad seems to have thought at first that he was bringing a version of Judaism to the Arabs. In Medina, when many of the Jews rejected him, he changed the *Qiblah* (direction of prayer) from Jerusalem to Mecca, symbolizing that this religion would now grow in a different direction. One of the major roots of Islam as it developed historically is, then, the Judaism of seventh-century Arabia.

- It gives us a way of approaching the *legal* emphasis of Islam: there are very strong parallels between Islamic law and Jewish law as both have developed through the centuries.[1] Comparisons with aspects of present-day Judaism can, then, help us to understand Islam and to see it as normal: of the three so-called 'Abrahamic' faiths, it is Christianity that is the 'odd one out' here.

- That leads to an important clue for *mission*: much of the New Testament deals with the purpose and limitations of the law, and the Gospels especially address people struggling to keep the law. We will find, therefore, that many of the gospel stories speak more directly to Muslims than they do to Christians who have never taken the law as seriously.

We offer the model of seeing Islam as growing out of Jewish roots as an alternative to two other common models. First, since the theologian John

---

1. J. Neusner and T. Sonn, *Comparing Religions through Law* (London: Routledge, 1999) gives a very helpful comparison of the sources, institutions, practices and categories of law in Islam and Judaism.

of Damascus, who died in AD 749,[2] Christians have tended to see Islam as a departure from Christianity – that is, as *a Christian heresy*. It is true that Islam developed in response to Christianity as well as in response to Judaism, and that it developed a strong anti-Christian polemic as the Muslim empires conquered and ruled over Christian populations. At the time of Muhammad, the nature of Christ was a big political question, and the Qur'an and the early Muslims got involved in that political argument. Although they sided against the powerful Byzantine Orthodox doctrine, they also sided against the Jews, telling them that they were wrong in persecuting Jesus because he was their Messiah. So it is possible to treat Islam primarily as a heresy that gets its Christology wrong. However, our analysis suggests that Islam goes back in time through sacred history towards the Law and the Prophets. It is from this backward step that Islam has developed forward into what it is today. Judaism also developed from the Law and the Prophets. The major difference is that, while Judaism rejects Jesus completely, Islam sees him as essentially the same as all the other prophets. Both effectively remove the transfiguration from history.

Second, people today often class Islam together with Judaism and Christianity as an *'Abrahamic' religion*. However, the biblical and qur'anic 'Abrahams' are very different, and Jewish, Christian and Muslim views of what it means to be 'Abrahamic' are therefore different. For example, the Qur'an has very little about God's covenant with Abraham, so his role as the father of the Jewish people is not emphasized. On the other hand, the Qur'an includes stories about how Abraham challenged the idolatry of his father and his people which are not in the Bible but which are in Jewish tradition (Surah 21. 51–71 and *Genesis Rabbah* 38). The Qur'an also tells a story of Abraham building the Kaaba at Mecca, with his son Ishmael (Surah 2. 125–129). So the qur'anic Abraham is a prophet who challenges idolatry, and his significance as a patriarch is more as the father of Ishmael than as the father of Isaac. Muslims see 'Abrahamic religion' as being like Islam.

From a Christian point of view, our study so far suggests that we should think of Islam together with Judaism as a *'Mosaic' religion*. Moses is the great figure in Judaism, and Moses is also a great figure in the Qur'an, where his life story has many parallels with that of Muhammad – to the extent that, as we have seen, Muslims see Muhammad as the 'prophet like Moses' promised

---

2. John of Damascus was a Syrian monk who is sometimes called 'the last of the church fathers' and is famous for his writings on iconoclasm. His *De Heresaebius* (*Concerning Heresies*) includes a chapter on Islam.

in Deuteronomy 18:18. Of course, rabbinic thinking has developed Judaism, and the Qur'an and Islamic thinking have developed Islam, so we can see that different plants have grown out of the Mosaic root; but at least there is a good measure of agreement on the nature of the root!

From this root, both Islam and Judaism have developed laws that build communities and govern every detail of life. Both have developed authoritative traditions for interpreting the message of the Bible – whether the Midrash, Mishnah and Talmud in Judaism, or the Qur'an, the Hadith and the shariah schools in Islam. Both are strongly monotheistic, both see prophecy as very important, both have set worship in a sacred language, both have sacred places, and both have strong emphases on their social and political identity as the people of God. However, there are also important differences. These differences can be seen not only as removing aspects of Judaism that Christians see as pointing to Jesus beyond the transfiguration, but also as consequences of beginning the faith with an ethnic group that is not Jewish and then taking the faith to the rest of the world.

Paul lists the privileges of the Jews thus: 'They are Israelites, and to them belong the adoption, the glory, the covenants, the giving of the law, the worship, and the promises. To them belong the patriarchs, and from their race, according to the flesh, is the Christ who is God over all, blessed for ever. Amen' (Rom 9:4–5). Muslims are not ethnically 'Israelites', but see themselves as descended from Ishmael and so related to the Jews. They also see their religion as the true successor to Israel, and claim the patriarchs (and the Messiah descended from the patriarchs) as their prophets. While they do not see themselves as 'adopted' sons of God, they do see themselves as his special people. They have a system of 'worship' that they believe was given by God, but without sacrifice and with the Kaaba instead of the temple. They speak of 'promises' and of 'covenants', but these are not the same as the biblical promises and covenants. They have 'law', which gives much common ground with Judaism, but in a different context. As we move on to consider some of the key differences between Islam and Judaism, we will see that what Muslims miss is 'the glory'.

Difference 1: Islam Proclaims Jesus to Be the Messiah

From a New Testament perspective, the key question for thinking about any system is, 'What does it do with Jesus?' The Qur'an removes the glory of the transfiguration but, despite all the limitations of Islamic views of Jesus that we have explored, Islam does affirm that Jesus is the Messiah. In this, the Qur'an challenges the Jews of its time, rebuking them for rejecting him.

Thinking this way can be a positive starting point for Muslim–Christian relations. If Christians think of Islam as a 'Christian heresy', discussions between Muslims and Christians are likely to focus on what the Qur'an denies about Jesus in its challenges to Christians. If Christians think of Islam as growing out of Jewish roots, discussions are more likely to begin from what the Qur'an affirms about Jesus in its challenges to Jews.

Difference 2: Islam is a Universal Faith

Judaism is the faith of ethnic Jews,[3] but Islam is a faith for all peoples.[4] This has important consequences for a faith that is built on law and on community.

Universalizing the faith in the way that Islam does means *universalizing the laws*. There are some laws that Jews see as dating to the covenant with Noah and therefore as applying to all humanity, but there are many that apply only to Jewish people – for example, circumcision, food laws, purity laws, and laws about family, community and worship. Islam has a history of calling more and more people to accept not only its beliefs but also the laws that cannot be separated from the beliefs. These include laws about circumcision, food, purity, family, community and worship, but also laws about the details of life, from how to brush one's teeth to how to greet a neighbour.

We might describe this as *universalizing a particular culture* – and this would not be far from the truth. The whole idea of Sunnah – the way of doing things that follows the example of Muhammad – comes from the idea that each Arabian tribal group had its own Sunnah, and that the groups were united as Muslims by following Muhammad's particular Sunnah. Just as Hebrew is the sacred language of the Jews, so Arabic is the sacred language of the Muslims. All Muslims, whatever their native language, need to use the language of the Arabian Peninsula in order to read the Qur'an and to worship.

---

3. Over the centuries, many non-Jews have accepted the Jewish faith and joined the Jewish people. However, for centuries Judaism has not been a missionary faith, and rabbis are required to discourage people from becoming Jewish before accepting them into the faith.

4. The Qur'an sees itself as sent in Arabic to the Arabs (Surahs 41. 2; 42.7), but it also sees Muhammad as the seal of the prophets (Surah 33. 40), and there are verses that are interpreted as meaning that he is a messenger for all people (7. 158; 25. 1; 34. 28). Some Christians therefore argue that Muhammad did not see himself as a prophet for the whole world, but only for the Arabs, but Muslims do not accept this argument.

In practice, Islam has adjusted to different cultures in many ways; but Sunnah and Arabic affect Muslim cultures, varied as they are, worldwide.

More controversial is the idea of the *universalizing of Islamic rule*. The early expansion of Islam, from the Arabian Peninsula across North Africa and the Middle East, was an expansion of the political rule of Muslims. As an area was conquered, it came under Islamic law. Only then, little by little and over the centuries, did people accept the Islamic faith. Muslims saw the expansion of Islamic rule as the expansion of the rule of God. Today, although many Muslims live under non-Islamic political rule, there are many who believe that, ideally, the way to peace is to live under Islamic rule, with non-Muslims allowed protected space under that rule. In contrast, even in biblical times, the Jews were never encouraged to take political control over anything beyond the Promised Land. Today, they may fight to keep control in Israel, but not to extend Jewish rule elsewhere.

In universalizing from the basis of Jewish roots, Islam is more like Christianity than like Judaism. Christianity, too, has universalized – but in opposite ways:

There were two options on *what to do with the law of Moses* when the gospel spread to non-Jews: either to make everyone keep all the same laws or to distinguish between laws that were for everyone and areas of life in which different peoples could choose what to do. It was not an easy decision to make, especially for those who had striven to uphold the letter of the law all their lives, as can be seen from Acts 10 – 15 and Galatians; but some of the apostles had seen the transfiguration and all knew that many aspects of the law were fulfilled in Jesus. It was decided that details of the laws about, for example, circumcision, food, purity, family, community and worship were applicable only to Jewish people. Neither was it an easy decision to live by: the apostles had to re-think Moses, to re-examine the purpose of the law and its place relating to salvation, and then to make sure that people attended to the underlying ethics that did apply to them.[5] The means of extending the church community was not by extending a standard set of rules but by releasing people from restrictions, in order that they might interact socially and live according to the law of love. In fact, a standardized legal structure would overturn God's plan for salvation: 'if you accept circumcision, Christ will be of no advantage to you' (Gal 5:2).

---

5. See, for example, Rom 6 and the letter of James.

There were two options as to *what to do with Hebrew language and culture* as the gospel spread: the options of either spreading the language and culture, or of letting everyone keep their own language and culture. By the time of Jesus, there were already Jews who were using the Greek language and adopting aspects of Greek culture. The New Testament continues this use of Greek, which a greater variety of people could understand than could understand Hebrew. Christians have taken this as an example which has led to the translation of the Bible into different languages and to the idea that the gospel should transform culture rather than replace it. Within the unity of the church there would be diverse people maintaining their distinct social structures along with their cultures and languages. This option, too, can be difficult to live out: we see plenty of examples of Christians imposing particular cultures, and also of Christians losing aspects of the gospel when they adapt to cultures. However, rightly understood, it is part of the good news. Just as God ordered peoples with their languages as well as their territories in Genesis 10, so he transforms and speaks to people through their own languages today. There will be no special sacred language when people from all nations gather around the throne of God: people of all languages will be welcome (Rev 7:9).

There were two options open to Jesus *regarding spreading the rule of God*: taking political power, or building a kingdom 'not of or from this world'. Faced with Elijah's problem of corrupt and largely foreign political power, Jesus took the second option, and so did the early church. But this option has not been easy either: again and again through history, we have seen Christians take political power when such power has been possible for them.

The question of how to call all peoples to faith in the One God is an important one for Christians relating to Muslims. The Islamic choices on universalizing the law of God and the rule of God may bring tensions, but so do the choices seen in the New Testament. Once again, we are challenged as to how we, as both fallen and redeemed, deal with all that is symbolized by Moses and Elijah. An underlying question is how the law relates to the covenants – with all peoples, with Israel and, through Jesus, with all peoples again.

Difference 3: Islam Reorders Law and Covenant

The Qur'an sees history in terms of God sending a series of prophets with a repeated message and developing laws, culminating in the final prophet with the final law for all peoples. The Bible sees history in terms of God calling a people for the purpose of blessing all other peoples, culminating in Christ; and that calling is expressed through a series of covenants, at the times of Noah, Abraham, Moses, David and Jesus. We include the Noahic covenant here because it is God's unconditional commitment to bless all the nations that the other biblical covenants fulfil. God's choice of Israel was not only for her own sake, but for the sake of all the peoples. The reason why Israel was given law and land, and the reason why she was given such stringent holiness requirements, was not only because she was God's chosen and beloved bride, but also because she was to be his light to others.

For the Jews, then, the law is a mark of God's covenant with them. God committed himself unconditionally to a people descended from Abraham to whom he would give a land and through whom he would bless the nations (Gen 12:1–3). He then brought that people out of Egypt and made an explicit covenant with the whole people. This was what was happening at Sinai: God was telling the people who he was and who they were, reminding them what he had done for them and announcing what he would do for them (Exod 19:4–6; 34:6–11). As part of this covenant, he gave them laws, and a ceremony took place at which they agreed to keep them (24:3–8). They were laws that would enable God's presence to go with them. They were laws of holiness and of sacrifice, but also laws that would mark them out as a special people and keep them away from other gods. The covenant ceremony itself, described in Exodus 24, was one of sacrifice and holiness, and, most importantly, it took place in the very presence of God.

An important clue to the nature of Jewish laws is found in the word *kosher*, which describes what is permissible for Jewish people. The word does not actually mean 'permissible' but 'pure' or 'appropriate'. The centre of Judaism is not, then, a system that tells Jews what to do but a covenant relationship with the holy God within which actions are judged by whether they are appropriate to that relationship. The laws do not make sense apart from the covenants.

The Qur'an also speaks of covenants (the words used in Arabic are 'ahd and *mithāq*), but the idea is rather different. Covenants are essentially about people agreeing to keep God's laws, in which case he will keep his side of the bargain. There is an original covenant wherein all humanity accepted their obligations towards God before creation (Surah 7. 172), and Muslims are promised paradise only if they keep their covenant (Surah 13. 19–26; cf. 5. 1; 16. 91; 57. 8), but most of the qur'anic references to covenants are about those made with the previous prophets – explicitly Noah, Abraham, Moses and Jesus (Surah 33. 7). Surah 3. 81 describes these covenants:

> God took a pledge [*mithāq*] from the prophets, saying, 'If, after I have bestowed Scripture and wisdom upon you, a messenger comes confirming what you have been given, you must believe in him and support him. Do you affirm this and accept My pledge [*iṣr*] as binding on you?' They said, 'We do.' He said, 'Then bear witness and I too will bear witness.'[6]

We see the idea that God 'takes' rather than 'gives' the covenants, which emphasizes God's initiative and the human responsibility that will follow. This is emphasized by the Arabic word *iṣr* that our translation renders 'pledge': it actually means 'load' or 'burden', the idea being that people are called to accept the responsibilities that God gives them. God's part is the gift of the message through the messengers, and the human part is obedience to the message; we know from elsewhere in the Qur'an that those who keep the covenant will then have God's blessing and attain paradise.

Qur'anic covenants are, then, about people acknowledging God's supremacy and agreeing to keep the laws that he gives. The law is right at the centre of the covenants; we could almost summarize them by saying that covenants are laws given to people that, if obeyed, lead to paradise and, if disobeyed, lead to hell. There is scarcely a hint of the unconditional commitment of God given in the biblical Noahic and Abrahamic covenants. The nearest we find is in Surah 2. 40–43, which speaks of special blessing given to Israel, but immediately goes on to an exhortation to keep the law:

> Children of Israel, remember how I blessed you. Honour your pledge to Me and I will honour My pledge to you: I am the One you should fear. Believe in the message I have sent down confirming what you already possess. Do not be the first to disbelieve in it, and do not sell My messages for a small price: I am the One of whom you should be mindful. Do not mix truth with falsehood, or hide the truth when you know it. Keep up the prayer, pay the prescribed alms, and bow your heads [in worship] with those who bow theirs.[7]

---

6. M. A. S. Abdel Haleem, *The Qur'an: A New Translation by M. A. S. Abdel Haleem* (Oxford: Oxford University Press, 2008), Used with permission.

7. Ibid.

Surah 2. 40 is the beginning of a long passage that continues to verse 96 and describes God's dealings with the Israelites, clearly referring to the Mosaic covenant. It tells of God's special favour in the choice of Israel, the rescue from Egypt, and the laws that were given. Again and again, Israel is told to keep the law, but, again and again, she is reminded of her failures. All this is part of a warning to the Jews to accept the prophethood of Muhammad.

The nature of the covenant with Israel is seen again in the Qur'an's brief treatment of the covenant ceremony of Exodus 19 – 24:

> God took a pledge from the Children of Israel. We made twelve leaders arise among them, and God said, 'I am with you: if you keep up the prayer, pay the prescribed alms, believe in My messengers and support them, and lend God a good loan, I will wipe out your sins and admit you into Gardens graced with flowing streams. Any of you who now ignore this [pledge] will be far from the right path.' But they broke their pledge, so We distanced them [from Us] and hardened their hearts. They distort the meaning of [revealed] words and have forgotten some of what they were told to remember: you [Prophet] will always find treachery in all but a few of them. Overlook this and pardon them: God loves those who do good (Surah 5. 12–13).[8]

This retains the idea that is so important in Exodus – that God is with Israel – but shifts the focus onto keeping the law as a basis for forgiveness of sins and entering paradise. Moreover, the laws that are given here are the laws that are central to Islam, and there is no hint of the Exodus laws on the tabernacle, the priesthood and the sacrifices. The whole covenant is expressed as something that is taken from Israel rather than as something that is given to Israel: it is the people's promise to obey (as in Exod 24:3, 7) that is emphasized.

Like Surah 2, the context of the passage focuses attention on the fact that the people broke their promise; and it goes on to say that God also took a covenant from the Christians, and that they also broke their promise (Surah 5. 14). This brings us to another important difference in the qur'anic view of covenants: they are conditional on people's obedience. In Surah 5 Muhammad is sometimes told to bear with the Jews, but he is also told that God is no longer with them; that is, they have broken their covenant, so God is no

---

8. M. A. S. Abdel Haleem, *The Qur'an: A New Translation by M. A. S. Abdel Haleem* (Oxford: Oxford University Press, 2008), Used with permission.

longer tied to his side of it. There seems to be a personal covenant with Moses that was not broken (Surah 7. 124; 43. 49), but much of the qur'anic material about Moses and the Jews focuses on the Jews' disobedience. The Qur'an has very little about the covenant made with Abraham. What it does say makes it clear that it will not apply to his descendants if they do evil (Surah 2. 124). It also seems that God's promise followed Abraham's obedience rather than, as in Genesis, Abraham's obedience following the promise.

In short, the Qur'an's focus is almost entirely on the conditional aspect of the Mosaic covenant. In the Torah, it is clear that people will lose God's blessing if they are disobedient, but the whole context of the Noahic and Abrahamic covenants and the story of God's dealings with Israel make it clear that God will somehow continue his relationship with his chosen people. He is able to deal with their disobedience. The Qur'an replaces the Noahic covenant with the conditional pre-creation covenant and the Abrahamic covenant with a covenant that will be lost if people disobey it. The idea of a steadfast covenant love that perseveres with people who rebel and disobey God is scandalous to many Muslims, because, they say, if God is good, he cannot love what is bad.[9]

Difference 4: Islam Replaces the Bible with the Qur'an

Jews and Christians share a large part of the Bible: what Christians call the Old Testament. The Qur'an sees itself as confirming the Torah, the Psalms and the previous prophets, but, in actual practice, it replaces them. Few Muslims read the Bible, and, when they do, many do it only to find fault and to try to prove that it has been corrupted. This is the most serious problem with the idea that we should think of Islam as a development from Judaism. Where Jews and Christians share the Old Testament writings, Muslims only accept their content in theory, and they have another book, the Qur'an, which has some serious differences from the Bible.

The Qur'an has a different view of sacred history from that of the Old Testament, so it puts the characters it shares with the Old Testament into a new framework. It does not see God as acting through the choice of a particular people through whom he will bring blessing to the whole world, but through a series of prophets sent to different peoples. It therefore has a very different view of the covenants that are so important to biblical history. This means that there are some ways in which Judaism is closer to Christianity than to

---

9. See also Surah 3. 134, 140: 'God loves those who do good . . . God does not love evildoers.'

Islam, so that we could think of Judaism and Christianity having a shared root, and Islam as having distorted that root.

However, we have seen that the Qur'an itself does not suggest that the Old Testament writings are wrong: rather, it chooses particular aspects of the Old Testament stories, and of the Jewish and Christian discussions of them. We can think of the Qur'an as entering into Jewish and Christian debates, sometimes taking one side and sometimes another. Very often, a problem raised by the Jewish rabbis is solved one way by the New Testament and another way by the Qur'an.

From a New Testament perspective, then, the Qur'an is built on Old Testament Judaism, but it builds on it in such a way as to change its interpretation of history and to undermine some of the key ideas that bring the glory of God to human beings. In particular, it leaves little room for either the coming of God or the pain of God seen in Jesus Christ.

Difference 5: Islam Sees the Coming of God as Impossible

> Return in mercy to Jerusalem Your city and dwell therein as You have promised . . . May our eyes behold Your return to Zion in mercy. Blessed are You L-rd, who restores His Divine Presence to Zion (From the Jewish daily prayers).

We said above that Islam does not have 'the glory' of Romans 9:4. What is that glory? Surely it refers to the glory of the presence of God seen on Sinai, in the tabernacle and in the temple – the presence of God that the Jews call *shekinah*. There is a Jewish tradition that the *shekinah* came to earth at the time of creation, but withdrew in stages to heaven in response to human sin.[10] It returned at Sinai, when it came to dwell in the tabernacle. The transfiguration shows us that same glory in Jesus, and the Holy Spirit brings the presence of God into the lives of believers in Jesus so that the church, too, has the glory.

There is a sense in which Judaism today has no glory. Ezekiel 10 gives us a vision of the departure of God's glory from the temple, and there was no return of the glory at the dedication of the second temple – only the return to Jerusalem of Ezra to teach the law (Ezra 6:16 – 7:6). Jewish tradition says that the glory will not return to Israel until the Messiah comes, and Jews are still awaiting his coming. However, the *shekinah* is believed to be present on

---

10. See C. G. Montefiore and H. Loewe, *A Rabbinic Anthology* (New York: Schocken Books, 1974), 82–85.

various occasions, particularly when Jews pray together; and expectation of future glory means that there is at least a possibility of God's coming.

As we saw in chapter 8, the Qur'an repeatedly omits almost all that pertains to the coming of God from its stories of biblical events. On the other hand, it calls people to seek God's face (see p. 130), and insists that God is nearer than our jugular vein (Surah 50. 16). It is not surprising, then, that there has been a great deal of discussion as to whether and how it is possible to experience God's presence, in this life or in the next life. It is the goal of Sufis. However, even for them, what is envisaged is a climbing towards God or a realization of his universal presence, and not God's coming to a particular place. In orthodox Islamic thinking, it is simply impossible for God to come, and for humans to see his glory. There is a sense in which God is everywhere, because he rules everywhere, sees everywhere and can bless everywhere; but he is not the sort of being who comes to us.

In parallel, there is Jewish discussion about what is meant by the glory – the *shekinah* which appeared visibly at these points in biblical history – and about how the presence of God is experienced today. For example, there is a tradition that the *shekinah* is over the head of a sick person. A popular website comments, 'It is a beautiful theology, imagining the Presence of God "hovering" (as it were) over someone who is suffering.' But it continues, 'Now, please understand, when a text says that God, or the Shechina, is present, it doesn't mean that God is absent or missing at other times – I believe these texts are talking about what we perceive and feel. Sometimes we feel that God is closer, and sometimes farther away.'[11] In these comments we can hear something of the struggle within Jewish thinking about what it might mean that the One transcendent God should come to us. Both Muslims and Christians have struggled with the same tensions, but we have resolved them in opposite ways. The Islamic solution is that God does not and cannot come; the Christian solution is that he has come in Jesus Christ, and continues to come in the Holy Spirit.

---

11. Rabbi Neal J. Loevinger, 'Feeling the Presence of God', http://www.myjewishlearning. com/texts/Bible/Weekly_Torah_Portion/vayechi_kolel5761.shtml?p=1; accessed October 2014.

The Crucial Question: What about the Pain in the Heart of God?

> Today God weeps over the situation in Palestine and Israel. Today God weeps over Gaza. With God, our hearts are broken when we see the carnage in Gaza and in Israel.[12]

So the Bethlehem Bible College begins its call to prayer for the situation of terrible conflict that is filling the news media at the time of writing this section. This small community of Palestinian Christians is grieving over sufferings inflicted on and by both Jews and Muslims, and calling both sides to peace. They are themselves committed to peaceful ways of dealing with the conflict; and their call and their commitment are based on their understanding that God himself grieves over the sufferings of Muslim, Jew and Christian alike. They are motivated by the pain in the heart of God that runs like a nerve through the Bible from before the flood, and leads to the glory of the cross and resurrection. But what about the Jews and the Muslims – do they see the pain in God's heart?

By this stage, it should be clear that we have come to the conclusion that Muslims are speaking about and seeking to worship the One God who is the subject of the Bible, but that they have some ideas about him that are different from biblical views in very important ways. As noted in the Introduction, we see no problem in translating the Arabic 'Allāh' by the English 'God', and we see no problem in translating the Hebrew *elohim* or the Greek *theos* with the Arabic word 'Allāh' in Bibles in languages spoken by Muslims.[13]

We have just dealt with the question of whether and how God can come to us, and suggested that Muslims and Christians have solved a question raised within Judaism in opposite ways. Life is not quite so simple: if we look at history, we see that a question like this keeps coming back and being discussed both within Islam and within Christianity. There are ongoing questions within the two faiths as well as between the two faiths. For example, the Christian solution to the question about the *shekinah* – that God comes in Jesus and in the Holy Spirit – is fine until we start asking exactly how the Father, Son and Holy Spirit can be One God.

---

12. 'A Statement by Bethlehem Bible College Regarding the Current Crisis in Gaza', Bethlehem Bible College, 25 July 2014, http://www.bethbc.org/news/statement-bethlehem-bible-college-regarding-current-crisis-gaza.

13. Some languages, like Arabic, have no other word for 'God'.

Understanding God is not easy; and it cannot be easy, because he is the one who made us, and our brains cannot be big enough to understand our Maker. So, nearly every time we consider an aspect of the nature of God, we are likely to find parallel discussions and disagreements in Judaism, Islam and Christianity. We are also likely to find that Islam and Christianity offer opposite solutions to questions that were raised by Jews, both before and after the time of Jesus Christ. The question of whether God grieves over his creation is one of the most difficult of these questions.

The question can be divided into two parts: Does God feel? And does what we do make a difference to God? There is a history of Jews, Christians and Muslims alike using the language and tools of philosophy to discuss these aspects under the technical term 'the passibility of God'.

The subject is raised in Jewish commentary on God's reaction to human evil in Genesis 6:6: 'And the LORD was sorry that he had made man on earth, and it grieved him to his heart.' Two questions are raised: How can a God who is all-powerful and who knows everything 'regret' something, and how can a God who is transcendent 'grieve'?

The ancient rabbinic discussions[14] explore these questions. They suggest that God regretted the error of having made creatures that could rebel against him. They also suggest that 'I regret' might actually mean 'I am comforted' (the Hebrew words are similar) and might refer to God's relief that he had put the human beings on earth and not in heaven, as they might otherwise have disrupted heaven too. They then raise the question of whether God knew what was going to happen, and give an answer that seems to contradict the idea that God made a mistake. They liken the creation of humankind to the birth of a child: the father rejoices at the son's birth, even though he knows that he will later grieve over the son's death. The grief of God is treated quite literally. God grieved for his world, says one rabbi, for the full traditional mourning period of seven days before he sent the flood. In short, this early discussion does not question the idea that God feels for his creation, although it does see the tensions in putting together God's all-knowing power and God's grief.

That tension has been considered over the centuries, and commentators have insisted that the 'regret' and the 'grief' should be seen as anthropomorphisms: that they use human pictures to describe something in

---

14. See the discussion of Gen 6:6–7 in *Genesis Rabbah* 27 and 28 (around the second century AD).

God that is not, in fact, like human beings at all. It only looks like 'regret' and 'grief' from our human point of view. Here is a discussion from a fifteenth-century rabbi quoted in a recent Jewish commentary:

> Since in human phraseology, when a king punishes those who have rebelled against him, he is said to be jealous and revengeful and full of wrath, so it is said of God when he punishes those who violate his will that He is a jealous and avenging God and is full of wrath, because the act which emanates from Him against those who transgress His will is similar to the act of a revengeful, grudging, jealous person. The attribution of sorrow to God must be explained in the same way. Just as human beings feel sorrow when necessity compels their works to be destroyed, so the Torah says, 'it grieved Him to His heart', and in the immediate sequel we read: 'And the LORD said, I will blot out man whom I have made . . . for I regret having made them.' 'Regret' is applied to God because He performs the act of a person who regrets what He has made and desires to destroy it.[15]

Despite this concern about referring to God in human terms, there are strong Jewish traditions, deeply based in Scripture, of understanding God as passionate about his creation. For example, parts of the Song of Solomon are seen as expressing God's love for Israel, and parts of Jeremiah are seen as expressing his weeping over Israel's sins.[16]

Most Muslims would say that God is definitely impassible (i.e. he cannot be hurt), and that what we do makes no difference to him. The Qur'an tells us that he is independent of everything that he has created,[17] and classical Islamic thought insists that nothing a human being does can hurt God in any way. Further, God does not reveal himself, but only his will. The Qur'an gives him many names, such as the Beneficent, the Merciful, the All Knowing, but these are understood only as attributes: they tell us something about what God does, but nothing about his essence, nothing about what he is in himself.

---

15. Joseph Albo, Ikkarim 3:14, quoted in M. Zlotowitz, *Bereishis: Genesis: New Translation with a Commentary Anthologized from Talmudic, Midrashic and Rabbinic Sources*, 2nd ed. (New York: Mesorah Publications, 1986), 190–91.

16. See Montefiore and Loewe, *A Rabbinic Anthology*, 58–60, on God's love for Israel, and p. 67 on God's weeping in Jer 13:17.

17. This is the implication of the word *ṣamad* in Surah 112. 2. It could be translated 'eternal', 'self-sufficient' or 'sought by all and seeking none'. This surah is so central to Islamic thinking about God that Muhammad said it was worth one-third of the Qur'an.

All this means that, even if God did experience something like emotions, they would be very different from human emotions, and we could not know about them.

So, what does the Qur'an mean when it describes God as, for example, angry? The classical commentator At-Tabari (AD 839–923) is considered authoritative by the vast majority of Muslim scholars. He addresses the question in his discussion of Surah 1. 6–7 ('Guide us to the straight path: the path of those You have blessed, those who incur no anger and who have not gone astray').[18] His argument is based on the ideas that God is perfect, that he is unlike human beings, and that the words used of God in the Qur'an describe what God does, and not what he is or what he feels. We notice that his questions and his solutions are similar to those expressed in the fifteenth-century Jewish quotation above.

> There is disagreement about the attribute of wrath in connection with God. Some say that God's wrath against one of His creatures . . . consists in His giving out His punishment to him either in his worldly life or in his afterlife, as He Himself has described: 'So, when they had angered Us, We took vengeance upon them, and we drowned them altogether' (Surah 43. 55). Others say that God's wrath against those He is angry with is a censure of them and their actions on His part, His words of rebuke to them. And yet others say that His 'wrath' has a conceptual meaning similar to that which is understood from the various ordinary meanings of 'wrath', although there is a difference between God's wrath and men's wrath. For men's wrath rouses and agitates them, is oppressive for them and causes them harm, but God can have no defect in His essence. Rather, 'wrath' is one of His attributes, like 'knowledge' or 'power'.[19]

So a standard Muslim response to the question of whether God can feel pain would be, 'No! God cannot "feel" in the way we do. That would mean that he changed in response to human beings, and would therefore imply that he was not perfect. When he is described as "angry", the Qur'an means that what he does looks like anger to us. Similarly, if God is described as

18. M. A. S. Abdel Haleem, *The Qur'an: A New Translation by M. A. S. Abdel Haleem* (Oxford: Oxford University Press, 2008), Used with permission.

19. This is a slightly simplified version of the translation by W. F. Madelung and A. Jones, *Al-Tabari: The Commentary on the Qur'an*, vol. 1 (Oxford: Oxford University Press, 1987), 78.

"merciful", it means that he acts in a way that we see as merciful, and we cannot say that he is being moved by an emotion. He certainly cannot feel pain, because that would mean that we could hurt him.'

However, some Muslims, especially those who have a lot of contact with Christians, do think that God feels and that he is saddened by human disobedience. He is loving and compassionate, they say, so he must feel. The classical Islamic discussion about whether God can feel emotions concerns the nature of his anger, but current discussions are more likely to be about the nature of his love. For example, there has been much recent discussion between Muslims and Christians about what we mean when we say that God is loving. This followed 'A Common Word', the open letter sent to Christian leaders by a group of Muslim leaders in 2007.[20] It calls Christians to begin their relationships with Muslims by agreeing that the central commandments in both Christianity and Islam are to love God and to love our neighbours. The question is, then, 'What does "love" to God and neighbour mean?' and 'Who is my neighbour?' This leads very quickly to the question of what it means that God loves us. Does it, or can it, mean that he can be hurt when we do not love him in return?

The discussion is mainly in English, and the words being discussed are in Arabic, so part of the problem lies in translation. In Islamic tradition, one of the ninety-nine beautiful names of God is *Al-Wadūd*, which is often translated into English as 'The Loving'. The root of the word is *wdd*, which carries meanings that are often nearer to the English 'friendship' or 'affection' than to 'love'. We might say that, as with so many Islamic descriptions of God, *Al-Wadūd* tells us about how God acts rather than about what he is in himself.

The root that more usually means 'love' is *ḥbb*, which is used to describe God loving in Surah 3. 31 and 5. 54:

> Say, 'If you love God, follow me, and God will love you and forgive you your sins; God is most forgiving, most merciful' (Surah 3. 31).[21]

> You who believe, if any of you go back on your faith, God will soon replace you with people He loves and who love Him, people who are humble towards the believers, hard on the disbelievers,

---

20. For the initial letter and a selection of the discussion that it generated, see http://www.acommonword.com/.

21. M. A. S. Abdel Haleem, *The Qur'an: A New Translation by M. A. S. Abdel Haleem* (Oxford: Oxford University Press, 2008), Used with permission.

and who strive in God's way without fearing anyone's reproach. Such is God's favour. He grants it to whoever He will. God has endless bounty and knowledge (Surah 5. 54).[22]

These verses make it clear that this kind of 'love' is conditional: if people follow Muhammad, God will love them; and if anyone goes back on their faith, God will not love them. Surah 2 makes this even clearer:[23]

God does not love those who overstep the limits (Surah 2. 190).

God loves those who do good (Surah 2. 195).

God loves those who turn to Him, and He loves those who keep themselves clean (Surah 2. 222).

He does not love the ungrateful sinner (Surah 2. 276).

Christians are often shocked by the idea that God should love good people but not love bad people; Muslims are often shocked when Christians say that God loves bad people. Obviously, we have different understandings of the word 'love'.

What about the idea that God is 'compassionate'? This English word has 'passion' at the centre, so it implies that God sympathizes and feels with us. The Arabic word that is often translated 'compassionate' is part of the phrase *bismillāh ir-raḥmān ir-raḥīm*, with which every surah except Surah 9 begins. Abdel Haleem, whose translation we are using in this book, translates this as, 'In the Name of God, the Lord of Mercy, the Giver of Mercy'.[24] He reflects the fact that the two names for God are based on the same Arabic root, *rḥm*, which has to do with mercy and does not have the emotional implications of the English word 'compassion'. 'Mercy' is one of the most important attributes of God in the Qur'an, but it is not the same as 'love'. Love between God and human beings can go in both directions, whereas mercy comes only in one direction. God loves us and we can love him back. God has mercy on us, but we cannot have mercy on him.

So, on the one hand, classical Islam answers the Jewish question about whether God can feel pain with a simple, 'No!' On the other hand, many Muslims perceive God as having some kind of emotional response to human beings. However, when the Qur'an uses words that can be translated into

---

22. M. A. S. Abdel Haleem, *The Qur'an: A New Translation by M. A. S. Abdel Haleem* (Oxford: Oxford University Press, 2008), Used with permission.

23. Ibid.

24. Ibid.

English as 'love' or 'compassion', it clearly means something different from what the New Testament means when it describes God as 'love'.

And what does the New Testament mean? The first epistle of John, which tells us that 'God is love' (4:8), also tells us what love means:

> By this we know love, that [Jesus] laid down his life for us (3:16).

> In this the love of God was made manifest among us, that God sent his only Son into the world, so that we might live through him. In this is love, not that we have loved God but that he loved us and sent his Son to be the propitiation for our sins (4:9–10).

We understand God's love, says John, when we look at Jesus and his death on the cross. It is, then, Jesus' pain on the cross that resolves the Jewish problem about the pain in the heart of God and, perhaps, answers the feeling of many Muslims that God must somehow feel with his creation. It is not a problem that the Old Testament uses 'anthropomorphisms' to describe God's emotions. The word 'anthropomorphism' literally means something that is 'in human shape'. In the Bible, God made human beings 'in his image', and, in Jesus, he did indeed come to this world in human shape.

Christians would, of course, agree with the classical Islamic idea that God's feelings must be different from human feelings, but for slightly different reasons. From a biblical perspective, God's feelings must be different from ours primarily because God is good, so his feelings cannot be like the human passions that drive us so strongly and so often take us into sin. For example, his anger must be a righteous anger: it must be caused only by things that are wrong, and it must lead only to responses that are just. Christians would also agree that there is nothing that we can do to diminish God – that is, to spoil his goodness or his power. But if Jesus is God-with-us, and if he is the means by which we know the love of God, then God is a self-giving God who somehow shares the pain of his creation. As we saw earlier from Genesis 6:6, the pain in the heart of God reflects the pain of the human beings in bearing children and in tilling the ground that resulted from the fall. Jesus, says Hebrews, was made perfect (or complete) through his sufferings (Heb 2:10). His death on the cross does not in any way diminish God's holiness and power: it is an essential part of it. It is the way in which God chooses to be affected by human sin.

Thinking Biblically about Islam

A faith similar to Judaism, but a faith that proclaims Jesus as Messiah, a faith that is universal, a faith that prioritizes law, a faith that sees God as everywhere but not as 'coming to us', and a faith that loses the pain in the heart of God . . . How can we summarize all this thinking about Islam?

In the light of the transfiguration, we can see Islam as a faith that takes people a long way towards understanding God and his will, but that stops short of the central revelation of God in the Son and the Holy Spirit, and that cuts out the central act of salvation in the cross and the resurrection.

In the light of Genesis 1 – 11, we can see Islam as a human development from this foundation that has been affected by the whole range of human dignity and human sinfulness. In both theory and practice, we can see much that is good and noble in Islam, but also much that is, from a biblical perspective, wrong, and that has led people into injustice and away from the gospel of Jesus Christ.

'But what', you may be asking, 'about the spiritual dimension of Islam? Can we see God at work in and through Islam? Can we see Satan at work in it? Why did God permit the growth of a faith that takes so many people away from all that the transfiguration signifies?' Our biblical studies have not produced any simple answer to these questions. We can say that, from a biblical perspective, there is much truth in Islam, and that God is, ultimately, the source of all truth. We can say that, from a biblical perspective, there is also error within Islam, and that error can come both from human beings and from satanic deception. We can say that, as anything else in this world, God can use Islam to his glory; but human beings can also use it for their own purposes, and Satan can use it for evil.

As God is concerned for and working among all human beings, he must be concerned for and working among the huge number of people – nearly a quarter of the world's population – who call themselves 'Muslim'. We need to be alert to God's work, to Satan's work, and to the longings and expectations as well as to the sins in every situation. The key question is not 'What is the spiritual origin of Islam?' but 'What is God doing here? And what, therefore, does he require of us?'

Should Christians Eat Ḥalāl Meat?

What Christians should 'think about Islam' is not just a theoretical question: there are also important practical questions. One question that has caused much concern in recent years is that of eating ḥalāl meat. Christians who think that 'Allāh' is an idol, and not the One Creator God, think of ḥalāl meat as 'food offered to idols' and use 1 Corinthians 8 – 10 as a basis for their thinking. Christians who think that 'Allāh' is the Creator point out that Jesus said that food cannot defile us (Mark 7:19), and see no difficulty in eating and serving ḥalāl food. Here is a reflection from an organization that has more concerns: it sees increased use of ḥalāl food in the West as part of the spread of Islam. The writer points out, first, that it is not only the method of killing but also the prayer used during the killing of the animal that makes the food ḥalāl, and, second, that this is an important aspect of shariah. He continues:

'Whether wittingly or unwittingly, major supermarket chains have applied sharia to the meat industry with the result that much of the meat . . . has been killed cruelly and prayed over according to Islamic law. Should it therefore be eaten? Again, the principle is that all food is good. If it is blessed and sanctified by Christian prayer, then there is no reason why Christians should not eat it. This is the case in many Muslim countries, where no other is available in the shops.

'However, food cannot be separated from its context. Having rejected Jewish law, should we as Christians now embrace Islamic law? The ḥalāl meat industry is part of a process of Islamization in which some Muslims are seeking to impose the legal requirements of Islam, not just on their own people, but also on the rest of society. Should we . . . submit to the diktat of Islamic law now being perpetuated by the British meat industry and through supermarket chains? In eating ḥalāl meat, it can be argued that Christians and other non-Muslims are now furthering the process of dawa (Islamic mission), the Islamization of society, and the imposition of Islamic law.'[25]

---

25. P. Sookdheo, 'Supermarket Halal', *Evangelicals Now*, Dec 2010. This quotation can be found at 'Should Christians Eat Halal Meat', Australian Prayer Network, http://ausprayernet. org.au/feature/feature_articles_34.php; accessed June 2015.

To Think About

What does the writer of the above passage think about Islam?

How far can Christians choose to do what shariah law requires?

How far should Christians be worried about 'the Islamization of society'?

And finally, in 'thinking about Islam':

Do You Remember What Ali Said?

'I think of the Bible as the sun: the source of light. The symbol of Islam is the crescent moon, and that is how I think of the Qur'an. The crescent reflects the light of the sun. It is only a small part of the light, but it is enough to make people want more light, and be glad to see the sun. When the sun comes out, the moon is still there, but you don't notice it.'

I ask, 'What about the dark part of the crescent moon?' Ali laughs. 'We don't worry about that,' he says. 'Talking with Muslims, we want to focus on the light – what we need is more light!'

'It does not really matter what they think of Muhammad: what matters is what they think of Jesus!'

To Think About

What 'really matters' in all this thinking about Islam?

Part 4

Transformation

Do not be conformed to this world, but be transformed by the renewal of your mind, that by testing you may discern what is the will of God, what is good and acceptable and perfect. For by the grace given to me I say to every one among you not to think of himself more highly than he ought to think, but to think with sober judgement, each according to the measure of faith that God has assigned (Rom 12:2–4).

Islam, we have said, effectively replaces the transfiguration with Muhammad and the Qur'an, and moves forward from there. In the last chapter, we thought about what that might mean for thinking biblically about Islam. But what about ourselves? How should we move forward from the transfiguration, and what difference does building on the transfiguration make to how we think about ourselves and to how we actually relate to Muslims?

You might have noticed that chapter 6 on Jesus did not complete the study of the transfiguration chiasmus. Here is the chiasmus again:

A Who is Jesus? (Luke 9:18–20): Peter's confession that he is the Messiah (v. 20b)

B Jesus predicts his sufferings (9:21–22); the call to all to 'take up the cross' (vv. 23–26)

C No one here will die before seeing the kingdom of God (v. 27)

D Transfiguration (vv. 28–36)

C' The healing of the boy with the unclean spirit (vv. 37–43)

B' Jesus predicts his sufferings (vv. 44–45)

A' Who is the greatest? (vv. 46–48)

We stopped at C' – at the healing of the boy with the unclean spirit that offered a glimpse of the kingdom of God – but the chiasmus does not stop there, and the healing of the boy has more to teach us. In Matthew and Mark, the focus in the story is on the weakness of Jesus' disciples, and in all the Synoptic Gospels the chiasmus finishes with another of the disciples' problems. The question in A was, 'Who is Jesus?' This is mirrored in A' by another question. After experiencing the amazing sight of the transfiguration, seeing the boy healed and then hearing about Jesus' sufferings to come, the question that occupies the disciples' thoughts in A' is, 'Who is the greatest?'

We started this book with Paul's exhortation in Romans 12:2 'Be transformed by the renewal of your mind'. This could have been translated, 'Be transfigured . . .', for the Greek word is the same as that translated 'transfigured' in Matthew 17:2 and Mark 9:2. The transfigured mind, says Paul, enables us to discern God's will; the key question for Christians seeking to think biblically about Islam is, 'Lord, what is your will? What do you want us to be and to do?' However, Paul goes straight on to a warning: 'to every one . . . not to think of himself more highly than he ought to think' (v. 3). Perhaps he had experience of people who, like the disciples, were always thinking about how they could be greater than others – is this Christian superior to that Christian? And are Christians superior to others? In this section, we will find resources both for discerning God's will and for dealing with our desires for greatness by looking again at Jesus, by journeying on from the Mount of Transfiguration with the disciples, and by reflecting on how Romans 12 – 13 can help disciples of Jesus as he sends them out into the world of Muslim people that we analysed through Genesis 1 – 11.

To Think About

What should have been filling the disciples' minds as they went on from the transfiguration?

What are the questions in your mind as you come to this last section?

13

Law, Zeal and the Cross

Now if the ministry of death, carved in letters on stone, came with such glory that the Israelites could not gaze at Moses' face because of its glory, which was being brought to an end, will not the ministry of the Spirit have even more glory?

And we all, with unveiled face, beholding the glory of the Lord, are being transformed [or *transfigured*] into the same image from one degree of glory to another. For this comes from the Lord who is the Spirit (2 Cor 3:7–8, 18).

The transfiguration demonstrates the glory of God come in Jesus. The way to transfiguration for his disciples is 'beholding', or looking at, 'the glory of the Lord'. In Luke 9, on the mountain top, Jesus tells us where that glory is to be seen as he talks about his departure and, woven into the chiasmus in B and B', his coming suffering. If we want to look at the glory, we have to look at the cross.

The cross is the answer to the problems in human nature seen in the Cain and Abel story. Hebrews 12:18–24 claims that the blood of Jesus 'speaks a better word than the blood of Abel'. Where the blood of Abel cried out in outrage against what his brother had done, the blood of Jesus shed on the cross is the way to forgiveness for all. Where Abel offered an acceptable sacrifice on his own behalf and was killed against his will, Jesus became the acceptable sacrifice on behalf of all people as he went willingly to the cross. Where the holiness of God made Sinai a terrifying and dangerous place until the sacrificial system could be set up, the sacrifice of Jesus enables us to come confidently into God's presence. Wherever and however Muslims are seeking God, the cross of Jesus Christ is the answer to their seeking.

The cross is the answer to the problems in human nature seen in the flood story. It is because the cross deals with evil that it is the acceptable sacrifice.

It is the one sacrifice that makes sense of God's commitment not to send another flood. In Islamic thinking, there is no need for this sacrifice, as God can, by his mercy, simply forgive sin. In biblical thinking, that is not enough: evil cannot just be 'forgiven', but has to be dealt with. In Islamic thinking, evil people attack Jesus but God rescues him: he is vindicated by this rescue and taken straight to paradise. In biblical thinking, Jesus battles with Satan and with sin on the cross. He appears to be defeated, but, in fact, he wins: the cross leads to the triumph of the resurrection, and only then to the ascension and glorification 'at the right hand of God'. Wherever and however Muslims are trying to deal with evil, the cross of Jesus Christ is the only lasting way to defeat it.

The cross must, then, also be the answer to the problems in human nature seen in the Babel story. In the transfiguration, we see a King whose authority comes not from this world but from God. Jesus told Pilate, 'My kingdom is not of [or from] this world' (John 18:36). That did not mean that Jesus ignored the earthly 'kingdoms' or the power struggles symbolized by Babel: rather, he struggled against those kingdoms and powers by keeping his focus on God's kingdom. He never fought with the weapons of political power. His priority was the cross.

Throughout the Gospels, Jesus is faced with the complex world we have seen in Genesis 4 – 11 – a world of personal need and family tensions, of pluralism and religious competition, of tyranny and political ferment. The 'world behind the text' of the Gospels is a world of power struggles, as the Roman Empire imposed its rule in Israel and as the leaders of Israel argued among themselves. The Gospels are full of the tensions caused by differing expectations of the Messiah: it was not easy for Jesus to keep to his priority.

The scene is set at the beginning of his ministry when, like Moses and Elijah, Jesus is led out into the wilderness (Luke 4:1–13). This follows Jesus' baptism, where, as at the transfiguration, the heavenly voice announces, 'You are my beloved Son; with you I am well pleased' (Luke 3:22). Like Moses and Elijah, Jesus was led far from the centres of power before returning to them to confront the rulers. He did not go alone: the Holy Spirit filled him, but the devil attempted to distract Jesus from his priority of bringing salvation on the cross. He did this by offering to help him to be a Messiah who was like Moses or Elijah, in power but not in weakness, and a Messiah who would not only give Israel power over her enemies but also take power for himself.

We can imagine Jesus going into the wilderness with the heavenly voice ringing in his ears. He is the messianic Son, and he is greatly loved; but how should he please his Father? From his answers to the devil, we can see which Bible passages were at the centre of his meditations. He quotes from Deuteronomy 6 and 8 – that is, from Moses' final teaching to the Israelites when they were gathered in the desert just outside the Promised Land – perhaps in the very place where Jesus now was. At the end of this teaching, Moses would go up Mount Nebo to his departure. Deuteronomy 6 – 8 is about the importance of the Israelites' remembering the Lord their God and keeping his law when they get into the land. The danger is that the very blessings that God gives them will tempt them to forget and to disobey. Deuteronomy 7 is about their political conquest of the land. The Israelites are to fight, to destroy idolaters and idolatry, and to keep separate from those who worship other gods (vv. 1–5). They are God's chosen and beloved people, but they must never imagine that their conquests are due to their own superiority, or that they will be any less liable to God's judgement than others if they turn to idolatry (vv. 6–11). God's blessing on them will depend on their keeping his law (vv. 12–15). They will not conquer because of their own strength, but because of what God will do (vv. 16–24). They must not look for any material gain from the idols they conquer (vv. 25–26). We note that Deuteronomy sees close links between right worship, law-keeping and political power. Power is not, in biblical thinking, in the hands of human beings, but in the hands of God.

Deuteronomy 7 raises so many difficult questions for first-century Israel that it is not surprising if Jesus took forty days to think and pray about it. First, there are questions about the history of Israel as they conquered the land but did not complete the job; as they fell deeper and deeper into idolatry; and as they were themselves conquered and lost the land. They had so often forgotten and disobeyed the laws! How much good had it done them to destroy other nations' idols? Had they ever really been 'holy to the LORD' (Deut 7:6)? Next, there are questions about the first-century situation. Israel had made a partial return from exile, but had seldom lived under her own sovereignty, and had never been at unity about who should have political power. The Roman takeover had largely come about because the Jews could not agree among themselves and had welcomed foreign intervention. Was that because, despite all the rabbis' discussions and the attempts of the various sects to keep the law, they had missed the heart of what the law was about? And that takes us to the big question for Jesus: what did God want now? Did he want to bless the Jews by giving them power in their land? Did he want them once again to fight and to conquer the worshippers of other gods who ruled them and lived among them? Whatever God wanted, his blessing would depend on Israel remembering him, keeping his laws and worshipping him alone. It was obvious that having the law of Moses had not been sufficient to make Israel do this, and it never would be. Even Moses himself had not kept it well enough to be allowed to enter the land.

The Gospels do not tell us what Jesus thought of such questions during his wilderness days, but they go on to show us how Jesus dealt with the power struggles among both political and religious leaders: this dealing took him to the cross. They do tell us how he dealt with the questions raised by the Mosaic laws, and how he identified and lived by the heart of the laws that so many people had missed: living like this took him to the cross. They do tell us how he fought idolatry and its roots: he conquered it on the cross. In the wilderness accounts, the Gospels take us to Jesus' confrontation with what is at the very heart of idolatry: they tell us how the devil tried to deflect him from what he believed was God's way of dealing with these questions. In each case, the devil tempted Jesus to do something for himself – for his own comfort, his own power, his own safety – rather than something to please his Father and to benefit other people:

- He tempted Jesus first with the idea of feeding himself. A meal could be arranged, he suggests. Would Jesus not prefer to stay safe and well fed? God had given bread to Israel in the wilderness through Moses, and had fed Elijah in the desert, so should Jesus not claim the same privilege? Jesus refused, using the words of Deuteronomy 8:3. The whole purpose of Israel's time in the desert, says Deuteronomy, was to humble them, to test them and to let them know that there was something much more important than bread: God's word and, therefore, God's laws. God was teaching them to keep his laws, and he was taking them into a good and rich land. But the Israelites had failed the test, and had never got to the point of really keeping God's laws. Jesus would go to the cross so that the laws could be written on people's hearts, bringing them into a place of blessing much greater than any physical blessing could be. And Jesus would keep the law himself, by keeping as his priority his Father's will and not his own safety.

- Then, from a very high mountain, the devil offered him all the kingdoms of the world. The means to political gain, however, was alliance with the devil – even the acceptance of his ultimate authority. There is a stark choice here between the kingdoms of the world and the kingdom of God. Jesus as Messiah is God's King, bringing God's kingdom. He rejects the kingdoms of the world as, in the words of Deuteronomy 6:13, he rejects the worship of the devil: 'It is the LORD your God you shall fear. Him you shall serve and by his name you shall swear.' This instruction is given in the context of the choice between the God who brought the Israelites out of Egypt into the Promised Land and the gods of the surrounding nations. So, in Jesus' temptation, idolatry is aligned with worship of the devil, and with the kingdoms of this world and with seeking personal power. Worship of the One True God is, as it was for Moses facing Pharaoh and for Elijah facing Ahab, a political decision: it is refusal of the kingdoms of this world that sets Jesus on the way to the cross.

- Finally, taking Jesus into Jerusalem, the devil suggested he do something dramatic to demonstrate his status as the Messiah, the Son of God. From the pinnacle of the temple, the devil told Jesus to 'throw yourself down' and see angels come to the rescue. The devil was using Psalm 91, which reassures the believer of God's protection of the righteous and judgement on the wicked. Miraculous rescue was what Israel had experienced again and again from the time of Moses and the exodus, whenever she had obeyed God. Divine protection was expected as a reward for keeping the law. The Messiah was expected to lead Israel to victory. Surely, says the devil, and on firm scriptural grounds, you can do this! Jesus' response is interesting. He does not argue about whether God will automatically protect the righteous, or say that God will raise him only after he has suffered. Instead, he quotes Deuteronomy 6:16 – he understands that what the devil is suggesting is that he should 'test God'. We noted above that, in the desert, God was testing Israel. The devil's suggestion is that Jesus should, as it were, turn the tables and test God, just as the Israelites did when they demanded miraculous provision for themselves at Massah (Exod 17:1–7). Jesus refuses to treat his Father like that. He is God's King, and he will obey God right up to the cross, with certainty that God will establish his kingdom in his own way.

Through the way of the cross, Jesus will enable the law to be kept and God's kingdom to come, and people will find a deeper rescue than any rescue from mere physical danger: eternal salvation will be open to all peoples.

When Muslims deny the cross, they lose all this. Muslims may try to keep the law, but how can they have God's intentions of love written on their hearts? Muslims may try to establish God's rule by extending Islamic rule, but how can they avoid this turning into seeking political power for themselves, which is idolatry? Most Muslims believe that God did miraculously rescue Jesus from the cross, so how can they know salvation from their own temptations to test God?

To Think About

It is August 2014. The news is full of 'the Islamic State' killing Yazidis in Iraq. The Yazidis follow an ancient religion which worships a fallen angel who was later reinstated. Many Muslims see them as 'devil worshippers'. 'The Islamic State' sees itself as taking their area for Islam, and it is, therefore, trying to wipe them out. It is literally following Surah 9. 5: 'wherever you encounter the idolaters, kill them, seize them, besiege them, wait for them at every lookout post . . .'[1] They are not taking into account the ways in which this verse has been interpreted through the centuries.[2]

Deuteronomy 7:2 tells the Israelites to defeat the idolaters in the Promised Land, and to 'devote them to complete destruction'. What is the difference between this and what 'the Islamic State' is trying to do? What difference does the cross make to how worshippers of the One True God should treat idolaters and idolatry?

Jesus would go to the cross to fulfil all to which the Mosaic law pointed. The cross would also fulfil all to which the work of Elijah pointed, and that would include Elijah's challenge to the corrupt powers of his day. As in Deuteronomy, the Bible's account of Elijah shows the link between wrong religion and wrong political power. Where Deuteronomy focuses on the importance of the keeping of God's laws, Elijah's ministry focused on

---

1. M. A. S. Abdel Haleem, *The Qur'an: A New Translation by M. A. S. Abdel Haleem* (Oxford: Oxford University Press, 2008), Used with permission.

2. Within the Qur'an itself, this verse is not a general commandment to kill all idolaters. The context of the verse is that the idolaters had broken their treaty with the Muslims, and the passage goes on to say that, should the idolaters ask for protection, they should be taken to a safe place.

challenging people's disobedience to those laws. If Moses was the law-giver, we might say that Elijah was the law-enforcer.

By New Testament times, Elijah's way of dealing with idolatry and disobedience to God was summarized in the word 'zeal'. Together with Phinehas, he was a model to the Jewish people of what zeal for God and his glory should look like (see also pp. 99 and 147) – and that included Phinehas' killing of the Israelite and his Moabite woman and Elijah's killing of the prophets of Baal. The word 'zeal' means something much more than enthusiasm and commitment to a cause; it means a desire to put God and his glory absolutely first, an attitude that will not put up with anyone or anything being put in God's place. It is a total commitment to getting rid of evil.

Elijah's zeal reflects an attribute of God himself, for, in the Old Testament, God is referred to as zealous, jealous or passionate (in Hebrew and Greek, the word 'zealous' is the same as 'jealous'): that is, single-mindedly committed and tolerating neither disloyalty nor dishonour. Israel was told that she should worship no other god, because the LORD's name is Jealous. His zeal accomplishes much: by his zeal, a remnant of Israel would be saved (2 Kgs 19:31), and, by his zeal, the reign of the Messiah would come to pass (Isa 9:7).

In Jesus' day, zeal was often expressed in political ways. The 'Zealots', of whom we read in the Gospels – at least one of whom was among Jesus' disciples (Luke 6:15) – had become one of the expressions of a Jewish resistance to the Roman occupation. They sought political liberation even with violence and upheld the honour of God, his temple and his laws. Paul described himself as 'zealous' when recounting how he had once upheld Israel's traditions by persecuting Christians (Phil 3:6). Here it is not hard to see a parallel for what is often seen as the 'fanatical' strain of religions, including Islam, today.

What about Jesus? Did he reflect the zeal of God as well as the 'pain in God's heart'? When he was tempted, he rejected the way of the Zealots, and he would also have rejected Paul's early idea that the way to deal with heretics was to persecute them and kill them if necessary. How, then, did Jesus show his single-minded commitment to God and his glory, and to dealing with the evil that he met?

The word 'zeal' is specifically used of Jesus in connection with the cleansing of the temple, when the disciples saw him driving out traders with cords lashed together for a whip and pushing over their stalls. The incident is very important, and is recorded in all four Gospels (Matt 21:12–13; Mark 11:15–18; Luke 19:45–46; John 2:14–17), probably because it signifies the return of God to his temple, as prophesied by Malachi 3:1–12.[3] The Jews have been waiting for the return of the *shekinah*, and here it is: the presence of God in the Messiah, Jesus. But, as Malachi warned, this is not a presence that starts by freeing them from the Romans: it is a presence that starts by purifying Israel. This is part of the pattern that we have already seen in Elijah's challenges to wrong worship and in John the Baptist's calls to repentance. While John's ministry at the Jordan implied that people could repent without going to the temple, Jesus took the challenge to the religious rulers much further by taking the call to repentance into the temple itself. John's gospel calls this 'zeal'.

Jesus is distressed to see people make an idol of money. Just as the Israelites earlier had listened to the lie of another powerful idol – 'one can serve both God and Baal' – here, the money-changers believe the lie that money whispers, 'one can serve both God and Mammon'. Jesus is violent, as Elijah had been before, in his insistence that Israel cease defiling herself by 'wavering between two options'. His behaviour reminds the disciples of a psalm in which a servant of God cries, 'Zeal for your house has consumed me' (Ps 69:9).

The reference draws us into this lament psalm of God's righteous servant. He is facing more enemies 'than the hairs of [his] head' (v. 4), alienation from his family and the pit closing its mouth over him. The enemies even mock him, by giving him vinegar when he is thirsty (v. 21). In this context, 'zeal has consumed me' does not, as in modern English, mean that the zeal is so eating into the psalmist that he has to act; the verse continues, 'and the reproaches of those who reproach you have fallen on me.' It seems that all the attacks on the psalmist have been provoked because of his zeal for God's house. He has put God first and has got into terrible trouble for it. The disciples were not thinking, 'Jesus has gone out of his mind with zeal', but, 'Jesus is going to get "eaten" by his enemies for his zeal'. And they were right. Mark notes that it was this incident that led directly to the religious leaders' 'seeking . . . to destroy him' (11:18).

The psalmist's zeal does not lead to his taking revenge on his persecutors, but it does lead to his calling down God's fury on them – desolation, pain and their being blotted out from the book of life. Jesus, however, at the moment of his worst affliction, when he too was given vinegar for his thirst, called out,

---

3. See Wright, *Jesus and the Victory of God*, 631–45, for a discussion of how the cleansing of the temple and the parables that went with it symbolized the 'return of God to Zion'.

'Father, forgive.' He allowed the insults of those who insult God to fall upon himself. Jesus literally allowed zeal for God's house to consume him, giving himself for others as he bore our sin and shame once for all time. He would not destroy the temple: he would allow the temple of his body to be destroyed. He who lashed together cords to make a whip was himself scourged. His zeal led him to the cross, and it was there that he dealt with evil.

Why I Deeply Admire Him

I've really learned to be very wary of religious people who have too many friends and are too popular, and keep banging on about 'relationships' and being nice.

Following Jesus for me means learning to reject the Victorian saccharine fiction . . . of 'gentle Jesus meek and mild', and seeing Jesus as someone who was gentle with the 'least of my brethren' and opened his personal fellowship to people the mosque and church look down on – while at the same time being a fractious, unpleasant and very not self-controlled, and very not restrained chastiser of powerful religious authorities. He was a rubbish politician – the complete opposite of Mr Pontius 'What is Truth?' Pilate.

I think Westerners who do Nice Middle Class Christianity forget that Jesus would not have fitted in socially at the church picnic. He, like the Prophet Muhammad, would have been disgusted at the British Muslim community's style of doing business, and its reduction of belief in the One God to a series of communal identity-affirming rituals.

Jesus wasn't a 'nice guy', and that's why I deeply admire him.[4]

To Think About

How far does this Muslim's view of Jesus fit the gospel accounts? What kind of zeal do you see in Jesus?

Jesus' zeal was different from Elijah's zeal in that it led him to die for his opponents rather than to kill them. It was similar to Elijah's zeal in that it was a single-minded commitment to pleasing God. Further, the cross fulfils something that is hinted at in Elijah's zealous confrontation with the Baal

---

4. Muhammad Al-Hussaini in *CMCS Newsletter* 6 (Autumn 2011).

prophets: his offer of a sacrifice that was accepted by God. Under the wood and the bull carcasses for that sacrifice were laid twelve stones, an ancient representation of the twelve tribes of Israel. Rock is incombustible, but God's fire burned it up, sparing those of the twelve tribes watching who were guilty of apostasy. Even the zeal of Elijah, so often thought of as being violently directed towards sinners, was directed towards sacrifice on behalf of others.

The New Testament deals with both violent zeal and sacrificial zeal, and with both wrongly and rightly directed zeal. For example, the high priests and Sadducees were zealous for what they saw as the security of their people and their religion. 'Filled with jealousy [literally 'zeal']', they imprisoned the apostles. To counter them, an angel of the Lord intervened and released the apostles (Acts 5:17–19). Paul deeply repented of his own wrongly directed zeal that led him to persecute Christians, and he describes the zeal of those in Israel who did not recognize Jesus as Messiah as 'unenlightened'. He understood the power of God to redirect zeal, so his response to wrong zeal was to pray for people's salvation (Rom 10:2).

The new Corinthian church displayed examples of rightly directed zeal, with zeal for Paul (2 Cor 7:7) and for their fellow believers (2 Cor 9:2); and they experienced it in Paul's own 'divine jealousy' for them (2 Cor 11:2). There is a right zeal for the purity of God's church, just as there was a right zeal for the purity of Israel. Titus 2:14 tells us that the purpose of Jesus' zealous self-giving was to purify a people for himself who would, in turn, be 'zealous for good works'.

Redirected Zeal

Hussain made his fellow believers in Jesus nervous.

First, he started handing out Bible tracts right outside their meeting place. 'If you have to risk causing a riot, can't you do it somewhere else?' they said. He moved; but one of the 'militant' Muslims who received a tract believed in Jesus.

Next, he decided to walk a hundred miles carrying a huge wooden cross through his Muslim country. 'You'll get lynched!' they said. He didn't: in fact, lots of people asked him what he was doing and he was able to tell them, and some asked for baptism. His testimony was that he had once been a member of a zealous, 'militant' Muslim group. Now, he was just as zealous for Jesus and wanted to honour his cross.

To Think About

What do you see of right and wrong zeal in the Muslims you know? And in the Christians you know?

Do you know of anyone who has repented of wrong zeal and changed the direction of their zeal? What motivated them to change? How do they demonstrate their zeal now?

14

Coming Down the Mountain

On the Mount of Transfiguration, Peter, James and John saw the glory of Jesus; but how far did seeing Jesus change them? Jesus was going to the cross to transform and fulfil the law of Moses and the zeal of Elijah; but what did that actually mean for his disciples? We have just been looking at Jesus; but how far have we understood what that means for our thinking about Islam and for our relationships with Muslims? In what ways does the cross change our law-keeping and our zeal?

We will follow Jesus and his disciples down the mountain to the series of confrontations with evil that met them in the world below. They call to mind Elijah's zealous confrontations with Israel's law-breaking.

Confrontation 1: With Sickness, Demons and Prayerlessness (Luke 9:37–43)

The first confrontation is with an unclean spirit. It is in the context of such confrontations, in a discussion about Beelzebul the prince of demons, that the name of Baal appears in the New Testament (Matt 10:25; 12:24–32; Mark 3:27; Luke 11:15–23). *Ba'al zebul* means, in Hebrew, 'Lord Baal'. The name does not appear in the Old Testament: instead, we find *Ba'al zebub*, which means 'Lord of the flies' and is probably a way of mocking Baal. It is *Ba'al zebub* whom Ahab's son Ahaziah tried to consult in 2 Kings 1, and whom Elijah challenged by calling down fire from heaven on Ahaziah's soldiers. The New Testament sees Jesus as fulfilling Elijah's ministry in his confrontation with demonic powers as well as in other ways.

There had been a violent, painful side to Baal worship on Mount Carmel: 'They . . . cut themselves . . . with swords and lances, until the blood gushed out upon them . . . they raved on' (1 Kgs 18:28–29). The disturbing nature of unclean spirits is seen again at the foot of the Mount of Transfiguration when a boy is brought to Jesus with a spirit who 'seizes him . . . cries . . . convulses him so that he foams at the mouth . . . shatters him . . . [throws] him to the ground' (Luke 9:39–42). Jesus rebukes this unclean spirit, heals the boy and restores him to his father. In this realm, Jesus is taking control and wielding power. The response is the same as the response on Carmel: people are amazed by God.

Elijah's ministry was dealing primarily with the faithlessness of Israel; this confrontation is also about the faithlessness of Israel and about the inability of the disciples to deal with the situation. It calls us, too, to confront our own faithlessness and prayerlessness when faced with powers that destroy people.

In Matthew, the disciples ask Jesus why they were unable to help the boy, and Jesus responds by saying that they need faith (Matt 17:20). In Mark, he says that they need to pray (Mark 9:29). In Luke, as we saw in chapter 6, the focus is on Jesus' response to the destructive power rather than on the need for prayer: 'O faithless and twisted generation, how long am I to be with you and bear with you?' (Luke 9:41).

We can hear something of the heart of God, agonizing over the destruction among his special people just as he did over the destruction in his creation in Genesis 6:6. We remember Moses pleading with God after the golden calf incident: 'Alas, this people has sinned a great sin' (Exod 32:31). Moses goes on to offer to be '[blotted] out of your book that you have written' if only God will forgive the people, but God tells him that Moses cannot bear the people's sin. We remember Elijah's agonizing at Horeb: 'The people of Israel have forsaken your covenant, thrown down your altars, and killed your prophets' (1 Kgs 19:10, 14). Elijah did not offer his life, but tried to save it: part of his complaint was, 'they seek my life, to take it away'. Jesus allowed others to 'seek [his] life, to take it away', by going to the cross so that the faithlessness and twistedness of Israel could be transformed.

To Think About

Today, the newspapers are full of destruction caused by Israel in the Middle East, and of destructive responses directed towards Israel and towards Jewish people. They are also full of destruction caused by and against Muslim people, and by and against people who call themselves 'Christian'.

Is the news very different 'today', when you are reading this, from how it was on the 'today' when the above paragraph was written?

How does the 'heart of God' respond to the twistedness of his people? What does this mean for your prayers?

At the foot of the Mount of Transfiguration, the twistedness in Israel was displayed in the life of a particular family: the dark shadows of evil, even of the demonic, that brought suffering to the demon-possessed boy whom Jesus met, bring suffering to many families across the world today. Sadly, they also overshadow many Muslim communities, especially those which engage in 'popular' practices that seek to placate the *jinn* and use religious formulae to gain health and prosperity. In relating to Muslims, do we have a zeal that makes us long to see people set free from spiritual bondage, and that leads us to a ministry of prayer and healing?

Later in the New Testament, James focuses our attention on Elijah when he writes about praying for the sick. God showed his jurisdiction over the realms of weather and fertility in his response to Elijah's simple prayer that 'there shall be neither dew nor rain . . . except by my word' (1 Kgs 17:1). 'He prayed again,' James says, 'and heaven gave rain, and the earth bore its fruit' (Jas 5:18). He encourages us to emulate Elijah by reminding us that he 'was a man with a nature like ours' (5:17).

When Jesus prayed to his Father, the responses often caused people to be amazed. There are parallels here with Muslim people today who are sometimes amazed at the power of prayer in Jesus' name as God does 'extraordinary things', as many of those who work among Muslims have testified. The only fire from heaven that fell in the lifetime of the apostles was that which came with the Holy Spirit at Pentecost. His power is the power they wielded as they went out into the nations. Can we be content to engage with Muslims, not with Elijah-style fireworks and not in our own power, but in the power of the Holy Spirit?

Hannah's Story: Talitha Cumi!

When Ishfaaq, a maulvi (religious scholar), joined my English class I was nervous at first. 'Will he disapprove of what I do? Is he here to check up on what I say as a Christian?' He did nothing to allay my fears, sitting at the back, scowling. His forehead bore the mark of a man who had bowed his head to the ground in unceasing prayer.

I continued to teach, encouraging my students to participate as much as possible to practise past perfect and simple in the right contexts. Little by little, Ishfaaq softened, joining in in his gruff voice and smiling at the jokey dialogues the other students performed.

'I hear you live near Holy Family Hospital, Ma'am,' he said to me after class one day. Before I could begin to worry that he knew my address, he continued, 'Ma'am, I know you are a Christian. Please could you visit my niece there? Pray for her, please. Her name is Adeela. She is fourteen and has hepatitis.'

It was a beautiful spring day when I first went to visit her. The windows were flung wide open to let in sunshine and fresh air. But how much it needed it! The place was filled with sickness. Even the mangy ward cat limping beneath drip stands had a broken leg. Adeela was surrounded by family members caring for her: the nurses were on strike. Her sister applied talcum powder and her brothers fetched cold drinks from the canteen. Her mother and aunt looked on, sick with worry. They made a space for me to join them by her bed, where I made feeble attempts to chat and offer comfort. Looking at Adeela's ashen face and almost rotten legs, however, I was fighting hopelessness. After an awkward silence her aunt raised her eyes heavenwards and gestured with her hands for me to pray. I stammered out a prayer in Jesus' name, knowing it was a risk, gambling all on God's power to do the amazing.

I continued to visit for nearly a month. I brought in picture books to cheer her up and told stories of Jesus' power to heal. Every time I waited to be invited to pray. Once they offered me money for praying. Adeela's condition deteriorated till one day I visited her while she was having a blood test. Blood sample slides littered the place and Adeela was skeletal. For the first time she did not smile at me. I hardly dared pray again and only managed to mumble through tears. When I said goodbye, I feared that would be the last time.

Two days later, they left for their village, realizing that the hospital was not making her better. I dreaded the phone call: 'Well, it was Allāh's will . . .' Summer grew hotter and I received an invitation to visit the family a day's journey to the south.

I got out of the hot car and blinked in the strong sunshine. It was good to be out of the city. Sheep were grazing among rocky outcrops on the low hills around us. Up the path came a tall young girl, clothed in bright blue and her face lit by a smile. 'As-salāmu 'alaykum Hannah!'

'Adeela!'

To Think About

Do you know people who have been healed after prayer in Jesus' name? What effect has it had on those who were healed and on those who saw them restored to health?

Confrontation 2: With Power-Seeking and Factions (Luke 9:46–49)

As Jesus goes to the cross, he will encounter the power dimensions of both Jewish and Roman religion. But before he does so, he challenges his own disciples about their power struggles. After all that they have seen of the glory of Jesus, they are still intent on deciding which one of them is 'the greatest'. In response, Jesus quietly takes a child and puts him right in the centre of the group (Luke 9:47). If they want to receive God's King, they are not to look for people with status, but to receive people who appear to be as unimportant as this small child. 'He who is least among all of you', he says, 'is the one who is great' (Luke 9:48). We are reminded, perhaps, of the foreign child healed by Elijah when all Israel was suffering from famine (1 Kgs 17:17–23). King Ahab might have thought that he was 'the greatest', but God sent Elijah first to this child, and Ahab had to wait his turn.

Immediately after this, John tells Jesus about someone who was casting out demons in his name. 'We tried to stop him', he says, 'because he does not follow with us' (Luke 9:49). The implication is that the group that travels with Jesus has a special status. John might now understand that there is no 'greatest' among the twelve, but he still thinks that the twelve are in some ways 'greater' than everyone else. Again, Jesus corrects him: he should accept anyone who accepts Jesus (v. 50). We are reminded, perhaps, of Elijah, exhausted by his zeal, and thinking that he is the only true worshipper of God left (1 Kgs 19:14). God told him that there were many more true worshippers of whom he did not know.

Jesus, too, had many more disciples than the twelve. Soon after this incident, he sends out seventy-two others, who will all have the authority to cast out demons in Jesus' name. When they come back rejoicing in what God has done through them, Jesus will rejoice that it is 'little children' who have been privileged to see what all the previous prophets longed to see (Luke 10:21–23). It is not 'greatness' that qualifies people to see the fulfilment of the law and the prophets; it is not worldly power; it is taking the humble place of the child that qualifies people to enter temples and palaces, legislative assemblies and forums to continue Jesus' ministry.

Luke 10:21–23 gives us another glimpse into Jesus' heart, as he bursts into a joyful prayer of thanksgiving. He has told the seventy-two not to rejoice in the submission of the demons but in their salvation (v. 20): now he is rejoicing 'in the Holy Spirit', not because of the power that the disciples have in his name, but because of the choice of his Father as to who would receive him. It was not the 'wise and understanding' – that is, not the elite, educated leaders; it was the ordinary and the humble people, and all depended on the Father's choice to open their eyes. In the midst of the power struggles of this world, can we share Jesus' heart for the 'ordinary' people?

The confrontations with the disciples' power struggles challenge us about our own desires to be 'the greatest'. There can be great competition among Christians about how they think about Islam: is this, that or the other writer 'the greatest'? There can be competition about how to reach Muslims for Christ: is this, that or the other method 'the greatest'? There are factions that argue about how to translate the Bible and about how new believers should relate to Islam, as well as others that argue about how far shariah law should be permitted in non-Muslim countries and about how to deal with violent extremism. There is also a great temptation for Christians to try to be 'greater' than Muslims in all sorts of ways. Many of these questions are important – but do we direct our zeal to the kingdom of God or to our individual or group 'greatness'? And how can we redirect our zeal towards the way of the cross?

Letter from a Church in the midst of Power Struggles, Egypt, 2013

When more than 85 Churches and institutions were viciously attacked and burned (a profound blow of disgrace and humiliation in this culture of 'honour'), the non-retaliation of Christians was both unexpected and unprecedented.

Immediately following these attacks, the leader of the Coptic Church, Pope Tawadros II said that if the destruction of these properties was the price Christians in Egypt have to pay to get a free Egypt, then that sacrifice is worthwhile! His – and all other Christian leaders' messages – have helped the Christian spirit of forgiveness to be powerfully demonstrated in Egypt . . .

Many Egyptian Christian leaders are reminding their flock that the Church consists of the people of God, Christ's body, and not the buildings in which we worship. Thus the Church can never be destroyed!

Egypt is not on the verge of civil war! On the contrary, most Egyptian Muslims and Christians are more united than ever in their common vision for the future, as together they have rejected extremist 'Political Islam', and are working towards the noble task of establishing a civil society which recognizes all Egyptians as equal citizens.

Egypt, however, faces incredible social, economic, cultural and political challenges as it tries to rebuild after three years of radical change and confusion. As a result many Egyptians are weary and pessimistic about the present situation in their country.

Most of our leaders, however, see beyond these difficulties towards a better Egypt. As a Bible Society we are seeking to make a positive contribution by providing a variety of Scripture products (print and electronic). One of our projects is a special edition of the Sermon on the Mount (in which Jesus presents principles of His Kingdom which reflect the aspirations of many Egyptians at this time), and a variety of tracts taken from it, for wide distribution. Some beautiful artwork for this product . . . says, 'You are the light of the world.'[1]

To Think About

What might bring joy to Jesus in this situation?

This letter was written by a Protestant evangelical, but many of the Christians of whom he writes are Coptic Orthodox. What enabled these Christians to resist the temptation to compete for power and honour among themselves? What enabled them to resist the temptation to compete for power with the Muslims around them?

---

1. Ramez Atallah, 'Bible Society of Egypt Newsletter', 12 September 2013, http://us6. campaign-archive2.com/?u=017b6b7c5bf6d7468fcc6aedc&id=ff25fb810a.

Confrontation 3: With Nationalistic Religion (Luke 9:51–56)

The third confrontation comes as Jesus 'set his face to go to Jerusalem' (Luke 9:51): that is, he is beginning his deliberate journey to the cross. On Jesus' route is a Samaritan village that rejects him. Some messengers sent ahead had tried to make arrangements for him to stay there, but the villagers had not cooperated. In keeping with the ethnic and religious prejudice between Jews and Samaritans, the disciples get angry and the stage is set for another confrontation. 'Lord, do you want us to tell fire to come down from heaven and consume them?' they ask, seeking to emulate Elijah. The allusion is not to the fire that devours Elijah's sacrifice on Carmel, but to the soldiers sent to Elijah by the Samaritan king Ahaziah, Ahab's son, in 2 Kings 1. Ahaziah is injured and wants to find out whether he will recover, so he sends messengers to inquire from the god Baal-zebub. In response, God sends Elijah to tell the messengers that the king will not recover, but also to rebuke the king for inquiring of Baal-zebub rather than the God of Israel. Furious, Ahaziah sends fifty soldiers to get Elijah. Elijah calls down fire from heaven, and that is the end of the soldiers. The king sends another fifty soldiers and, again, they are devoured by heavenly fire. Finally, the king sends another fifty soldiers, but this time God tells Elijah to go with them; he goes and delivers the same message in person to Ahaziah, and Ahaziah dies.

This third confrontation in Luke has to do with dealing with people who reject Jesus just as King Ahaziah rejected the God of Israel. It also has to do with the ethnic and national dimension of religion that Jesus had already challenged in his reference to Elijah and the widow of Zarephath in Luke 4. The disciples did not, as far as we know, want to call down fire from heaven on any of Jesus' Jewish opponents. Here, Jesus confronts the Jewish–Samaritan hostility by rebuking the disciples: 'You do not know what manner of spirit you are of, for the Son of Man came not to destroy people's lives but to save them' (v. 55, margin). He has just 'set his face' to go to the cross because his preference is for the way of the sacrifice, and not for the way of the flood.

So, instead of calling down fire, the disciples had to follow him 'to another village', presumably among the same people. Jesus is doing exactly what he told the twelve to do when he sent them out (Luke 9:4–5). When people receive him, he stays with them; when they reject him, he moves on.

Moving on with Jesus, the disciples are again faced with the potential cost of following him through an area in which he is likely to be rejected (vv. 57–62). They might find no hospitable house, they might have to leave their own families, and they will have to focus on bringing God's kingdom to others rather on those in their own homes. As Jesus then sends out the seventy-two (10:1–16), he is very clear that they will be faced with opposition. They will be 'as lambs in the midst of wolves' (Luke 10:3), but the instructions are not to fight back or to call down fire from heaven; rather, they are to warn the town, just as Jonah did Nineveh (Jonah 3). We remember that Nineveh, Israel's greatest enemy, repented. The wicked Gentile towns of Tyre and Sidon, says Jesus, would also have repented. If the Samaritan and Jewish towns do not repent, says Jesus, they will come under judgement, but the judgement will be in the hands of God, and it is not for the disciples to call down fire from heaven. They should not take rejection personally. They are only disciples: if they are rejected, it is Jesus who is being rejected.

As Jesus continues his journey through Samaria towards Jerusalem, Luke has two more specific references to Samaritans. Towards the end of their trip, nearing Jerusalem, Jesus heals ten lepers in the region between Samaria and Galilee. Only one returns to thank him. Luke spells out that 'he was a Samaritan' (17:11–19). The other reference is Jesus' well-known answer to the question 'Who is my neighbour?' (10:25–37). Jesus makes a Samaritan the hero of the story: it is a very different response than calling down fire!

Ida's Story: This Really Happened!

The sun was going down and it was nearly time to break the Ramadan fast. Muslims, dressed in clean clothes, were making their way to the mosque and David, my husband, would soon be home. He was hungry and thirsty and his mind was on the chink of cups that he could hear as the tea stall was prepared for customers coming out after prayer. He had eaten nothing all day, because he did not want to eat or drink when his Muslim friends were fasting.

Disaster! Not looking where he was going, David slipped and fell into an open, stinking, 4-foot-deep drain, and could not get out. The passing people watched his struggles, but no one wanted to dirty his clothes, or his prayers would be invalid. Then one man stopped. He was an older man, dressed in spotless white. He helped David out: no longer spotless, he wouldn't be able to go to the mosque now. 'My son,' he said, 'God has been good to you!' 'My father, how has God been good to me?' asked David, standing there filthy and bruised. 'Many cows have fallen into that ditch,' said his rescuer, 'and they have all broken at least one leg. Your legs are whole. You should thank God.' And he poured clean water over David and brought him home.

To Think About

How do you respond to people who reject Jesus? Does it make any difference what ethnic or religious group they belong to?

Jesus' parable of the good Samaritan takes us to the heart of law-keeping and zeal. It is Jesus' answer to an expert in religious law who, like so many experts in Islamic law, wanted to reach paradise. The law-keeping and the zeal of the two Jewish religious leaders made them avoid the unclean, wounded man. The Samaritan put the heart of the law into action by showing love, and his zeal led him to give his own time and money to save the wounded man.

There are several parallels between Samaritan–Jewish differences in New Testament times and the differences between Muslims and Christians today. The Jews and Samaritans had a long history of antagonism, and they lived separately, even though the Samaritan territory was right in the middle of Jewish territory. Most Jews would have taken the longer journey around Samaria rather than walking through it as Jesus did. Likewise, in many places today, there is a long history of mutual suspicion and separation, with Christians and Muslims living within their separate communities even if they do, as it were, pass through each other's territories, meeting at work or at school but not visiting each other's homes or understanding each other's hearts. So Jesus' interactions with Samaritans have much to teach us. Could it be that some Muslims are more open to Jesus' healing power than we are? Or that some are more compassionate than we are?

The Gospels' treatment of Samaritans is especially relevant for our relationships with Muslims who are in minority situations or who are marginalized by society. Many Christian women working among Muslim women in Europe say that Jesus' meeting with the Samaritan woman in John 4 is the gospel passage that most helps them in their ministry.

We can find many parallels between the situation of Jesus and the Samaritan woman and the situation of Christians and Muslims today. The Jews and the Samaritans shared aspects of a common heritage: Jesus and the woman met at Jacob's well and both acknowledged Jacob as a patriarch. Christians and Muslims often find that the Old Testament patriarchs and prophets are good 'meeting points', places to situate dialogue. However, the woman at the well was reluctant to accept anyone greater than Jacob, just as Muslims are reluctant to accept that there could be any human being greater than a prophet. The woman quickly accepted Jesus as a prophet just as Muslims do. She moved towards acknowledging Jesus as the Christ, just as Muslims regard him as the Messiah while only partially understanding the implications of this title.

The different temples for Samaritans and Jews remind us of the different places and forms of worship of Muslims and Christians. The Samaritans and Muslims share a concern with a territorial positioning of their religious practice: 'Our fathers worshipped on this mountain, but you say that in Jerusalem is the place where people ought to worship,' the woman stated (John 4:20). Muslims also pray towards a specific place, Mecca, and seek to visit it for the hajj. Jesus challenged the woman, saying that her community worshipped what it did not know (4:22). Likewise, Muslims generally see God as unknowable.

Relating to Samaritans was controversial. We have seen what the disciples wanted to do to the village that refused entry to Jesus. When they found Jesus talking to the Samaritan woman they were triply shocked (4:27): how could a religious teacher sit with a woman, one who had a bad reputation and who was a Samaritan? The woman herself was surprised that he would reach across their religious and ethnic divide to ask for water. There are some in the church who oppose church members having warm relations with Muslims, and who would suggest they should not 'bother with them'.

Just as in Luke 9, when messengers went ahead to ask Samaritans to prepare a place for Jesus to stay, Jesus begins the relationship with this woman from a position of need. He is tired from his journey and asks for a drink. Could expressing need and weakness like this be a way of being childlike in the Muslim world, of going out without 'money bag . . . knapsack . . . [or] sandals' (Luke 10:4)?

If you live in a traditional Muslim society, you will probably be able to imagine the position of this woman who had had five husbands. Most probably, she had been rejected by each husband in turn. She might have been unfaithful, but it is more likely that she was childless or had a health problem of some kind. She would not have been able to live securely without a husband, and was now forced to live with a man who had not married her. We do not know how far she was at fault and how far she was a victim, but she was clearly an outcast from her community or she would not have had to come alone to the well at midday. Jesus understood her. He did not ignore her condition or condone it, but he got her to talk about it. Can we understand and listen to people in such difficult situations?

The first gospel readers would not only have been shocked at Jesus' sitting and talking with this sinful Samaritan woman: they would also have been shocked that she is the first person to whom Jesus reveals his identity in John's gospel. In John 2:23–25, we read that Jesus decided not to reveal his true identity and 'entrust himself' to Jews in Jerusalem during the Passover. In chapter 3, a notable religious leader struggles to understand Jesus' teaching. Now, Jesus declares himself to be the Messiah (4:26), and, through this woman, the message of who he is gets declared to the Samaritans before it is declared to the Jews.

Despite all the differences between Jews and Samaritans, Jesus tells this woman that if she knew the gift of God, she would be free to ask for it and would be given it (John 4:10). He transforms her shameful past of rejection and adultery into the context for her glowing testimony, 'Come, see a man who told me all that I ever did' (v. 29). It is in her village that it starts to become clear that Jesus' is the Saviour of the *world*, not just of Israel.

Finally, this conversation prompts Jesus to observe that 'the fields are white for harvest. Already the one who reaps is receiving wages and gathering fruit for eternal life' (vv. 35–36). This Samaritan woman is part of the harvest, but she immediately becomes a reaper, and many from her town believe. Can this story give us faith that Jesus can do amazing things within communities we consider too hard to reach with the news of his salvation?

Hannah's Story: You Teach Muslim Children?

The light went out – an explosion of black in our faces. For a split second there was nothing, then recollection. The power had gone. It went every night, but we never got used to the sudden blindness.

I was on study leave, visiting an area far from where I lived, being hosted by relatives of friends. 'Uncle' fumbled around for a candle, muttering in frustration as he did so. He had so much wanted to put on a good evening for me. From a house nearby came the sound of a woman's coarse laughter and suggestive jokes. The fans came to a standstill and the air grew thick and heavy. A mosquito whined and a baby cried.

By the time Mr Masih (his name means 'Messiah') had lit the candle, giving the grubbiness a golden glow, he was full of the cares of the world. 'This place is bad,' he sighed. 'What we need is education. Our children don't know how to read and the young people are taking on bad habits.' I had smelt liquor on someone's breath earlier; I knew what he meant.

'What can you do to help us? The Christians here need an NGO to come . . . or a convent.'

I didn't know what to say. I wasn't in a position to suddenly relocate to this town. 'I'm sorry, I don't live here. I teach up in the mountains – my team is based there.' I already had a job, far away, in a different province – where there were few Christians.

'You teach Muslim children?' He looked appalled. 'But they will be greedy for all they can get out of you. They will make you work for them.' He was furious. 'They will take from you but only hate you in their hearts. Come to our people; we are Christians like you.'

To Think About

What would you want to say to Mr Masih?

15

Sending Out the Disciples

Luke 9 starts with Jesus sending out the twelve disciples; Luke 10 starts with Jesus sending out seventy-two more. We can, therefore, look at the transfiguration as being at the heart of a section of Luke's gospel that is not only about who Jesus is, but also about what the disciples are called to do. If we want to find the answer to the question, 'Lord, what do you want of us?' we need to look at this wider setting of the transfiguration.

Both the accounts of sending out the disciples emphasize the *authority of Jesus* that Peter, James and John glimpsed in the transfiguration and that was publicly demonstrated in the healing of the demon-possessed boy. Jesus' initial sending of the twelve shows that he has enough authority to delegate to them authority over demons and diseases (9:1). The sending of the seventy-two finishes with Jesus' vision of Satan falling, and with him saying again that he has given the disciples authority over 'all the power of the enemy' (10:19). The transfiguration gives us a glimpse of what it means that Jesus is Messiah – God's anointed King; and these two passages give us a glimpse of what it means to be disciples of that King. It means working under his authority and not our own; and it means doing it his way and not ours. The theme continues throughout Luke 9: verses 23–26 call us to deny ourselves and to follow in the way of the cross; verses 57–62 remind the prospective disciple that, just as Jesus had no fixed home, so the disciple might have no fixed home. When we look at Jesus in Luke 9, we see him on the way to the cross. When we look at the disciples, we see what it looks like to follow him there. Sharing in the dishonour of Jesus' cross is the only way to share in the honour of Jesus' kingdom.

What is it that the disciples were sent to do, and that might lead them into dishonour? In both the sendings, the job is two-fold: to heal people and to proclaim the coming of the kingdom of God (9:2; 10:9). In both cases, the disciples are told to take nothing with them, to stay in homes wherever they are welcome, and to 'shake off the dust from [their] feet' and move on when they are not welcome. The second sending passage gives extra details: the seventy-two are to go in pairs, they are to pray for more labourers, and what they are doing could be dangerous. Just as Jesus would be rejected and killed, so might they be rejected and killed. But, where people accepted Jesus, they would be accepted too (10:16).

It is easy to focus on the difficulties of living and proclaiming the kingdom of God, but, if we read Luke 10:1–20 carefully, we will see that the emphasis is not on those who rejected the disciples but on those who accepted them. The disciples returned to Jesus in joy, not in shame, and we read nothing of their rejection. We can suppose that there were some who rejected them and that they simply 'shook off the dust from their feet' against them and went on, leaving their judgement in God's hands and praying for their repentance –but we know nothing of that. The emphasis on acceptance is reflected even in the instructions they were given: they were to be so confident that some homes would receive them that they took no provisions at all. And they were to begin every visit with a greeting of peace. This is especially important for our thinking about relationships with Muslims, since they, too, have what they believe to be a God-given greeting: *as-salāmu 'alaykum*, which means 'Peace be with you'.

Following Jesus' Instruction

Francis of Assisi took Jesus' instructions in Luke 10 and in Matthew 10 quite literally in his preaching of the gospel and in his own instructions to the Franciscan brothers. They were to go among unbelievers, including Muslims, with nothing, to stay with them, to keep their laws and, when it seemed good to them and to the Holy Spirit, to tell them about Jesus. This was during the middle of the Crusades, so they were to be prepared for martyrdom. On the basis of these passages, and from Jesus' greeting of 'Peace' to his disciples after the resurrection (John 20:26), Francis believed that God revealed to him a greeting that should be used by all the Franciscans. It was, in Latin, *pax et bonum*, which means, 'Peace and good.'

Francis put his own teaching into practice: in the middle of the third Crusade, he crossed the lines from the Christian army to the Muslim army, unarmed and accompanied by one Franciscan brother. He took with him the greeting of peace, and was welcomed by the Sultan himself. Following their talks, the Franciscans were made guardians of the Christian holy places in the Holy Land, and were free to go and minister in the Sultan's territories.[1]

To Think About

What had the disciples learned about Jesus and about the kingdom of God between the sending out of the twelve and the sending out of the seventy-two? What difference might that have made to how the seventy-two proclaimed the kingdom of God? What difference might it make to how you and your church relate to Muslim people?

What is the relevance of Jesus' instructions about mission in your own context?

As we think about our mission among Muslims, a key question is our purpose. Jesus warns the seventy-two not to rejoice in the power they have over demons, but in their salvation (10:20). That should warn us not to give in to the temptation to power, but, like Jesus in the wilderness, to keep our focus on the cross. Luke tells us what Jesus' purpose was in sending out these disciples: it was to prepare people for his own coming (9:1; 10:9). Similarly, our mission is not to demonstrate the power of Christianity over Islam, but to prepare Muslims to receive Jesus.

Christian mission is, say the missiologists, getting involved in the *missio Dei* – the mission of God himself. God is a sending God. He sends Abraham, Moses, Elijah and the other prophets, He sends his Son, he sends the Holy Spirit, he sends the apostles, and he sends his church. What we need to do is to find our place in that sending. The missiologists are right, but Muslims also know that God is a sending God: the whole of qur'anic sacred history is, after all, about God sending prophets. Comparison with Islam might prompt us to seek out the distinctively biblical model. We have seen that, in contrast to a focus on simply sending, the whole of biblical history is about God's desire to live among human beings.

---

1. See C. Mallouhi, *Waging Peace on Islam* (Downers Grove: IVP, 2002); and Ida's *Crusade Sermons, Francis of Assisi and Martin Luther: What Does It Mean to 'Take up the Cross' in the Context of Islam?*, Crowther Centre Monograph No. 14 (Oxford: Church Mission Society, 2010).

We therefore need to find our place not only in God's sending, but also in God's coming. Rather than thinking about God sending prophets, we can think about God coming to Abraham, about God coming to Moses, and about God choosing Israel as a people among whom he could dwell and through whom his presence could come and be seen in his world. God did not only send Jesus: he came in Jesus. God did not only send the Holy Spirit: he came in the Holy Spirit, and he still comes to be present in our lives.

So the church is now God's dwelling place: where even two or three are gathered in the name of Jesus, there God dwells. Whether you are part of a huge church in Korea or the USA, or part of a tiny fellowship of believers in Jesus in a Muslim country, or even the only follower of Jesus in your area, you are the place where people can see the presence of God. And your mission among your Muslim neighbours is the same mission that Jesus gave the seventy-two: it is to prepare people to receive the presence of God in Jesus. That will involve healings, it will involve service, it will involve calling to repentance, and it will involve explaining what Jesus' kingdom is about and how the cross fulfils and transforms both law and zeal.

Ida's Story: A Few Flowers among the Weeds and Rubbish

My next-door-neighbour-but-one had died. I only spoke a few words of her language, but I had loved her, prayed for her and greeted her every day as she lovingly tended the roses in her garden. Apart from my own garden and one other, hers was the only garden in the street with flowers: the others were full of rubbish and weeds, with just a few growing spinach and coriander. That reflected the area. Our street had a lot of new immigrants from rural Bangladesh and Pakistan, and they grew the vegetables. There were some flats rented out to students, and a scattering of elderly white people. At the bottom of the road was an estate that was entirely 'white' because all the non-whites had experienced so much racial harassment that the council had moved them elsewhere. We had 80 per cent unemployment and there was so much crime (mainly from the 'white' people) that the police and social workers always worked in pairs and no firm would insure a car against fire or theft in our street. I was trying to help the small local church to reach out to its Muslim neighbours. My flowers were part of my attempt to bring a glimpse of God's life and light to the area.

The old lady's two granddaughters knocked on my door. They were beautiful children who came regularly to the children's club that I held in my home six afternoons a week (with a Bible story on Sundays), and I visited their home whenever I could. 'Just before she died, Grandmother started to talk about you,' they said. 'She'd watched you, and she said that you were kind and good, and that Christianity was not as bad as she'd thought. Then she told us all that she knew about Jesus from the Qur'an, and then told us that we should always honour him. We thought you'd like to know.'

To Think About

In what ways do you think that Ida was following Jesus' instructions about mission in what she says in this story? In what ways might you follow his instructions in your own context?

Transfigured Minds

'I appeal to you therefore, brothers, by the mercies of God, to present your bodies as a living sacrifice, holy and acceptable to God, which is your spiritual worship . . . be transformed [transfigured] by the renewal of your mind,' says Paul to the Romans (Rom 12:1–2). What is the basis of this appeal? What does Paul mean by the 'mercies of God'? To what is his 'therefore' referring? We might say that, at this stage in Romans, Paul is referring to the whole of the gospel that he explained in chapters 1 – 8; but between chapter 8 and this appeal lie chapters 9 – 11, which are about God's dealings with the Jews. Chapters 1 – 8 tell us about the gospel which is for everyone; chapters 9 – 11 ask about the place of God's special people. One of the questions in the 'world behind the text' of Romans is how Jews and Gentiles relate to God and to each other. These are questions to do with law, but also to do with history, nationalism and ethnicity.

In his argument, Paul turns in 11:2–5 to the zealous disappointment of Elijah with Israel. In Nazareth, Jesus had cited Elijah's compassion on the Sidonian widow to challenge the nationalistic religion of the Galileans: the Gentiles, he implies, have always been God's concern, and they might be the first to enter the kingdom of God (Luke 4:25–26). Here, Paul looks at the other side of the question. He uses Elijah's experience to explain that God also continues to include the Jews in his kingdom. Paul reminds his readers of the despair Elijah felt when he feared that Israel would be completely extinguished. He quotes Elijah's prayer: 'Lord, they have killed your prophets, they have demolished your altars, and I alone am left, and they seek my life.' Paul uses God's reply to him, 'I have kept for myself seven thousand men who have not bowed the knee to Baal' (11:4), to demonstrate that God did not abandon the Jews. He concludes, 'So too at the present time there is a remnant, chosen by grace' (v. 5).

By highlighting this aspect of the account of Elijah and the prophets of Baal, Paul expands our vision of God's compassionate heart. The cross represents God's pain on behalf of all peoples: God is concerned for the non-Israelites *and* is saving and using many Israelites whose stories we are not told. The transformed mind that has accepted God's mercies in Christ will, like Paul, share Jesus' zealous concern for the salvation of all peoples – Muslims and Christians, Jews and Gentiles, secular people and Hindus. The most important transformation of our minds towards thinking biblically about Islam is the place where we started this book: seeing Muslims as human beings, created by God and loved by him, and as much in need of his mercies as we are.

Romans 12 goes on to tell us the result of the renewed mind: it is discernment of the will of God. Doing the will of God is central to Islam, but, for Muslims, God's will is mainly discerned through law. The cross of Christ changes this focus by changing us, so that the law is written on our hearts. But we still need some guiding principles to help us: you would not be reading this book had you not realized that you needed some help in discerning what God wanted of you in thinking about Islam and in relating to Muslims. So Paul goes on to give the Christians in first-century Rome instructions on how to live. These instructions offer principles that we can take into our living among Muslims in the twenty-first-century world.

Do Not Think More Highly of Yourself than You Ought to Think! (12:3–5)

There is no room for the argument about who is the greatest that beset Jesus' first disciples. The immediate context here is the church: we are not to think that we are more important than anyone else within the church, but to recognize that we are all dependent on each other. However, the principle extends much wider: we need to get ourselves into perspective as small people with a very big God. The Islamic shout is *allāhu akbar* – God is greater. That is something on which Christians can agree: the One True God is greater than all of us, and is able to do far more than we can ever ask or think.

Use the Gifts That God Has Given You! (12:6–8)

There is no one gift and no one ministry that is needed in relating with Muslims – we need all of God's people with all of their gifts. We need prophecy: Christians need to hear God's word in relationship to Muslims, and Muslims need to hear God's word to them. We need service: Muslims share the needs of the human race. We need teachers: to teach Christians about Islam, about Muslim people, about relationships with them; and to teach Muslims about the Christian faith. We need exhortation: both Christians and Muslims need encouragement to do what is right. We need generosity: relationships are built through giving and receiving of all kinds. We need leadership: informed, godly leadership, which knows the grieving heart of God. We need acts of mercy: in a world of so much strife, where Muslims and Christians so often blame each other, we need people who will mirror the mercy of God.

Prophecy is to be based on faith, and in accordance with the faith in the crucified and risen Lord. For the next three gifts listed by Paul, the use of the gift is emphasized by a repeated word: service in serving, teaching in teaching, exhorting in exhortation. The final three each have a word about the attitude with which they are to be used. Giving is to be 'generous' – literally 'in simplicity', which implies a sincere heart, open to other people. Acts of mercy are to be done 'with cheerfulness' – the Greek word is *hilarotes*, which indicates readiness and eagerness. It is leadership, being 'out in front', that is to be carried out 'with zeal'. The Greek word here is not *zelotes*, meaning 'zeal', but *spoude*, meaning 'speed', which then comes to mean diligence, earnestness and striving to do the job. The English word 'zeal', used in the ESV, translates that idea well.

We are not just to use our gifts, turning Paul's exhortation into a new kind of law. All the gifts differ 'according to the grace given to us' (v. 6) – we use them recognizing that they are indeed gifts from God, privileges written inside us rather than tasks imposed from outside. Keeping the law means, here, being what God has made us to be. And we are to do this vigorously, using all the energy that God gives us: this is the zeal to which we are called.

Love Your Neighbours! (12:9–13)

This passage continues the short phrases of the previous sentence: in Greek, it is all part of the same sentence, so its first application is to relationships with fellow Christians. This is important in Islamic contexts, as Muslims judge our faith by what they see in us. Too often, they see disunity and disagreement, and they can find very little of the 'compassion and mercy' that the Qur'an says God put into the hearts of Jesus' followers (Surah 57. 27). They might see more of the rebellion and transgression of which the same qur'anic verse accuses Christians. Muslims know that Christianity claims to be a religion of peace and of love, but they see a history of colonialism and war. They hear Christians denigrating Islam, they watch Western television, and they conclude that Christianity has failed. Where will they see redeemed people, with God's laws written on their hearts?

The exhortation is clear: we are to have real, not pretended, love. Literally, in verse 9, love is to be 'the opposite of hypocritical'. No play-acting, no pretence, no ulterior motives! This is real love, love that does not put up with evil but that holds onto whatever is good. It leads us to prayer, to sharing, and to hospitable community life. This kind of love can only be maintained if it is centred on our Lord – it is he who enables us to keep hoping even when everything looks hopeless, and to bear patiently the difficulties in our relationships. But we can only keep this law of love if we have a right zeal, and if our focus is on serving the Lord rather than on trying to show everyone that Christians are 'the greatest' when it comes to loving one another. The competition is not for honour or 'greatness' for ourselves, but for showing honour to other people. There are two words of zeal in verse 11. First, we are not to be lazy in *spoude* – in the diligent, focused hard work that this love is going to take. Second, we are to be on fire (*zeontes*, which is from the same root as the usual word for 'zeal') in the Spirit – it is only the power of the Holy Spirit that can transform our spirits towards this love. The fire of destruction must be directed towards our own sin and selfishness, and not towards other people. Even if other people persecute us, we are to call down God's blessings on them, and not be like the disciples who wanted to call down fire on the Samaritan village.

Love Your Enemies! (12:14–21)

You might at this stage be thinking of Islam as a friend of the gospel, or you might be thinking of it as an enemy of the gospel. You might be thinking of Muslims as part of your family and your people, as friends of your family and your people, or as enemies of your family and people. It doesn't really matter, because God's call is the same: friends or enemies, we should love them, bless them, help them if they are in need, and pray for them. We should never respond to evil with more evil, but with good. This is the key to peace: that someone should stop the cycle of enmity by refraining from vengeance. This is not to ignore the evil of persecution or other hostility, but to recognize that evil can never be overcome by evil, but only by good. It is this sort of love for enemies that took Jesus to the cross. A flood does not, in the long run, solve the problem of evil, but his sacrifice does.

Be Subject to the Governing Authorities! (13:1–7)

This is a difficult passage to obey in some circumstances, and it is tempting to assume that it was written to Christians living under a benevolent regime. It was not: the reverse is true. They were under the rule of pagan Rome, and were often under suspicion and subject to persecution. Paul's advice is that these Christians should not try to overthrow or undermine the regime, but should be model citizens. Being subject to the authorities does not mean assuming that these authorities are good; rather, it is part of overcoming evil by good. This was also Jeremiah's advice to the Jews who went into exile: they were to work and pray for the welfare of the pagan imperial city of Babylon (Jer 29:7). God had called Israel to be a blessing to the nations, even to Babylon, and the Israelites would do well only as the whole city did well.

Roman rule was ordered and mostly peaceful, so we cannot extend this passage to say that Christians should never object to unjust and violent rulers. It does not tell us how to deal with war and revolutions. However, it does tell us that we can live under non-Christian rule. Since the rise of Islam, life for Christians under Muslim rule has been very varied: there have been times of oppression and even of genocide, and there have been times of peace and security – but Christians have usually been considered as citizens in a different category from Muslims, especially for taxation. Over the centuries, many Christians have fled or have converted to Islam under the pressure. Many others have stood firm, paid their taxes and lived by the light of the gospel. Currently, some Christians in the West are worried that numbers of Muslims are rising, and that their countries might eventually come under Islamic rule.

This passage implies that, in terms of the kingdom of God, it does not matter very much what kind of earthly kingdom we live under. This contrasts with Islamic legal thinking, where there has been a lot of discussion about whether Muslims can live under non-Muslim rule. For example, when the British colonized Nigeria, one writer advised that Muslims should first fight to try to prevent non-Muslim rule but then, if they were defeated, they would have to flee to a Muslim-ruled area. If they had to stay, they would have to keep Islamic rule in their hearts, and only keep the laws of the colonizers outwardly.[2] The many millions of Muslims living under non-Islamic rule today have to think through these classical ideas, and to use different categories. For example, one classical idea is that Muslims can live in a place where they have a treaty whereby they can practise their faith in safety, and countries in the West can be seen in those terms.[3] However, while Islam started with Muslims living under Islamic rule, the first Christians neither lived under Christian rule nor tried to do so. It might not be easy, but we can live under the kingdom of heaven whoever our earthly rulers are.

Owe Nothing but Love! (13:8–10)

This is what it means to live under the kingdom of heaven. This is the summary and fulfilment of that kingdom's laws that Jesus illustrated in the parable of the good Samaritan. He finished the parable by saying to the expert in religious law, 'You go, and do likewise' (Luke 10:37). Whatever we think of 'Islam', Muslims are our fellow human beings. Whatever we need for ourselves we should want for them too.

Love towards Muslims, like love towards any other human beings, is not optional. It is commanded, and it is a debt to be paid. There are wonderful examples of Christian love towards Muslims, but there have also been many times in history when Christians have been anything but loving. So many of us have focused on the ways in which Islam opposes the gospel and not on the ways in which it points people to things that are true. 'But,' some may ask, 'what about the debts that Muslims owe to us? What about the times when Muslims have conquered Christians, and have tried to destroy the faith of Christians?' Jesus tells us to pray, 'forgive us our debts, as we also have forgiven our debtors', and then warns us that, if we do not forgive people who have sinned against us, neither will God forgive us our sins (Matt 6:12–15). We are to pay our debt of love, and to forgive any debts that we think are owed to us.

---

2. See Muhammad S. Umar, *Islam and Colonialism: Intellectual Responses of Muslims of Northern Nigeria to British Colonial Rule* (Leiden: E. J. Brill, 2005).

3. See, for example, T. Ramadan, *Western Muslims and the Future of Islam* (Oxford: Oxford University Press, 2004).

Moreover, we are not to keep this law reluctantly, but from our hearts. Love has already been explained in Romans 12:9–13. It has to be genuine, hopeful, patient and driven by the fire of the Spirit. What does love look like? It looks like Jesus, who loved us and gave himself for us, even when we were his enemies (1 John 3:16; 4:10; Rom 5:6–8). And how can we even begin to love with that love? Only as we are transfigured through him. Paul summarizes his relationship with the law in Galatians 2:19–20: 'Through the law I died to the law, so that I might live to God. I have been crucified with Christ. It is no longer I who live, but Christ who lives in me. And the life I now live in the flesh I live by faith in the Son of God, who loved me and gave himself for me.'

The key to this kind of living is Jesus' own exhortation to his disciples before the transfiguration: to take up the cross daily (Luke 9:23). Prophets like Moses and Elijah had to bear suffering and shame as they conveyed God's message to sinful people. Jesus suffered as he bore all our guilt and shame by carrying the cross. We, as disciples, follow. We 'carry the cross' as we are prepared to give up everything, even our lives, for Jesus and for the people to whom he calls us. We 'carry the cross' in a different way when we explain its meaning to Muslims as witnesses to our crucified and risen Lord.

The cross is at the centre of biblical history and of Jesus' thinking, but it is almost universally denied by Muslims. A focus on the cross should therefore take us not only to the centre of what it means to think biblically about Islam, but also to the heart of how Christian thought and action should be different from Islamic thought and action. This book has aimed to show that thinking biblically about Islam is a complex and multifaceted task; however, the ultimate test of our thinking is simple: does it reflect the cross of Christ?

During the Crusades, 'carrying the cross' meant wearing a red cloth cross and going to fight Muslims in the Holy Land. The Muslims had conquered the land, and European Christians launched crusade after crusade to try to win it back. They slaughtered many Jews and eastern Christians as well as Muslims. Jesus had laid down his life for them in the Holy Land, the soldiers were told, so they should lay down their lives for him in that same Holy Land; then they would be sure of the salvation that was won on that cross. Looking back, we can see that this was a mirror image of some militant Islamic ideas, as Islam itself mirrored some of the Byzantine ideas of a Christian empire.

When 'the cross' becomes a symbol for a group seeking power such as 'Christendom', 'the Christian West' or 'the Christian community', people start defending it against those they perceive to be threats to the group. A church in a Muslim neighbourhood that Hannah used to pass on her way to work had a sign outside which depicted a sword mounted on a cross. When people lift up the cross as a rallying point against 'the other', they dangerously link religion and power in the way God hates. Even a cross like that can become a tower of Babel.

So, what difference does the cross make? How does the cross of Christ fulfil and transform the law? It makes, at last, a way for people to keep the law by writing it on their hearts. It transforms people, and enables them to keep its deepest intent. How does the cross of Christ fulfil and transform zeal? It cleanses idolatry in people and transforms the zeal that kills idolaters into the zeal that is ready to be killed to bring them salvation.

The central challenge in the Elijah story is relevant to all our dealings with Muslims: which god will we follow? This is not about whether we can call God 'Allāh', but about what kind of god we believe in, and how, therefore, we serve him. In practice, what is our object of worship? Are we serving a god of numbers, noise, power politics and ritual? Or are we serving the God who has been at work throughout the history of Israel, who actually provides for us, even if we are in a minority of one, whose focus is on the widow, who challenges all other powers and who will honour his own name? What kind of God do we see on the cross?

Ida's Story

I was in Qatar at a conference of Christian and Muslim scholars on 9 April 2003, when the allied troops toppled the statue of Saddam Hussein in Baghdad. I remember vividly the shock of the Muslims present as they took in the fact that the ancient centre of the Islamic empire had fallen to non-Muslims: it was as if the Vatican had been taken over by Saudi Arabians. It was not that they had any admiration for Saddam Hussein: they knew that he was a tyrant, and that his rule violated their Islamic principles. It was the loss of a symbol of their people and of their faith that was so difficult.

Even more vividly, I remember the Bible passage that I had been opening up for my study group the previous day. I had been allocated the book of Jonah, and our small group of Muslims and Christians had been deeply moved as we read of God's concern for Nineveh, then the capital of the area that is today's Iraq. In Jonah's time, Nineveh headed a powerful imperial nation and was Israel's greatest enemy. God did not send an army to conquer Nineveh, but a prophet to call her to repentance. The story of Jonah's reluctance and of Nineveh's repentance is well known. At the end of the book, in response to Jonah's complaint about his lack of shade, God asks, 'Should not I pity Nineveh, that great city, in which there are more than 120,000 persons who do not know their right hand from their left?' (Jonah 4:11).

The ancient Nineveh is the modern Mosul. Christians living there have for centuries kept an annual fast in memory of the repentance of their ancestors at the time of Jonah, and there has long been a shrine to him which has been a centre for prayer for Muslims as well as for Christians. Today, that shrine is no more – it was recently destroyed by the militant group that calls itself 'the Islamic State'. I do not know how many Christians, and how many Shi'ite and Sufi Muslims judged by 'the Islamic State' also to be infidels, have been killed and put to flight in recent weeks. I do not know exactly what is motivating the current terrible violence – history, politics, religion, personal anger and despair. And I have no idea what could put a stop to it all. But I can hear God's voice to all who would prefer sending armies to calling people to repentance, 'Should not I pity that great city . . . ?'

To Think About

What is in God's heart as he sees the Muslims in your country?

'That . . . you may discern what is the will of God, what is good and acceptable and perfect' (Rom 12:2). Peace for our communities, freedom for our children, preserving our cultures, preventing suffering for our Christian sisters and brothers, security in our countries: these are not bad aims. The Table of Nations in Genesis 10 shows that God's good order of blessing for humanity has peoples in their own places and with their own languages and cultures; and the biblical picture of God's future blessing fulfilled in Jesus is of creatures as well as peoples at peace (e.g. Isa 11:1–9). If we turn these things into ultimate objectives, however, and if we link them with our religion and look for peace only for ourselves, we are always going to be in danger of sliding into the religion of Babel in Genesis 11. Jesus was not a Messiah who fought for people, land and power, but the Messiah of the transfiguration who went to the cross in order to achieve what no fighting could ever achieve. Like him, we need a higher objective; like him, we want to be God's children with whom he is well pleased.

We finish with the words of one of the greatest Christian scholars of Islam of the last century: 'The objective is not, as the crusaders believed, the repossession of what Christendom has lost, but the restoration to Muslims of the Christ whom they have missed . . . To restore Christ transcends all else.'[4] The only way we can move towards this objective is the way of Jesus to the cross. And let us leave the resurrection up to God!

---

4. Cragg, *The Call of the Minaret*, 220, 230.

Bibliography

Abdallah, B. M. *Zilzāl al-arḍ al-'aẓīm fī al-Qur'ān al-Karīm wa-al-sunnah wa-al-Injīl wa-al-'Ahd al-Qadīm* . Cairo: n. p., 1991.

Adil al-Haqqani, Sheikh Nazim. 'The Coming of the Mystery Imam al-Mahdi.' http://khidr.org/al-mahdi.htm; accessed June 2015.

Akhtar, Shabbir. *Be Careful with Muhammad! The Salman Rushdie Affair.* London: Bellew Publishing, 1989.

Al-Busiri, *Qaṣida al-Burda* or *The Poem of the Cloak* (13th century). Selection of stanzas from the translation by Hamza Yusuf available at http://syedsalman.buzznet.com/user/journal/60429/blessed-burdah-poem-cloak-noble/; accessed October 2014.

Alexander, Paul. 'The Apocalypse of Pseudo-Methodius.' In *The Byzantine Apocalyptic Tradition*, edited by Paul Alexander, 13–50. Berkeley: University of California Press, 1985.

Anonymous. 'What Does the Bible Say about the Church?'. *Barnabas Aid*, July–August 2012.

'A Statement by Bethlehem Bible College Regarding the Current Crisis in Gaza', Bethlehem Bible College, 25 July 2014, http://www.bethbc.org/news/statement-bethlehem-bible-college-regarding-current-crisis-gaza.

Atallah, Ramez. 'Bible Society of Egypt Newsletter.' 12 September 2013, http://us6.campaign-archive2.com/?u=017b6b7c5bf6d7468fcc6aedc&id=ff25fb810a.

Ayoub, Mahmoud. *Islam: Faith and History.* Oxford: Oneworld, 2004.

Badawi, Dr Jamal. 'Muhammad the Last Messenger of Allāh – Muhammad and the Abrahamic Tree IV: Moses' Prophecy', in answer to the question 'Are There Any Other Prophesies [sic] of Prophet Muhammad May Peace Be Upon Him in What Is Commonly Referred to as the Torah?', http://jamalbadawi.org/index.php?option=com_content&view=article&id=211:124-muhammad-the-last-messenger-of-allah-muhammad-a-the-abrahamic-tree-iv-moses-prophecy&catid=25:volume-12-muhammad-the-last-messenger-of-allah&Itemid=13; accessed October 2014.

Bhaumik, Subir. 'Nobody's People in a No-Man's Land.' *Aljazeera*, 16 August 2012, http://www.aljazeera.com.

Bienkowski, P., and A. Millard, eds. *Dictionary of the Ancient Near East.* London: British Museum Press, 2000.

Bowker, John. *The Complete Bible Handbook: An Illustrated Companion.* London: Dorling Kindersley, 1998.

Brown, D. *A New Introduction to Islam.* Chichester: Wiley-Blackwell, 2009.

———. *Rethinking Tradition in Modern Islamic Thought.* Cambridge: Cambridge University Press, 1996.

Brown, Daniel W. *A New Introduction to Islam*, 2nd ed. Oxford: Wiley-Blackwell, 2009.

Constable, O. R., ed. *Medieval Iberia: Readings from Christian, Muslim, and Jewish Sources.* Philadelphia: University of Pennsylvania Press, 1997.

Cook, D. 'The Figure of the Antichrist.' In *Contemporary Muslim Apocalyptic Literature*, edited by D. Cook. New York: Syracuse University Press, 2005.

———. *Understanding Jihad.* Berkeley: University of California Press, 2005.

Cook, M. *Studies in Muslim Apocalyptic.* Princeton: Darwin Press, 2002.

———. *The Koran: A Very Short Introduction.* Oxford: Oxford University Press, 2000.

'Concerns about Islamic Extremism on the Rise in Middle East.' Pew Research, 1 July 2014, http://www.pewglobal.org/2014/07/01/concerns-about-islamic-extremism-on-the-rise-in-middle-east/.

Cragg, K. *The Call of the Minaret.* Oxford: Oxford University Press, 1956.

Dalrymple, William. *The Last Mughal: The Fall of a Dynasty, Delhi, 1857.* London: Bloomsbury, 2006.

Decalogue. Translation available online in *The Works of Philo Judaeus*, trans. C. D. Yonge. London: H. G. Bohn, 1854–90. www.earlyjewishwritings.com/text/philo/book26.html.

'Declaration of the Islamic State', June 2014, https://ia902505.us.archive.org/28/items/poa_25984/EN.pdf.

Doi, A. R. *Shari'ah: The Islamic Law.* London: Ta Ha, 1984.

'Dua Nudba / The Supplication of Lamentation.' Qul library, http://www.qul.org.au/library/duas-supplications/410-dua-nudba-the-supplication-of-lamentation; accessed June 2015.

Glaser, I. 'Towards a Mutual Understanding of Christian and Islamic Concepts of Revelation.' *Themelios* 7, no. 3 (April 1982): 16–22, available at http://www.medievalchurch.org.uk/pdf/islamic-revelation_glaser.pdf.

———. *Crusade Sermons, Francis of Assisi and Martin Luther: What Does It Mean to 'Take up the Cross' in the Context of Islam?*, Crowther Centre Monograph No. 14. Oxford: Church Mission Society, 2010.

———. 'Reading the Bible.' In *The Bible and Other Faiths: What Does the Lord Require of Us?* Leicester: Inter-Varsity Press, 2005.

———. *The Bible and Other Faiths: What Does the Lord Require of Us?.* Leicester: Inter-Varsity Press, 2005.

Goldingay, J. *Old Testament Theology, Vol. 1: Israel's Gospel.* Downers Grove: IVP; Milton Keynes: Paternoster, 2003.

Green, M. *2 Peter and Jude: An Introduction and Commentary.* Leicester: Inter-Varsity Press, 1968.

Guerin, Orla. 'Pakistani Christian Asia Bibi "Has Price on Her Head".' BBC News, 7 December 2010, http://www.bbc.co.uk/news/world-south-asia-11930849.

Habib, Irfan. 'The Coming of 1857.' *Social Scientist* 26, no. 12 (January–April 1998): 8.

Haleem, M. A. Abdel. *The Qur'an: A New Translation by M. A. S. Abdel Haleem* (Oxford: Oxford University Press, 2008), Used with permission.

'Haqiqah: What Is the Truth Behind ISIS?', http://imamsonline.com/blog/haqiqah-what-is-the-truth-behind-isis/.

Hertz, J. H., ed. *The Pentateuch and Haftorahs.* London: Soncino, 1960.

Herzog, C., and M. Gichon. *Battles of the Bible.* New York: Random House, 1978.

Hijazi, Maulana Khatr. *Qiṣaṣ al-Anbiyā.* Lahore: Nashran-o-tajran kitab, 1978.

Hirsch, Emil G., Eduard König, Solomon Schechter, Louis Ginzberg, M. Seligsohn, and Kaufmann Kohler. 'Elijah.' In *The Jewish Encyclopaedia*, 1906, JewishEncyclopedia.com, http://jewishencyclopedia.com/articles/5634-elijah.

Holmes, Arthur F. *All Truth Is God's Truth.* First British edition. Leicester: IVP, 1979.

Hoyland, R. *Seeing Islam As Others Saw It: A Survey and Evaluation of Christian, Jewish and Zoroastrian Writing on Early Islam.* Princeton: Darwin Press, 1997.

In Reach Ministry, www.inreachministry.wix.com/inreach .

Iqbal, Muhammad. *Zabūr-i-'Ajam* in *Kulliyat-i-Iqbal.* Lahore: Iqbal Academy, 1990.

Ishaq, I. *The Life of Muhammad: A Translation of Ibn Ishaq's Sirāt Rasūl Allāh.* Translated by A. Guillaume. Oxford: Oxford University Press, 1955.

'Islam Is the Prophesied Beast System (Revelation Chapters 13–18).' Apocalypse Prophesied 2008–2015, http://www.apocalypse2008-2015.com/Beast_System-Islam.html, accessed October 2014.

Josephus, *Antiquities of the Jews*, 3:80, trans. H. St J. Thackeray. Loeb Classical Library, 1930.

Just, A. A., ed. *Luke.* Ancient Christian Commentary on Scripture: New Testament vol. 3. Downers Grove: IVP Academic, 2003.

Kathir, Ibn. Commentary on Surah 75. 22–23, avalaible in English online at www.qtafsir.com.

Khan, Aamer Ahmed. 'What Motives Led to Shahbaz Bhatti's Murder in Pakistan?'. BBC News, 2 March 2011, http://www.bbc.co.uk/news/world-south-asia-12622080.

King, L. W., trans. 'The Code of Hammurabi', http://www.sacred-texts.com/ane/ham/index.htm .

Kyle, R .G. *Apocalyptic Fever: End-Time Prophecies in Modern America*. Eugene: Cascade Books, 2012.

Latifzadeh, Afshin. 'The Sword and the Praise (Psalm 149:6).' Pars Theological Centre, http://www.parstheology.com/message-of-the-week/the-sword-and-the-praise-psalm-1496/; accessed October 2014. Used with his permission.

Lawson, T. *Crucifixion and the Qur'an: A Study in the History of Muslim Thought*. Oxford: Oneworld, 2009.

'Letter to SAARC on Improving Protections for Migrant Workers.' Human Rights Watch, 17 December 2013, http://www.hrw.org/news/2013/12/17/letter-saarc-improving-protections-migrant-workers.

Loevinger, Rabbi Neal J. 'Feeling the Presence of God.' http://www.myjewishlearning.com/texts/Bible/Weekly_Torah_Portion/vayechi_kolel5761.shtml?p=1; accessed October 2014.

Maalouf, Tony. *Arabs in the Shadow of Israel: The Unfolding of God's Prophetic Plan for Ishmael's Line*. Grand Rapids: Kregel, 2003.

Madelung, W. F., and A. Jones. *Al-Tabari: The Commentary on the Qur'an*, vol. 1. Oxford: Oxford University Press, 1987.

Magonet, J. *A Rabbi's Bible*. London: SCM, 1991.

Mallouhi, C. *Waging Peace on Islam*. Downers Grove: IVP, 2002.

Marshall, D. *God, Muhammad and the Unbelievers*. Richmond: Curzon Press, 1999.

Maududi, S. A. A. *Tafhīm al-Qur'ān*, 1988–93, translated as *Towards Understanding the Qur'an* by Z. I. Ansari. Leicester: The Islamic Foundation, 1988–93, volumes 1–4.

Mernissi, Fatima. *Women and Islam: An Historical and Theological Enquiry*. Oxford: Blackwell, 1991.

Mingana, A., trans. 'Timothy I, Apology for Christianity (1928)', http://www.tertullian.org/fathers/timothy_i_apology_01_text.htm ; accessed October 2014.

Montefiore, C. G., and H. Loewe. *A Rabbinic Anthology*. New York: Schocken Books, 1974.

Moucarry, C. *Faith to Faith: Christianity and Islam in Dialogue*. Leicester: IVP, 2001.

————. *The Search for Forgiveness: Pardon and Punishment in Islam and Christianity*. Nottingham: IVP, 2004.

Muhammad Al-Hussaini in *CMCS Newsletter* 6 (Autumn 2011).

Negev, Avraham, ed. *The Archaeological Encyclopedia of the Holy Land*, 3rd ed. New York: Prentice Hall Press, 1990.

Neusner, J., and T. Sonn, *Comparing Religions through Law*. London: Routledge, 1999.

Neuwirth, A., N. Sinai and M. Marx, eds. *The Qur'an in Context: Historical and Literary Investigations into the Qur'anic Milieu*. Leiden: Brill, 2010.

Nye, Catrin. 'Converting to Islam: The White Britons Becoming Muslims.' *BBC News UK*, 4 January 2011, http://www.bbc.co.uk/news/uk-12075931.

'Open Letter to Al-Baghdadi', http://www.lettertobaghdadi.com/.

Padwick, C. *Muslim Devotions*, 2nd ed. Oxford: Oneworld, 1996.

Parrinder, G. *Jesus in the Qur'an*. Oxford: Oneworld, 1965.

Pew Research Center. 'Muslim-Majority Countries.' *Pew Research*, 27 January 2011, http://www.pewforum.org/2011/01/27/future-of-the-global-muslim-population-muslim-majority/.

Protoevangelium of James. Available in translation at http://www.earlychristianwritings.com/infancyjames.html.

'Punjab Governor Salman Taseer Assassinated in Islamabad.' BBC News, 4 January 2011, http://www.bbc.co.uk/news/world-south-asia-12111831.

'Qatar 2022: Reactions.' Fifa.com, 2 December 2010, http://www.fifa.com/worldcup/qatar2022/news/newsid=1344979/index.html.

Qummi, M. *The Promised Mahdi: the Deliverer of the Whole of Mankind*. Isfahan: Amir-Ul-Mu'mineen Library, 2008.

Ramadan, T. *Western Muslims and the Future of Islam*. Oxford: Oxford University Press, 2004.

Rashid, Ahmed. 'After 1,700 Years, Buddhas Fall to Taliban Dynamite.' *The Telegraph*, 12 March 2012, http://www.telegraph.co.uk/news/worldnews/asia/afghanistan/1326063/After-1700-years-Buddhas-fall-to-Taliban-dynamite.html.

Richardson, J. *The Islamic Antichrist*. Los Angeles: WND Books, 2015.

Rieff, David. 'Were Sanctions Right?' *New York Times Magazine*, 27 July 2003, http://www.nytimes.com/2003/07/27/magazine/were-sanctions-right.html.

Rippin, A., ed. *The Blackwell Companion to the Qur'an*. Oxford: Blackwell, 2006.

Robinson, Neal. 'Jesus.' *Encyclopaedia of the Qur'ān*. ed. Jane Dammen McAuliffe. Georgetown University, Washington DC: Brill Online, 2014

Roosenberg, Tim. 'Islam and Christianity Daniel 11 Seminar.' Sealing Time Ministries, http://www.sealingtime.com/resources/featured-speakers/tim-

roosenberg/islam-and-christianity-daniel-11-seminar-tim-roosenberg.
html, accessed October 2014.

Rushdie, Salman. *The Satanic Verses.* New York: Viking, 1988.

Ruston, M. 'Approaches to Proximity and Distance in Early Sufism.' *Mystics Quarterly* (2007): 1–25. Available at www.jstor.org.

Ṣaḥīḥ Bukhārī and *Ṣaḥīḥ Muslim I,* both available on www.sunnah.com.

Ṣaḥīḥ Muslim, Book 1, No. 309, at www.usc.edu/org/cmje/religious-texts/
hadith/muslim/001-smt.php.

'Should Christians Eat Halal Meat.' Australian Prayer Network, http://
ausprayernet.org.au/feature/feature_articles_34.php; accessed June 2015.

Silverstein, A. *Islamic History: A Very Short Introduction.* Oxford: Oxford
University Press, 2010.

Simonetti, M., ed. *Matthew 14 – 28.* Ancient Christian Commentary on
Scripture: New Testament vol. 1b. Downers Grove: IVP Academic, 2002.

Small, K. *Holy Books Have a History: Textual Histories of the New Testament and
the Qur'an.* Kansas City: Avant, 2009.

Smith, J. *Islam: The Cloak of the Antichrist.* USA: WinePress, 2011.

Sookdheo, P. 'Supermarket Halal.' *Evangelicals Now,* Dec 2010.

'Sufism.' The School of Sufi Teaching, Singapore, http://singapore.sufischool.
org/.

Taha, Mahmud Muhammad. *The Second Message of Islam,* trans. Abdullah al-
Naim. New York: Syracuse University Press, 1987.

The Corpus Coranicum project, http://koran.bbaw.de/.

The World Evangelical Alliance's panel on the translation of divine filial
language. The panel's report (April 2013) can be found at http://www.
worldea.org/images/wimg/files/2013_0429-Final%20Report%20of%20
the%20WEA%20Independent%20Bible%20Translation%20Review%20
Panel.pdf.

Tottoli, Roberto. 'Elijah.' *Encyclopaedia of the Qur'an,* ed. Jane Dammen
McAuliffe. Georgetown University, Washington DC: Brill Online, 2014.

Tusi, Shaykh. Articles on 'Monotheism', 'Tenets of Islam', http://www.al-islam.
org/gallery/kids/Books/tenets/monotheism.htm; accessed October 2014.

Umar, Muhammad S. *Islam and Colonialism: Intellectual Responses of Muslims
of Northern Nigeria to British Colonial Rule.* Leiden: E. J. Brill, 2005.

Usmani, S. A. *Tafseer-e-Usmani,* translated as *The Noble Qur'an* by M. A.
Ahmad. Lahore: Aalameen Publications, 1991.

Van Kooten, G. H. 'Why Did Paul Include an Exegesis of Moses' Shining Face
(Exod 34) in 2 Cor 3?'. In *The Significance of Sinai: Traditions about Sinai
and Divine Revelation in Judaism and Christianity,* edited by George J.
Brooke, H. Najman and L. Stuckenbruck, 149–182. Leiden: Brill, 2008.

Von Denffer, A. *'Ulūm Al-Qurʾān: Introduction to the Sciences of the Qurʾan*, 2nd ed. Leicester: The Islamic Foundation, 2005.

Weil, Simone. *Waiting on God: The Essence of Her Thought*. London: Fontana, 1959.

Wilders, Geert. 'Who Lost Europe?', Apocalypse Prophesied 2008–2015, http://www.apocalypse2008-2015.com/Beast_System-Islam.html, accessed October 2014.

'WPO Poll Analysis: American Evangelicals Are Divided on International Policy.' 2 October 2006, World Public Opinon.org, http://www.worldpublicopinion.org/pipa/articles/brunitedstatescanadara/270.php?nid=&id=&pnt=270.

Wright, N. T. *Jesus and the Victory of God*. London: SPCK, 1996.

———. *The New Testament and the People of God*. London: SPCK, 1992.

Yusuf Ali, A. *The Holy Qurʾan: Text, Translation and Commentary*. Jeddah: Islamic Education Centre, 1946.

Zlotowitz, M. *Bereishis: Genesis: New Translation with a Commentary Anthologized from Talmudic, Midrashic and Rabbinic Sources*, 2nd ed. New York: Mesorah Publications, 1986.

Zwiep, A. W. *The Ascension of the Messiah in Jewish Lukan Christology*. Leiden: Brill, 1997.

Langham Literature and its imprints are a ministry of Langham Partnership.

Langham Partnership is a global fellowship working in pursuit of the vision God entrusted to its founder John Stott –

to facilitate the growth of the church in maturity and Christ-likeness through raising the standards of biblical preaching and teaching.

Our vision is to see churches in the majority world equipped for mission and growing to maturity in Christ through the ministry of pastors and leaders who believe, teach and live by the Word of God.

Our mission is to strengthen the ministry of the Word of God through:
- nurturing national movements for biblical preaching
- fostering the creation and distribution of evangelical literature
- enhancing evangelical theological education

especially in countries where churches are under-resourced.

Our ministry

Langham Preaching partners with national leaders to nurture indigenous biblical preaching movements for pastors and lay preachers all around the world. With the support of a team of trainers from many countries, a multi-level programme of seminars provides practical training, and is followed by a programme for training local facilitators. Local preachers' groups and national and regional networks ensure continuity and ongoing development, seeking to build vigorous movements committed to Bible exposition.

Langham Literature provides majority world preachers, scholars and seminary libraries with evangelical books and electronic resources through publishing and distribution, grants and discounts. The programme also fosters the creation of indigenous evangelical books in many languages, through writer's grants, strengthening local evangelical publishing houses, and investment in major regional literature projects, such as one volume Bible commentaries like *The Africa Bible Commentary* and *The South Asia Bible Commentary*.

Langham Scholars provides financial support for evangelical doctoral students from the majority world so that, when they return home, they may train pastors and other Christian leaders with sound, biblical and theological teaching. This programme equips those who equip others. Langham Scholars also works in partnership with majority world seminaries in strengthening evangelical theological education. A growing number of Langham Scholars study in high quality doctoral programmes in the majority world itself. As well as teaching the next generation of pastors, graduated Langham Scholars exercise significant influence through their writing and leadership.

To learn more about Langham Partnership and the work we do visit **langham.org**

Lightning Source UK Ltd.
Milton Keynes UK
UKOW06f1012110316

270017UK00013B/228/P

9 781783 689125